D1222610

Tennessee Silversmiths

Tennessee Silversmiths

Benjamin Hubbard Caldwell, Jr.

The Frank L. Horton Series

The Museum of Early Southern Decorative Arts
Winston-Salem

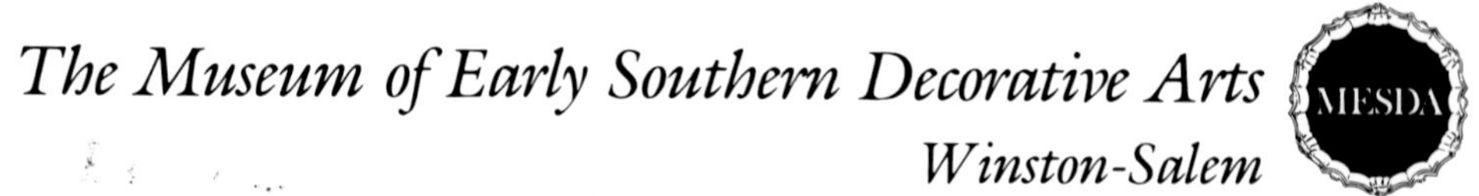

Distributed for MESDA by
The University of North Carolina Press
Chapel Hill and London

828844

Mitchell Memorial Library
Mississippi State University

The preparation of this book was made possible in part by research grants from the Research Tools and Reference Works Program of the National Endowment for the Humanities, an independent federal agency.

Copyright © 1988
The Museum of Early Southern Decorative Arts

Frontispiece. Cream pitcher marked by Campbell and Donigan, 1855, Nashville. Courtesy of the Tennessee State Museum, photograph by Wesley Stewart.

ISBN: 0-945578-01-6

LC: 8863431

To the late Pauline and L. A. Cox
of Rocky Mount, North Carolina,
who first taught Gertrude and me
to appreciate southern decorative arts,
and to my late father Ben
and my mother Thelma Jackson Caldwell
for stimulating my interest in history and antiques.

Contents

Ladle made by John Campbell, 1850–55, engraved "David & Willie," Nashville. LOA: 11½". Private collection.

Preface

"How do you *know* it's a Nashville piece?" I quizzed the affable owner of a local shop one day in 1964 as he showed me a handsome silver ladle.

"Because," he said, "a family member who wishes to remain nameless gave it to me to sell."

I turned the ladle over, letting the light define "J. Campbell" stamped on its shaft. "That man was a Philadelphia maker," I thought, and I set out to prove my friendly shop owner wrong. I figured there were no local silversmiths.

First, I visited Stanley Horn, the late Tennessee Historian, who told me that the ladle's engraving, "David and Willie" (he pronounced it "Why'-lee"), probably indicated David and Willie McGavock, who built "Two Rivers" about 1852, shortly after their wedding. The mansion stands just north of Nashville in a neighborhood still known as "Two Rivers." "Worked into the brickwork on the side of the house are the names 'David' and 'Willie,'" Horn said.

With that information in hand I checked local newspapers of the 1850s at the Tennessee State Library and Archives. Lo and behold, there was indeed a John Campbell, silversmith, who advertised and worked in Nashville. I had found my first Tennessee silversmith, with the help from friends, while still a resident at Vanderbilt University Hospital's Department of Obstetrics and Gynecology.

Not long thereafter, Miss Ima Hogg, the prominent Houston collector and philanthropist, visited me and offered (with a twinkle in her eye) a great sum for the ladle, sorely tempting this struggling physician. I refused, explaining to her that I thought Tennessee pieces should stay in Tennessee, and she agreed, with that same twinkle in her eye; I assume it was the gleam of approval. And therein lies one of the major reasons for this book . . . to encourage Tennesseans specifically, and Southerners in general, to take pride in their true heritage. We may admire old silver and furniture from centers to the north and east of us, but there is much to be treasured right here.

In 1952 an exhibition of southern decorative arts was organized at the Virginia Museum of Fine Arts in Richmond, promulgating fine antique pieces made in the South. David B. Warren's 1968 exhibition entitled *Southern Silver* at the Museum of Fine Arts in Houston reinforced the idea of taking pride in local treasures. The latter exhibition ultimately led to my 1971 article on Tennessee silversmiths in *Antiques* magazine, and, finally, to this book.

I have felt a sense of urgency about getting as many facts as possible gathered together *now*. Modern-day living separates families; histories die. In the last few years, as we have brought this study to completion, we have often found ourselves in contact with a lawyer for an estate rather than the correspondent who had responded to my original article.

My initial idea was to search federal censuses, city directories, state gazetteers, and old Tennessee newspapers to document the silversmiths practicing their craft in the state prior to 1860, citing at least one source for each craftsman. The destruction of the census records of Tennessee for 1800 and 1810 (except for Rutherford and Grainger counties) by English troops during the War of 1812, however, hampers all those who use census records for local histories. Inaccuracies in the census—caused by transpositions from query to listing or for whatever reason—create further difficulties. In the 1850 census for Davidson County, for example, there were two listings for Thomas Kent, a Nashville silversmith. The first listing stated that Thomas Kent was a silversmith, aged 32, and that he was born in Ohio. Two females were listed in his household: Matilda Kent, aged 28, born in Ireland, and Isabella Armitage, aged 22, also born in Ireland. The second listing stated that "T. Kent," silversmith, aged 33, was born in Ohio. Three females were listed in this household: Matilda, aged 29, born in Ireland, Lucy, aged 5, born in Tennessee, and Isabella Armitage, aged 20, born in Ireland.

Problems also arise regarding newspaper research. Some silversmiths chose not to advertise, often for a year or two, perhaps because business was good or if the firm had no new merchandise to sell. The researcher frequently is puzzled about whether the man remained in town or even remained in business during the lapse of published advertisements.

Through the generosity of many individuals, the primary research for this study has been augmented by the inclusion of family oral histories and letters. Undoubtedly, some information has been omitted or filed incompletely, and time has not allowed me to examine court records—especially wills—fully enough. I hope other research will emerge to fill in our knowledge of the silversmiths and untangle some of their accounts.

My book attempts to record the silversmith trade in Tennessee from its inception in 1792, the year George Bean began making silver in Bean's Station, Tennessee. The cut-off date for this study is 1860. The Civil War interrupted the course of normal living and destroyed much southern decorative art; thereafter, of course, with the decline of our agrarian society and the inception of the Industrial Revolution, a good deal of the silver was produced by the roll-plate process or stamped out in bulk by machines.

You will see that I have included in my listings a number of men who called themselves watchmakers, jewelers, and silver platers, because we have found objects made by these men. I have even included men who called themselves clock sellers or those who merchandised silver and jewelry products in "variety houses," the "Sears" of their day. Thus, if their labeled pieces are ever found, later students will have a point of reference from which to embark on their own historical journeys. I have not included men who were primarily gunsmiths—even though they may have made silver gun mounts; counterfeiters and engravers have been omitted, although in some cases their trades overlapped with silversmithing.

Several final points must be made regarding methodology, principally concerning entry headings for each individual.

1. I have adhered to a journalistic "who-what-when-where" approach in formulating entry headings, trying to list each man at his principal Tennessee locations as he chose to identify himself. Even this approach was fraught with difficulty because a tradesman's concept of his own work as well as a community's need for specific services constantly shifted.

2. When the *only* reference to a man's work was the *State Gazetteer's* all-encompassing "Jewelry, Watches, Clocks, &c.," his title entry heading identifies him as a "jeweler, watch and clockmaker." This category includes known silversmiths, watchmakers, jewelers, and even one physician, who may have retailed jewelry, watches, and clocks.

3. Each silversmith has been listed in the county where he lived or worked, using the county's name as found. In a few cases the county's name may have changed since the silversmith worked there; many later Tennessee counties were formed from earlier, larger Tennessee counties.

4. A man's name is listed first according to the spelling found most frequently with commonly appearing variations in parentheses immediately following.

5. I have shown either a mark or a photograph of an object with each silversmith if known silver exists (unless otherwise noted). The majority of the photographs of the marks are not credited. Many were photographed by Jack Shwab. The description of marks is defined by the form of the two types of dies in use: the intaglio die, the face of which was engraved with letters, and when struck left a sunken impression with raised letters, and the cameo die, the face of which was formed by letters raised from the surface with gravers, chisels, and files, and which, when struck, left only the letters themselves —not the face of the die—sunk into the surface. "Cameo," in other words, is the reverse of "intaglio." The marks left by the cameo die have been known incorrectly as "incuse," "incused," or even "incised." The actual definition of incuse simply means "struck in," which would apply to the intaglio mark as well, while "incised" literally means "cut," which is applicable to a burin, but not a stamped mark. Generally speaking, cameo dies were not in use in America before the nineteenth century. Although far more difficult to create, cameo dies distorted less metal when struck, in contrast with the considerable distortion caused by the broad face of an intaglio die.

6. Question marks have been used in entry headings to indicate lack of complete documentation. For example, if an advertisement reveals that a man worked in Kentucky in 1830 as a silversmith, and the 1840 census for Tennessee records that two children were born to a silversmith with the same name in Tennessee between 1833 and 1836, one can assume the Kentucky artisan became a Tennessee resident sometime after 1830. If he chose not to advertise, however, his place of work remains unknown until documentation by the 1840 census. Furthermore, since occupations were not recorded in the federal census until 1850, it is often difficult to document that artisans working before that time continued in the trade. Therefore, we may list a man as 1833?–50. Also in regard to dates in the entry headings, a man's death date is only given in the heading if it is known that he died while still practicing his trade. If a silversmith was working past 1860, his working date is listed as 1860 and later; however, if the year he stopped working was found in documents, and it was not at his death, the full working range is given, e.g. 1845–72. In the chapter entitled "The Setting," the mention of various Tennessee silversmiths was not felt to require reference since documentation regarding these individuals may be found in their entries.

During the course of my fifteen years of research many people unstintingly have offered advice, encouragement, time and effort. I especially would like to thank Barbara Swift, without whose help this book would not have been possible. My gratitude also is extended to: Orrin W. June, whose organization of the Historic Sites Federation of Tennessee led to the publication of *Antiques in Tennessee* in 1971; Alice Winchester and Wendell Garrett, editors of *Antiques* magazine, for their support and interest in the *Tennessee* issue; Ellen Beasley, for her help in the preparation of the *Antiques* article; Crawford Barnett, whose discussions spurred me to further research; J. Russell MacBeth, Thomas K. Connor, Richard H. Hulan, and Owen Meredith for their part in the *Made in Tennessee* exhibit at the Tennessee Botanical Gardens and Fine Arts Center at Cheekwood; Frank Horton, for his encouragement, and John Bivins, Forsyth Alexander, Sara Lee Barnes, Wes Stewart, and the entire MESDA staff for their patience with this project; the late Stanley Horn and Dale Kirby for their encouragement; Jack

Shwab, the photographer responsible for most of the illustrations in this book; and for their concern over the preparation of the manuscript, Evelyn Byrd Blackmon, Mary Ellen McCabe, Gay S. Pepper, and Dot Solgot.

A special thanks is extended to the following individuals and institutions: Crenshaw Adams, Mrs. Elliott Adams, Dr. and Mrs. Justin H. Adler, Mr. and Mrs. J. C. Askew, William P. Beall, the Belle Meade Mansion, Swannee Bennett, Frances Colley Bowman, Dana C. Brooks, Betty and Martin Brown, Beverly S. Burbage, Dr. and Mrs. B. F. Byrd, William T. Chumney, Margaret Wemyss Connor, Mrs. Sims Crownover, Amelia Edwards, Dr. Frank B. Galyon, the late Mrs. Stanley Horn, Dr. G. William Huckaba, Mrs. Charles W. Jewell, the Ladies Hermitage Association, Mrs. E. R. Lewis, Mrs. Jeanette Noel, Dr. Thomas Parrish, Jerome Redfearn, Margaret Reid, Mrs. Campbell Ridley, William R. Selden, Mrs. Jesse Short, Jr., Edward Stone, Jr., Robert R. Van Deventer, and Irene and Ridley Wills.

I acknowledge as well the help of the staff members at the Tennessee State Library and Archives, the Nashville Public Library, the Tennessee State Museum in Nashville, the Dixon Gallery and Gardens in Memphis, the Knoxville Public Library, the Memphis Public Library, Western Reserve Historical Society in Cleveland, Ohio, the Museum of Fine Arts in Boston, Massachusetts, the Public Library of Cincinnati and Hamilton County, the San Antonio Museum Association, the San Antonio Conservation Foundation, the University of Kentucky at Lexington's Library, and Vanderbilt University Library's Special Collections.

Among many others whose assistance has been invaluable (and I fear I may have forgotten some) are the following: Robert Abels, Ann Alley, Clifton Anderson, Dorothy Winton Apfel, Rosemary Arneson, Catherine P. Avery, H. Parrott Bacot, Ursula S. Beach, V. H. Beckman, Marylin Bell, Clarence Berson, Mrs. W. G. Berson, Ann Sides Bishop, Bates Black, Marquis Boultinghouse, Virginia Bowman, Mrs. Ralph Brickell, William R. Calhoun, Mary Elizabeth Cayce, William R. Chamberlain, Isabel E. Chenoweth, Mrs. Meyer Cohen, Mrs. G. Dallas Coons, The Corcoran Gallery of Art, Stephen D. Cox, Richard O. Deaderick, Douglas Drake, Steve Driver, Miriam F. Dulaney, John Egerton, Basil Elliston, Fred Engel, Frances Ewald, Jonathan Fairbanks, Ken Feith, Donald L. Fennimore, Brenda Ford, Douglas Fuller, Jill L. Garrett, Edward Gildersleeve, Ruth Ann Griggs, Evelyn Cayce Guy, Robin Hale, Susan Haltom, James L. Hansen, Mrs. Frances Haynes, Mary Glenn Hearn, Virginia L. Hewitt, Mrs. Roger Holland, Stanley Horn, Jr., William Howell, Charles Hummell, Irma Jackson, Elizabeth Jacobs, Colin James, A. L. Jobe, Marion Jobe, Dr. Jim Johnson of Memphis, John Rison Jones, Jr., Everett E. Kelley, Dr. James Kelly, Alan Kerley, Jane Kerley, George H. S. King, John Kiser, Katherine Kovacs, Florence Langford, Annette Levy, Mitzi Lemons, A. E. Lightfort, T. Vance Little, Helen D. Lockhart, Mrs. Sidney McAllister, A. A. McCampbell, Betsy McCampbell, Claire McCann, Dr. William J. MacArthur, Charlotte Fowler Maclellan, Walter Nold Mathis, Sydney F. Martin, C. Somers Miller, Inez Moncrief, Jennifer Moody, Chaddra Moore, Robert Y. Moses, Genella Olker, Reba Ann Orman, Grace B. Paine, Jane M. Pairo, Dr. Tom Parrish, Frances Parsley, Herschel Payne, Mary Reynolds Peacock, Mary Prueher, Leslie Pritikin, Laura Rehmert, Mrs. Herbert Richards, Mr. and Mrs. E. A. Robertson, Amelea Rudisill, Reba Russell, Carolyn Sartor, Frances Schell, Charles A. Sherrill, Mrs. Frank Smith III, Gus Smith, Mrs. Sidney Adair Smith, R. C. Snapp, Carolyn W. Stanley, Marshall Steanet, Cecilia Steinfeldt, Everlyn Stephenson, Cynthia Stow, Martha Strayhorn, Samuel B. Stuffle, Dr. Charles Trabue, Louis L. Tucker, Jim Van Story, Marion Vickers, Hugh Walker, Ronald J. Walker, David B. Warren, Mr. and Mrs. Richard Weesner, Mary West, Martha Wetherington, Ralph Whitesell, Mary Jane Whiteside, Lisa Whitlow, Charlotte Wilcoxen, Henry Williamson, Barbara P. Willis, Mrs. Jesse Eli Wills, Elizabeth Woosley, Betty Young, and Dean Zimmerman.

Finally, I appreciate the years of understanding on the part of my wife, Gertrude Sharp, and my children, Sarah and David, Trudy, and Ben III.

Benjamin Hubbard Caldwell, Jr.

Part I
The Setting

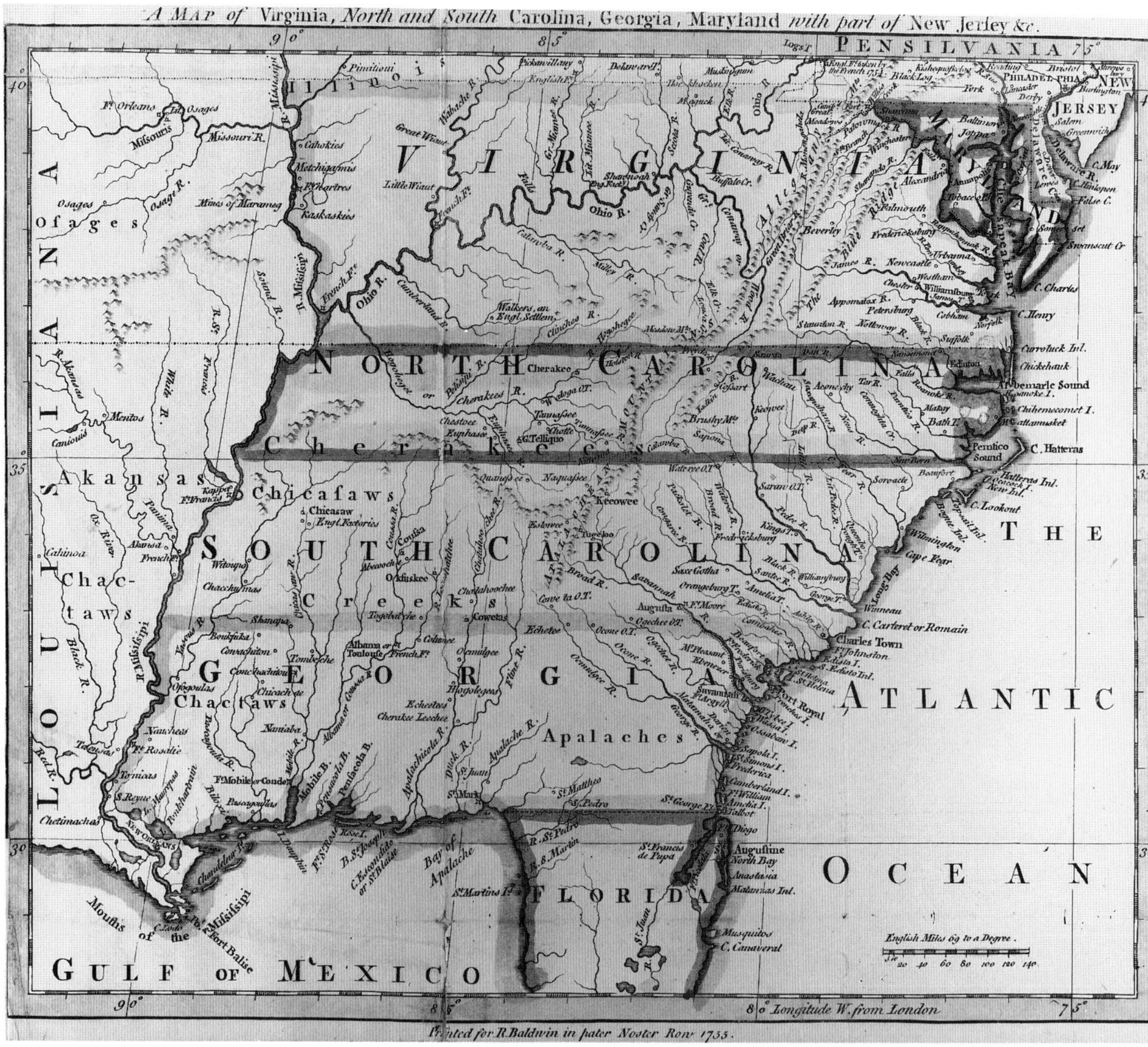
A MAP of Virginia, North and South Carolina, Georgia, Maryland with part of New Jersey &c.
PENSILVANIA
VIRGINIA
NORTH CAROLINA
Cherakees
SOUTH CAROLINA
Creeks
GEORGIA
Apalaches
FLORIDA
LOUISIANA
Akansas
Chicasaws
Chactaws
Osages
THE ATLANTIC OCEAN
GULF OF MEXICO
Bay of Apalache
Mouths of the Misisipi
NEW JERSEY
PHILADELPHIA
Albemarle Sound
C. Hatteras
Pamtico Sound
C. Lookout
Cape Fear
Charles Town
Port Royal
Augustine
C. Canaveral
English Miles 69 to a Degree.
8 0 Longitude W. from London
Printed for R. Baldwin in pater Noster Row 1755.

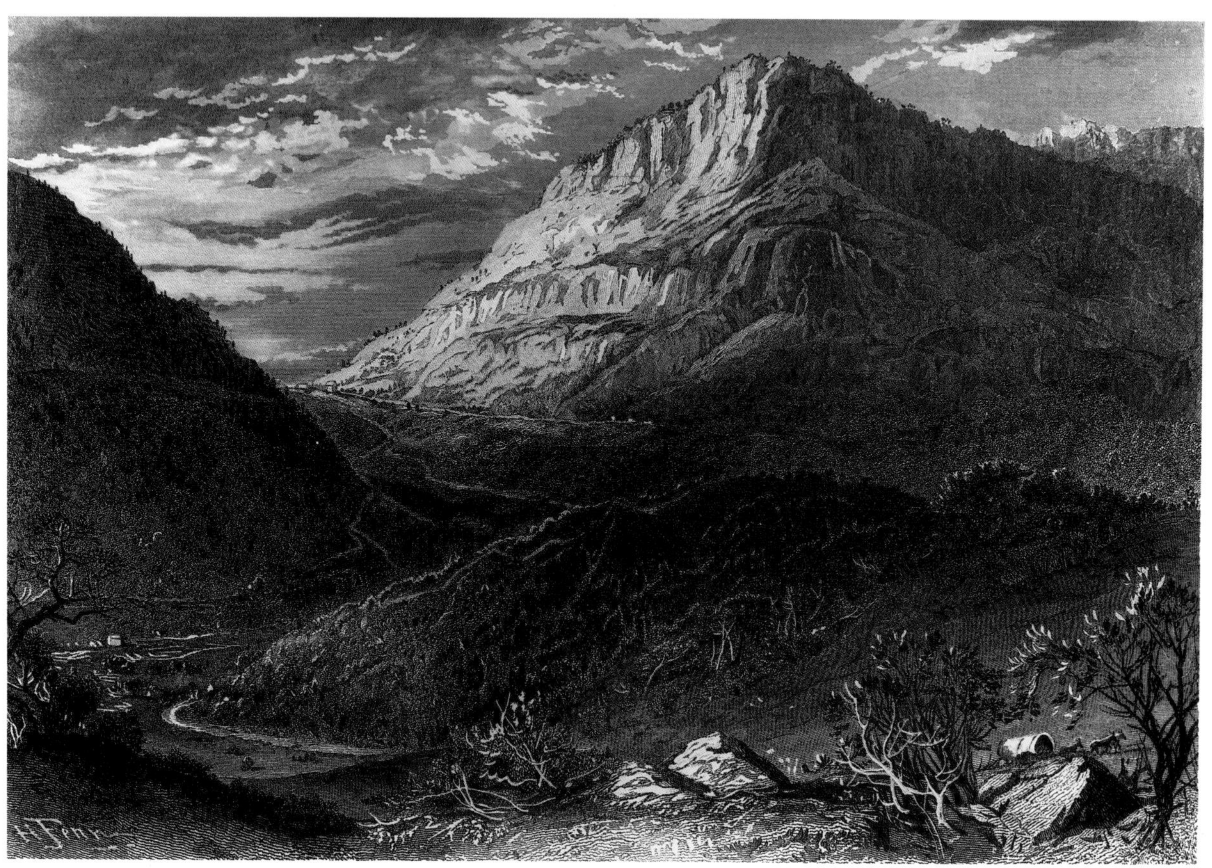

The Setting

At the time of the American Revolution, the period that American decorative arts collectors seem to admire the most, the region now known as Tennessee was still wilderness. A part of North Carolina (fig. 1), it was called simply "the Territory South of the River Ohio" or "the Old Southwest Territory." Its central basin provided a hunting ground for a number of Indian tribes; the Cherokee occupied its periphery. Consequently the story of the artisans who made silver in Tennessee is quite different from that of Boston, Philadelphia, and Charleston silversmiths who were making spoons, beakers, and teapots fifty to one hundred years earlier. Understanding the reasons for Tennessee's late settlement helps to explain some of these differences. Although weaving into whole cloth the many strands of the state's beginnings —of its men's desires and ambitions—is far too complex a task for this study, some background is necessary.

The late emergence of Tennessee settlements was effected by diverse factors. The coastal areas of North America were settled first, and the mountains between the Southwest Territory and the colonies provided a discouraging barrier to expansion. As historian Archibald Henderson said so effectively, "the difficulties of cutting a passage through the towering wall of living green long proved an effective obstacle. . . ."[1] The first white men who journeyed beyond those natural walls were explorers and traders. As early as 1541 Hernando de Soto, searching for silver and gold, reached a site on the Mississippi near what later became the city of Memphis. In 1673 Father Jacques Marquette and Louis Jolliet descended the Mississippi River from Canada; during the same year James Needham and Gabriel Arthur explored the region, perhaps the first Englishmen to do so. In 1682 Robert Cavelier de La Salle claimed the Mississippi River Valley for France[2], thereby extending the continuing struggle between France and England into the region.

Charles I in 1629 had granted the province of "Carolana" (with boundaries from the ocean on the east to "soe fare as the Continent extends" on the west between the thirty-first and thirty-sixth parallels) to his Attorney General, Sir Robert Heath. Subsequently, Charles II deeded much of the same land to Lord Clarendon and seven other court favorites who declared Heath's grant void because he had failed to colonize the territory. Seven of the eight proprietors later sold their claims to King George II, but Lord John Carteret, who was to become the Earl of Granville, retained title to one-eighth of the land, a strip about sixty-five miles wide extending west from the Atlantic to the Pacific through what is now the upper two-thirds of Tennessee. It later became known as Granville's District.[3]

Before 1692 Martin Chartier, a French trader, explored the Cumberland River, and about 1700 Jean Couture was probably the first white man to explore the Tennessee River in its entirety.[4] Fourteen years later Frenchman Jean du Charleville established a trading post near what is now Nashville. In 1750 Dr. Thomas Walker, a Virginia physician and explorer, recorded his discovery of an opening between the ridges of mountains separating the eastern colonies from the area now called Tennessee and Kentucky. The discovery of this gap (fig. 2), which Walker named for the Duke of Cumberland, later aided the area's first settlement by Virginians and North Carolinians.[5]

Long hunters like Daniel Boone followed the explorers and traders, further blazing the way for the earliest settlers. These men traveled Indian trails that may have been established by the ancient mound builders, and even before these Indians by the buffalo that had chosen the paths of least resistance across rugged terrain in search of salt licks and feeding grounds. A myriad of these trails crisscrossed the territory in all directions.

The Great Warrior Path had been used by the five Indian nations of western New York to fight the southern Indians.[6] Settlers from Pennsylvania, New England, Maryland, North Carolina, and Virginia later followed its narrow lead, widening it for the use of packhorses. This great path was really two north-south trails paralleling each side of the Allegheny and Appalachian mountains. The eastern branch passed through Pennsylvania east of the Alleghenies, traversing Virginia to the piedmont area of North Carolina, eventually extending to South Carolina and Georgia. The alternate path led through western Pennsylvania down the Shenandoah Valley west of the Alleghenies, forging into northeastern Tennessee. At that point it connected with roads from Salisbury, Charlotte, and Morganton in North Carolina,[7] becoming the Wilderness Road or Boone's Trail, the name most used after 1775. With its branches the Wilderness Road provided further access to eastern Tennessee. A north fork, the Kentucky Road, led off toward Boonesboro.

Travelers on a passage down the Ohio River could

1. A Map of Virginia, North and South Carolina, Georgia, Maryland with part of New Jersey &c.. *1755, published for R. Baldwin, London. HOA: 8¼", WOA: 10³⁄₁₆". MESDA Research File (MRF) S-14,202.*

2. *A view of Cumberland Gap from* Picturesque America *by William Cullent Bryant (New York: D. Appleton & Co., 1872). HOA: 5¼", WOA: 7⅞". MRF S-14,200.*

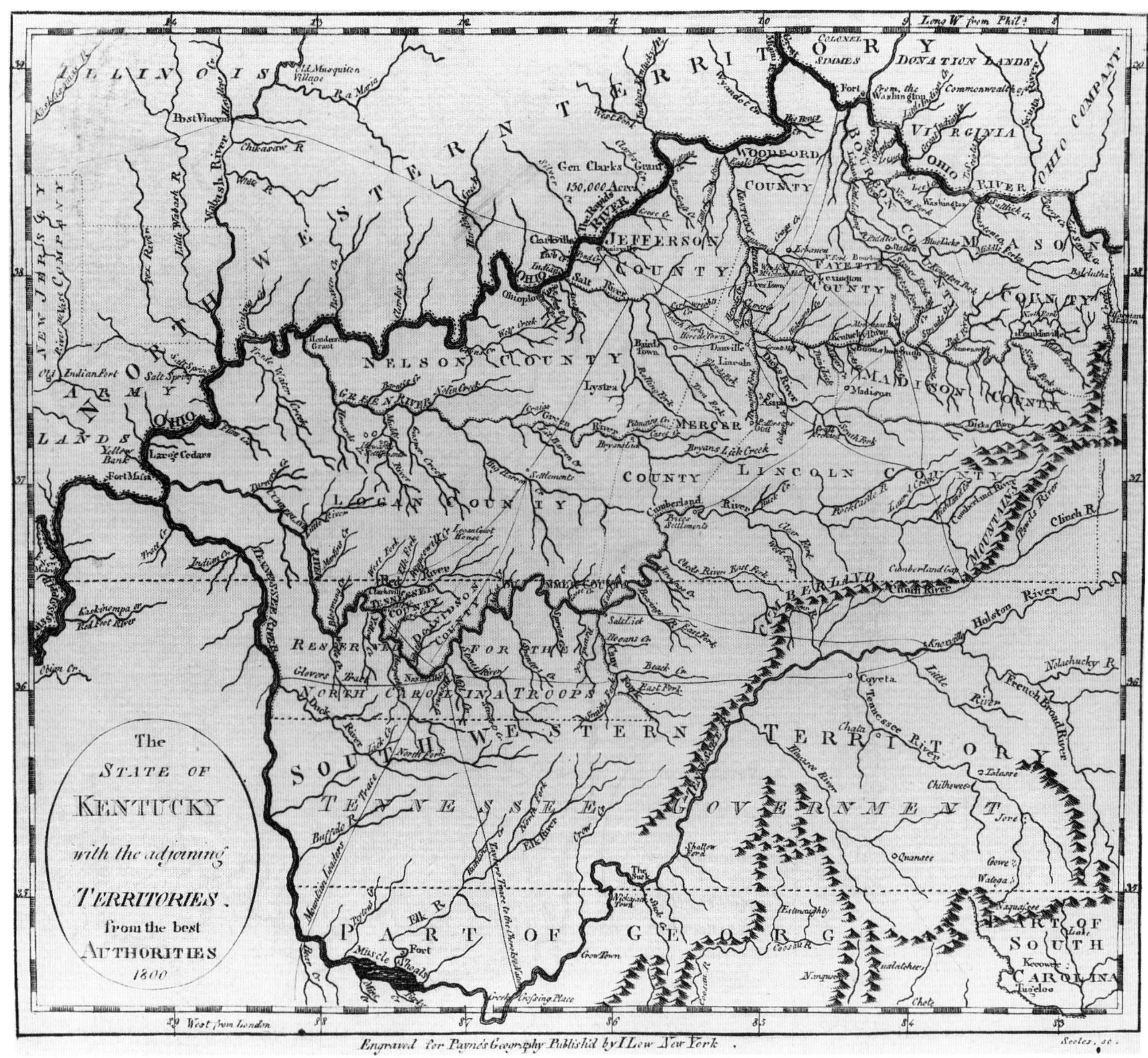

3. *A map of* The State of Kentucky with the adjoining Territories from the best Authorities, *1800, engraved for* Payne's Geography, *published by I. Low, New York. HOA: 8½", WOA: 9½". MRF S-14,210.*

journey in Kentucky from Maysville, Lexington, and Danville, southwest to Bardstown, Bowling Green, Russellville, and Logan's Court House, and thence into Tennessee through White's Creek and on to Nashville. Those from the Louisville area (see Clarksville in what is now Indiana on Payne's map, fig. 3) traveled through Elizabethtown, and on to Nashville through White's Creek. From the Watauga country in eastern Tennessee —Greeneville, Jonesboro, and Elizabethton—settlers could take the Wilderness Road toward Nashville from Knoxville via the Salt Lick, or Carthage, and Gallatin. A southern branch of this road reached Nashville through Kingston, near the Indian village of Coyeta (figs. 4, 4a), through the towns of Washington, Madison, McMinnville, and Jefferson. J. Russell used explorer's names on his 1794 map (fig. 5) to identify the following routes out of Nashville: Taylor's Trace to the Cherokee nation, to Huntsville, Alabama, and southward into Georgia; the Mountain Leader Trail across the Tennessee River into present-day Mississippi, closely paralleling the recently completed Natchez Trace Parkway; and Glover's Trace, which ran directly westward into the Louisiana Purchase.

Rivers also were heavily traveled even before the steamboat era. Traders drifted their flatboats down the Missis-

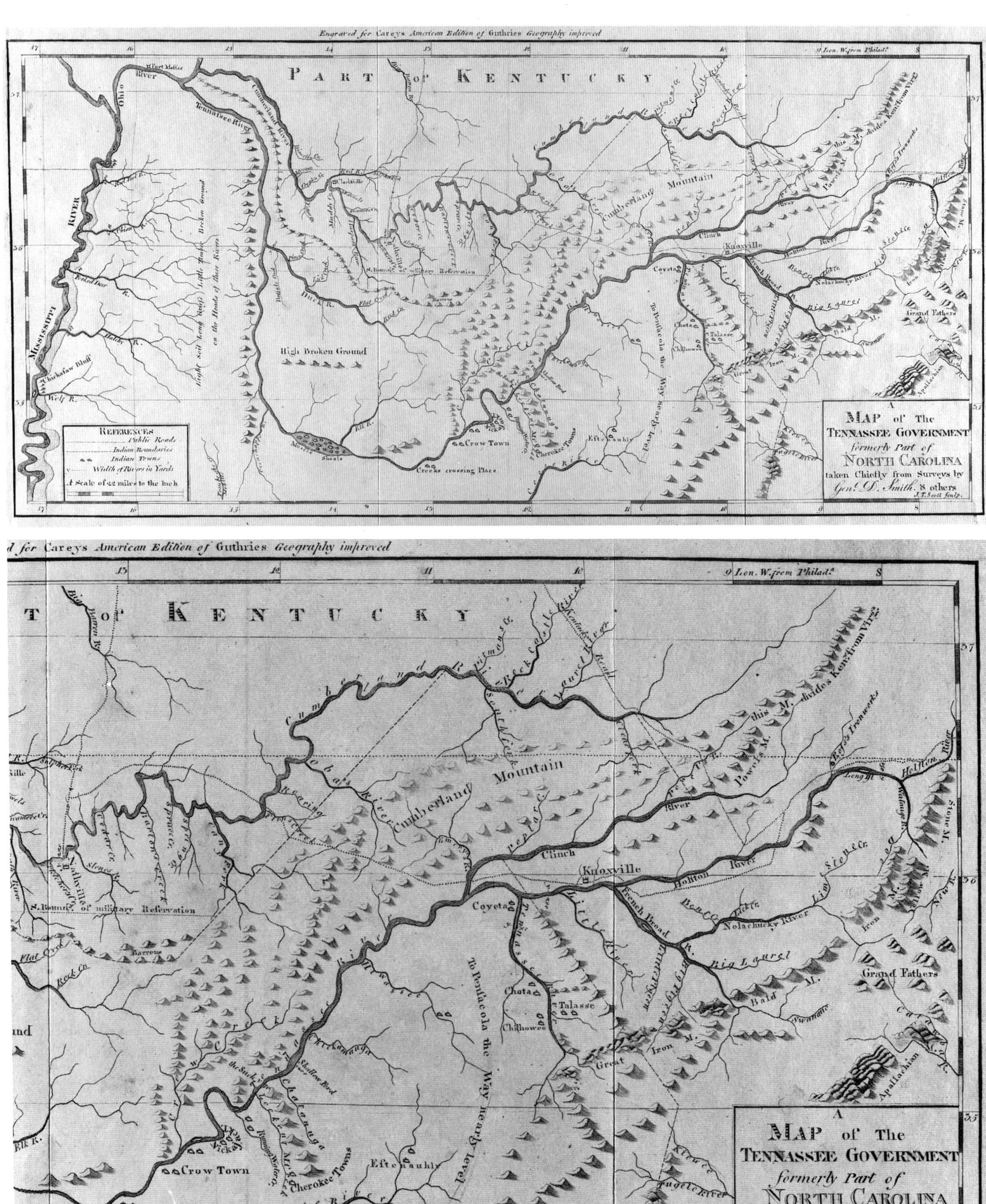

4, 4a. A Map of the Tennassee government formerly part of North Carolina taken Chiefly from Surveys by Genl. D. Smith & others, *1796, engraved by J. T. Scott, Philadelphia. HOA: 9¼", WOA: 20³⁄₁₀". MRF S-14,207. Indian and settlers' routes are illustrated in fig. 4a.*

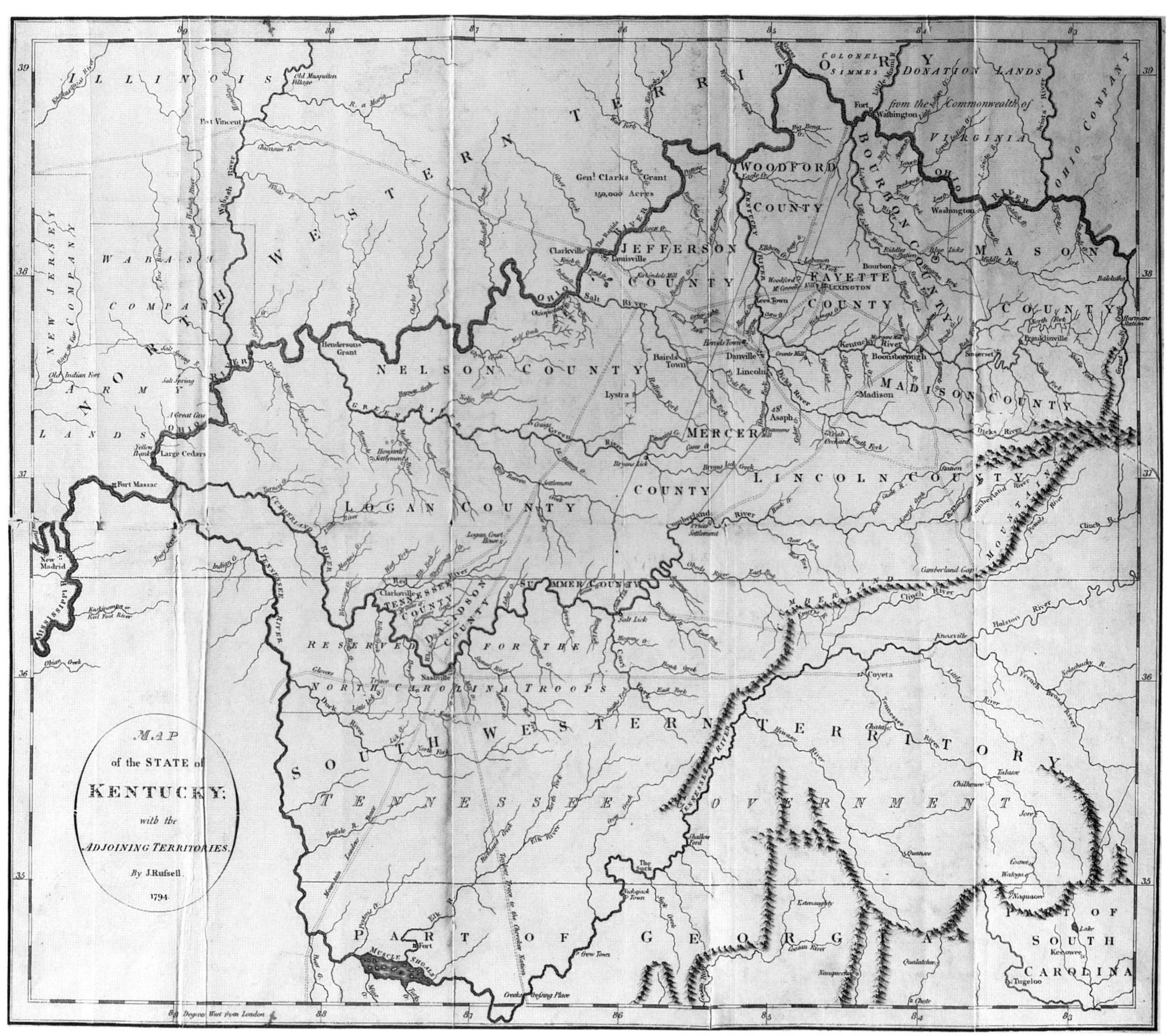

5. Map of the State of Kentucky; with the Adjoining Territories, *1794, by J. Russell, published by H. D. Symonds, London. HOA: 14½", WOA: 17½". MRF S-14,209.*

sippi to New Orleans where such boats were broken up and sold for lumber. The boatmen then returned by land.[8]

The first official survey, which examined a portion of the northeastern line of what is now Tennessee, was run in 1749. In that year Peter Jefferson (Thomas Jefferson's father) and Joshua Fry, commissioners for Virginia, along with William Churton and Daniel Weldon, commissioners for North Carolina, extended the line established in 1728, which delineated the North Carolina and Virginia boundary, ninety-three miles westward across the Alleghenies to an area on the south fork of the Holston River, now part of Johnson County, Tennessee's most northeasterly division.[9] Although both the French and the English coveted this "overhill" land, it is unlikely that any white men had settled there at the time the Fry-Jefferson survey was published. Acreage could not be legally bought and sold in a land over which a surveyor's line had not yet been run, and in fact ownership of this territory remained in dispute for years to come.

At the Albany Conference of 1754 Benjamin Franklin advocated the establishment of colonies in the "west" to check French expansion, but the following decade only fomented further episodes in the struggle between the Spanish, the Indians, the French, and the British for the land. During that period near the Indian town of Tuskegee, Fort Loudon was established at the urging of the Cherokee, but it was destroyed by the tribe three

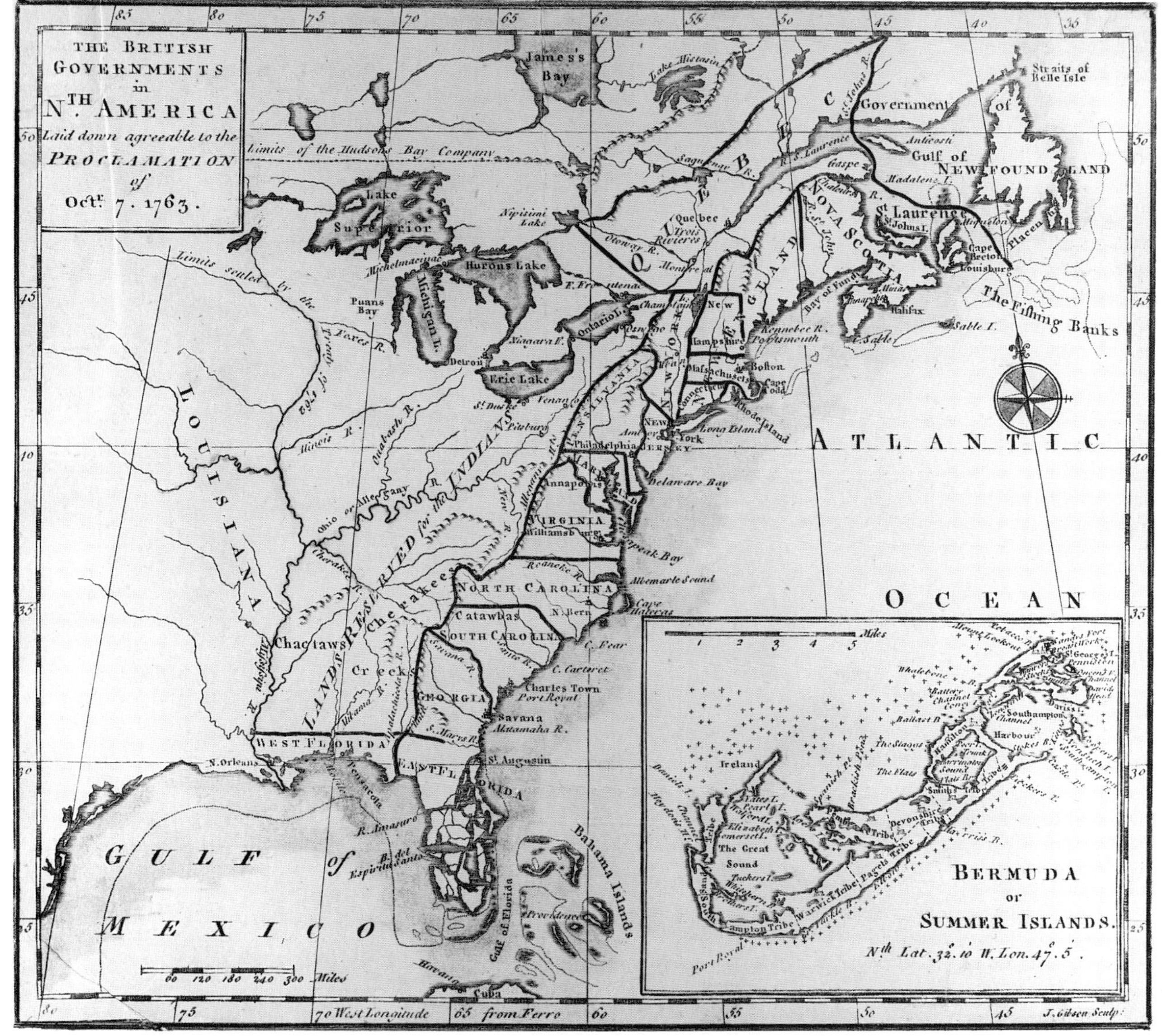

6. The British Governments in Nth. America Laid down agreeable to the Proclamation of Octr. 7, 1763, *engraved by J. Gibson, HOA: 14½", WOA: 17½", MRF S-14,201.*

years later.[10] It was not until 1763 that a treaty between the English and French made possible the beginnings of what might be considered settlement in the area.[11]

Other impediments to progress remained. Although many individuals, including "Virginia gentlemen" such as the Washingtons and Patrick Henry, were interested in purchasing acreage, the original charters of Charles I and Charles II stood in the way of land speculation.[12] Further, in 1763 George III issued a proclamation that forbade governors to issue warrants and surveys for lands beyond the Blue Ridge Mountains. The Crown reserved for the Indians all the land west of the line running down the watershed of the Appalachians, yet interest in this territory (fig. 6) could not be quashed. In 1765 Virginian Henry Timberlake published in London an account of his journey along the Holston River and his winter's stay among the overhill Indians. His narrative describing the potential of the "overhill" region became a popular volume.[13] Two years later, in the spirit of the time, settlers began to ignore the Royal Proclamation of 1763, just as some had refused to pay taxes on their land to representatives of the Crown. The North Carolina government collected or "regulated" quit-rents for the Crown, but a group of men who refused to pay earned the name of "Regulators." Some drifted westward, encouraged by land speculators, while others fought and were soundly defeated at the battle of Alamance in 1771.[14] There was a basic difference between the Regulators and the frontiersmen of Virginia and the Mecklenberg area of North Carolina. The latter purchased their land as soon as it came on the market, while the former staked out claims before the land became available.[15]

In 1775 North Carolina merchant Richard Henderson formed the Transylvania Company and, acknowledging Indian ownership of the land, purchased nearly twenty million acres from the tribes at a price of about two and a half cents per acre. This land was situated in the central basin of Tennessee and lower Kentucky. Henderson observed that "the country might invite a prince from his palace, merely for the pleasure of contemplating its beauty and excellence, but only add the rapturous idea of property, and what allurements can the world offer for the loss of so glorious a prospect?"[16] Other North Carolinians bought large portions of Granville's tract,[17] the south line of which would have run, had it been surveyed, near the present town of Sweetwater above Chattanooga in East Tennessee to Covington in the west near the Mississippi.[18]

The first known permanent settler in eastern Tennessee was William Bean. In 1769 he emigrated from southwest Virginia with his son, George Bean, who was to become the state's first silversmith (see fig. 34).[19] The family settled on Boone Creek near the Watauga River where a settlement sprang up before the Revolutionary War. James Robertson moved to Watauga in 1770; nine years later he helped found Nashville.[20] The Jacob Brown settlement and trading post, first established by Regulator John Ryan on the Nolichucky River, and the Carter settlement and store on the Holston River, rank with Watauga as the earliest settlements in Tennessee.[21] The inhabitants of this region were not aristocracy, but rather common people willing to travel by horseback along trails often too narrow to afford passage for a wagon. Many wore clothing of dressed skins, and most carried only the barest necessities. Their wills and inventories reveal the paucity of their possessions, often just a quilt, a "kittle," and perhaps a mare, yet these Wataugans initiated "the first independent governmental body organized by . . . Americans."[22] James Robertson and John Bean negotiated a ten-year lease with the Cherokee for the Wataugans' use of the land,[23] thereby bringing about a somewhat interrupted and uneasy peace with the natives.

According to historian Marcus Lewis, "no less than 70,000 people moved through the Cumberland Gap and over the 'Wilderness Road'" in the years 1774–90.[24] In 1789 North Carolina ceded "that tract of land south of the Ohio river" to the United States, perhaps as a result of the unrest of the settlers in that district. Because the state of North Carolina provided no protection from the Indians but required taxes nevertheless, a number of citizens formed the short-lived (1784–88) state of Franklin in East Tennessee. The federal census of 1790 recorded a total of 35,691 inhabitants in the counties of the Southwest Territory. Historians do not always agree on the origins of these intrepid men and women. Samuel Cole Williams quoted an estimate from *A Century of Population Growth,* 1790–1900, which suggested that eighty-three percent of the settlers were of English origin and only eleven percent were Scots-Irish; the remainder during the decade of the 1790s were said to be German, Irish, Welsh, or Huguenot. Williams believed that during the Revolutionary period twenty-five percent of the pioneers had been Scots-Irish, "almost all of whom came from the Valley of Virginia or from Pennsylvania."[25] In 1794 Jebidiah Morse's London-published *American Geography* described early Tennesseans as chiefly of Scottish descent, from Pennsylvania and the part of Virginia lying west of the Blue Ridge. Morse noted that simplicity of manner prevailed among these men and women who came to secure and work the land. Historian Thomas Perkins Abernethy, from a more distant perspective, added Germans to the newcomers "who came down the valley of Virginia from Pennsylvania." He contrasted the hard-working German "thrifty farmers and mechanics" with the Scots-Irish "adventurers and politicians," who "blazed trails, fought Indians, established governments, and speculated in lands."[26]

North Carolina's granting of land warrants in the Tennessee area to men who had served in the Continental army brought more settlers to the territory. Some came to claim their land; others sold their grants. Daniel Smith recorded in his *Short Description of the Tennessee Government* that by 1793 the territory was divided into western and eastern sections, separated by the Cumberland Mountains. He observed that farmers living in the eastern sector would find a ready market in Richmond, while those in the western sector would send their goods down the Mississippi River to New Orleans.[27]

In June 1796 forty-two thousand square miles of territory south of the Ohio became known as the state of Tennessee, even though the region contained acreage that belonged to the Indians. The territory then contained ten counties: Blount, Davidson, Sullivan, Greene, Jefferson, Sevier, Hawkins, Sumner, Washington, and Tennessee (now Robertson and Montgomery).[28] It was not until 1818 when Isaac Shelby and Andrew Jackson purchased West Tennessee from the Chickasaw Indians that the state's three geographical areas were made politically contiguous. These regions (fig. 7) were defined by the ridges and valleys of East Tennessee lying between the Appalachian and Cumberland mountains, the highland-rimmed central basin of Middle Tennessee between the Cumberland and Tennessee rivers, and the "gentle undulating surface"[29] of West Tennessee, stretching from the Tennessee River to the Mississippi.

The history of silversmithing in Tennessee parallels the growth and settlement of those geographical areas; a study of the trade can be divided into three periods. The first immediately follows the transition from territory to statehood in 1796, and lasts until about 1820 with the end of the frontier. The second period spans the 1820–40

7. A map of Tennessee engraved by E. Colin, undated, published by Arnoul, Paris. HOA: 11", WOA: 17½. MRF S-14,205.

period when steamboats and stagecoaches helped to make Tennessee the fifth most populous state in the Union. The third and final period of study, 1840–60, encompasses the introduction of electroplating and rail travel; it was brought to a close by the developing Civil War.

George Bean was working at the silversmithing trade in East Tennessee as early as 1792. Within a few years, Joseph T. Elliston earned his first fifty cents repairing a watch in Nashville. Such services increasingly were required in Middle Tennessee as the state's central basin attracted more and more people.[30] By 1800 trails into East Tennessee had been widened enough to allow wagon passage.[31] Samuel Cole Williams recorded three "first roads": the Island Road from Chilhowie, Virginia, to what is now Kingsport; a wagon route from Burke County, North Carolina, to Jonesboro; and the Walton Road from Campbell's Station near Knoxville to Nashville.[32] In 1802 Andre Michaux described the road between those two cities as "wide and as well beaten as those in the environs of Philadelphia."[33] Other roads (fig. 8) were planned. Along these overland routes surged a growing number of emigrants from Virginia, North Carolina, Massachusetts, Pennsylvania, Kentucky, Maryland, France, Scotland, and England.[34] In addition, exports and imports moved to and from Baltimore and Philadelphia over the same routes.[35]

Gentlemen Washington Feb. 23. 1803.

It is upwards of a twelvemonth since my attention was drawn to the importance of a road which should enable the inhabitants of Tenisee & Kentucky to seek a market on the Savannah, and instructions were immediately given to our Commissrs. Genl. Wilkinson & others to negotiate with the Cherokees for permission to the states interested to open the road through their country. it was stiffly rejected at first; but they have been made sensible of the urgency of the case, and have latterly shewn better dispositions. instructions have been given to bring it to a close, and when obtained we shall adopt the best means we can for having it judiciously conducted. you may assure your government that no unnecessary delay will be admitted so far as our operation is necessary. Accept my friendly salutations & assurances of respect.

Th: Jefferson

8. President Thomas Jefferson's letter of 23 February 1803 indicating his support for the building of a road "... which should enable the inhabitants of Tenisee and Kentucky to seek a market on the Savannah ..." and stating that negotiations were underway with "... the Cherokees for permission to the states interested to open the road through their country. ..." Courtesy of the Tennessee State Library and Archives.

DIVISIONS CIVILES ET POPULATION.

Comtés.	*Blancs.*	*Noirs libres.*	*Esclaves*	*Divers.*	*Total.*
Anderson.	4,295	24	349	0	4.668
Bedford.	12,334	88	3,590	0	16,012
Bledsoe.	3.616	23	361	0	4,005
Blount.	10.154	54	1,050	0	11,258
Campbell. . . .	4.093	35	116	0	4,244
Carter.	4,484	6	345	0	4,835
Claiborne. . . .	5,101	30	377	0	5,508
Cock.	4,409	15	468	0	4,892
Davidson.	12,066	189	7.899	0	20,154
Dickson.	3 861	24	1,305	0	5,190
Franklin.	12.338	66	4.167	0	16.571
Giles.	9,272	25	2,261	0	11,558
Granger.	6,796	199	656	0	7,651
Greene.	10.465	30	829	0	11,324
Hamilton.	766	16	39	0	821
Hardman. . . .	1,317	9	136	0	1,462
Hawkins.	9 308	310	1,331	0	10,949
Hickman	5,371	9	700	0	6,080
Humphries. . . .	3,522	3	542	0	4,067
Jackson.	6,734	109	750	0	7,593
Jefferson.	8,030	31	882	0	8,943
Knox.	11,666	83	1,205	0	12,954
Lawrence. . . .	3,066	1	294	0	3,631
Lincoln.	12,506	5	2,250	0	14,761
Minn.	1,452	18	153	0	1.623
Marion.	3,719	2	167	0	3,888
Maury.	15.620	49	6,420	52	22,141
Montgomery. . .	7,491	65	4.663	0	12.219
Monroe.	2,351	22	156	0	2,529
Morgan.	1,630	0	46	0	1,676
Overton.	6.431	32	665	0	7,128
Perry.	2,161	0	223	0	2,384
Rhea.	3.858	23	334	0	4,215
Roane.	7,025	56	814	0	7,895
Robinson.	7.379	39	2,520	0	9,938
Rutherford . . .	14,165	2 0	2,187	0	16,552
Sevier.	4,469	13	290	0	4,772
Shelby.	251	0	103	0	354
Smith.	13.938	88	3,554	0	17,580
Stewart.	6,997	48	1,352	0	8,397
Sullivan.	6 083	96	836	0	7,015
Sumner.	13.701	143	5,362	0	19,211
Washington. . .	8,506	72	979	0	9,557
Wayne.	2,387	0	72	0	2,459
Warren.	9,385	12	950	0	10,347
White.	7,981	127	593	0	8,701
Williamson. . .	13,593	75	6,972	0	20,640
Wilson.	14,724	162	3,844	0	18,730
	340,867	2737	79,157	52	422,813

La population était, en 1790, de 35,691 habitants.
en 1800, de 105,602.
en 1810, de 261,727.

9. *A table from J. Carez's* Carte Geographique, Statisque and Historique du Tennessee, *(No. xxxii), published about 1825, appeared again in Eastin Morris's 1834 publication,* Tennessee Gazetteer, or Topographical Dictionary, *demonstrating the increase in Tennessee's population from 1790–1825.*

Federal censuses recorded the influx of settlers. By 1800 the state had attained a population of 105,802; by 1810, this figure had more than doubled, rising to 261,727, and by 1820, the population of 1800 had almost quadrupled, reaching 422,813 (fig. 9).[36] Archibald Henderson, in *Conquest of the Old Southwest*, provided a reason for this surge, noting that the settlers' "prime determinative . . . was the passion for the acquisition of land."[37] Tennessee settlers during the first several decades of the state's history primarily were concerned with the development of productive farms rather than the amenities; even recreation such as card games is said to have been a "rare amusement."[38] As a result only about fifty pieces of silverware, almost none of them hollow ware, have been found from this period. The marks on early Tennessee silver often seem out of proportion, too large for the silver on which they were stamped. Spoons predominate; an occasional ladle, and a few presentation cups reveal the work of men like the Ellistons, John Garner, Thomas Cain, and William Hilliard.[39] No work by the Atkinsons, George Bean, Benjamin Barton, Francis Fleshart, and others has come to light.

These early silversmiths settled in the towns that grew around the crossroads of the early trails, usually in the center of good farm land, not far from river trade routes. Such towns included Dandridge, Elizabethton, Jonesboro, Knoxville, and Maryville in East Tennessee; and Carthage, Franklin, Nashville, Clarksville, Columbia, Murfreesboro, and Winchester in Middle Tennessee. Trade at the time was principally with the East—Baltimore, Richmond, and Philadelphia, the latter lying about 650 miles distant from Knoxville. Most of Middle Tennessee's imports came by wagon from Philadelphia to Pittsburgh, then down the Ohio River and up the Cumberland, or by river routes to Kentucky and then overland via Lexington.[40]

Seventy names make up the list of early-period craftsmen. Of that seventy, fifty-one called themselves silversmiths, and eighteen mentioned the word "goldsmith" in their advertisements Some, like Thomas Deaderick, had no doubt served a complete apprenticeship[41] before reaching Tennessee. These men advertised for apprentices (fig. 10) and used the terms "goldsmith and silversmith" to indicate their experience. A second group trained under silversmiths but may not have completed a seven-year apprenticeship. Joseph T. Elliston, for example, was apprenticed to kinsman Samuel Ayres in Kentucky at the age of sixteen, yet three or four years later he was working on his own in Nashville.[42] Others in this group were runaways (fig. 11). Indented apprentice Alfred Parrot ran away from silversmiths Richmond & Flint (see fig. 103) of Nashville and three years later, he was advertising in Cairo. Some silversmiths such as Thomas Cain (fig. 12) also called themselves watch and clockmakers, while some, like A. R. Freeman of Nashville, advertised as silver platers. Before the invention of

LIBERAL ENCOURAGEMENT &
CONSTANT EMPLOY,
will be given to one or two
JOURNEYMEN
At the Gold and Silver Smith business, and to one at the Clock & Watch busines. Also, wanted an Apprentice of a good family between the age of 14 and 16 years.

G. G. GARNER.

Knoxville, August 3, tf.

10. *Silversmith Griffin G. Garner advertised in the* Knoxville Register *of 10 August 1816 for journeymen and "an Apprentice of a good family. . . ." All advertisements illustrated herein are courtesy of the Tennessee State Library and Archives.*

STRAY DOGS.

RAN AWAY from the subscriber, within a week past, two dogs, neither of them very valuable. One was a large dog, nearly 6 feet high, dark complexion and eyes—named AARON WINSLOW—has a father living some place in Albama. The smaller was named TRIP—he had a white face, and was as pretty a little fellow as you would wish to see—it is not known whether he has a father or not. The big dog ran away on Sunday last, and made for the south. The little one ran away on Monday—and made for—no body knows where. A reward of one cent and no thanks will be given for the big dog—fifty cents and all reasonable expences paid for the little one.

Any person seeing these dogs will please give information to the undersigned by letter or otherwise, and confine them in jail so I may get them again—& moreover, all persons are hereby cautioned against trading with or harboring said dogs—particularly the dog Aaron as a body is very apt to smell bad after being in his company. The little fellar' Trip, 'never hurts nobody.'

THOS. A. THOMSON.

27th June, 1823.

11. *Silversmith Thomas A. Thomson announced in the Franklin* Independent Gazette *of 4 July 1823 that his two "Stray Dogs" had run away: "A reward of one cent and no thanks will be given for the big dog—fifty cents and all reasonable expences paid for the little one."*

THOMAS CAIN,
CLOCK & WATCH MAKER,

INFORMS the public that he has commenced business in the house opposite Mr. Haynes's tavern. He assures those who may think proper to favor him with their custom, that their commands shall be faithfully executed, on the most reasonable terms. October 14, 1809.

12. *Silversmith Thomas Cain identified himself as a "Clock & Watchmaker" in the* Knoxville Gazette *of 14 October 1809.*

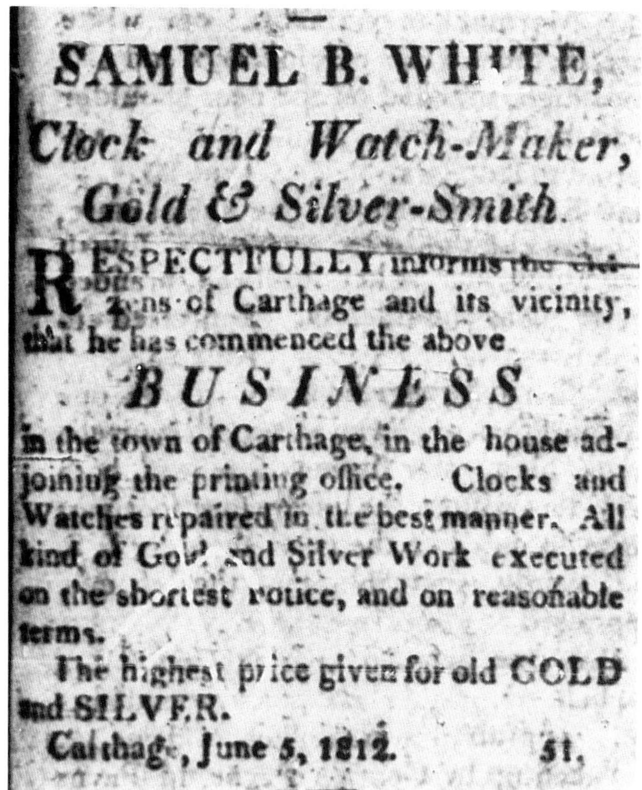
SAMUEL B. WHITE,
Clock and Watch-Maker,
Gold & Silver-Smith.
RESPECTFULLY informs the citizens of Carthage and its vicinity, that he has commenced the above
BUSINESS
in the town of Carthage, in the house adjoining the printing office. Clocks and Watches repaired in the best manner. All kind of Gold and Silver Work executed on the shortest notice, and on reasonable terms.
The highest price given for old GOLD and SILVER.
Carthage, June 5, 1812. 51.

13. *Samuel B. White, "Clock and Watch-Maker, Gold & Silver-Smith" announced the commencement of his business in the* Carthage Gazette *of 8 July 1812.*

THE Subscriber having furnished himself with all the necessary apparatus for carrying on the Clock, Watch-Making and Silver Smith business, in Gallatin, is now ready to receive any business that he may be favored with and by his assiduity will endeavour to merit the custom of those who may employ him.
D. H. WHIPPLE.

14. *D. H. Whipple advertised in the Nashville* Democratic Clarion & Tennessee Gazette *of 2 April 1811 that he had "furnished himself with all the necessary apparatus for carrying on the Clock, Watch-Making and Silver-Smith business, in Gallatin. . . ."*

electroplating, these tradesmen probably used close-plating, which combined heat, tin, a soldering iron, and pressure to make a thin foil of silver adhere to a base metal. John Campbell's 1845 stock inventory (Appendix II) listed a plate mill and bellows; these items most likely were utilized for this purpose. The technique was used most successfully with small articles such as teaspoons, spurs, or harness parts. These platers may have made Sheffield plate, but no documented example or evidence has been found.

The advertisements of these early craftsmen were straightforward notices (figs. 13, 14) supplying names, addresses, and services performed. Joseph T. Elliston and Thomas Deaderick of Nashville varied that pattern, using lotteries to encourage business. In 1803 Elliston urged "Fortunes Favorites!!!" to purchase tickets at three dollars each, thereby gaining a chance to win anything from silver teaspoons and silver sleeve buttons to an "elegant gold watch." The purchase of a lottery ticket for acquisition of such niceties may have been more acceptable to the frontiersmen of early nineteenth century Tennessee than an outright purchase.

An examination of the 1820 federal census of manufactures revealed that silversmiths resided in at least seven counties: Bedford, Davidson, Green, Hawkins, Maury, Rutherford, and Smith. According to that survey the craftsmen made clocks and watches, gold and silverware, dirks, and rings. They used silver from Spanish milled dollars (see figs. 65, 65a) and "all kinds of gold," noted Robert Fletcher of Rutherford County, "with the exception of American coins."[43] The population census for 1820 indicated seven additional counties with working silversmiths. Perhaps these men generated more income from farming, gunsmithing, or some other pursuit, much as Vermont's silversmiths worked at a variety of tasks to "eke out a livelihood,"[44] and so were not considered silversmiths in the census of manufactures. The census of manufactures was inconsistent in its trade listing.

By the second decade of the nineteenth century, life became more prosperous for Tennesseans, especially in the Cumberland Basin, due to rapidly-expanding agricultural production. The price of cotton soared[45] during the years 1815–18, bringing even more people into the western community, and the value of real estate rose. At the beginning of the 1820s, however, land values fell, for the panic of 1819 had driven down the price of cotton.[46] A depression swept the Cumberland Basin, its effects appearing in the notices (fig. 15) of Tennessee's silversmiths. According to Abernethy, "Out of the war, the boom, and the panic, there emerged a new order of

All persons indebted to me

BY bond, note, or book account, are requested to come forward immediately and discharge the same, as I am so situated I can't wait longer than the 15th of September, at which time all unpaid I shall be obliged to hand to an officer for collection. This measure I am driven to by necessity.

G. G. GARNER.

Knoxville, August 24, 1819. tf

15. *Griffin G. Garner's notice in the* Knoxville Register *of 24 August 1819 reflects the desperation caused by the 1819 depression.*

things. Tennessee had ceased to be a frontier and had come to be an agricultural commonwealth . . . trade was occupying the attention of the rising towns, and steamboats and stage coaches were taking the place of keelboats and packhorses."[47]

During 1820–40 the state matured rapidly. Its geographical destiny had been reached with Jackson's and Shelby's purchase of West Tennessee from the Chickasaw in 1818. During this time Tennessee became a significant producer of agricultural products, particularly in its central basin. Federal censuses detail the state's growth after the first quarter of the century. The population had risen to 684,000 by 1830; by 1840 Tennessee had become the fifth most populous state in the Union with a population of more than 850,000.[48] Commerce grew accordingly. From 1821–36, Governor William Carroll established "Jacksonian Democracy" in Tennessee, and his answer to the economic disaster of 1819 was economy and retrenchment. He favored business on a specie basis, and expected banks, either state or federal, to act conservatively. Nashville exported one million dollars' worth of cotton in 1825, and by 1833 was exporting four and one-half million dollars' worth of goods, importing goods worth three and one-half million. Abernethy writes of Nashville: "The frontier outpost had grown into a western commercial center . . . the simplicity of the early years was replaced by a society which thought much of dress and manners and social activities."[49]

Transportation within Tennessee and into the state had become more efficient. Governor Carroll backed improvements in the navigational systems of Tennessee's rivers and in fact was the owner of the first steamboat to reach Nashville. He also envisioned roads that would permit easier access to major markets.[50] S. Augustus Mitchell's *Tourist Pocket Map of 1836* listed nine regular stagecoach routes out of Nashville, and four out of Knoxville. The Murfreesboro to Huntsville, Alabama, stage ran three days each a week. Stages traveled with similar frequency between Blountville and Abingdon, Virginia, from McMinnville to Huntsville, Alabama, and between Columbia and Florence, Alabama. Frances Trollope's description of stage travel in 1830 dismissed any idea of comfort. She wrote that "the coach had three rows of seats, each calculated to holdthree persons, and we were only six . . . we were for some miles tossed about like a few potatoes in a wheel-barrow. Our knees, elbows, and heads required too much care for their protection to allow us leisure to look out of the windows; but at length the road became smoother, and we became more skillful in the art of balancing ourselves, so as to

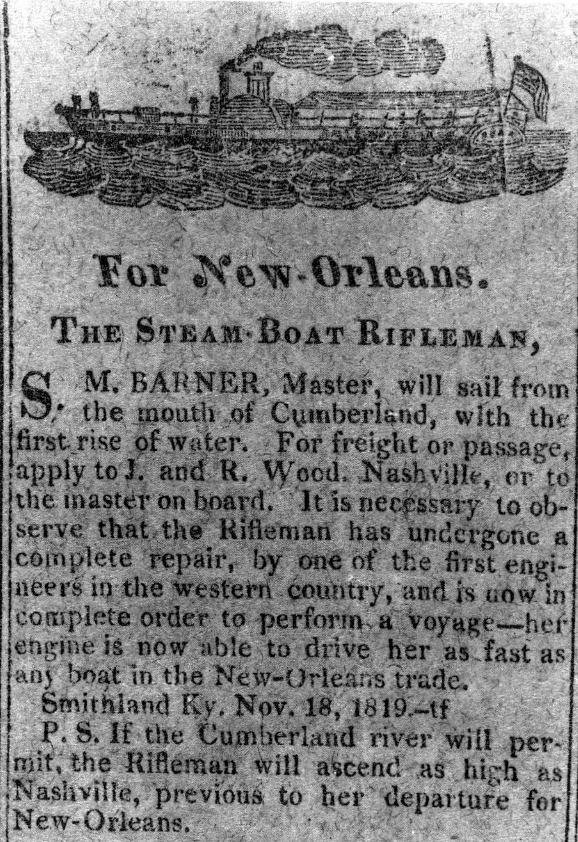

For New-Orleans.

THE STEAM-BOAT RIFLEMAN,

S. M. BARNER, Master, will sail from the mouth of Cumberland, with the first rise of water. For freight or passage, apply to J. and R. Wood. Nashville, or to the master on board. It is necessary to observe that the Rifleman has undergone a complete repair, by one of the first engineers in the western country, and is now in complete order to perform a voyage—her engine is now able to drive her as fast as any boat in the New-Orleans trade.

Smithland Ky. Nov. 18, 1819.–tf

P. S. If the Cumberland river will permit, the Rifleman will ascend as high as Nashville, previous to her departure for New-Orleans.

16, 16a. *Fast transportation became increasingly important to Tennessee's economic well-being. The rise of the steam-boat saw the decline of the frontier and the beginning of a new era for the young state (*Nashville Clarion, *18 Nov. 1819). By the 1850s the sight of a steamboat on the Cumberland River was common enough to warrant its inclusion in an 1859 lithograph of Nashville's Zollicoffer Bridge and Levee printed by J. E. Wagner. HOA: 12½", WOA: 18½". Private Collection.*

meet the concussion with less danger of dislocation."[51] Steamboats represented a tremendous savings in time and in the cost of shipping (figs. 16, 16a). A trip by flatboat to New Orleans and return by keelboat or overland route might have taken a year.[52] A steamboat could reach New Orleans from Nashville in a week and return in about seventeen days.[53] Such shipping made it easier for Tennesseans to send their produce and wares to market, thereby increasing personal wealth. Steamboats also made the importation of competing products possible. An advertisement of 2 July 1830 in the Gallatin *Examiner*, for example, informed local readers of a change of address by Bailey & Company, a jewelry firm located within the Philadelphia city limits.

These developments were directly responsible for increasing the size of the Tennessee silversmithing trade. Listings for silversmiths and clock and watchmakers rose from fifty in the earlier period to one hundred and seven in the middle period. Of that number, seventy-seven used

John Nuckolls,
GOLD & SILVER-SMITH, WATCH MAKER AND JEWELLER.
HAS commenced the above business, in this place, and is prepared to execute any business in his line, with neatness and despatch.
Jackson, May 29.—3m

17. *John Nuckolls's advertisement in the* Jackson Gazette *of 29 May 1824 simply and directly stated his services.*

REMOVAL.
THE subscriber has removed his SILVER-SMITH SHOP to the east corner of the public square, to the white framed house lately occupied by S. Holland, and formerly by L. & J. Thompson, as a Saddler's shop, where all work in his line can be had on the most accommodating terms.
☞ WATCHES and CLOCKS repaired carefully at the cheapest rates.
☞ SILVER-WORK done in the neatest manner.
☞ A neat assortment of JEWELRY on hand, and a constant supply kept.
☞ *AN APPRENTICE WANTED.* A smart, active boy, of a good family, between 14 and 17 years of age, would be taken on favorable terms, if immediate application be made.
THOS. A. THOMSON.
Franklin, Oct. 3, 1823. 16.3t

18. *As early as 1823, in addition to producing silver flatware and repairing watches, Thomas A. Thomson was "merchandizing" jewelry. (Franklin* Independent Gazette, *3 Oct. 1823).*

the term "silversmith" in their advertisements; only ten mentioned the word "goldsmith." The author has found the birthplaces of just forty-three of the one hundred and seven, but these origins may be fairly representative of the entire trade: Virginia, nine; North Carolina, six; Tennessee, five; New England, five; Kentucky, four; Pennsylvania, three; Maryland, three; Scotland, two; Ireland, two; France, South Carolina, Germany, and Santo Domingo, one each. It is possible that few of these men had served the usual silversmith's seven-year apprenticeship,[54] yet a considerable amount of silver was made in Tennessee during the 1820–40 period, perhaps more than in either the earlier or later periods. John Campbell and Paul Negrin made fine silver (see figs. 48c, 102a) during this period, as did Samuel Bell, William Calhoun, C. Guiteau, and James Hodge, although the work (see figs. 35e, 47, 76, and 81) of the latter four spans both the middle and later periods.

J. Brown's advertisement of 1820 establishes the theme of this transitional middle period (see fig. 42). Although Brown had served his apprenticeship in London, he did not rely solely on the work of his own hands or on special orders after establishing himself in Knoxville. He stocked jewelry and silver work, some of it probably his own work and some perhaps imported from Philadelphia or New York. Some silversmiths' advertisements (fig. 17) retained the earlier period's simple statement of service approach; these men, particularly in the smaller towns like Bolivar, Madison, Franklin (fig. 18), and Jackson, probably conducted business much as it had been carried on in the earlier years. The touchmarks (see figs. 110b, 119a) of men such as Elijah M. Ringo and John M. Smith retained the appearance of an earlier time, although Smith's marks (see figs. 119c, 119d, and 119e) evolved with some degree of sophistication. Silversmiths in larger towns, like Knoxville's Samuel Bell, continued to make silver, but also advertised (fig. 19) an added variety of new items to meet the shifting tastes of their customers. The first quarter of the nineteenth century had transformed some of Tennessee's frontiersmen into sizeable landholders (fig. 20).[55] They began to acquire possessions to grace their homes, although relatively little silver was recorded in their inventories. Perhaps the conservative nature of some individuals prohibited their "overdoing" luxuries. James McGavock, for example, arrived in Middle Tennessee in the late eighteenth century

JEWELRY.

THE SUBSCRIBER

HAS JUST RECEIVED IN ADDITION TO HIS FORMER STOCK, A

NEW SUPPLY

OF

JEWELRY,

Consisting in part, of the following articles, (TO WIT:)

Finger Rings, Breast Pins, Ear Rings, } *Pearl, Garnet, Jet, Topaz, Paste, & Christal.*
Gilt, Steel and Jet Buckles,
do. Reticle and waist Clasps,
Fine Steel Watch Chains, Keys and Seals.
Common do.
Silver spectacles, with green & plain glasses,
Gold and Silver Tooth Picks,
Silver pencil cases, with knives, calendar and plain,
Set and plain Collar Buttons,
Table, Tea, Desert, Cream, Mustard, Gravy Soup, & Salt } **SPOONS**
Sugar Tongs,
Sugar Bowls and Cream Jugs,
Silver mounted Cocoa Nut shells,
Silver Spurs, plain and chased,
Fine & Jewelers Gold chains,
Chased & Set fine, and Jewelers gold Seals and Keys,
Fine Gold chain for Necklaces.
Silver Thimbles,
Steel purses,
Fine and Jewelers gold, set and plain clasps,
Gold mounted Jet Beads,
Eight Day Brass *CLOCKS,*
First rate *ENGLISH WATCHES,*
Swiss and French do.

First rate *ENGLISH WATCHES,*
Swiss and French do.
Toy - - - do.
Gilt breast pins, watch chains, seals and keys,
A large assortment of Dirks,
Swords, brass and silver mounted,
Ladies Scissors and knives,
Fine Scissors,
Silver and plated Scissors chains,
Pocket Compasses,
Fine Lead pencils.

ALSO, A FULL ASSORTMENT OF
Watch Makers' Tools and materials,
Scotch stone,
Pumice stone,
Borax, and
Refined Saltpetre.

ALSO, AN ASSORTMENT

OF

Fine pen, pruning & common knives,
Whips, Walking Canes, with & without spears,
Fashionable Beads and Fans,
Tortoise and mock tortoise shell side and tuck combs,
Fine and common pocket combs,
Pocket Books and Snuff Boxes,
Spring and thumb Lancets,
Sealing wax,
Brass Candlesticks,
Fine steel Snuffers,
Steel and brass barrelled *POCKET PISTOLS,*
Britiania Tea Pots,
Plated castor stands,
Violins, violin strings, and flutes,
First quality Spanish Segars,
Windsor, Rosin and transparent Soap,
Scenting bottles,
Sponges,

GOLD LEAF,

Carpenters' Pencils,
Snuff and snuff Beans,
Tooth brushes, and
Brass heel plates.

ALSO,

An Assortment of

Confectionary Articles,

(SUCH AS,)

Hoarhound, Peppermint, and Lemon, } **CANDIES,**
Sugar almonds & secrets,
Raisins, English Currens,
Almonds, Figs and Cocoa Nuts.

ALSO,

GROCERIES.

Sugar & Coffee,
Copperas & Madder,

WINDOW GLASS,

Pepper, Allspice, Indigo, Ginger and Allum.

ALSO, AN ASSORTMENT

OF

STONE WARE.

All of which the Subscriber flatters himself he can sell as low for CASH, (as he is determined to sell for cash alone,) as they can be sold in this market.

Samuel Bell.

N. B.—CLOCKS and WATCHES repaired in the neatest and best manner. Travellers can have their Watches put in first rate order in a short time.

GOLD & SILVER WORK

Made to any pattern, in the neatest style.

☞ The highest price will be given in CASH FOR BEES-WAX.

S. B.

Knoxville, June 9, 1825. 12m.

19. *Samuel Bell offered an extensive line of goods when he advertised his "New Supply of Jewelry," assorted silver flatware, "A Full Assortment of Watch Makers' Tools" and materials, and general merchandise. Silversmithing was added only as a postscript: "Gold and Silver Work Made to any pattern, in the neatest style"* (Knoxville Register, *9 June 1825*).

Table XIII. Showing the number of persons engaged in Agriculture, Commerce, and Manufactures, and also the number of foreigners not naturalized in each of the United States; together with the proportion which each class forms of the whole population.

States.	Persons engaged in						Foreigners, not naturalized.	
	Agriculture.		Commerce.		Manufactures.			
	Number.	Proportion.	Number.	Proportion.	Number.	Proportion.	Number.	Proportion.
Maine,	55,031	18.5	4,297	1.5	7,643	2.5	1,680	.5
New-Hampshire,	52,384	21.4	1,068	.4	8,699	3.5	124	.05
Massachusetts,	63,460	12.1	13,301	2.5	33,464	6.4	3,425	.6
Rhode Island,	12,559	15.1	1,162	1.4	6,091	7.3	237	.28
Connecticut,	50,518	18.4	3,581	1.3	17,541	6.4	568	.2
Vermont,	50,951	21.6	776	.3	8,484	3.6	935	.4
New-York,	247,648	18.0	9,113	.66	60,038	4.3	15,101	1.1
New-Jersey,	40,812	14.4	1,830	.66	15,941	5.7	1,529	.6
Pennsylvania,	140,801	13.4	7,083	.67	60,215	5.7	10,728	1.0
Delaware,	13,259	18.2	533	.73	2,821	4.0	331	.4
Maryland,	79,135	19.4	4,771	1.2	18,640	4.5	3,776	.9
Virginia,	276,422	25.9	4,509	.4	32,336	3.0	2,142	.2
North Carolina,	174,196	27.3	2,551	.4	11,844	1.8	415	.06
South Carolina,	161,560	32.9	2,588	.5	6,488	1.3	1,205	.2
Georgia,	101,185	29.6	2,139	.6	3,557	1.0	453	.1
Alabama,	30,642	24.0	452	.3	1,412	1.1	162	.1
Mississippi,	22,033	29.2	294	.4	650	.9	181	.2
Louisiana,	53,941	35.1	6,251	4.1	6,041	4.0	3,145	2.0
Tennessee,	101,919	24.1	882	.2	7,860	1.8	312	.07
Kentucky,	132,161	23.4	1,617	.3	11,779	2.0	529	.1
Ohio,	110,991	19.0	1,459	.2	18,956	3.3	3,495	.6
Indiana,	31,074	21.1	429	.3	3,229	2.2	833	.5
Illinois,	12,395	22.5	233	.4	1,007	1.8	598	1.1
Missouri,	14,247	21.4	495	.8	1,952	3.0	497	.8
Michigan Ter.	1,468	16.6	392	4.4	196	2.0	656	7.5
Arkansas Ter.	3,613	25.4	79	.5	179	1.2	34	2
Columbia D.	853	2.6	512	1.6	2,184	6.6	564	1.7
Total,	2,065,499	21.4	72,397	.75	349,247	3.5	53,655	.55

20. *The figures in table 13 from Jedidiah and Richard Morse's* New Universal Gazetteer. . . . *(New Haven, Conn.: S. Morse, 1823) underscore the agrarian nature of Tennessee in 1823.*

and became one of the wealthiest landowners in the Southwest, living "in simple pioneer frugality, a frontiersman till his death in 1812." Although his dwelling was of log construction,[56] his sons built fine homes. Teaspoons and tablespoons still predominated in most households, but middle-period inventories disclose several or even "a sett" as opposed to single spoons found in earlier-period listings. More specialized forms begin to appear at this time, such as silver thimbles, cream spoons, casters, and waiters.

A search for silver items in a sampling of estate inventories in several counties, beginning with the year each respective county was formed, revealed the following silver items: Smith County, during 1799–1831, 62 tablespoons, 79 teaspoons, 3 ladles, 7 watches, and 9 miscellaneous items; McMinn County (1819–31), 6 tablespoons and 6 teaspoons; Montgomery County (1796–1840), 166 tablespoons, 158 teaspoons, 5 ladles, 24 watches, and 29 miscellaneous items. The fact that so little silver was recorded is puzzling; the veracity of these inventories appears dubious. Perhaps they support the theory of frontier frugality as well as the notion that silver holdings really should not be a matter of public record! Middle Tennessee attorney-historian T. Vance Little pointed out that nineteenth century decedents' household items passed to their wives free from creditors. "The fact that they were exempt from claims is no reason for their omission from the estate inventory," observed Little, "but there could have been some laxity since those items on the inventory were subject to attachment."[57]

One factor seems to remain constant throughout all the decades of silversmithing in Tennessee: the difficulty of collecting debts (figs. 21, 21a). The fact that some farmers paid their accounts annually no doubt contributed to this problem. Both Donigan's and Campbell's inventories reveal pages of accounts due. In the early years accounts often were settled with barter items such as beeswax, feathers, and whiskey. This sort of trade led to pleas for cash by tradesmen whose financial state was further weakened near the end of the 1830s by the economic chaos that followed Jackson's failure to renew the national bank charter. In Nashville, banks suspended spe-

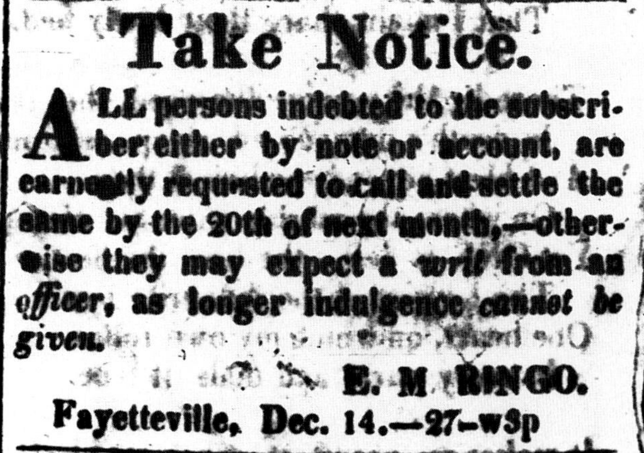
Take Notice.

ALL persons indebted to the subscriber either by note or account, are earnestly requested to call and settle the same by the 20th of next month,—otherwise they may expect a writ from an officer, as longer indulgence cannot be given.

E. M. RINGO.

Fayetteville, Dec. 14.—27-w3p

PAY UP! PAY UP!!

ALL those indebted to the subscriber by note or account are earnestly requested to come forward and settle immediately.

SAMUEL SIMPSON.

P. S. He intends doing a cash business and wishes all his old accounts settled by cash or note by the first of March—longer indulgence cannot be given.

Feb. 6, 1840—tf. S. S.

21, 21a. *An example of the difficulty silversmiths had collecting payment is the advertisement placed by E. M. Ringo in the Fayetteville* Village Messenger *of 14 December 1827. Samuel Simpson's notice to "PAY UP! PAY UP" in the* Clarksville Chronicle *of 29 October 1840 was another of the many pleas for debtors to settle their accounts.*

cie payments in 1837 and did not resume them until 1842.[58]

Perhaps because of the state of the economy, along with increased competition from retailers who could easily and cheaply import the "latest" goods, eight silversmiths met on Christmas night of 1836 to form the "Association of the Watch-Makers, Silversmiths & Jewellers of Nashville" (Appendix I). They established a bill of rates on all watch repair work, and all agreed to adhere to the prices, "knowing and feeling the necessity of union and harmony." The secretary of the association was to inform all newly-arrived watchmakers, silversmiths, and jewelers of the rates agreed upon. Notably missing among the men present was Thomas Gowdey, who may have represented the source of the association's fiercest competition: the dollar-wise retailer. Whether Gowdey actually made silver himself remains uncertain. He either was not invited to attend the association's two meetings in 1836, or simply chose not to join, although six years later he formed a partnership with association member John Peabody. The association's minute book, found by the author at the nineteenth-century Crockett house (still standing on Wilson Pike near Franklin in Williamson County) represents the first record located in the South of a silversmiths' guild, with the exception of Pleasant and Sill's circa 1809 account of an organized group in Baltimore.[59] Although the Nashville association planned an annual December meeting, nothing further is known of its accomplishments.

Had they but known, those Nashville silversmiths, watchmakers, and jewelers were to face even fiercer competition in the following two decades. Railroads created the same measure of excitement and growth that steamboats had provided earlier, and the mechanization of silver work brought diverse marketing challenges to the period from 1840–60. This later period in the history of silversmithing in Tennessee represents yet another transition, in this instance firmly interweaving the threads of mechanized silver manufacture and the increasing ease of transportation into one seamless cloth.

In 1845 Middle Tennessee boasted 410 miles of macadamized roads, paved with layers of broken stone, thus increasing the speed of stage travel from three or four miles per hour to seven or eight.[60] The pages of Nashville's newspapers during the 1840s provided an impressive display of steamboat activity: new goods arriving from New York only sixteen days after shipment, and the steamboat making a voyage to St. Louis every ten days. One advertisement offered heartfelt thanks to the people of Tennessee for their patronage on the Smithland, Kentucky, packet; Smithland lies on the Ohio River at the confluence of the Cumberland and Ohio rivers. Railroads became a significant factor by about 1854 when nine lines within the state utilized about 400 miles of track, and almost 700 additional miles were under construction.[61]

The resulting changes not only brought more competing goods into the region, but also produced an acceleration of migration to and from the state. Tradesmen who were not as successful as they might have liked found it easier to leave the state, and thus Tennessee "played a significant role in the colonizing of other states" in the 1850s.[62] An analysis of the 1850 Tennessee population reveals that thirty-five percent of Arkansas settlers had been born in Tennessee; twenty-one percent of Texas settlers and nineteen percent of the Missouri population had the same roots. Similarly, settlers dissatisfied with their lot elsewhere moved into Tennessee. The same study of the state's population of 850,000 in 1850 indicated that forty-two percent had been born in North Carolina, twenty-seven percent in Virginia, and nine percent in South Carolina.[63] A search of 1860 census records revealed the pattern of emigration followed by some Tennessee silversmiths: B. Archerman sailed from England to New York, moving from there to Ohio, and then to Tullahoma in Coffee County; E. R. Kerley emigrated from Wales to Boston and thence to North Carolina and Virginia, finally taking residence in Gallatin in Sumner County.

Records of the 1840–60 period documented 354 men working in silversmithing and related trades.[64] Of that number, seventy-three called themselves silversmiths; seventy-four were watch-and-clockmakers; fifty-five referred to themselves as jewelers, and the remainder used a combination of these terms. Only three used "goldsmith" in their advertisements. In some instances, the migration of silversmiths into Tennessee has made the certain attribution of marks difficult. For example, an "A. Beach" has been recorded in Hartford, Connecticut, circa 1823; an "Albert Beach" was working in New York City circa 1839–47.[65] An Andrew Beach arrived in Tennessee about 1841, and his birthplace was either "N.Y." or "N.J."; the handwriting of the 1850 census taker is difficult to read. A spoon found in Tennessee bears a mark that Ensko attributed to A. Beach of Hartford (see fig. 33). Did A. Beach leave Hartford, or did some settler carry the spoon with him to Tennessee?

For years collectors have been confused by Ensko's attribution of Nashville silversmith Joseph T. Elliston's mark to Peter Ellison of New York. Many such mysteries remain unsolved, although it should not be considered unusual that northern silversmiths, facing the rapidly expanding competition brought about by mechanized production, left the North for new territory. Among these in Tennessee were artisans like F. H. Clark, E. B. Cunningham, and Robert Wilcox. At least fifteen Tennessee silversmiths and watchmakers with names like Schmidt, Steindler, and Kirchner crossed the Atlantic, no doubt hoping to gain a better existence than they had enjoyed in such German states as Prussia, Hesse, Saxony, and Bavaria. Some of these men worked for themselves, while others went to work for established shops like those of George Washington Donigan in Nashville or James

To Silversmiths & Jewelers.
J. FOWLKES & Co. have on hand an extensive assortment of sand and blk. lead CRUCIBLES.
may 19.

22. *It is evident from this 1843 advertisement offering "an extensive assortment of sand and "Crucibles" that there were some precious metals still being hand cast in the 1840s and perhaps even later (*Memphis Weekly Appeal, *7 July 1843).*

Merriman and F. H. Clark in Memphis. The use of journeymen continued throughout all three periods of Tennessee silversmithing, but it seemed on the increase in the middle and later periods. As a result, silver made in Tennessee that bears a particular silversmith's mark may not always have been made totally by him, unless the piece was the work of a one-man shop.

The influx of people and goods brought technological advances in making silver to the forefront in Tennessee. Perhaps the earliest of these was the machine that made possible the rolling of flat sheets of silver; this work had formerly required extensive forging by hand. Invented in England, this labor and time-saving device produced a flat silver sheet from the ingot. By the late eighteenth century, the machine was used by some American silversmiths. A second mechanical development employed rolling dies capable of producing elaborate banding or beading on thin strips of silver. A third innovation permitted the manufacture of silver hollow ware—even those with curved sides—by spinning thin rolled silver on a lathe and burnishing it over multiple-part wooden forms also mounted on the lathe. Spinning thereby superceded the time-consuming process of raising hollow ware by hand. Finally, the invention of electroplating in 1840 led to the large firms' production of less expensive silver plate.[66]

Tennessee silversmiths were slow to grasp these changes, some, perhaps, for lack of capital. As a result, the art's development in Tennessee may have been ten to twenty years behind that in eastern urban areas, and it is likely that before 1845 Tennessee silversmiths knew little of these methods. Trained in the earlier techniques, they continued to produce what was needed just as they always had; J. Fowlkes's 1843 advertisement (fig. 22) in a Memphis newspaper documents this conservative attitude. After the mid-1840s, however, some Tennessee silversmiths began to utilize the new mechanization either by importing rolled silver and ornamental work or by retailing completed pieces of silver—especially hollow ware—made on the eastern seaboard. In fact, it is likely that much of the hollow ware with repoussee decoration, die struck handles, and milled banding illustrated in this book are of northern manufacture. The same can be said for most of the spoons and forks with die formed handles.

23, 23a. *These two unmarked cups were awarded as prizes at fairs in Middle Tennessee in 1855. On the interior of the cup on the left are the planishing marks left from hand-raising. The example on the right has concentric rings left from spinning the body of the goblet over a wooden form chucked in a lathe. Both goblets appear to have a rolled banding at the rim and foot, and the beading on the stem of the left example also may be rolled. Fig. 23a, HOA: 4⅞".* Private collection.

New Watches, Jewelry, &c.

J. CAMPBELL,

WOULD respectfully invite the attention of those who have heretofore favored him, and the public generally, to his present new and handsome assortment of fine WATCHES, *rich and fashionable* JEWELRY, SILVER-WARE, *Plated and Britannia Ware, fine* CUTLERY. MILITARY and other GOODS usually connected with his line of business, which he has lately selected in *New York and Philadelphia*, with great care both as to *quality and prices* —and offers for sale at very moderate *advances on cost.*

He will continue to devote strict attention to the repairing of WATCHES and CLOCKS—Manufacturing and repairing of JEWELRY—manufacturing SILVER SPOONS--mounting Canes, &c. and hopes by an endeavour to merit, to receive a continuance of patronage.

October 10, 1843—tf

24, 24a. *Two of John Campbell's advertisements illustrate how a jeweler's business evolved. Campbell's notice dated 10 October 1843, in the* Nashville Union *of 4 November 1843, stated that he had on hand "rich and fashionable JEWELRY, SILVER-WARE, Plated and Britannia Ware" and that he continued "manufacturing SILVER SPOONS." His later advertisement dated 28 January 1845, in the* Nashville Union *of 8 July 1845, did not mention manufacturing.*

J. CAMPBELL

WOULD respectfully inform the public that he has returned to his former stand on the Square, and that having rebuilt and enlarged his establishment, he is prepared to execute in the best manner any business in his line with which he may be favored. He has for sale a large and handsome assortment of

Splendid Watches and Jewelry,

Of the latest and most fashionable patterns. Also a large stock of

SILVER WARE,

Consisting of Spoons, Forks. Butter-Knives, Cups, Ladles, Sugar-tongs, etc. Also—Rich silver-mounted and plated *Castors, Cake and Fruit Baskets and Waiters;* fine Branch and other *Candlesticks*; together with

Plated and Britania Urns & Pitchers,

Tea and Coffee Pots: Plates and Goblets; German-Silver Goods; Fine table Cutlery, Mats, &c. An assortment of richly painted and japanned *Tea Trays* and *Waiters*, with various other articles, such as

Spectacles, fine Pocket and Pen-Knives, Scissors, Razors and Razor-Strops, Diamond-pointed Gold & Steel Pens, Pearl and shell Card-cases and Snuff-boxes, Purses and Pocket Books, Chessmen, Backgammon Boards, Walking Canes, Revolving and Belt Pistols,

Surveyors' Compasses and Chains,

Mathematical Instruments, Tape Measurers, with a general assortment of Watch-makers' Tools and Materials.

January 28.

Two presentation cups (figs. 23, 23a) given at Sumner County fairs in 1855 document the technological dichotomy in silversmithing during the later period. No doubt some silversmiths such as Samuel Bell and James Hodge produced good-quality handmade silver throughout their Tennessee careers, while others, like William H. Calhoun and John Campbell, both of Nashville, combined both ancient and modern techniques in their production, adding as well the term "jewelers" to their advertisements (figs. 24, 24a).

Some intaglio and cameo marks (figs. 25, 25a) on Tennessee silver dating just before the Civil War were placed there by retailers who either had never picked up a raising hammer or had long given it up. For example, the marks of four so-called silversmiths and two firms operating before and after 1860 are preceded by marks used by Wood and Hughes (1840–99) of New York City. George R. Calhoun (see fig. 46b), James Merriman (see fig. 99h), Bruno Hugo Stief (see fig. 121a), and A. J. Warren (see fig. 126), Gates and Pohlman (see fig. 71a), and Hope and Miller (see fig. 84) apparently all had some of their silver made by the New York firm.

25, 25a. *Two pieces of silver with overstrikes have been found in Tennessee. The first example shows the mark of William H. Calhoun of Nashville which partially obliterated the mark of Obadiah Rich of Boston. The second illustrates how James Gowdey of Nashville tried to obliterate the mark of A. B. Warden of Philadelphia by overstriking with pseudo-hallmarks (see fig. 73). Private collection.*

26, 26a. *Beaker, unmarked, 1854, engraved "Premium D. C. A. &/ M. Association/ to W. G. Harding/ for Aged Mule" on its side. HOA: $3\frac{3}{16}$". Courtesy of Belle Mead Mansion. This beaker was found in Tennessee. Its incising is such that often has been attributed to Eastern wholesalers, but the beaker may have been made in Tennessee.*

Some silver (figs. 26, 26a) was produced by hand in Tennessee as late as 1855, and perhaps even later. Author Jill Garrett discovered town records of 1871 describing James Hodge's "*recently* built silversmith shop"; Goodspeed's *History of Tennessee* recorded the presence of silversmiths M. A. Rainbow of Shelbyville in 1880 and Leon Godfroy and J. A. Casey of Pulaski in 1886.[67] The interruption caused by the Civil War and the rapid industrialization of the South following the war, however, provided a natural terminus to this study.

Because Tennessee was settled late, its tradesmen enjoyed a narrow span of years to produce wrought ware before the onset of mechanization. Among the Protestant sects that settled the area, Presbyterians, Methodists, and Baptists predominated, and their avoidance of lending importance to the material world has insured that no hoard of beautiful old church silver will be uncovered.[68] Many historians and collectors have presumed that large quantities of silver were confiscated during the Civil War, and there is certainly some evidence to that effect, but it is more likely that silver was used in the difficult post-war years as loan collateral or for barter. Regardless of whether it was melted down or traded away, silver tended to migrate to more prosperous regions of the country.

The vicissitudes of Tennessee's history have conspired against collectors of the region's silver. The largest collection is on display at the Tennessee State Museum in Nashville. The Memphis Brooks Museum of Art, the Belle Meade Mansion in Nashville, and the Bayou Bend Collection in Houston all own Tennessee silver, and a few private collectors continue the search. The collector can be grateful for the Tennessee silver he has found, even pieces made elsewhere and then stamped with a local mark, for such imported wares reveal patterns in living that are a part of the history of silversmithing in Tennessee.

Part II
The Silversmiths of Tennessee

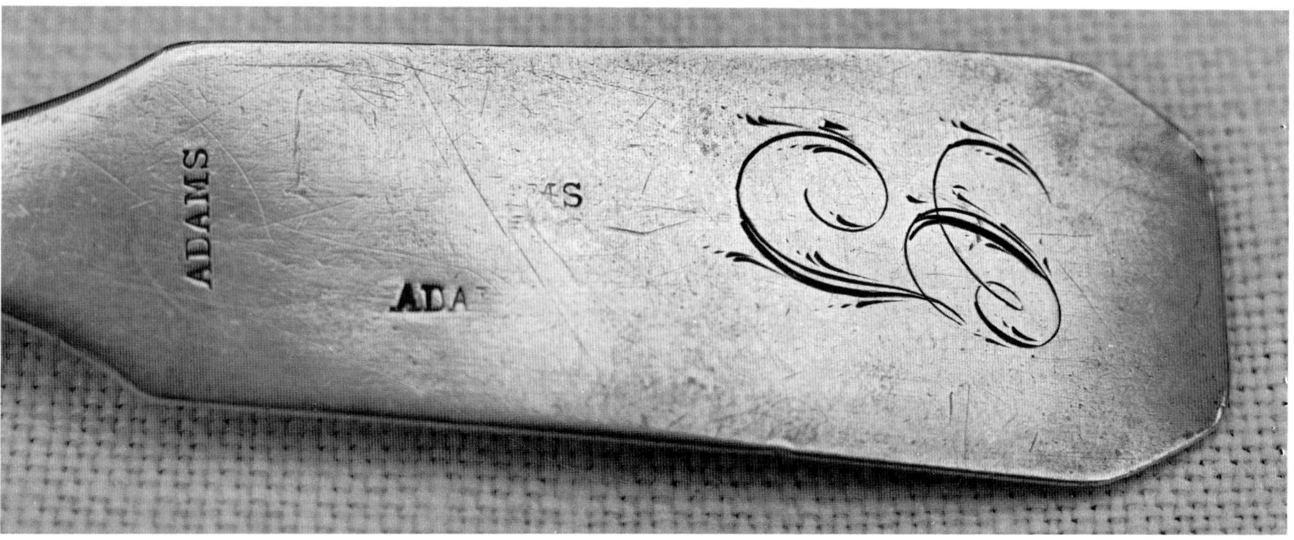

27, 27a. *Teaspoon marked on the obverse by Daniel Adams and on the reverse "Watson," 1840–50, engraved with a "G." LOA: 5⅞". Private collection. The mark illustrated in fig. 27a is that of James Watson (1821–71) of Philadelphia.*

27b, 27c. *Gold medal, engraved on the front "Peace hath her victories. Presented to Mark R. Cockrill by the state of Tennessee as a testimonial of distinguished merit for his unrivalled success in wool culture and other agricultural pursuits, Nashville, Tenn., 1854." and on the back "Dan. Adams Engraver." Diameter: 2⅜". Courtesy of the Tennessee State Museum, photograph by Stephen D. Cox.*

ADAMS, Daniel. Engraver, silversmith? Nashville, Davidson County, 1847?–d. 1885.

Daniel Adams was a Nashville engraver whom tradition has identified as a silversmith. Born the son of David and Jane Gillespie Adams in Ireland on 10 March 1810, he emigrated to the United States in 1832.[1] No record remains of when he began work in Nashville, but a spoon survives which bears his mark (figs. 27, 27a). By 1847 he was listed as a property owner on the Nashville list of taxable property.[2] In a *Nashville Daily Gazette* advertisement dated 10 January 1849, Adams respectfully informed the "citizens of Nashville and surrounding country" that he was prepared to execute "daguerreotype likenesses of all sizes in the best manner." City directories from 1855–70s list him variously as an "engraver," "engraver and daguerreotypist," and "engraver and photographer."[3] The last daguerreotype made of Andrew Jackson shortly before his death is attributed to Adams.[4]

In the collection of the Tennessee State Museum in Nashville is a gold medal (figs. 27b, 27c) presented to Mark Robertson Cockrill by the state in 1854 as a prize for his work in developing award-winning wool. If Adams made it as well as engraved it, this medal would represent the earliest marked example of Tennessee-made gold found to date.

When Adams was captured and imprisoned in the battle of Nashville during the Civil War, it is said that he first refused to accede to a Union officer's request to remove the engraving from some silver in the officer's possession. Being a practical man, Adams later consented to the task in exchange for his release. A surviving example of Adams's later work is an elaborate silver necklace (fig. 27d), which was presented to Adams's sister-in-law, Mary Jane Strickler Adams, on 25 December 1878. Adams was buried 12 September 1885 in Mt. Olivet Cemetery, Nashville.[5] Family records report that he remained a bachelor all his life.[6]

27d. *Silver necklace made, engraved, and presented by Daniel Adams to his sister-in-law, Mary Jane Strickler Adams, 25 December 1878, Nashville. LOA: 16½", center shield: HOA: 2⅝", WOA: 2⅛". Private collection.*

ADAMS, John. Clock and watchmaker, jeweler, silversmith. Knoxville, Knox County, 1809.

John Adams, a clock and watchmaker, silversmith and jeweler, announced the opening of his Knoxville shop in May 1809; he was located in a store "lately occupied by Messrs. Allen and M'Auly." The relationship, if any, between John Adam of Alexandria, Virginia (c.1791–1817), and John Adams of Knoxville is not known.[7]

ROBERT ANDERSON,

Clock & Watch Maker,

KNOXVILLE, TENNESSEE,

RETURNS his sincere thanks to the public, for their liberality since he commenced business in this place, and informs them that he occupies the same SHOP, one door east of Dr. Strong's drug and medicine store, where all

Watches, Clocks, &c.

Left for repair, will be well taken care of, and done at the shortest notice, and on reasonable terms for cash.

He has lately received in addition to his former stock, a very elegant assortment of

JEWELRY,

Consisting in part of the following articles, viz:

Gold and Gilt Watch Chains, Ear Rings, Finger Rings, Gold and Gilt Seals and Keys, Neck-Laces, &c. together with a choice assortment of

SILVER WATCHES, &c.

All of which will be sold on accommodating terms.

☞One or two JOURNEYMEN wanted immediately, who are acquainted with the Silversmith and Watch repairing business. None need apply but first rate workmen. Also an apprentice is wanted to the above business, a steady youth from the country would be preferred

December 21, 1819.

28. *Robert Anderson's advertisement in the* Knoxville Register *of 21 December 1819 asked for one or two journeymen "acquainted with the Silversmith and Watch repairing business" and stated that he would prefer "a steady youth from the country" as an apprentice.*

ADAMS, Samuel F. Watchmaker. Knoxville, Knox County, 1819.

The only known reference to Samuel F. Adams's work as a watchmaker appeared in the *Knoxville Register* for 15 June 1819 when D. W. Davis (q.v.) advertised that he was moving into the "white frame house on Market Street" formerly occupied by Samuel F. Adams as a watchmaking shop.[8]

AERTSEN and EICHBAUM. Retailers, jewelers, watch repairers. Nashville, Davidson County, 1828–29.

During 1828–29 Aertsen and Eichbaum advertised their "New Jewellery and Fancy Store!!!" on the west corner of the public square, opposite the U. S. Bank in Nashville. In addition to their stock, which represented the "newest fashion," they also repaired watches and jewelry.[9]

ALLEN, Samuel. Silversmith. Knoxville, Knox County, 1817.

A *Knoxville Register* advertisement placed Samuel Allen in that city in 1817, where he appears to have been managing a silversmithing shop for G. G. Garner (q.v.). Garner opened a new shop in the "southeast corner of a commodious brick building belonging to Thomas Humes' estate," leaving Allen in charge of the original shop.[10]

ALLEN, V. F. Watchmaker. Chattanooga, Hamilton County, 1860.

V. F. Allen was born in Baden, Germany, about 1807 and was working as a watchmaker on Market Street in Chattanooga by 1860. The *State Gazeteer* that year listed him under "Jewelry, Watches, Clocks, etc." The 1860 census recorded the value of his personal estate at $2,500.[11]

ALLISON, James R. Watchmaker, jeweler. Chattanooga, Hamilton County, 1857–60 and later.

Born in Tennessee about 1815, James R. Allison kept shop as a jeweler, watch, and clockmaker on Market Street in Chattanooga from 1857–60 and later. In the 1860 census his real estate was valued at $2,500 and his personal estate at $3,000.[12]

ANDERSON, Robert. Watch and clockmaker. Knoxville, Knox County, 1819.

Robert Anderson served an apprenticeship in Scotland before arriving in Knoxville in early 1819. As a watch and clockmaker he repaired timepieces and music boxes as well as offering for sale a "very elegant assortment of jewelry." His business was large enough to require the help of two "journeymen acquainted with the silversmith and watch repairing business" (fig. 28) as well as an apprentice for the same trades.[13]

ANDREWS, David. Watch and clockmaker, jeweler. Memphis, Shelby County, 1843.

David Andrews worked as a jeweler, watchmaker, and clockmaker in Memphis in 1843. At his shop on Front Street, one door south of the railroad, he cleaned and repaired timepieces and offered an assortment of jewelry for sale.[14]

ARCHER, William T. Jeweler. Memphis, Shelby County, 1860.

William T. Archer, who was born about 1828 in South Carolina, was living in Memphis by 1860. There he was one of the associates in A. J. Warren and Company (q.v.), a firm that dealt in silverware, jewelry, watches and fancy goods at its 293 Main Street shop. Archer's personal estate was valued at $8,000 in 1860.[15]

Edgecombe County, North Carolina, court records (May Term 1791) mention a silversmith named William Archer who took orphan John Whitehouse as an apprentice.[16] Perhaps this William was William T. Archer's father or grandfather.

ARCHERMAN, B. Silversmith. Tullahoma, Coffee County, 1860.

Born in England about 1826, B. Archerman was working as a silversmith in Tullahoma in 1860 as recorded by the federal census for that year. Archerman and Julia, his wife, had two sons: six-year-old John, born in New York, and two-year-old Walton, born in Ohio.

ATKINS (ADKINS), John. Silversmith. Sneedville, Hancock County, 1860.

In 1860 John Atkins was a partner in Rose and Atkins (q.v.), a clock and watchmaking firm in Sneedville; aged 29, he was living in the household of William and Mary Rose along with the Roses' nine children. In the federal census for 1860 this Virginia-born craftsman listed his occupation as silversmith.[17]

ATKINSON, Holland L. Silversmith, jeweler. Nashville, Davidson County, 1850–60.

H. L. Atkinson was born in Tennessee in 1828. The 1850 census recorded that he was living in the Nashville household of Charles Sayers, a shoe and bootmaker, and was working as a silversmith. From 1853–60, Atkinson appeared in Nashville directories as a jeweler, first at 15 Public Square, then at 16 Public Square, and finally at William H. Calhoun's (q.v.), a Nashville jewelry and silversmithing firm located at the corner of College Street and the public square.[18]

ATKINSON, James. Silversmith. Jonesboro, Washington County, 1860.

James Atkinson, the twenty-four-year-old son of Martha and Wilton Atkinson (q.v.), was recorded as a silversmith in the 1860 census for Washington County. Probably a former apprentice of his father, who was an invalid by 1860, James was providing at least partial support for the family. Other household members were John Atkinson, also twenty-four, who was a day laborer, and William, twenty-three, and Henry, seventeen, both of whom worked as "tinners."

ATKINSON, Matthew. Silversmith, watch and clockmaker. Jonesboro, Washington County, 1801–05?.

Matthew Atkinson sailed from France to the United States with his widowed mother, who was a practicing silversmith, and two brothers. They settled in Baltimore, Maryland, where Anne Maria Atkinson (circa 1796–1817) pursued the watch and clockmaking trades.[19] The 18 September 1787 *Baltimore Advertiser* contained a notice that Matthew and William Atkinson (q.v.) had moved their clock and watchmaking shop to the corner of Market and Holliday streets.

The brothers moved to Jonesboro, Tennessee, sometime thereafter, for in 1801 the Tennessee State Assembly commissioned Matthew and William Atkinson to create a press die for the first Tennessee state seal (fig. 29).[20]

29. Matthew and William Atkinson were commissioned in 1801 to make the press die for the state seal. This impression in parchment of their "Great Seal of the State of Tennessee" appears on Land Grant No. 2206 to William Shelton for acreage in Jackson County. Dated 8 October 1831, it was signed by Gov. William Carroll. Private collection.

The last known evidence of Matthew Atkinson's presence in Tennessee was not work-related. He was involved in two court cases in 1805 with former Tennessee Governor John Sevier, first as a witness for defendant Sevier and then as the defendant in a suit brought by Sevier.[21]

ATKINSON, William A. Silversmith, watch and clockmaker. Jonesboro, Washington County, 1793?–1801; Grainger County, 1810.

William A. Atkinson was born in France and arrived in this country as a young man with two brothers and his widowed mother, as a working silversmith. It is possible that the family supported the royal cause and fled France during the tumult of the French Revolution. One family member bore the name "Leroy," conceivably in support of the monarchy. William A. Atkinson named his own son William Leroy (q.v.). The Atkinsons settled in Baltimore, Maryland where William A. and Matthew Atkinson were working as watch and clockmakers by 1787.[22]

In 1792 William married Mary Massengill of Lincoln County, North Carolina, the daughter of a wealthy landowner.[23] Three years later Halifax's *North Carolina Journal* for 5 January 1795 reported that thieves had

> . . . broke open the shop of William A. Atkinson, watch maker in Lincolnton, and robbed [him] of seven silver watches of the following names and mumbers, viz. Robt. Ridges, London, No. 267, Alex. Anderson, London, No. 9698, Fran. Briggs, London, No. 1511, R. Stanhope, London, No. 400. Jas. Thornton, London, No. 327. P. Pagne, London, No. 583. John Carrell, Philadelphia, Number no[t] known; it turns the hour in a small circle at one side of the face, and the day of the month in another small circle, a second hand moves in the centre—the hands are gold. Also one hundred ounces of silver, of the following description, viz. an old sword mounting, an odd shoe and knee-buckle, cut money, filings, one dozen and a half of teaspoons unfinished, three pairs of finished scissars [sic], 40 small files for watchmaking, and a number of main springs. . . .

Following the birth of William and Mary Atkinson's son, Wilton, about 1793, the couple settled in Jonesboro, Washington County, Tennessee.[24] There the Tennessee State Assembly commissioned William and Matthew Atkinson to make the state's first seal (see fig. 29) in 1801. The first document stamped with the new seal was the warrant directing payment in full for one hundred dollars to the two men for their work.[25]

Atkinson and his wife had a total of seven children. An 1810 census listed a William Atkinson in Grainger County where it appears that he had relocated his family. His son Wilton (q.v.) remained in Jonesboro where he practiced the silversmithing trade. Atkinson's son William Leroy worked at the same trade in Bean Station, Grainger County.[26]

ATKINSON, William L. Jeweler. Nashville, Davidson County, 1860.

The 1860 census for Davidson County recorded a William L. Atkinson working as a jeweler in Nashville's First Ward. Born in Tennessee, the thirty-year-old probably was related to earlier Atkinson silversmiths, but his family connection has not been established.

ATKINSON, William Leroy. Silversmith. Grainger County, 1821?–60.

William Leroy Atkinson was born in Tennessee about 1793, the son of one of Tennessee's early silversmiths, William A. Atkinson (q.v.). In 1821 he married Elizabeth Cobb, and the couple took up residence in Bean Station where he worked as a silversmith.[27]

In 1826 when Atkinson's apprentice William Sword (q.v.) ran away, Atkinson offered a one-cent reward but vowed he would "pay no charges nor give any thanks" for Sword's return. Atkinson was convinced his charge had been persuaded to leave "by some degraded person in the neighborhood."[28]

Atkinson continued to work in Grainger County through at least 1860 when he appeared in the federal census as a silversmith living in Rutledge with his wife and six children whose ages ranged from eighteen to thirty-three.

ATKINSON, Wilton. Silversmith, jeweler. Jonesboro, Washington County, 1825–60 and later.

Wilton Atkinson was born about 1793 in North Carolina, the son of silversmith William A. Atkinson (q.v.) and Mary, his wife.[29] The family moved to Jonesboro sometime after Wilton's birth. As a young man, Wilton served under General Andrew Jackson in the War of 1812, surviving to return to Jonesboro and practice his father's profession.[30] In 1825 Atkinson and William Boyce formed the firm of Atkinson and Boyce (q.v.), offering their services as silversmiths along with a stock of jewelry, spoons, and dirks.[31]

In 1848 Wilton Atkinson was one of the fifteen men of Jonesboro who sold stock to raise funds for building the East Tennessee and Virginia Railroad which would link Knoxville to the state of Virginia "east of Bays Mountain between Holston and Nolichucky Rivers." Paul Fink, in his *Jonesborough: The First Century of Tennessee's First Town*, gives credit to the men of Jonesboro for their contribution toward completion of the railroad in 1858.[32]

Wilton married a Tennessee woman, Martha B[...?] and continued to live in Washington County. In 1850 his real estate was valued at $800. The 1860 census recorded that five adult children were living with Wilton and Martha. Wilton worked as a silversmith until the Civil War.[33]

ATKINSON and BOYCE. Silversmiths, goldsmiths, clock and watch repairers, jewelers. Jonesboro, Washington County, 1825–33?.

Wilton Atkinson (q.v.) and William Boyce (q.v.), Jonesboro silversmiths, formed the partnership of Atkinson and Boyce (fig. 30) in December 1825. Their services included clock and watch repairing as well as gold and silver work.[34]

In September 1833 Boyce conveyed to Wilton Atkinson a deed to property on the north side of East Main Street "having had buildings thereon destroyed by fire, together with many of the adjoining buildings."[35] The partnership may have been dissolved after this property sale.

AYCOCK (AYECOCK), A. J. (Jack). Watch and clockmaker, jeweler. Dover, Stewart County, 1860.

In 1860 twenty-six-year old Jack Aycock was living with Elizabeth, his wife, and two young daughters in Dover, Stewart County, where he worked as a watchmaker. The "A. J. Ayecock" listed that year in the *State Gazetteer* under "Jewelry, Watches, Clocks, Etc." probably was the same man.[36]

BADOUX, F. S. Jeweler, watchmaker. Nashville, Davidson County, 1855–60 and later.

F. S. Badoux was born in Switzerland about 1831. By the age of twenty-three he was living in Tennessee and working as a jeweler and watchmaker; his and his wife Catharine's first child was born there. In 1855 his shop was located at 31 Union Street in Nashville; his residence was located at Line and McLemore streets where he remained through 1860 and beyond.[1] The 1860 census for Davidson County evaluated his real property at $3,700 and his personal property at $1,000.

Badoux probably was related to L. Badoux (q.v.) who also appeared in the Nashville directories for 1855 and 1857 as a watchmaker at the same address. A man named Ozanne was also listed at Badoux's address during this period. King's *Nashville Directory* listed a shop in the name of Mrs. F. Badoux at 31 North Cherry Street as late as 1870.[2]

BADOUX, L. Watchmaker. Nashville, Davidson County, 1855–57.

L. Badoux was working in Nashville as a watchmaker at 31 Union Street from 1855–57. He probably was related to F. S. Badoux (q.v.).

PARTNERSHIP.

W. ATKINSON & WM. BOYCE.

Return their individual thanks to the public for the very liberal support they have heretofore received in their seperate establishments. They have now the pleasure of informing their friends and the public generally, that they have united their establishments together and will hereafter do business under the firm of

ATKINSON & BOYCE.

And will continue to repair in the neatest and best manner

CLOCKS & WATCHES.

Of every description.

GOLD & SILVER WORK,

Will also be made to any pattern in the neatest style.

They will constantly keep on hand or make at a very short notice, the following articles of

JEWELRY.

Finger Rings, Breast Pins, Ear Rings, } GOLD.

Fine steel, gold and gilt Watch Chains.

Keys and Seals,

Table, Tea, Desert, Cream, Mustard, Gravy, Soup, & Salt } *SPOONS.*

Silver Spurs,

Gold Necklaces,

Gold Clasps.

Handsome Silver & Gold mounted } DIRKS.

Ladies Scissors' Chains &c.

Together with every other article that can be called for in their line of Business. They promise the public their united exertions shall be made to give satisfaction to all who may please to deal with them—and that their work shall be well executed upon the most reasonable terms. A continuation of public patronage is very respectfully solicited.

Dec., 9,—tf.—

30. *Silversmiths Wilton Atkinson and William Boyce announced their new partnership with the promise that their ". . . united exertions shall be made to give satisfaction to all who may please to deal with them. . ." (Jonesboro,* Farmers Journal, *16 Dec. 1825).*

6 1-4 Cents Reward.

RANAWAY from the ſubſcriber on the 13th of December, 1803, an apprentice to the ſilver ſmiths buſineſs, by the name of Robert Barret, about 19 years of age, about five feet ten inches high, ſhort hare, heavy made, and dark complection; whoever will deliver me ſaid apprentice, in Naſhville, Tenneſſee, ſhall have the above reward but no charges paid.

J. T. Elliſton.

Diſtrict of Weſt Tenneſſee, to wit; November term. 1803.

31. *Silversmith Joseph T. Elliston offered a small reward "but no charges paid" for runaway apprentice Robert Barret (Nashville* Tennessee Gazette and Mero District Advertiser, *4 Jan. 1804).*

NOTICE.

ON Tuesday, 18th October next, will be sold, on a credit of twelve months, the house and lot where Benjamin Barton lived in the town of Carthage. Also, a complete set of watch makers tools, clock makers tools, and black smith tools; together with various other tools and instruments for different purposes in the silver smiths trade. Two new clocks will be sold, and materals for several more. Bond with sufficient security will be required of the purchacers.

Leonard Ballew,
Tamsey Barton,
Administrators.

Carthage 10th Sept. 1808. 3.f

32. *Benjamin Barton's administrators placed a notice in the* Carthage Gazette *of 10 September 1808 that demonstrates the various trades in which he was versed.*

BAIN, John. Silver plater. Memphis, Shelby County, 1860.

John Bain was a twenty-one-year-old bachelor from Illinois when the 1860 census listed him as a silver plater in the Seventh Ward of Memphis. He lived on Linden between Causey and Hernando streets.[4]

BARMAN, Charles. Watchmaker. Clarksville, Montgomery County, 1860.

Charles Barman was born about 1836 in Connecticut and was listed as a watchmaker in the 1860 federal census for Davidson County. He lived at the residence of W. W. Warfield "north and east of the Cumberland River."

BARNHEIM, F. W. Watchmaker. Nashville, Davidson County, 1855–56.

F. W. Barnheim was working in Nashville as a watchmaker during 1855–56. His residence was located at 46 Line Street.[5]

BARRET, Robert. Silversmith's apprentice. Nashville, Davidson County, 1804.

Robert Barret was apprenticed to Nashville silversmith Joseph T. Elliston (q.v.). On 4 January 1804, at about the age of nineteen, Barret ran away and his master advertised (fig. 31) in the *Tennessee Gazette and Mero District Advertiser* for his apprentice's return, offering a six-and-one-quarter cent reward. He described Barret as "five feet ten inches high, short hare, heavy made, and dark complection."

Although the outcome of that episode in Barret's life is unknown, twelve years later a Robert Barrett, born in 1784 and believed to be the same man, opened a silversmithing shop in Greensburg, Kentucky. Barrett served three terms in the Kentucky State Legislature, worked as Justice of the Peace, served in the War of 1812, and attained the rank of major in the militia. He died in 1821.[6]

32a. *"B. BARTON" mark from sugar tongs, c. 1810. Private collection.*

BARTON, Benjamin. Silversmith, watch and clockmaker, blacksmith. Carthage, Smith County, d. 1808.

According to Smith County records, just before his death on 10 June 1808 Benjamin Barton requested that J. J. Wells and William Martin sell his house and tools "to the best advantage" for the express purpose of discharging his debts. Accordingly, the *Carthage Gazette and Friend of the People* of 12 September 1808 carried an advertisement (fig. 32) offering for sale his home and lot, along with his watchmaking, clockmaking, and blacksmithing tools "together with various other tools and instruments for different purposes in the silversmiths trade." The firm of Davis and Jones (q.v.) purchased his silversmithing tools.[7]

In *Silversmiths of Virginia*, George Barton Cutten recorded an English-born silversmith, Benjamin Barton, working in Alexandria from 1801 until his death in 1816.[8] No connection between the two has been found. A pair of sugar tongs purchased in Nashville are marked "B. BARTON" (fig. 32a); the mark resembles that of the Virginia silversmith, but it has a different cartouche.

BAUGH, Mikel (Michael). Silversmith. Rogersville, Hawkins County, 1834?–35; Cleveland, Bradley County, 1850.

Mikel Baugh was born in Virginia in 1805. Baugh had settled in Tennessee with his New Hampshire-born wife, Isabella, by 1834; the Baugh's eldest child, John, was born that year. Goodspeed's *History of Tennessee* recorded that Baugh was located in Rogersville, Hawkins County, in 1835; by 1850 he was working as a silversmith in Bradley County.[9]

Valentine Baugh, an Abingdon, Virginia, silversmith working circa 1800, may have been Mikel Baugh's father.[10]

BAYNE, Fred. Watchmaker. Memphis, Shelby County, 1860.

Born in Prussia about 1829, Fred Bayne was working as a watchmaker and living in the First Ward of Memphis at the time of the 1860 federal census.

BEACH (BEECH), Andrew S. Silversmith, jeweler. Nashville, Davidson County, 1847–57.

Andrew S. Beach was born in New Jersey about 1812. He had emigrated to Tennessee by at least 1841 when his eldest child, Emma, was born there. His wife, Caroline, was a native of Tennessee. The 1847 listing of taxable property in Nashville recorded that Beach owned property on Spruce Street valued at $500. During the same year he employed William Hutchinson (q.v.), who may have been an apprentice or even a silversmith in his own right. Beach kept shop on the "Alley near the Banner office" in 1853 and lived at 176 South Market Street, where he remained through at least 1857.[11]

Ensko and Kovel noted an "A. Beach" in Hartford, Connecticut, (circa 1823) and Belden listed an Albert Beach in New York (circa 1839–47); however, no connection has been established.[12]

33. *"A. BEACH" mark from the reverse side of a silver teaspoon with a Tennessee provenance, 1841–55. LOA: 6". Courtesy of the Tennessee State Museum, photograph by Stephen D. Cox. Although this mark has been attributed to several northeastern silversmiths, it is possible that, because of the spoon's provenance, the mark is that of Tennessee silversmith Andrew Beach.*

THIS ſubſcriber informs the public, that he carries on the Goldſmith's and Jeweller's buſineſs, at his houſe near Bean's ſtation, on German Creek, Hawkins county. He likewiſe makes Rifle Guns in the neateſt and moſt approved manner. Thoſe who pleaſe to employ him in either of the above branches, may depend on having their commands faithfully executed.

GEORGE BEAN.

German Creek, October 4, 1792.

34. *George Bean was the first silversmith in Tennessee. His offer to make "Rifle Guns" not only reflects the diversification of a competent metal worker, but also the necessity of such items in an unsettled land (*Knoxville Gazette*, 6 Oct. 1792, advertisement date 4 Oct. 1792).*

BEAN, George. Goldsmith, jeweler, gunsmith. Bean Station, Grainger County, 1792–1801; Rutherford County, 1804; Franklin County, d. 1820.

George Bean, the son of William Bean and Lydia Russell Bean, was born in Pittsylvania, Virginia, in 1754. In 1776 George, William, Robert, and Jesse Bean established what was then called "Bean's" Station in Hawkins (later Grainger) County at the crossing of the Baltimore-Nashville and Louisville-Charleston roads. There he married his first wife, Jane; he later married Prudence Cope.[13] In 1792 Bean advertised (fig. 34) his services as a goldsmith, jeweler, and gunsmith at his home on German Creek near Bean Station.[14]

In 1801 he lost all his Grainger County property in a

lawsuit with Matthew English, and he purchased land in Rutherford County in 1804. Bean, the state's earliest known gold and silversmith, died in Franklin County in 1820.[15]

BEATY, John. Merchant. Nashville, Davidson County, 1850.

In 1850 John Beaty of Nashville offered for sale "cheap for CASH only" gold lever and other fine watches.[16]

BECKWITH, George. Merchant? Smithville, DeKalb County, 1838, 1860.

Although George Beckwith was listed in Goodspeed's *History of Tennessee* as one of the "merchants" of Smithville, DeKalb County, in 1838 (the year the town was founded), there was no evidence that he was working as a clock and watchmaker/ jeweler in that town until the 1860 *State Gazetter* listed him under "Jewelry, Watches, Clocks, Etc."[17] In that year's census Beckwith was listed as a "merchant."

Kovel noted a Robert W. Beckwith working as a silversmith in Raleigh, North Carolina, circa 1840–43, and in Charlotte, North Carolina, circa 1858. No connection has been established.[18]

BEDET, Henry A. Jeweler. Memphis, Shelby County, 1855–56.

Henry A. Bedet appeared in the 1855–56 *Memphis City Directory* as a jeweler. He boarded at 116 Second Street.[19]

BELL, David. Silversmith. Knoxville, Knox County, 1850–52.

David Bell was born in 1831, the son of noted Knoxville silversmith Samuel Bell (q.v.). The 1850 census listed Bell as a silversmith living in his father's household. By 1852 he had moved to Texas where he, with his father and brothers, continued to work in the silversmithing trade, using the mark "J. G. and D. Bell." By 1863 the firm was known as Bell and Brothers.[20]

BELL, F. Watchmaker. Cornersville, Giles County, 1860.

The 1860 census for Giles County recorded that F. Bell, born in Kentucky about 1830, was working as a watchmaker in Cornersville, then a Giles County town. Bell evaluated his personal estate at $200.

BELL, John. Silversmith. Dresden, Weakley County, 1850.

John Bell was born in North Carolina about 1799. The 1850 census for Dresden, Weakley County, listed Bell as a silversmith residing in the household of N. Nailing, a farmer. Other members of the household included fifty-seven-year-old Dr. P. B. Bell, Sarah Bell, forty-four, and Bell children ranging in age from eight to twenty-two.

35. *Wood engraving of Samuel Bell (1797–1881), from the 1891–92* Knoxville City Directory. *Courtesy of the McClung Historical Collection, Knoxville-Knox County Public Library.*

BELL, Samuel. Silversmith. Knoxville, Knox County, 1819–52.

Samuel Bell (fig. 35), believed to be Knoxville's best-known silversmith, worked for thirty-three years in that city, becoming one of its leading citizens. At the age of fifty-four he moved to Texas with his family and continued in the trade there until he died at the age of eighty-four.[21]

Born of English parents 15 July 1798 in Washington County, Pennsylvania, near Pittsburgh, Samuel Bell was apprenticed at an early age to an arms manufacturer in Pittsburgh. At fourteen he was making blades for swords used in the War of 1812.[22] By 1819 he had moved to Knoxville where he formed Bell, Dyer and Simpson (q.v.), "Watch and Clock Makers, Silversmiths, Gilders, and Jewelers, and Sword and Dirk Makers."[23]

Newspaper accounts gave many glimpses of his endeavors. In April 1820 his original partnership had been dissolved, but Bell and Simpson (q.v.) continued to work together at the same location on Gay Street. Two years later Simpson died, and shortly thereafter Bell made plans to leave Knoxville. In mid-1822 he asked customers to retrieve their watches, pay their accounts, and present

35a

35c

35b

35a, 35b, 35c, 35d. *Four marks known to have been used by Samuel Bell during his tenure (1819–52) in Knoxville. Figs. 35a, 35c courtesy of the Tennessee State Museum, photograph by Stephen D. Cox. Fig. 35d, private collection, photograph by Jack Shwab.*

35d

any claims against him; at the same time he offered a quantity of sheet iron with which he planned to make stove pipes. Bell apparently remained in Knoxville, for about a year later he announced that he had opened a shop one door north of his "old stand" and had taken in David Bell, a tailor, possibly his brother.[24]

In July 1824 Bell offered "the highest prices in cash for any quantity of Bees Wax." In addition to his skills as a silversmith and jeweler, his shop offered groceries, candies, stoneware, and window glass.[25]

For more than a decade Bell's advertisements sought payment from his customers, pointing out that one could not "carry on business without cash," and that he had incurred debts that required payment. Bell's ire particularly was aroused when Winston C. N. Lusk, a law student, left town without paying his bill. In a somewhat convoluted newspaper message, Bell advised "all gentlemen who wish to contract debts and not pay them not to come to me as I am determined to advertise every person who does it."[26]

Knoxville newspapers carried at least three accounts of Bell's activities during 1826. When one of his silversmithing apprentices ran away, Bell offered a six-and-one-quarter cents reward. Later, Bell and a man named Delancy (q.v.) formed a partnership (Bell and Delancy, q.v.). The two men worked at Bell's Gay Street shop, one door north of Morgan and Jacobs, opposite the Knoxville Hotel. At the end of the year, Bell's infant son, James, died; the Bells later had another son whom they named either James or Jessup.[27]

By 1832 the partnership of Bell and Delancy had been dissolved, and Samuel Bell once again shared a shop with David Bell, tailor, although at a new location, 198 Merchants Row. Advertisements that Bell placed at this time carried more flamboyant promises than his former notices. One, for example, mentioned an assortment of merchandise "purchased lower than any goods ever had been sold or ever will be bought upon the face of the earth." The two Bells shared a shop and advertising space, although they worked at separate tasks. The duration of this arrangement is uncertain, for by 1839 Samuel had returned to his Gay Street shop where he advertised as "Samuel Bell, Watch-Maker, Jeweller, Etc." and offered to perform dental surgery.[28]

Bell served two terms as Knoxville's mayor, first from 1840–42 and then again from 1844–46. An ordinance

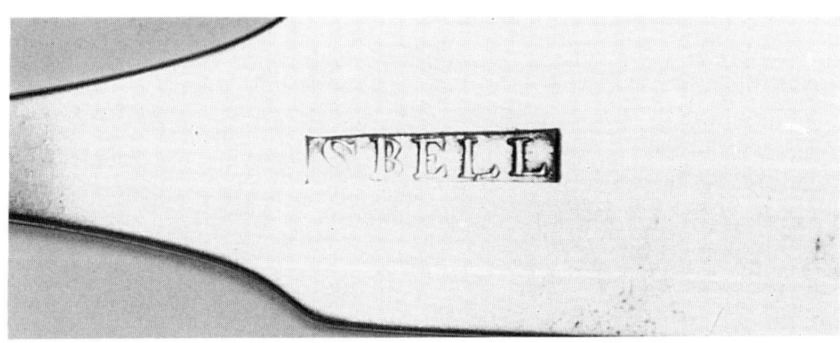

35e, 35f. *Mustard spoon marked "S. BELL," 1819–52, engraved "Jam," Knoxville. LOA: 5¾". Dessert spoons (reverse and obverse views) marked "S. Bell" (fig. 35f20), 1819–52, engraved "JLC," Knoxville. LOA: 7¾". Private collection, photograph by Helga Photo Studio, Inc. for* Antiques.

35g. *Spoon punches used by Samuel Bell, probably in both his Knoxville and San Antonio, Texas shops. Far left, teaspoon; center left, tablespoon, LOA: 6", width of bowl: 1½"; center right, demitasse, LOA: 5½", width of bowl: ¾"; far right, serving spoon, LOA: 7¾", width of bowl: 1¾". Courtesy of the San Antonio Museum Association on loan from the San Antonio Conservation Society, San Antonio, Texas. Spoon punches were used to establish the hollows of spoon bowls. The spoon blank, a flat piece of silver, was placed on a block of lead or pitch, and the shaped end of the spoon punch was driven into the blank to form a bowl.*

Bell prepared with his aldermen early in his first term attempted to prevent the furious driving of carts "for hauling water or otherwise" in Knoxville, promising fifty-cent fines to all minor drivers—on second offence—and their guardians, "all freemen of color . . . all white men over twenty-one. . . .[29] During the 1840s Bell also became a director of the Knoxville Marine Fire Insurance and Life and Trust Company, chartered with capital of $300,000.[30]

The 1850 census for Knox County listed Bell and his wife, Eliza Carr, with six children: David, Ann Maria, Hampton (Powhatan), James M. (Jessup M.), Margaret A., and Dutler; Bell had assets valued at $4,400. Three silversmiths lived in the Bell household: Samuel, his nineteen-year-old son, David (q.v.), and a nineteen-year-old boarder, James Felty (Felts) (q.v.). At least two other sons, Hampton and James, became silversmiths at a later date.[31]

According to the Knox County census of manufactures for 1850, Bell had invested $4,400 worth of real and personal property in his business. He used annually $1,500 worth of gold, silver, and brass, which the firm of five men fashioned into an annual production worth $4,000. His average monthly capital expended for labor amounted to $150.

In 1852 Bell sold his business to David Large Hope (q.v.), an established Knoxville silversmith who had worked with Bell. Bell moved his family to San Antonio, Texas, where he established himself as a "jeweller and silversmith." Recognized as one of the most prolific and proficient of Texas artisans, Bell was particularly known for his Bowie-style knives, prized for their excellent blades. Other work ranged from jewelry, silver spoons, cups, swords, "pistol and sword handles mounted in gold and set with precious stones" to a pair of silver spurs made for General Sam Houston and actually worn in action.[32] Bell's sons joined him in his Texas trade, producing silver under various marks such as "J. G. & D. Bell" and "Bell & Bros."[33]

Samuel Bell died on 2 March 1881 at the home of his son David. A San Antonio paper remembered him as the central figure in a scene that had taken place when federal troops entered San Antonio in 1865. At that time Bell had waved the stars and stripes from the top of the Alamo, extending the "olive branch of peace . . . to our suffering people." In another long article printed at his death, the *San Antonio Light* observed that "up to the day of his death he had preserved his strength and lived and labored almost right on to the end. He was a man who was happy only when at work, and he could not be persuaded to give it up. His life has been marked by temperance and frugality. . . ."[34]

It is possible that this Knoxville and San Antonio silversmith may have been related to William Bell, who was working in Philadelphia about 1805. Samuel Bell was born in Pennsylvania and returned to Pittsburgh in 1820 to marry an English-born woman, Eliza Carr; his Tennessee firm quoted prices from a Philadelphia price list, and his advertisements proclaimed experience gained in other parts of the country.[35] This possible relationship, however, remains indefinite; similarly, any connection with two other Samuel Bells, a blacksmith in Nashville, circa 1810–18, and a Boston clockmaker, circa 1813, 1819, is unknown.

BELL and DELANCY. Gold and silversmiths. Knoxville, Knox County, 1826.

Samuel Bell (q.v.) and an individual named Delancy (q.v.), whose first name is unknown, formed a partnership in early 1826. They pursued the clock and watchmaking, gold and silversmithing business in Bell's shop on Gay Street. The firm did not last more than two years, for by 1828 Bell again ran notices under his own name.[36]

BELL, DYER and SIMPSON. Watch and clockmakers, silversmiths, gilders, jewelers. Knoxville, Knox County, 1819–20.

Samuel Bell (q.v.), Edmund B. Dyer (q.v.), and James Simpson (q.v.) formed one of Knoxville's earliest silversmithing partnerships in late 1819. They offered their collective talents as "WATCH and CLOCK MAKERS, SILVERSMITHS, Gilders and Jewelers, and Sword and Dirk Makers" at their shop on Gay Street, formerly owned by G. G. Garner, another Knoxville silversmith. In 1820 Dyer left the partnership, which was re-formed as Bell and Simpson.[37]

BELL and SIMPSON. Silversmiths, watch and clockmakers, jewelers. Knoxville, Knox County, 1820–21.

Samuel Bell (q.v.) and James Simpson (q.v.) first worked together in 1819 as partners in the firm of Bell, Dyer and Simpson; they remained together as Bell and Simpson in the same shop on Gay Street in Knoxville when Dyer left in 1820. There they charged for their services according to prices "agreed upon by those in like trade in Philadelphia" and offered as their price-source a "printed book . . . for those who wished to consult it." Their advertisement referred to experience the partners had garnered "in different parts of the United States." Bell had served an apprenticeship in Pittsburgh,[38] and Simpson had worked in Ireland before emigrating.[39]

The partnership terminated in September 1821 with the death of Simpson. At Simpson's death, Bell purchased the entire stock belonging to the firm of Bell and Simpson for approximately $1,700.[40]

BERLSCHY (BEITSCHY, BERTSCHY), R. Jeweler, watchmaker. Memphis, Shelby County, 1860.

R. Berlschy worked as a jeweler and watchmaker in Memphis on Beale Street, opposite the market house, in 1860.[41]

36. *Solomon Augustus Wood Berson (b.1810-d.1883), oil, 1837–46, artist unknown. HOA: 35½", WOA: 27½". Private collection.*

BERSON, Guillaume. Jeweler. Brownsville, Haywood County, 1860.

Guillaume Berson, the son of Lucinda Van Pelt and Solomon Wood Berson (q.v.), followed his father into the jewelry business, thereby representing the third generation of Bersons involved in the trade. Born in Tennessee about 1839, Guillaume lived with his mother and father in Brownsville at the time the 1860 census for Haywood County was taken.

BERSON, Solomon Augustus Wood. Watchmaker, jeweler, silversmith. Franklin, Williamson County, 1833–38; Brownsville, Haywood County, 1846–d. 1883.

In 1810 Solomon Augustus Wood Berson was born in Salem, Massachusetts, the second son of William Berson, Sr. (q.v.) and his wife Eunice. Solomon's father, a French gentleman who lost his inheritance in 1796, learned the clockmaker's and jeweler's trade to replace his lost income. He later taught these skills to his sons.[42]

Solomon Berson moved to Tennessee with his family

36a, 36b. *Lucinda Van Pelt Berson, wife of Soloman Augustus Wood Berson, oil, 1837–46, artist unknown. HOA: 35½", WOA: 27½". Private collection. It is possible that the jewelry Lucinda is wearing was made by a member of the Berson family.*

from the Boston area[43] and advertised with his brother William (q.v.) in Franklin as W. and S. Berson (q.v.) as early as November 1833. At that time the brothers announced the removal of their jewelry and watch establishment from the public square next door to Doyle and Poebles to a shop immediately opposite William R. Owens. They requested that their old friends and customers call on them as before. Numerous advertisements appeared thereafter through 1838. In May of that year, Solomon's brother and partner, William, died. Shortly thereafter, Solomon notified the public that his business would be continued as William Berson and Son (q.v.).[44] Young Berson probably had joined his father to form the partnership.

An 1846 letter to Solomon's wife, the former Lucinda Van Pelt, from her father, Henry Van Pelt, founder of the *Memphis Commercial Appeal*, placed the couple in Brownsville, Haywood County, Tennessee, at that date. The letter inquired solicitously about Lucinda's health and alerted her to the arrival of a parcel of oysters, bear meat, and soda biscuits.[45] The young couple evidently had followed Berson's father to Brownsville after their marriage in 1837.[46]

At the time of the 1850 census for Haywood County, Solomon Berson and his three children were living with his sister and father in Brownsville. Lucinda apparently had died by then. By the time of the 1860 Haywood County census, Solomon, aged fifty, listed his occupation as jeweler, his real property at a value of $6,000 and his personal property at $6,000. His oldest son, Guillaume (q.v.), was also a jeweler. A nineteen-year-old daughter and an eighteen-year-old son lived with Solomon at his Brownsville residence, as did two young nephews with the last name of Kelly (q.v.), who were jewelers, a young woman named E. A. McLemiere and her three-month-old son, and three sisters for whom Berson had succeeded in securing at least a part of the indemnity due them as rightful heirs of William Berson, Sr.[47]

Solomon Berson died on 4 June 1883. Portraits (figs. 36, 36a) of Solomon and Lucinda Van Pelt Berson remain among family members in Tennessee.[48]

37. *Detail from portrait of Guillaume (William) Louis Rose Fortune Berson (b. 1779-d. 1855), oil, 1805–15, artist unknown. HOA: 35", WOA: 27". Private collection, photograph by Clement Photographers, Brownsville, Tennessee.*

BERSON, William, Jr. Watch and clockmaker, silversmith. Franklin, Williamson County, 1833–d. 1838.

William Berson, Jr., was born 28 July 1805, in Dracut, Massachusetts. His father (q.v.) eventually brought the family to Franklin, Tennessee, where William, Jr., pursued his father's occupation.[49] In Franklin, William, Jr., and his brother Solomon worked as partners as early as 1833. They advertised frequently and took apprentices on a regular basis.[50] The partnership dissolved when William Berson, Jr., died in Franklin at thirty-three on 9 May 1838.[51]

BERSON, William, Sr. (Guillaume Louis Rose Fortune). Watch and clockmaker, jeweler, silversmith, goldsmith. Franklin, Williamson County, 1833–43; Brownsville, Haywood County, 1843–d. 1855.

William Berson, Sr., was born in Port-au-Prince, Santo Domingo, on 21 June 1779, where his father was both solicitor for the Crown, and Royal Admiralty Judge for the district Petit Goave. He attended school in Paris from 1788–96, when slave insurrections in Santo Domingo inspired by the French Revolution caused the loss of his entire inheritance. At that time his uncle in Paris advised him to learn a trade, and Berson chose to become a jeweler and watchmaker. He practiced this trade for some years, as did his sons and his grandsons.[52]

About 1798 Berson joined the French Navy and was captured by the English and later by the Americans. Arriving in Boston by late 1800, he married Eunice Wood and resumed work as a watchmaker and jeweler. The Berson's first child, Annette, was born in 1803.[53]

Before 1805 the couple moved to Dracut, Massachusetts, where their oldest son, William, and a daughter, Jeanette, were born. From Dracut the family moved to Salem where Solomon, Juliette Montagnac, and Harriette Eunice were born. In 1815 William Berson closed his Salem shop and, hoping to improve his fortune, set sail on the schooner *Elizabeth* with his family on an ill-fated trip to the West Indies. The ship was forced to return from Guadeloupe, which was consumed with yellow fever; the ship's captain and first mate perished *en route*. Berson and the second mate managed to see the ship through a hurricane and eventually anchored the vessel safely in Norfolk harbor. Mrs. Berson died shortly thereafter at the age of thirty-five.[54]

Family records show that "Berson moved his family to East Tennessee, first to Blountville, then to Greeneville," but he first may have worked his way down the east coast to Washington, North Carolina. There, in 1816, the firm of Berson and Roberts commenced business in "Gold and Silver Work, Engraving and Hair Work," clock and watch repair. By the time Berson reached Franklin in 1836 he had added silversmithing to his talents. He occupied the shop formerly occupied by silversmith William Cayce (q.v.) on the north corner of the public square, where he cleaned and repaired clocks and watches as well as making and mending all kinds of gold and silver work. His business was large enough to require the help of two apprentices that year.[55]

Two years later at the death of William Berson, Jr., Berson and his second son, Solomon, formed W. Berson and Son (q.v.), an active clock, watch, and silversmithing firm in Franklin. In 1843 Berson and his family moved to Brownsville where he remained until his death on 25 January 1855.[56]

BERSON, W. and S. Jewelers, watch and clockmakers, silversmiths. Franklin, Williamson County, 1833–38.

William and Solomon Berson were both sons of William Berson, Sr. (q.v.), a Tennessee clockmaker, watchmaker, and silversmith. William and Solomon moved to Tennessee with their father, and having learned their father's trades, apparently formed the partnership of W.

38. *Watchpaper engraved "W. & S. BERSON/ WATCH & CLOCK MAKERS/ GOLD & SILVER SMITHS/ FRANKLIN/ TENN Watches & Clocks Repaired and Warranted 12 Months" signed and dated on the reverse by J. S. Claybrook, watch repairer, 17 August 1833, Franklin. Diameter: 1¾". Courtesy of the Tennessee State Museum. The paper itself was engraved in "Philada"; however, "Til—e—" is all that remains of the engraver's name. Watchpapers originally were used as cushioning for inner works and protecting fragile parts from dirt particles. Repairers frequently signed and dated watchpapers, and it is not uncommon to find more than one in a case.*

38a. *Cream ladle marked "W. & S. BERSON./ FRANKLIN," 1835–38, engraved on the obverse "Mc" for McDaniel. LOA: 7¾", width across bowl: 1 9/16", rise: 1¼". Private collection.*

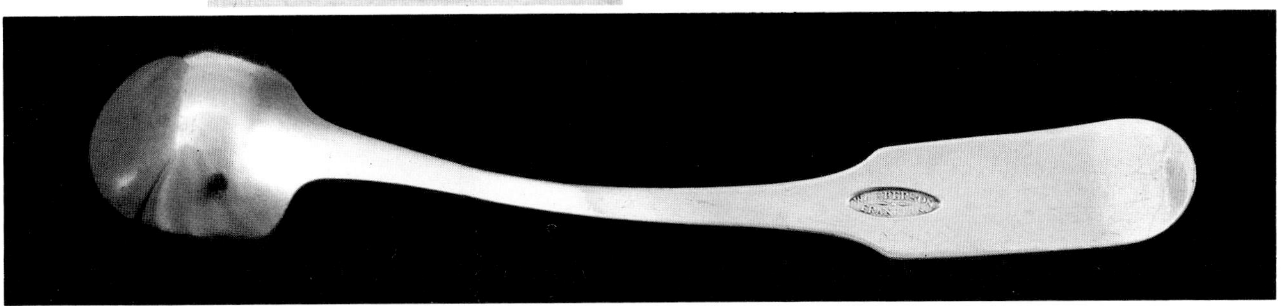

38b. *Cream ladle marked "W & S BERSON/ FRANKLIN," 1835–45. LOA: 6½". Private collection.*

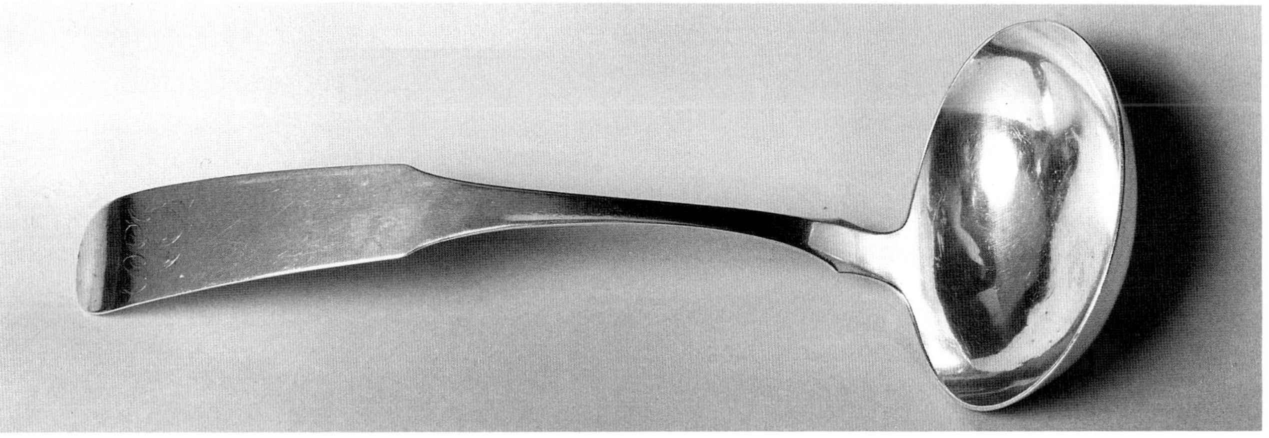

and S. Berson in Franklin as early as 1833.[57] The following year they announced the receipt of a "splendid stock of New Jewelry" and requested two or three apprentices to learn the "Gold and Smith business," and an 1835 notice promised the latest in jewelry, music boxes, and silver. By 1838 they needed two additional apprentices, "boys between the age of 12 and 15," to the "Watch and Clock making business."[58] The Tennessee State Museum owns a watchpaper used by the firm (fig. 38). A ladle (fig. 38a) marked "W & S Berson" has remained in the possession of one Tennessee family since its purchase.

The partnership was dissolved in May 1838 with the death of William, Jr.; at that time Solomon Berson and his father established the firm of William Berson and Son.[59]

39. *Watchpaper inscribed "W. BERSON & SON,/ Watch & Clock Makers/ Gold & Silver Smiths/ Franklin,/ Ten./ Watches and Clocks repaired & warranted twelve months," 1838–44?, signed and dated on the back by J. S. Claybrook, 6 June 1833. Private collection. Although the content of the inscription is the same as that of fig. 38, this printed watchpaper is simpler than the elaborately engraved and imported watchpaper of the other example.*

BERSON, William and Son. Watch and clockmakers, jewelers, silversmiths, goldsmiths. Franklin, Williamson County, 1838–44?; Brownsville, Haywood County, 1844?.

William Berson, Sr. (q.v.), and his son, Solomon Berson (q.v.), both skilled clockmakers, watchmakers, and silversmiths of Franklin, formed the partnership of William Berson and Son in May 1838.[60] The duration of the partnership is unclear. Both men moved to Brownsville, Tennessee, about 1844[61] and may have continued work there as a firm with the same name. A watchpaper (fig. 39) from the Bersons' watchmaking years in Franklin, Tennessee, is in a private collection.

BIDDLE, (....?). Jeweler, silversmith?, clock and watchmaker. Nashville, Davidson County, 1814–17.

Biddle, whose first name is unknown, joined E. Raworth (q.v.) to form a partnership in Nashville about 1814. In December of that year the partners offered clock and watch repair work as well as a stock of jewelry received from Philadelphia. The firm was dissolved by mutual consent in October 1817.[62]

Cutten recorded that a John S. Biddle, silversmith/jeweler, was working in Wheeling, Virginia (now West Virginia), about 1807.[63] Wheeling was located on the westward trade route many settlers followed to Tennessee. It is possible that John S. Biddle may have joined that movement and settled in Nashville.

BINGIM, Francis F. Silversmith. Clarksville, Montgomery County, 1850.

The 1850 Montgomery County census does not record the place of Francis F. Bingim's 1830 birth; however, in 1850 he was working in Clarksville as a silversmith and living in the the household of Samuel Simpson (q.v.), another silversmith.[64]

BLACKBURN, Burwin. Silversmith. Rogersville, Hawkins County, 1831? 1850.

Burwin Blackburn was born in Virginia about 1801 and arrived in Tennessee as early as 1831. At the time of the 1850 census for Hawkins County he and his wife Elizabeth lived in Rogersville where he worked as a silversmith. His estate at the time was valued at $2,000.

A "Blackburn" whose first name is unknown, was recorded as working in Shelbyville, Kentucky, circa 1812. No tie between the two silversmiths has been established.[65]

BLUM, Robert David. Jeweler, engraver, silversmith? Nashville, Davidson County, 1857–60 and later.

Robert David Blum, who was born in 1826, and his wife Frances emigrated to the United States via England where their first child was born in 1849. Blum settled in New York and then briefly in Pennsylvania and Ohio before moving to a permanent home in Nashville by 1857. There Blum kept a jeweler's shop on Deaderick Street, then Cedar Street, and finally North College Street.[66]

Described as "Nashville Jewry's greatest artist of this period," Blum made two plates for the Mogen David Synagogue; the plates were engraved with the Ten Commandments in large gilt letters. These plates were arranged over the ark; a small silver plaque beneath them bore Blum's name and "1859," the date of his gift. At that time he also served as one of the trustees of the congregation.[67] Later, Blum carved letters on the cornerstone of the new Temple and made a silver crown for the Torah in preparation for dedication services. Blum remained active in community affairs until his death in 1885.[68]

BLYTHE and CONWAY. Retailers. Paris, Henry County, 1857.

Blythe and Conway operated a "variety house" in Paris, Henry County, which offered almost "anything you could want." In a March 1857 *Sentinel* advertisement headed "NEW REMEDY TO SOFTEN THE HARD TIMES," the partners offered all sorts of jewelry—finger rings, watch keys, watches, breast pins, and ear bobs in addition to assorted comestibles, household needs, gunpowder, and wines.[69]

BOND, H. B. Jeweler. Gallatin, Sumner County, 1860.

H. B. Bond, born in 1830 in Tennessee, was listed as a jeweler of Gallatin in Sumner County's 1860 census. He lived in the same hotel as E. R. Kerley (q.v.).

BOSKERN, Edward. Jeweler. Memphis, Shelby County, 1860.

Edward Boskern was born in New York about 1840 and was working as a jeweler at the time of the 1860 census. He lived in the Eighth Ward of Memphis at the residence of James Pooley (q.v.); another jeweler, George Keller (q.v.), was also living there.

BOSTLE (BOSTLEMAN), Charles. Watchmaker. Nashville, Davidson County, 1859–60 and later.

In 1859 Charles Bostle(man) worked as a watchmaker at M. C. Bruce's, an auction house at the corner of Cedar and Cherry streets in Nashville. He continued to work in the city long after 1860.[70]

BOSTLEMAN, W. Clock repairer, gunsmith. Nashville, Davidson County, 1853–59.

W. Bostleman, a Nashville clock repairer and gunsmith, lived at 1½ South Market Street in 1853. In 1859 he was working at 13 North Market Street.[71] Bostleman and Charles Bostle(man) (q.v.), another Nashville watchmaker, may have been related.

BOURGUINE, H. Watchmaker. Nashville, Davidson County, 1859.

In 1859 H. Bourguine was working as a watchmaker at 30 South Market Street in Nashville.[72]

BOWDEN, G. W. Silversmith. Mount Pelia (sic), Weakley County, 1860.

In 1860 G. W. Bowden, born in Tennessee, was working as a silversmith in Weakley County's District Fourteen. According to the census that year, the twenty-three-year-old Bowden and Nancy, his wife, had real property valued at $400 and personal property valued at $740.

BOWEN, H. Jeweler. Memphis, Shelby County, 1848?–50.

H. Bowen was born in Vermont in 1822. Bowen, with Elizabeth, his New York-born wife, and children arrived in Tennessee sometime after 1848; by 1850 they were living in Memphis where he worked as a jeweler.[73]

BOWLAND, William. Silversmith. Henry County, 1860.

William Bowland, born about 1832 in Kentucky, was working as a silversmith in District Two of Henry County at the time of the 1860 census. Bowland evaluated his real property at $1000 and his personal property at $100. William and Sarah Bowland had one son, William, born in Tennessee in 1858.

W. W. BOWMAN,
Watchmaker and Jeweler,
PARIS, TENN.

HAVING permanently located in Paris, respectfully solicits a share of patronage in his line of business. All work entrusted to his care will be executed with neatness and dispatch, and warranted to be well done. A good lot of

NEW AND FASHIONABLE JEWELRY

of all kinds warranted as represented. Also an assortment of CLOCKS of all kinds—from $2 up. WATCHES of all kinds, warranted to keep good time, together with a variety of

FANCY GOODS, &c.

Every article warranted to be what it is sold for.
Room on the East side of the square.

40. *W. W. Bowman, "Watchmaker and Jeweler," announced in the* Paris Sentinel *of 13 March 1857 that he had "permanently located in Paris."*

BOWMAN, W. W. (M.) Silversmith, watchmaker, jeweler. Paris, Henry County, 1857–60.

W. W. Bowman, a Kentucky native, advertised (fig. 40) as a watchmaker and jeweler in the Paris *Sentinel* for 13 March 1857. The 1860 census listed his occupation as "silversmith." The thirty-year-old Bowman and his wife Virginia, also a Kentucky native, had three young children, all born in Tennessee.

Marquis Boultinghouse recorded a W. W. Bowman, who was a dealer in jewelry and silverware, in Murray, Kentucky, during 1870–71.[74] Also, an Elias Bowman worked in Rochester, New York, circa 1834, but no connection between Elias and W. W. Bowman has been established.

BOYCE, William. Silversmith, jeweler. Jonesboro, Washington County, 1825?–50; Greene County, 1860.

William Boyce was born about 1807 in Maryland and appeared in Jonesboro, Tennessee, sometime before 1825. In December of that year Boyce and Wilton Atkinson (q.v.) announced that they were combining previously separate establishments into the firm of Atkinson and Boyce (q.v.) and that they repaired clocks and watches and produced gold and silver work. The same newspaper that carried this notice revealed that Boyce also served as secretary of his Masonic Lodge.[75] Census tabulations from 1830–50 documented William Boyce's continued residence in Washington County; however, by the time of the 1860 census, the fifty-three-year-old silversmith was living in Greene County. His household included three children ranging in age from one to nine, as well as an Ann Chapman and her young son.

Pleasant and Sills, in *Maryland Silversmiths*, recorded a William Boyce who was apprenticed by his father to silversmith George Aiken on 27 October 1806. This is not the same man as Tennessee's William Boyce.

BOYD, Henry D. Silversmith. Henry County, 1860.

Henry D. Boyd, born in Kentucky about 1837, was working as a silversmith in Henry County by time of the 1860 census. He lived in the county's Fourteenth District with his nineteen-year-old wife, Nancy, a native of Tennessee.

The following five names represent what this author refers to as a "snarl of Brittains." Although two appear on the same page in the 1857 Nashville Directory *listings, (Brittain, Britton), and one Britain signed the Nashville association of watchmakers, silversmiths, and jewelers agreement in 1836, the relationships of the men remain entangled. A good indication of the Britain confusion was found in "The Book of the Association of the Watch-Makers, Silversmiths & Jewellers of Nashville." The secretary of that organization listed one of its members as John Britton, yet that member signed his own name on the following page as John S. Britain (see Appendix I). Lacking the definite proof to untie the knots, the author has reported the facts as found.*

BRITAIN, J. S. Watchmaker, jeweler, silversmith. Columbia, Maury County, 1839.

The Columbia Observer for 24 October 1839 announced that J. S. Britain had begun business as a "Watchmaker, Jeweler and Silver Smith" opposite Union Bank in Columbia (fig. 41).

BRITAIN, John S. Watchmaker, silversmith, jeweler. Nashville, Davidson County, 1835–36.

In 1835 John S. Britain and his partner, D. A. Webb, purchased J. M. Smith's establishment on College Street, two doors above Yeatman and Wood's bank.[76] It is possible that Webb left Nashville shortly thereafter, for on 25 December 1836, John S. Britain affixed his signature to the list of silversmiths who formed the "Association of the Watch-Makers, Silversmiths & Jewellers of Nashville." Webb's name is not among the signatures. The association's nine men set out to establish fees for services rendered and to share information that would lead to "union and harmony" among association members.[77]

BRITTAIN, J. S. Watchmaker. Nashville, Davidson County, 1859.

In 1859 J. S. Brittain lived in Nashville on South Field Street and worked as a watchmaker for George W. Donigan (q.v.).[78]

BRITTAIN, John. Silversmith, watchmaker. Nashville, Davidson County, 1850–57.

John Brittain was born in Tennessee about 1820. By 1850 he was a resident in the Davidson County household of James Moss, a tavern keeper, and was working as a silversmith. In 1855 and 1857 he was listed as a watchmaker at 38 North College Street in.[79]

A "Brittain" whose first name is unkown worked with Robert W. Beckwith in Charlotte, North Carolina, circa 1858. No connection is known.[80]

BRITTON, John S. Silversmith. Nashville, Davidson County, 1855–d. 1860.

John S. Britton, silversmith, born about 1813, worked at a Vine Street shop and lived on South Field in Nashville from 1855 to 1857. He died in April 1860 and was buried in the old city cemetery in Nashville. Britton's ties, if any, to the Philadelphia Brittons of about the same period remain uncertain, as do any possible connections with either J. S. or John S. Britain (q.q.v.) other than the similarity of their Nashville addresses.[81]

J. S. BRITAIN

Watch-Maker, Jeweler & Silver Smith,

RESPECTFULLY informs the citizens of Columbia and its vicinity, that he has opened an establishment opposite the Union Bank for the purpose of repairing watches, clocks and Jewelry of all descriptions. His work will be neatly executed. Spoons made to order.

June 27, 1739—tf.

41. *J. S. Britain's advertisement in the* Columbia Observer *of 24 October 1839 announced the opening of an establishment for the purpose of repairing watches, clocks, and jewelry. The placement of his statement "Spoons made to order," at the end of the notice indicates that by the later period outlined in this study, the silversmithing business took second place to repair work and goods importation.*

41a, 41b. *Spoon marked "JB," engraved "EBD," Nashville. LOA: 7¾". Private collection. This spoon may be the work of one of the Nashville silversmiths using the names Britain, Brittain, and Britton.*

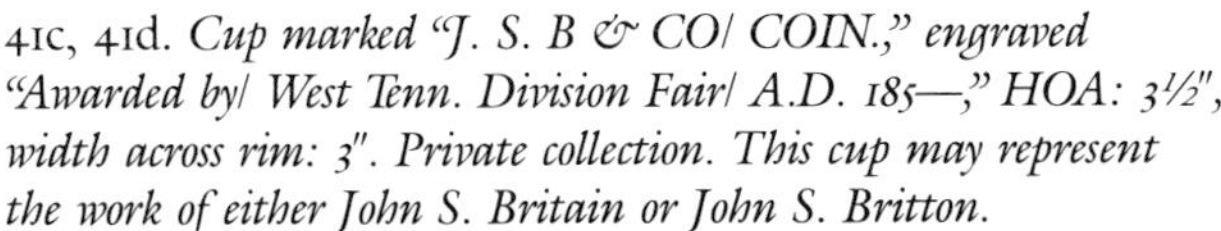

41c, 41d. *Cup marked "J. S. B & CO/ COIN.," engraved "Awarded by/ West Tenn. Division Fair/ A.D. 185—," HOA: 3½", width across rim: 3". Private collection. This cup may represent the work of either John S. Britain or John S. Britton.*

J. BROWN & co.

BEG leave to inform the inhabitants of Knoxville and its vicinity that they have commenced the

Watch repairing Business,

In the shop on Cumberland street formerly occupied by G. G. Garner, and hope by strict attention to this branch, to merit their encouragement.

J B. has served seven years in the city of London to the above business, and flatters himself that he can turn out any kind of

WATCH WORK

In complete order, VIZ;
Musical Watches, Repeaters, Patent Leavers, &c. &c. &c.

They have on hand and will keep a constant supply of

JEWELRY

AND

SILVER WORK.

Knoxville, June 6. tf

42. *J. Brown flattered himself that he was fit for the watch repairing business in a notice stating that he had "served seven years in the city of London"* (Knoxville Register, *20 June 1820, advertisement dated 6 June 1820).*

BROADBRIDGE, William. Watchmaker. Nashville, Davidson County, 1855–57.

William Broadbridge was working in Nashville as a watchmaker from 1855–57. City directories listed him then at 62 North Sumner Street. No relationship has been established with silversmith James Broadbridge of Newburgh, New York, circa 1806–32.[82]

BROWN, J. and Company. Watchmaker, jeweler?, silversmith?. Knoxville, Knox County, 1820.

J. Brown worked as a watch repairer in London for seven years before emigrating to the United States. A *Knoxville Register* advertisement of 6 June 1820 indicated that Brown took over G. G. Garner's (q.v.) shop on Cumberland Street in Knoxville, where he performed "any kind of WATCHWORK" and kept on hand a supply of jewelry and silver work.

BUCKNER, W. L. Silversmith. Clifton, Wayne County, 1859?–60; Manchester, Coffee County, 1860.

W. L. Buckner's presence in Tennessee was first noted in an 1860 *State Gazetteer* listing for Clifton, Wayne County, under "Jewelry, Watches, Clocks, &c." By the summer of 1860, however, the federal census taker recorded him as living with his wife and their son William H. (q.v.) in Manchester, Coffee County. The forty-nine-year-old Buckner, a native of Virginia, valued his personal estate at $200.[83]

BUCKNER, William H. Silversmith. Clifton, Wayne County, 1859?–60; Manchester, Coffee County, 1860.

A listing for W. H. and W. L. Buckner (q.v.) appears in the *State Gazetteer* for 1860; this record presumably predated the 1860 census taker's placement of the twenty-six-year-old silversmith in Manchester, Coffee County. Buckner lived with his wife and two young children in the home of his father, W. L. Buckner (q.v.).[84]

BURKE, Edmund K. Silversmith, jeweler, watchmaker. Nashville, Davidson County, 1847–50.

Edmund K. Burke was born in New York in 1820. Before arriving in Nashville in 1847, he lived in Louisville, Kentucky, where about 1841 he worked for silversmith George Griffin; Burke was in St. Louis, Missouri, circa 1842.[85]

In the *Nashville Daily Union* for 25 January 1848, Burke advertised his skills as a "manufacturing jeweler, silversmith and gilder." The *Nashville Whig* for 22 August 1848 noted his "new and splendid assortment of Jewelry from the East" and a supply of Masonic regalia and jewels, all of which he had for sale.

In 1849 Burke and Landay Shoemake (q.v.), formerly of Smith County, Tennessee, joined in a watchmaking, silversmithing, and jewelry firm on College Street "next door to the Nashville Insurance office, between Union St. and the Square." Although Burke appeared in the

43. *"E. K. BURKE" mark, possibly that of Edmund K. Burke.*

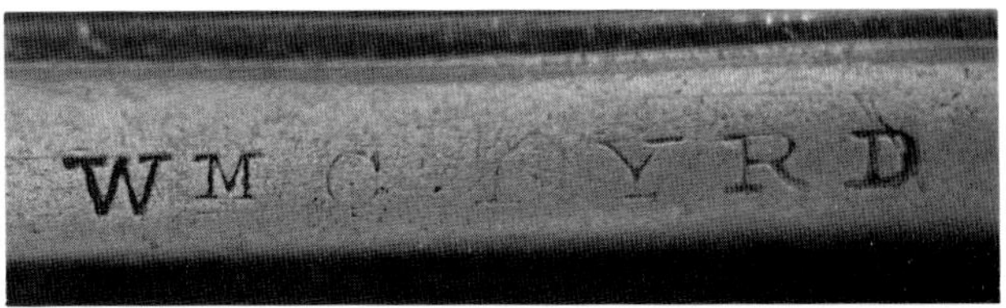

44. *Watchmaker and retailer William C. Byrd's mark, c. 1860. Courtesy of the Tennessee State Museum, photograph by Stephen D. Cox.*

44a. *"C. L. BYRD & CO." mark, c. 1875. Courtesy of the Tennessee State Museum, photograph by Stephen D. Cox. C. L. Byrd and Sarah Bird continued the retailing business after William's death in 1874.*

1850 census for Nashville as "K. Burke," a July advertisement in the *Nashville Daily Union* that year revealed that his tools had been purchased by the firm of Wolfe and Bailey (q.v).[86]

BURKE and SHOEMAKE. Watchmakers, silversmiths, jewelers. Nashville, Davidson County, 1849.

In 1849 Edmund K. Burke (q.v.) and Landay Shoemake (q.v.) formed the partnership of Burke and Shoemake in Nashville. They advertised as "Watchmakers, Silversmiths, and Jewellers" on College Street, prepared to manufacture and repair all kinds of jewelry and silverware. They also kept in stock a selection of jewelry, plated ware, and lodge regalia.[87]

BURN, Joseph. Silversmith. Sullivan County, 1860.

At the time of the 1860 census for Sullivan County, Joseph Burn was working as a silversmith and living in a hotel in the county's Seventeenth District. The thirty-four-year old artisan was a native of Pennsylvania.

BURTON, Joseph T. Silverplater. Memphis, Shelby County, 1859.

In 1859 Joseph T. Burton was listed as the owner of a fancy goods/jewelry store and also as a silver plater at 331 Main Street, Memphis. He lived on Vance Street between DeSoto and Hernando Streets.[88]

BYNUM (BYRUM?), John R. Jeweler. Bolivar, Hardeman County, 1860.

According to the census of 1860 for Hardeman County, John R. Bynum was a "M[aster] Jeweller." The eighteen-year-old native of Tennessee lived with Sarah D. Bynum, fifty-seven, a native of North Carolina.

BYRD, William C. Jeweler. Memphis, Shelby County, 1859–d. 1874.

In 1859 William C. Byrd was living on Union street near Bayou in Memphis and working as a watchmaker, probably at J. E. Merriman and Company.[89] The 1860 federal census for Shelby County listed William C. "Bird," 26, Sarah Bird, 24, and their three-year-old daughter as members of the James E. Merriman household. The census also noted Byrd's birthplace as Ohio and quoted the value of his real property at $4,000; his personal property was valued at $100.

By 1865 the city directory listed Byrd as one of Merriman's partners, and the following year the firm was reorganized as Merriman, Byrd and Company. Byrd lived at the Overton Hotel on Main and Poplar Streets at the time; the Shelby County Courthouse now occupies the site. Byrd eventually went into business for himself as "successor" to Merriman, Byrd and Company, offering watches, silverware, and jewelry at 275 Main Street.[90]

Byrd's brother, C. L. Byrd, fought in the Civil War as a young boy and afterwards joined William as a bookkeeper. When William died in 1874, his widow and brother formed C. L. Byrd and Company (fig. 44a). That partnership, at the corner of Main and Madison, offered the "most extensive selection" of jewelry "in the south" until C. L.'s death about 1905.[91] No relationship has been established between Byrd and the William Byrd who worked as a silversmith in both Augusta, Georgia, and Charleston, South Carolina, circa 1800.[92]

CAIN, C. Watch and clockmaker, silver and goldsmith. Knoxville, Knox County, 1812.

C. Cain advertised, with T. Cain in *Wilson's Knoxville Gazette* for 3 May 1812, his willingness to attend to watch and clock repairs or gold and silversmithing tasks. He

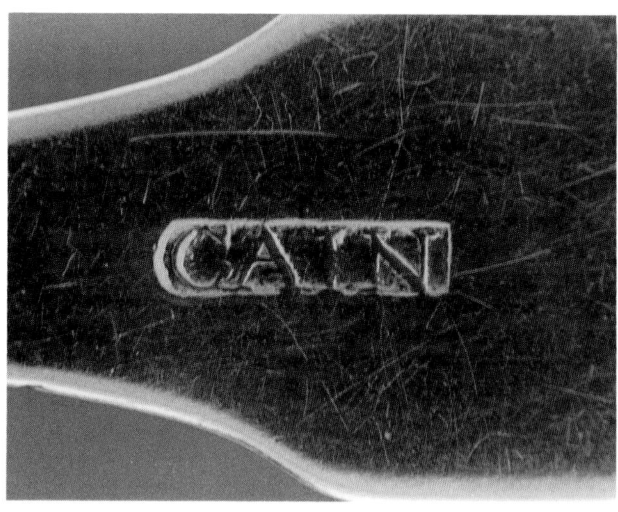

45. *"CAIN" mark, c. 1810. This mark may have been used by Thomas Cain, C. Cain, or both.*

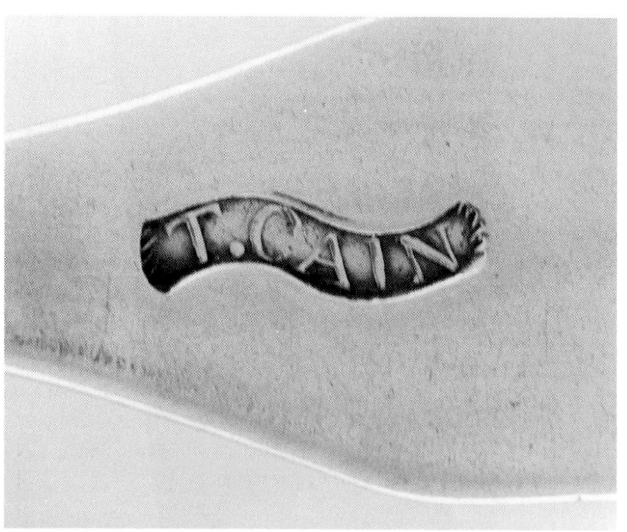

45a, 45b. *Two marks attributed to Thomas Cain, c. 1820 and 1830, respectively. Fig. 45b courtesy of the Tennessee State Museum, photograph by Stephen D. Cox.*

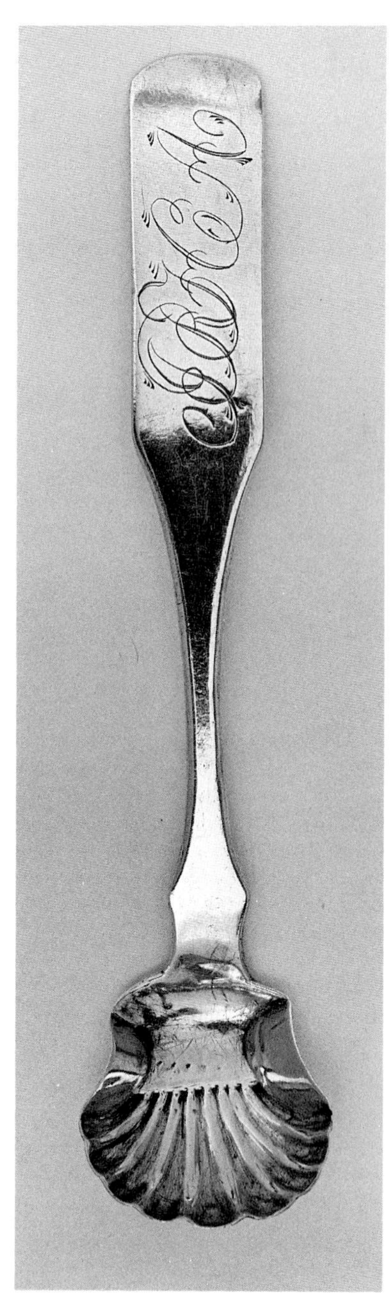

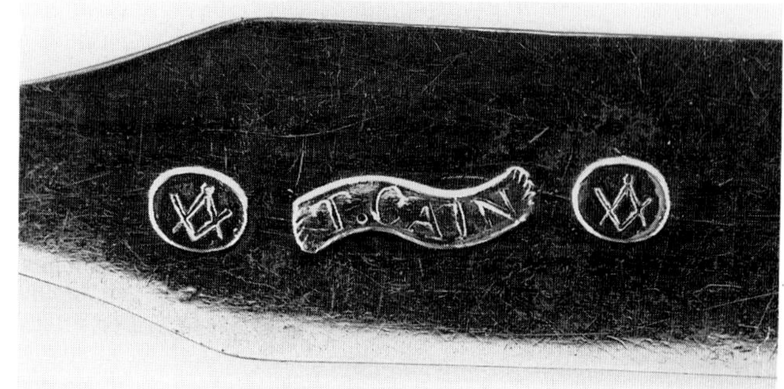

45c, 45d. *Sugar spoon marked "T. CAIN" flanked by Masonic emblems, c. 1830, engraved "JFRCA." LOA: 4⅞". Private collection. MRF 13,435. The mark illustrated in fig. 45d is the same as that of fig. 45a with the addition of Masonic emblems and also is attributed to Thomas Cain.*

also offered to "paint miniatures, fancy pieces and morning devices." He may have been related to Claiborn W. Cain of Petersburg, Virginia (circa 1817–24), or perhaps have been the same man. No mention of C. Cain in Tennessee after 1812 has been found.[1]

CAIN, Thomas. Watchmaker, gold and silversmith. Knoxville, Knox County, 1809–13.

In 1807 Thomas Cain offered an "elegant Assortment of JEWELLRY" on Fayetteville Street in Raleigh, North Carolina; however, by 1809 Cain was in Knoxville where he and John Garner (q.v.) formed the partnership of Garner and Cain (q.v.). The firm was listed as "Watch-Makers, Gold and Silver Smiths" in Knoxville. Later that year the partnership was dissolved by mutual consent, and Garner remained in the old shop; Cain opened his own establishment "opposite Mr. Hanes's tavern." By 1811 Garner had left Knoxville, and Cain had taken over his former partner's shop as "successor of John Garner." In 1812 Thomas Cain was associated with the firm of T. and C. Cain (q.v.), Knoxville watch and clockmakers and gold and silversmiths. In 1813 Frances Fleshart (q.v.), the son of Knoxville silversmith Frances Fleshart (q.v.), was apprenticed to Thomas Cain by order of the Knox County court. That same year Cain was in partnership with Abner Harrison; the firm was known as Cain and Harrison (q.v.).[2]

CAIN, T. and C. Watch and clockmakers, gold and silversmiths. Knoxville, Knox County, 1812.

T. and C. Cain were working as gold and silversmiths, watch and clockmakers at their Knoxville shop in 1812. The firm attended "punctually" to watches or orders sent "by stage or otherwise" and offered a "fresh assortment of Watch Glass."[3]

T. Cain was probably Thomas Cain (q.v.), a Knoxville silversmith. C. Cain (q.v.) may have been related to Claiborn W. Cain of Petersburg, Virginia (circa 1817–24).[4]

CAIN and HARRISON. Watch and clockmakers, gold and silversmiths. Knoxville, Knox County, 1813.

In Knoxville in late 1813 Thomas Cain (q.v.) and Abner Harrison (q.v.) advertised that they wanted "immediately" a journeyman gold and silversmith who understood watch repair and could come well recommended; in return, the journeyman would receive "liberal wages and long employment." The two men also requested editors of both the *Virginia Argus* and *Lynchburg Star* to insert the advertisement twice and forward charges to the offices of *Wilson's Knoxville Gazette*.[5]

No documentation for Abner Harrison in census records has been found earlier than 1840 when an Abner Harrison was listed in Robertson County. The 1850 census revealed that this Virginian was a farmer. Another Abner Harrison, also a farmer, was listed in the same census for Overton County.

46. *George Reid Calhoun (b. 1834-d. 1903), c. 1865. HOA: 3¼", WOA: 2". Private collection, photograph courtesy of C. G. Giers Photograph Gallery, Nashville.*

CALHOUN, George Reid. Silversmith, jeweler. Nashville, Davidson County, 1847–d. 1903.

George Reid Calhoun (fig. 46) was born in Ijamsville, Ohio on 29 June 1834.[6] According to information from George Calhoun's granddaughter, George's father, Hugh Calhoun, had arrived in Nashville as a young man from Philadelphia where his immigrant parents had settled. Hugh Calhoun left the Brown's Creek area near Nolensville Pike in Nashville to fight in the War of 1812 and then settled in Ohio.[7]

By 1847 George had moved to Nashville where he lived with his half brother, William H. Calhoun (q.v.), and worked in William's jewelry shop in the public square. Many years later George wrote that he had "slept in the store, 1849 to 1858, with the goods in cases; no safes to put the goods in, as we have now, no gas lights in the houses or the streets."[8]

In 1855 William made George a partner, and the two men worked together on the public square, at the second door up from Market Street. In the fall of 1858 the

46a, 46b. *Fork marked "W & H/ STERLING" and "G. R. CALHOUN & Co.," c. 1850, engraved "ACO." Dimensions not recorded. Private collection, MRF S-13,429. The "W & H" mark illustrated in fig. 46b is one of several used by Wood & Hughes (1840–99), a New York firm; Gates & Pohlman (1865–80) of Nashville and Hope & Miller (1870s) are only two of the several firms whose silver bears the same mark (see figs. 71a, 84, 99b, 121a, and 126a).*

46c. *Postcard with a view (extreme right) of George R. Calhoun's shop on the corner of Union and Fifth Avenue in Nashville, 1880s. Private collection, photograph by Bradford L. Rauschenberg.*

firm moved to the corner of College Street where they remained for a number of years.

At William's death in 1865, George established his own shop, George R. Calhoun and Company, which was first located on the square at the second door from Market Street. Calhoun later moved to a corner shop in the Maxwell House, located at Fourth and Church Streets. Twenty years later, he relocated his store two doors south of Union Street on Fourth Avenue; his final move was to the corner of Fifth and Union streets (fig. 46c) where he remained until his death in 1903. His farm on Twenty-First Avenue later provided the site for present-day Hillsboro Village. Calhoun's sons, George and Tyler, worked in their father's shop.[9] Much of this information was derived from a family history compiled by Tyler Calhoun, George's second son.

The "W & H" mark (fig. 46b) struck with a cameo die (Wood and Hughes of New York, circa 1840–99)[10] that accompanies George Calhoun's mark indicates that his silver, at least in later years, was made elsewhere.

CALHOUN, William Henry. Silversmith, jeweler. Nashville, Davidson County, 1835–d. 1865.

William Henry Calhoun was born about 1815 in Pennsylvania, probably Philadelphia, where his immigrant grandparents had settled. His father, Hugh Calhoun, a whitesmith and toolmaker, moved to Nashville, fought in the War of 1812, and then settled in Ohio. Hugh Calhoun later sent William Henry to Philadelphia to learn the silversmith trade.[11] (William Henry Calhoun owned silver by Philadelphia silversmiths A. Dubois and Joseph Richardson; it is now at Andrew Jackson's Hermitage.)

William moved to Nashville and opened a jewelry store there in 1835. He was to become perhaps Nashville's most prolific silversmith. By 1840 Calhoun and J. Flowers (q.v.) were operating a shop there under the name of Calhoun and Flowers (q.v.). The partnership was still intact in 1844 when it moved from its Union Street address to the public square.[12]

By 1847 when his half brother, George (q.v.), came to work for him, Calhoun probably had ventured on his own again in Nashville, establishing a "cheap cash store." His motto, "small profits and quick sales," served him well; the store proffered a large stock of watches, clocks, jewelry, silver, silver plate, and Britannia ware from New York and Philadelphia, as well as the services of a staff experienced in repairs.[13]

According to the Davidson County census for 1850, Calhoun's household included his Pennsylvania-born wife, a daughter, Mary Ella (born 1839), a son, William, Calhoun's half brother, George (also a silversmith at fifteen), and an A. M. Richless. His assets at the time amounted to $3,400. The 1860 census for Davidson County listed an evaluation of his real property at $84,300 and his personal property at $40,000.

47, 47a. *Salt spoon marked "W. H. CALHOUN TY.," 1840–50, Nashville. LOA: 3 7/16". Private collection, MRF S-13,434.*

47b, 47c, 47d, 47e. *Four marks used by William Henry Calhoun, 1845–50, 1850–55, c. 1855, and 1865 respectively. Fig. 47d courtesy of the Tennessee State Museum, photograph by Stephen D. Cox. The mark illustrated in fig. 47e may have been the last that Calhoun used; he died in 1865.*

47h. *Cup marked by William H. Calhoun, c. 1852, engraved "For my Husband/ St. John 4:14," and on the opposite side "Col. Robt. Hatton Tenn." HOA: 4½", width at widest point 4¼". Tennessee State Museum collection, photograph courtesy of Helga Photo Studio, Inc. for* Antiques.

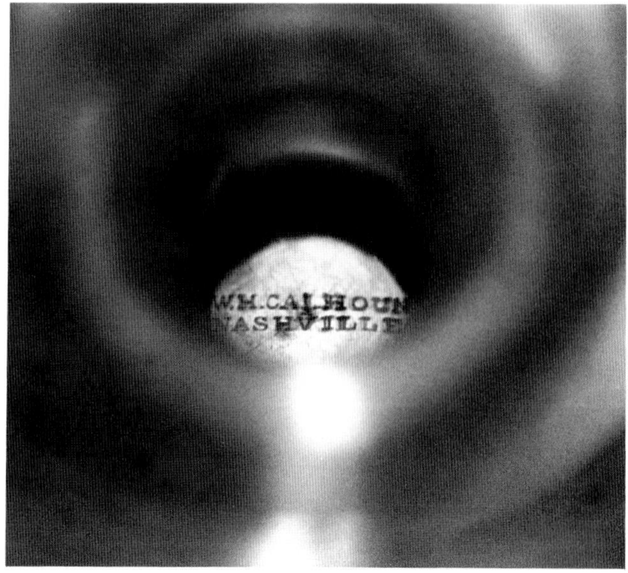

47f, 47g. *Cup marked "W. H. CALHOUN/ NASHVILLE," engraved "To Epsilon/ 2nd Div. Fair M. Tenn./& 3rd S.A. & M.S./1855." HOA: 5⅛", width across rim: 3⅜". Courtesy of Belle Meade Mansion, Nashville.*

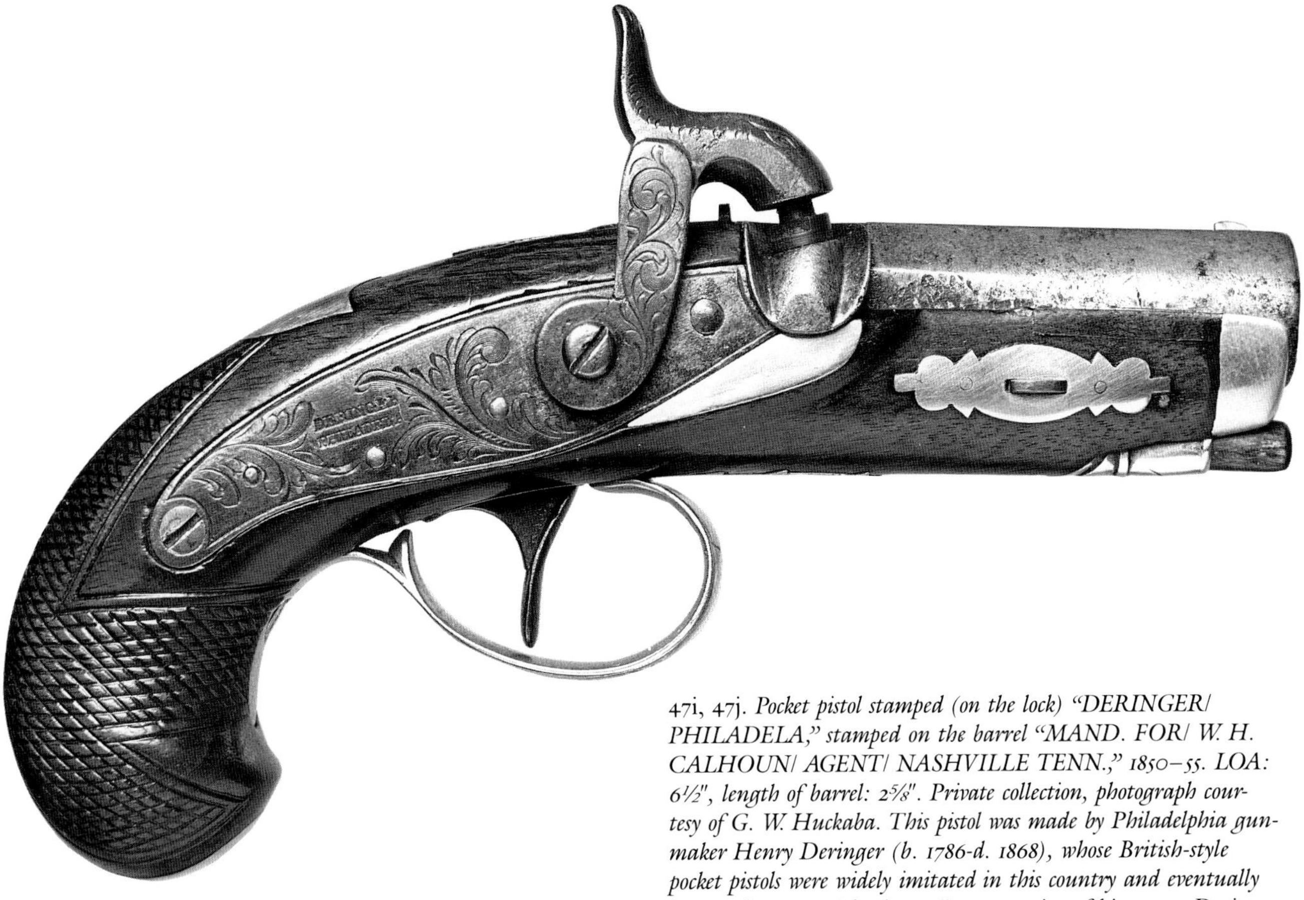

47i, 47j. *Pocket pistol stamped (on the lock) "DERINGER/ PHILADELA," stamped on the barrel "MAND. FOR/ W. H. CALHOUN/ AGENT/ NASHVILLE TENN.," 1850–55. LOA: 6½", length of barrel: 2⅝". Private collection, photograph courtesy of G. W. Huckaba. This pistol was made by Philadelphia gunmaker Henry Deringer (b. 1786-d. 1868), whose British-style pocket pistols were widely imitated in this country and eventually became known as "derringers," a corruption of his name. Deringer also made other handguns; a pistol he made for F. H. Clark & Co. of Memphis is illustrated in figs. 54h, 54i.*

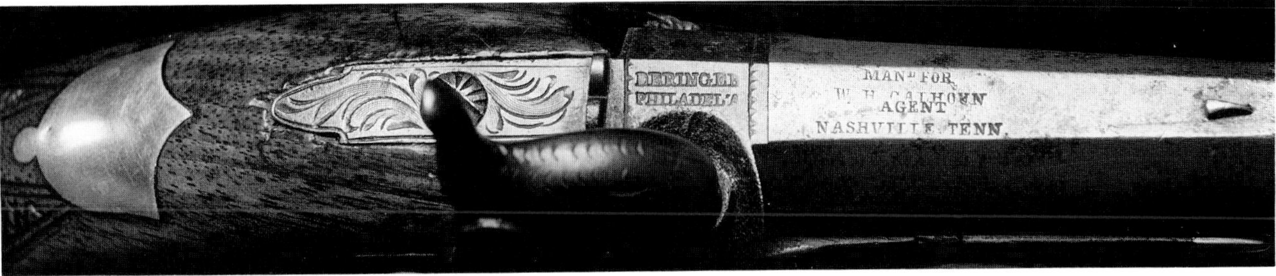

In the collection of the Tennessee State Museum is a Calhoun cup (fig. 47h), which was returned to Lebanon, Tennessee, in General Robert Hatton's baggage after his death at the battle of Seven Pines, Virginia, on 31 May 1862.

Calhoun operated a successful establishment for many years, employing numerous workmen.[14] A large vault constructed upon Calhoun's death in 1865 bears witness to his success in business, as does the William H. Calhoun Hall erected at Vanderbilt University with a large bequest from his daughter, Mary Ella. Mary Ella, who married twice but had no children, apparently foresaw disputes over the requested disbursement of her estate, for her will specifically stated that the Vanderbilt bequest "was all Calhoun money."[15] Calhoun's two sons, Frank and William, died as young men; neither married.[16]

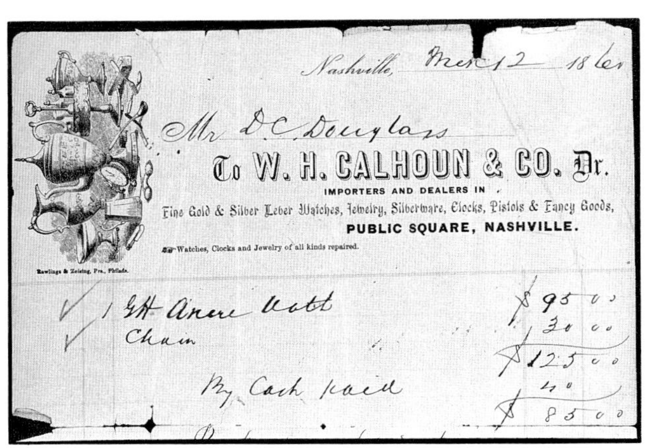

Nashville, Mar 12 1860

Mr D C Douglass

To W. H. CALHOUN & CO. Dr.

IMPORTERS AND DEALERS IN

Fine Gold & Silver Lever Watches, Jewelry, Silverware, Clocks, Pistols & Fancy Goods,

PUBLIC SQUARE, NASHVILLE.

Watches, Clocks and Jewelry of all kinds repaired.

1 [illegible]		$95 00
Chain		30 00
		$125 00
By Cash paid		40
		$85 00

47k. *Invoice with "W. H. Calhoun & Co." letterhead, 1860, Nashville. HOA: 8¼", WOA: 6¾". Private collection.*

47l, 47m, 47n. *Tea set marked by William H. Calhoun," 1850–52, engraved "I. F. Lanier," Nashville. Teapot (fig. 47l), HOA: 9½". Sugar bowl (fig. 47m), HOA: 9". Cream pitcher (fig. 47n), HOA: 7". Each piece has grape and vine feet and a strawberry nob lid. Courtesy of the Tennessee State Museum.*

47o. *Pitcher marked "W. H. CALHOUN/ NASHVILLE" 1855–60. HOA: 17³⁄₁₆", WOA: 8⁷⁄₁₆", DOA: 6½. Private collection, photograph by Bradford L. Rauschenberg.*

CALHOUN and FLOWERS. Silversmiths, jewelers, watch repairers. Nashville, Davidson County, 1840–44.

William H. Calhoun (q.v.), the noted Nashville silversmith, and J. Flowers, probably Joshua Flowers (q.v.), established the firm of Calhoun and Flowers in Nashville about 1840. At their shop on Union Street "next door to H. R. W. Hill's office," Calhoun made and repaired jewelry, while Flowers devoted his time to the watch business. Their stock included watches, jewelry, thimbles, spectacles, and pencils. In 1843 the firm moved from Union Street to the public square, "three doors from Nichol's corner," where they carried on much the same business through at least part of 1844.[17]

CAMP, A. G. Jeweler? watch and clockmaker? Purdy, McNairy County, 1860.

A. G. Camp appeared in the 1860 *State Gazetteer* listings under "Jewelry, Watches, Clocks, Etc." for Purdy, McNairy County.[18]

CAMPBELL, James. Retailer? clock and watchmaker? Knoxville, Knox County, 1818.

In 1818 James Campbell was working at his "old stand" opposite the shop of C. G. and R. Morgan. There he kept on hand a general assortment of "seasonal goods," which he was determined to sell "as low as anyone in the state . . . a few London Made CLOCKS and WATCHES, and a genteel Gig with Harness."[19]

A year earlier, a silversmith with the name James Campbell was working in Steubenville, Ohio;[20] no connection with the Knoxville man has been established. According to Knittle's *Early Ohio Silversmiths*, the Steubenville Campbell originally emigrated from Maryland.[21] There was, however, no mention of him in Pleasants and Sills's book *Maryland Silversmiths, 1715–1830*.

CAMPBELL, John. Silversmith, watch and clockmaker, jeweler. Nashville, Davidson County, 1836–57?.

John Campbell was born in Scotland on 6 May 1803. In September 1818 he was apprenticed to John Selph, a silversmith in Fayetteville, North Carolina. By December 1827 the two men were partners in the firm of Selph and Campbell, operating two shops in Fayetteville. The partnership was dissolved two years later, but Campbell continued to work independently.[22] In 1831 a fire destroyed most of Campbell's tools, apparently not an insurmountable complication; by 1834 he had formed the partnership of Campbell and Prior; Warren Prior was the other principal. This venture lasted until 1836 when Campbell advertised his intention to move to Nashville. His subsequent move to Tennessee was via Cheraw, South Carolina.[23]

Campbell's first work in Nashville was in an 1836–37 partnership with John Peabody (q.v.).[24] Campbell was one (fig. 48d) of nine men who formed a group in 1836 to promote harmony and union among the profession's members. The "Association of the Watch-Makers, Silversmiths & Jewellers of Nashville" established price guidelines for the manufacture and repair of clocks, watches, silver, and jewelry.[25] Whether the group succeeded in its pursuit of trade cooperation is not known; no further mention of its existence has been found.

Campbell worked independently for a number of years at a shop that he rebuilt and enlarged on the south side of the square in Nashville. He advertised his services there as a clock and watchmaker/ repairer, jeweler, gold and silversmith. An example of his work was found in twelve matching tablespoons made for the Washington family at Wesyngton, the family home near Springfield. Six (fig. 48c) of these spoons are illustrated. Stock inventories dated May 1843, April 1844, and January 1845 indicated a value of goods and materials on hand ranging from $6000 to $14,000. An 1847 Nashville tax list evaluated his real property on Spruce Street at $1,000, and his personal property, consisting of one slave, at $400.[26]

Campbell entered into at least two other partnerships; Campbell and Stevens (q.v.), 1849–50, and Campbell and Donigan (q.v.), 1853–55. His name appeared in the 1857 *Nashville Directory* when his residence was listed as 19 North Vine Street; no business address was given. In 1856 Campbell purchased 206 acres and a house (fig. 48e) still standing outside Franklin, Tennessee, and he died there in 1875.[27]

According to one source, President Andrew Johnson owned silver bearing the "J. Campbell" mark as well as silver with the mark of E. Wiggers (q.v.), a later Nashville silversmith.[28] Johnson was elected governor of Tennessee in 1853.

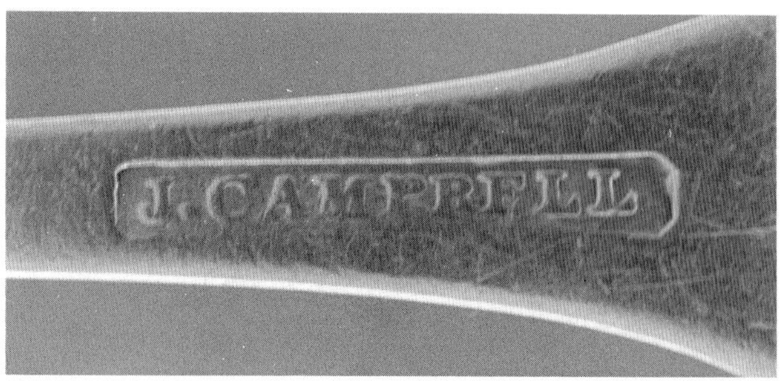

48, 48a, 48b. *Three marks used by John Campbell, 1840–50, c. 1850, and 1850–55, respectively.*

48c. *Six tablespoons marked "J. CAMPBELL," c. 1850, engraved "W," Nashville. LOA: 7⅝". Private collection.*

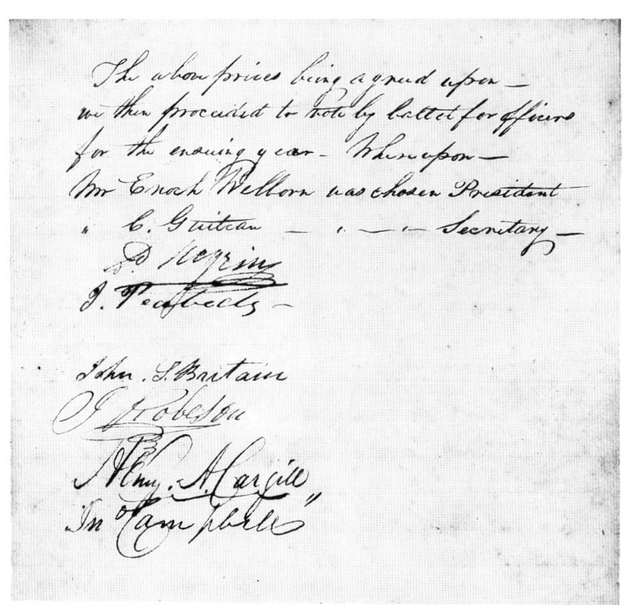

The above prices being agreed upon —
we then proceeded to vote by ballot for officers
for the ensuing year — Whereupon —
Mr Enoch Wellorn was chosen President
" C. Guiteau — " — " Secretary —
[illegible]
[illegible]

John. S. Britain
J. Robeson
Alexr. A. Cargill
Jn° Campbell

48d. *The signature of John Campbell affixed to a membership agreement in the "Association of the Watch-makers, Silversmiths and Jewelers of Nashville," 1836. Private collection.*

48e. *This Franklin house, probably built in the 1820s on land purchased by Judge Thomas Stuart in 1818, housed John Campbell and his wife from 1856–75. It still stands on Spencer Creek Road. Photograph by Arthur R. Ezell.*

49

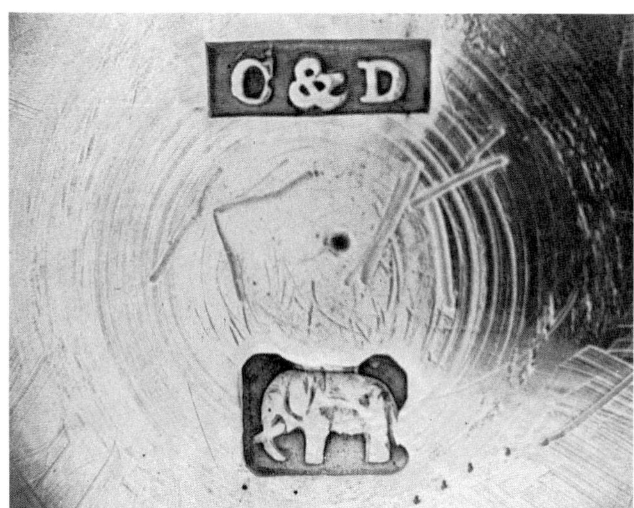

49a

49b

49c

CAMPBELL and DONIGAN. Silversmiths, watchmakers, jewelers. Nashville, Davidson County, 1853–55.

John Campbell (q.v.) and George Washington Donigan (q.v.) worked together in the partnership of Campbell and Donigan at the corner of College and Union streets in Nashville from 1853–55.[29] They produced a quantity of silver items identifiable today by an unusual elephant hallmark (figs. 49a, 49b) used in conjunction with either "C & D" or "Campbell and Donigan" marks. The elephant hallmark was used on East Indian export silver as a symbol of standard. It was also used on platinum to denote its purity, and for these reasons was adapted by some British metal workers other than silvermsiths; the elephant mark is rare in America.

49d. *Beaker marked "CAMPBELL & DONIGAN" with two elephants, engraved "M.C.A. & M.L./..to../ Leda,/ 1855.," Nashville. HOA: 3¾", width across the rim: 2¾". Courtesy of Belle Meade Mansion, Nashville. Four other similar beakers have been recorded by the author. They were given as prizes for equestrian events at the Maury County Agricultural and Mechanical Society (M. C. A. & M. S.) and the Davidson County Agricultural and Mechanical Association (D. C. A. & M. A.).*

49, 49a, 49b, 49c. *Two cream pitchers and a child's cup marked by Campbell and Donigan. Left: Cream pitcher marked "C & D" with an elephant (fig. 49a), engraved "Premium to Locomotive/ At the State Fair of Tenn./ 1855. LOA: 6½". Center: Child's cup marked "C & D" with an elephant, engraved "Wm. Martin Settle,/ from his grandpa,/ Wm. L. Martin./ Decr. 25, 1855" (fig. 49c). HOA: 3¼". Right: Cream pitcher marked "CAMPBELL & DONIGAN" with two elephants (fig. 49b), engraved "D. C. A. & M. A. to Castor, 1855." HOA: 5¼" Private collection. The "Castor" mentioned in the engraving on one of the cream pitchers was William G. Harding's horse at Belle Meade in Nashville.*

CAMPBELL and STEVENS. Silversmiths, watch repairers, jewelers. Nashville, Davidson County, 1849–50.

John Campbell (q.v.) and Stevens, whose first name is unknown, advertised a large assortment of jewelry, watches, and fancy goods at their store on the corner of College and Union streets during 1849–50.[30] A spoon bearing the Campbell and Stevens mark has been recorded; however, permission to photograph it was not secured.

CANE, James. Watchmaker. Memphis, Shelby County, 1850–57.

James Cane was born in Alabama in 1816. The birth of his oldest child in 1844 established his residence in Tennessee by at least that year. By 1850 Cane, his Tennessee-born wife, Lavinia, and his family had moved to Memphis where he worked as a watchmaker. Memphis directories listed J. Cane on Market Street from 1855–57.[31]

CANOVEN, M. B. Watchmaker. Nashville, Davidson County, 1860.

M. B. Canoven appeared in the 1860 *Nashville Business Directory* as a watchmaker at 41 Union Street and as a resident of the Edgefield District; W. O. Conover (also Canoven, q.v.), a jeweler and watchmaker, was listed at both the same shop and the same area of residence.[32]

50a, 50b. *Serving spoons marked "CARGILL.," 1836–39, engraved "JNB," Nashville. LOA: 8¾". Courtesy of the Tennessee State Museum.*

50. *"H. A. CARGILL" with a "G" mark used by Henry A. Cargill of Nashville, 1836–39.*

CAPSHAW, David (B. D.). Silversmith, jeweler, watch and clockmaker. Livingston, Overton County, 1850, 1860.

David Capshaw was born in Tennessee about 1818 and was working as a silversmith and living in the Overton County household of William G. Roberts, an innkeeper, at the time of the 1850 census.[33]

According to the 1860 *State Gazetteer*, B. D. Capshaw was a resident of the town of Livingston in the same county, where he was listed as a jeweler, watchmaker, and clockmaker.[34]

CAPSHAW, William P. Silversmith. McMinnville, Warren County, 1850.

William P. Capshaw was born about 1814 in North Carolina. The birth of his eldest child in Tennessee established his residence in the state as early as 1843. Capshaw listed his occupation as "silversmith" in the 1850 census when he, his Tennessee-born wife, and his family were living in McMinnville, Warren County.[35]

CARGILL, Henry A. Silversmith, clock and watch repairer, jeweler. Nashville, Davidson County, 1836–39.

In October 1836 Henry A. Cargill opened his silversmithing, watch and clockmaking shop on Union Street. Three months later he signed (see fig. 48d) "The Book of the Association of the Watch-Makers, Silversmiths & Jewellers of Nashville" at the group's second meeting on 28 December 1836.[36] The following year, Cargill advertised his return from the North with a splendid assortment of watches, jewelry, and military goods. He also announced his readiness to manufacture all kinds of silverware, to repair clocks and watches, and to mend jewelry. Cargill continued to advertise throughout the following year; in one notice he offered a piano forte for sale, and in another he noted that he was moving to a new location on the public square, "next door to W. T. Berry's book shop."[37]

In late 1838 Cargill sold the contents of his shop at reduced prices for cash, perhaps because of the nationwide depression taking place at that time. By the following year another Nashville silversmith, Henry Thomas (q.v.), had purchased Cargill's stock of goods and was offering it for sale at Cargill's former public square location.[38]

CASBURN, John M. Watchmaker. Ripley, Lauderdale County, 1846?–50.

John M. Casburn was born in England about 1816, married a North Carolina woman, Elizabeth W(....?), and by 1846 had arrived in Tennessee. The 1850 census listed Casburn and his family in Ripley, Lauderdale County, where he was working as a watchmaker.[39]

CAYCE, Eldred B. Silversmith, jeweler, watchmaker. Franklin, Williamson County, 1852–98.

Eldred Beverly Cayce was born in 1837 in Tuscumbia, Alabama, where his father, the Franklin silversmith William Cayce, had settled in the hope of finding gold. When the family returned to Franklin, Cayce (often called "E. B.") was an apprentice to his brother, John M. Cayce (q.v.), from 1853–57. Thereafter, E. B. Cayce earned a law degree, served in the Confederate army, and after the war supported his wife, Jennie E. McCulloch, and their children by rejoining the family jewelry business in Franklin. When illness forced him to retire in 1898, he was succeeded in the family business by his son, E. B. Cayce, Jr., who later became a physician.[40]

While maintaining his business, E. B. Cayce also was ordained and served as a minister for four years in the Christian Church of Franklin. He died in Franklin on 11 June 1905.[41]

51. *Eldred B. Cayce (b. 1837-d.1905), c. 1856. Private collection.*

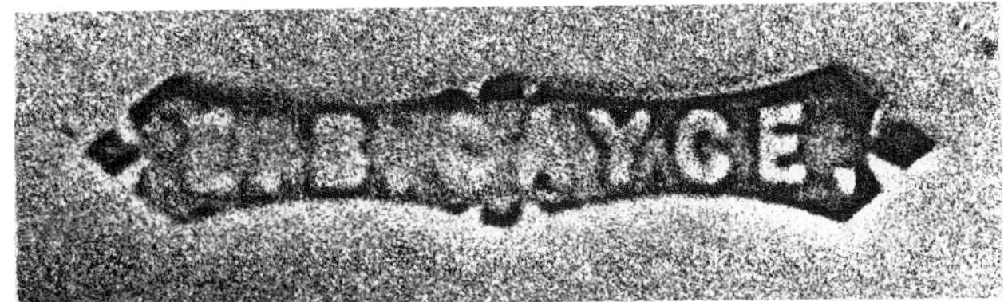

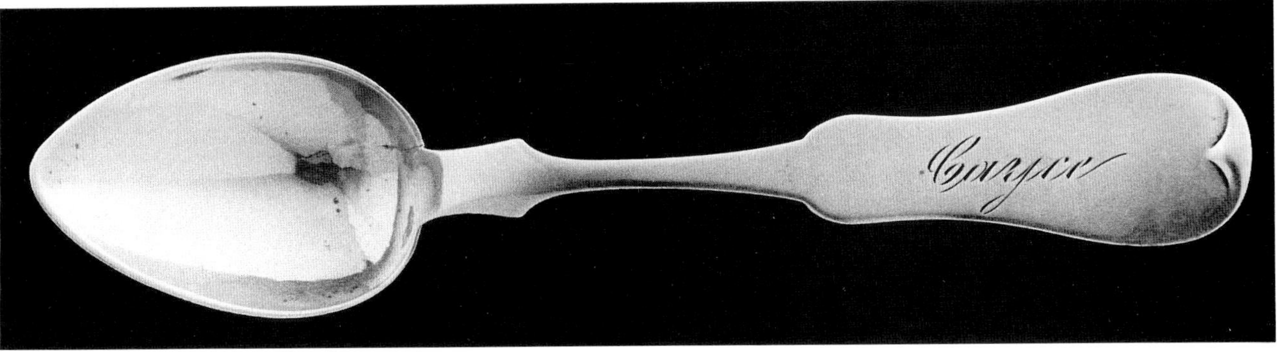

51a, 51b. *Teaspoon marked "E. B. CAYCE.," c. 1860, engraved "Cayce," Franklin. LOA: 6". Private collection.*

51c. *E. B. Cayce (left) and employee in front of his Franklin store, c. 1880. Courtesy of Mrs. Dana C. Brooks. Note the display and storage of the pocketwatches in the window to the left and the spectacles over the door.*

CAYCE, John M. Silversmith, watchmaker. Franklin, Williamson County, 1850–70.

John M. Cayce was born in November 1827 at Cayce Springs in Williamson County, the oldest son of William (q.v.) and Sarah Cayce. The 1850 census indicated that John M. Cayce was working as a silversmith at the family jewelry store in Franklin; he had been apprenticed to his father. According to the *Williamson County News*, he assumed control of the business in 1854.[42] Cayce inherited much of his father's mechanical genius and was granted fifteen patents on devices ranging from a pair of watchmaker's pliers designed to reshape cogs, to a portable forge and a "sporting and life boat."[43]

Cayce served in the ordnance department of the Confederate army, making and repairing guns, and at the end of the war in 1865 married Jennie Irene Cayce of Memphis. Cayce ran the family business until 1870 when he moved to Nashville. He died in 1902, at his daughter's home in Charleston, Mississippi, at the age of seventy-five.[44]

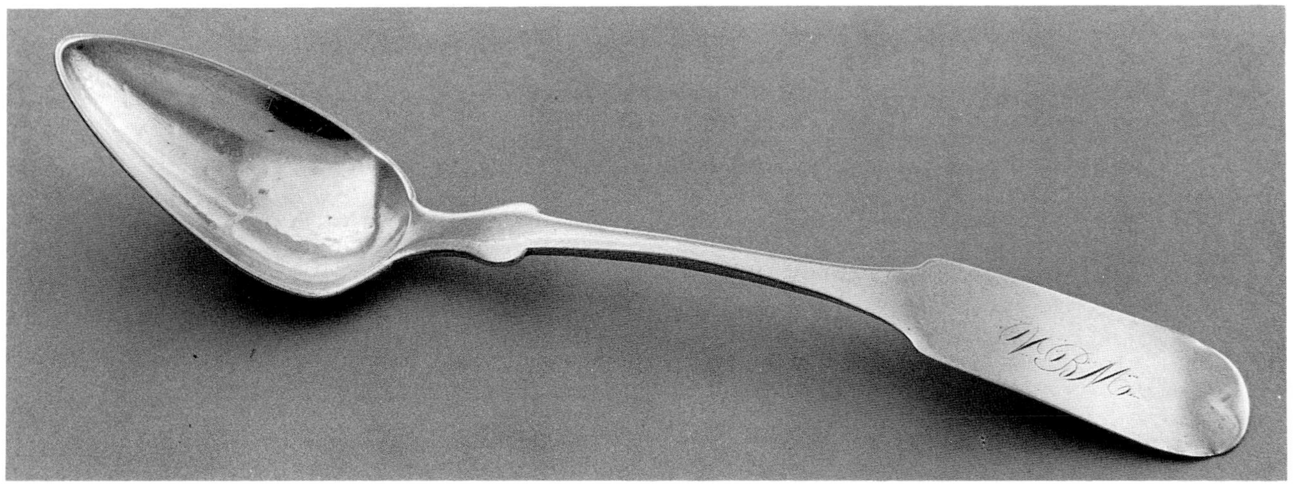

52, 52a. *Dessert spoon marked "J. M. CAYCE.," 1855, engraved "VBM," Franklin. LOA: 7". Courtesy of the Tennessee State Museum.*

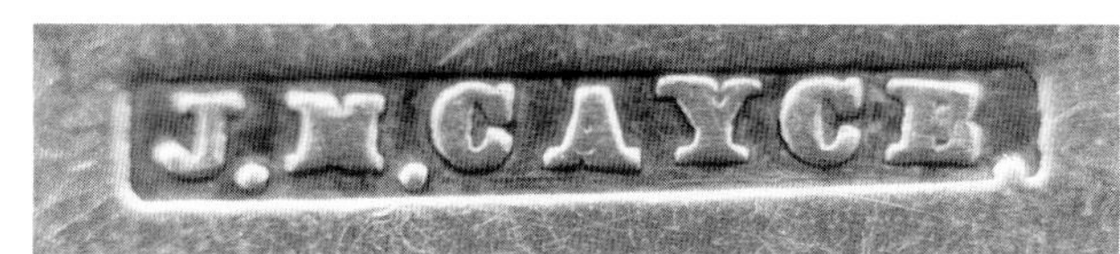

CAYCE, William. Silversmith, watchmaker, jeweler. Franklin, Williamson County, 1820–d. 1878.

According to family history, William Cayce was born 16 April 1803, one of thirteen children of Shadrach Cayce, Jr.,[45] a Virginia entrepreneur who had moved to Williamson County, Tennessee, about 1800 with his wife, Mary Ann Dodson (Dotson), and their first three children. The family initially settled between Franklin and Nashville; Shadrach then moved to Georgia and finally to Lawrenceville, Lawrence County, Tennessee; William Cayce, however, remained in Franklin.[46] As a boy William had access to his father's blacksmith shop and tools; it is said that he made a set of watch-repair tools and repaired several watches acquired in "youthful trading."[47]

In 1820, at the age of 17, William Cayce opened his own jewelry shop in Franklin on the north side of West Main Street; "Cayce's" store was to remain in operation for three generations, not closing until 1907.[48]

William Cayce married his cousin Sarah Cayce in 1824 and continued to run a successful jewelry business. On 5 July 1826, he and his brother Shadrach purchased forty-eight acres of land on Murfree's Creek, ten miles south of Franklin. The site later became a resort known as "Cayce Springs."[49]

Franklin newspaper advertisements of the day supplied glimpses into Cayce's business activities. In 1831 he requested that his customers pay their accounts or risk facing a collections officer. In his Main Street shop, Cayce repaired timepieces and developed a business large enough to require the help of a silversmithing apprentice. In early 1836 Cayce requested that his patrons pay their bills as he planned to move to Tuscumbia, Alabama. In preparation for the move, Nashville silversmith Barton Richmond (q.v.) signed an advertisement announcing the sale of Cayce's home and lot in Franklin.[50] Cayce and Richmond may have had a business connection, but the nature of such a possible relationship is unclear.

Cayce's move to Tuscumbia followed the discovery of gold in Alabama. He remained there for about six years, returning to his jewelry store in Franklin by 1842. A brother presumably had run the business during William's absence.[51]

At the time of the 1850 census William Cayce and his family were still living in Franklin; his net worth at the time was $3,000. Four years later the *Western Weekly Review*, a Franklin paper, noted that William Cayce had received a patent for an improved lock, an "ingenious piece of mechanism . . . entirely unpickable."[52] He died at Cayce Springs in 1878 at the age of seventy-five and was buried in the family graveyard there.[53]

CHAMBERLAIN, S. E. Watchmaker. Nashville, Davidson County, 1860.

In 1860 S. E. Chamberlain was working as a watchmaker at the shop of noted silversmith and jeweler William H. Calhoun (q.v.); this shop was on the corner of College Street and the public square in Nashville.[54] A spoon marked "S. CHAMBERLAIN" with a Tennessee history has been recorded in the MESDA files. It is possible that this was S. E. Chamberlain's mark, although no certain attribution has been made.

CHEEK, F. M. Watchmaker, jeweler. Paris, Henry County, 1856.

In January 1856 F. M. Cheek purchased the stock and tools of J. B. Johnson's (q.v.) watch and jewelry establishment in Paris, Henry County. Cheek promised to complete with dispatch all work entrusted to him and offered to sell a fine lot of jewelry "cheap for Cash and cash only."[55]

CISSNA, William. Clock and watch repairer, silversmith, jeweler, dental surgeon. Memphis, Shelby County, 1836–37.

William Cissna first appeared in Memphis in April 1836. At that time Cissna and J. R. Garland (q.v.) announced their association as clock and watch repairers, silversmiths, and jewelers. The same *Memphis Enquirer* advertisement noted Cissna's readiness to practice "the art of Surgeon Dentistry." The partnership was short-lived, for by June 1836 Cissna had moved to the room previously occupied by N. B. Starr, a tailor, on Main Street, one door south of McKee and Hester's store. From this new location Cissna advertised twelve-month guarantees on his watch-repair work and offered to repair jewelry "in the neatest possible manner."[56] By May 1837 Cissna had formed the partnership of Cissna and Robert (q.v.) which retailed clocks, watches, and guns.[57]

The pocket and long Steel Rifles.

THE subscribers have just received, and will constantly keep on hand, a large and general stock of the PATENT STEEL POCKET and LONG RIFLES, drilled of Steel from the Solid Bar, thereby avoiding the liability of seams and scales in welding. Many remarkable shots have been made by those that have been accustomed to shoot them. The Long Rifle being said to shoot ONE THOUSAND YARDS; ☞but try them.

CISSNA & ROBERT.

May 6–10,

N. B. Fine watches repaired and warranted to perform well.

53. *"Cissna & Robert" offered "Patent Steel Pocket and Long Rifles" for sale in the* Memphis Enquirer *of 6 May 1837. "Fine Watches repaired and warranted to perform well" was added only as a postscript.*

CISSNA and ROBERT. Clock and watch repairers, silversmiths, gunsmiths. Memphis, Shelby County, 1837.

Probably early in 1837, William Cissna (q.v.) and Robert (q.v.) formed Cissna and Robert, a Memphis clock and watch shop that also sold and possibly made guns. Cissna had worked in the partnership of Garland and Cissna (q.v.) with J. R. Garland (q.v.) during the previous year;[58] Robert was probably A. J. Robert, later of Nashville and Murfreesboro.

In May 1837 the firm advertised (fig. 53) a new supply of "patent steel POCKET and LONG RIFLES." The latter, the partners noted, were drilled from a solid bar of steel "thereby avoiding the liability of seams." The long rifle was said to shoot one thousand yards.[59]

53a. *Mark, possibly that of the firm of Cissna and Robert(s), Memphis, 1837.*

CLARK, Frederick Harvey. Merchant, jeweler, dentist. Murfreesboro, Rutherford County, 1838; Memphis, Shelby County, 1841–d. 1866.

Frederick Harvey Clark was born in Danbury, Connecticut, in 1811, the son of James and Elizabeth Starr Clark. New York City directories listed him as a watchmaker from 1829–34. In 1841 Clark and James E. Merriman (q.v.) formed a partnership; their shop was located on Exchange Square in Memphis. They continued to work together through 1847, advertising with great frequency.[60]

By 1850 Clark had formed F. H. Clark and Company. At that time he was living in the household of James S. Wilkins (q.v.), a watchmaker and future partner; A. C. Wursbach (q.v.), who was later to join Clark as a partner, also was living with Wilkins. Several other jewelers, watchmakers, and clerks were members of the same household.[61]

F. H. Clark and Company, which was located at "1 Clark's Marble Block," at Main and Madison streets, subscribed to a full-page advertisement in the 1855 *Memphis City Directory*. By that time Wursbach had joined Clark as a partner; the firm sold watches, jewelry, and silverware, repaired timepieces, and made daguerreotypes. The 1856 *Memphis City Directory* noted the addition of J. S. Wilkins (q.v.) and Thomas Hill (q.v.) as partners. Directories through 1866 continued to list Clark as a jeweler. He died in Memphis on 21 January 1866 and was buried in Danbury, Connecticut.[62]

54, 54a, 54b, 54c. *Four marks used by the Memphis firm of F. H. Clark and Co., 1840–50 (fig. 54), c. 1850 (figs. 54a, 54b), c. 1860 (Fig. 54c). Fig. 54 courtesy of the H. F. du Pont Winterthur Museum, Decorative Arts Photographic Collection. The "MEMPHIS" of the mark in fig. 54b also appears on silver marked by James Merriman and James Pooley (see figs. 99c and 105a).*

54d, 54e. *Pair of beakers marked "F. H. CLARK & Co./ MEMPHIS," 1847–60, engraved "CMA," Memphis. HOA: 3½", diameter at rim: 3½". Courtesy of the Tennessee State Museum, photograph by Stephen D. Cox.*

54f, 54g. *Pistol marked "MAND. FOR/ F. H. Clark & CO./ MEMPHIS TENN/ AGENT," 1850s, also marked DERINGER/ PHILAD—."* Private collection. *This pistol was made by Henry Deringer (b. 1786-d.1868) for F. H. Clark; Deringer made a similar pistol for William H. Calhoun of Nashville (see figs. 47i, 47j.).*

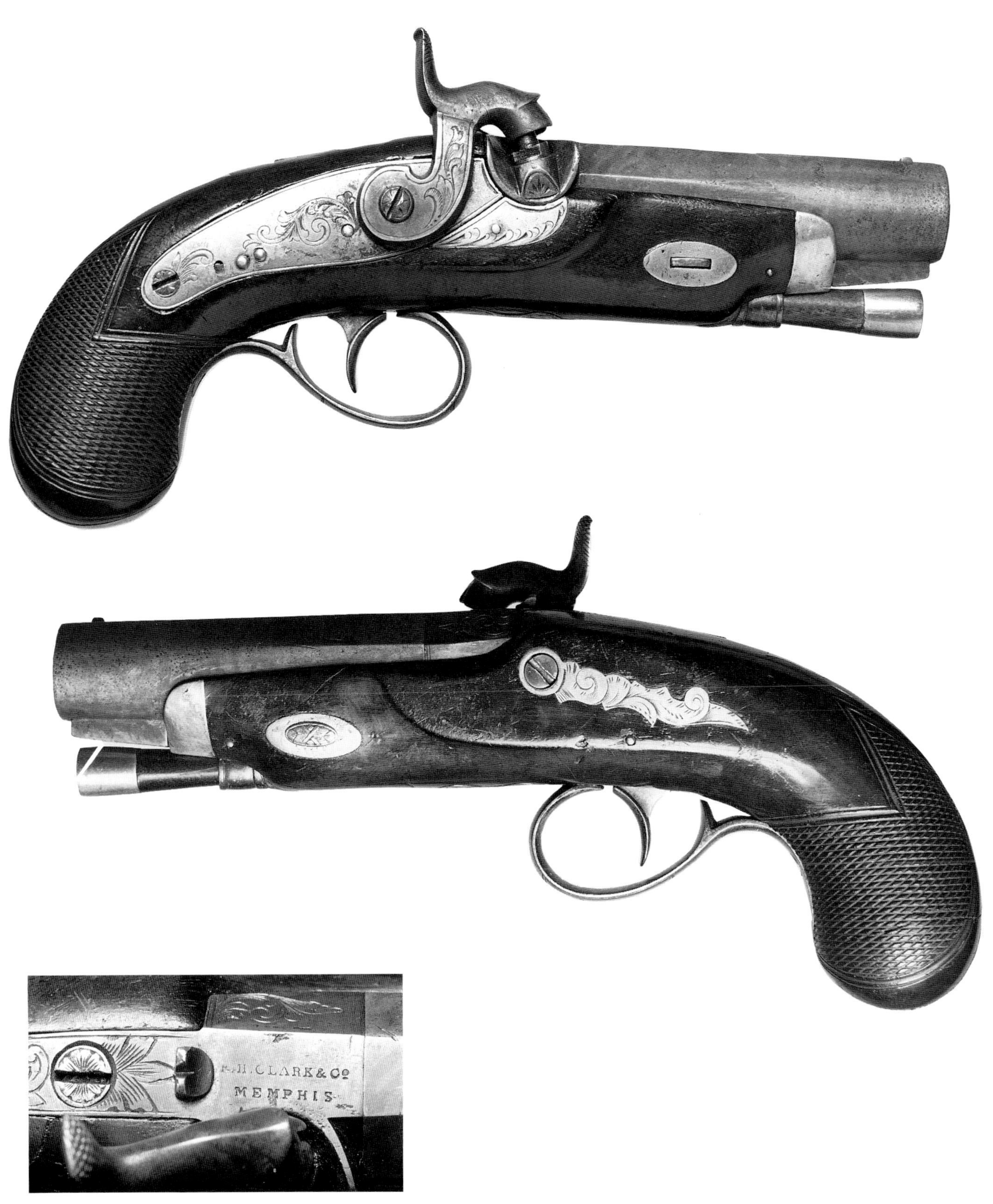

54h, 54i, 54j. *Pistol marked "F. H. CLARK & CO/ MEMPHIS," 1850s, unknown maker, possibly Memphis. LOA: 7½". Private collection.*

54k. *Surveyor's compass engraved "F. H. Clark & Co. Memphis, Tenn.," 1847–60. LOA: 14½". Courtesy of the Tennessee State Museum, photograph by Stephen D. Cox. This brass surveyor's compass, or circumferentor, is missing its alidades, cover, and spirit levels.*

54l. *Punch ladle marked by F. H. Clark & Co., 1855, engraved "Bankhead," Memphis. LOA: 13", width across bowl: 4¼", rise of shaft: 1½". Private collection.*

COHEN (COHN), Henry. Watchmaker, jeweler. Nashville, Davidson County, 1855–60 and later.

Henry Cohen was born about 1826; he emigrated from Poland with his wife Rosa and lived in New York for a few years before settling in Nashville during the 1850s. Cohen, a watchmaker and jeweler, kept shop at a number of locations, including 159 North Market Street in 1855, 26 Market in 1857, 30 Market in 1859, and at several South Market Street sites after 1860.[63]

An active member of the Mogen David Congregation, Cohen held several offices and eventually served as the congregation president. He also was a member of the Cattles Company of Hawkins Battalion, Nashville's military police, during the Civil War. Cohen died in 1884.[64]

COLEMAN, S. K. (H.). Jeweler. Nashville, Davidson County, 1855–d. 1859.

S. K. Coleman worked as a jeweler at 39 North Market Street in Nashville from 1855–57. He is believed to have been the same jeweler as S. H. Coleman, who was a trustee of the Mogen David Congregation from 1857–58. Coleman died on 18 September 1859 at the age of sixty-three, leaving a wife and three children.[65]

COLLINS, Henry M. Jeweler. Chattanooga, Hamilton County, 1850–53; Cleveland, Bradley County, 1860.

Henry M. Collins was born in Georgia about 1822. At the time of the 1850 census he was working as a jeweler and living in the Chattanooga household of watchmaker James J. Mulkey (q.v.). Collins remained at a shop on Market Street in Chattanooga for three years, but by 1860 he had moved to Cleveland, Bradley County, where he dealt in dry goods, jewelry, watches and clocks.[66]

The following paragraphs describe the "confusion of Connelleys" which resulted from a study of directories and census records. Dates and locations overlap; spellings differ. No conclusions have been drawn, the facts are presented as they were recorded, and a solution to this mystery is hoped for from those with more information.

CONLEY, James. Silversmith. Nashville, Davidson County, 1855–60.

James Conley was working as a silversmith in Nashville from 1855–57 at a shop on Vine Street; he lived in South Field. Conley is listed in the city's 1860 directory; the entry gave the same addresses.[67]

CONNELLEY (CONNELLY), J. B. Watch and clockmaker, silversmith, jeweler. Jackson, Madison County, 1825–26.

Early in 1825, the *Jackson Gazette* announced that J. B. Connelley had established himself as a watch and clockmaker at a shop on Main Street in Jackson, a few doors below Bell Tavern; he made silverware, "musical watches," and jewelry "inferior to none in the state." A year later he requested (fig. 55) payment of debts owed

I HAVE but little owing to me, but it will possibly help pay my debts, and it will save me cost by getting my money immediately.
J. B. CONNELLEY.
Jan. 28–3t
☞AN APPRENTICE would be taken to learn the Clock and Watch making business.

55. *J. B. Connelley placed this advertisement in the* Jackson Gazette *of 28 January 1826.*

him and sought an apprentice to the clock and watchmaking business.[68]

CONNELLY, J. (Jas.) B. Watchmaker. Nashville, Davidson County, 1859–60.

During 1859–60 J. B. Connelly worked as a watchmaker in Nashville, probably in his residence on Vine Street near Wilson's Springs.[69]

CONNELY and WEAVER. Watch & clock repairers. Nashville, Davidson County, 1850.

In February 1850 Connely and Weaver opened their watch and clock repairing shop on Market Street in Nashville, "opposite Charles Nichol's Store."[70]

CONNLEY, J. B. Watchmaker. Nashville, Davidson County, 1859.

J. B. Connley worked as a watchmaker at 30 South Market Street, Nashville, in 1859.[71]

CONONLY, James. Watchmaker. Nashville, Davidson County, 1860.

James Cononly, born about 1792 in Pennsylvania, was working as a watchmaker at the time of the 1860 census for Davidson County. He lived in Nashville's District Ten with Ann, his wife, and Eugine, his fourteen-year-old son who was born in Tennessee.

CONOVER, (....?). Watch repairer. Fayetteville, Lincoln County, 1860.

The 1860 census for Lincoln County listed twenty-year-old Conover as a watch repairer in Fayetteville. A native of Pennsylvania, Conover lived in the home of Elzira Ringo, who may have been Elijah Ringo (q.v.).

CONOVER (CANOVEN), W. O. (W. V., W. G.) Jeweler, watchmaker. Nashville, Davidson County, 1859–60.

The 1860 census for Davidson County listed twenty-seven-year-old W. O. Conover as a jeweler and a native of New Jersey. He lived in Edgefield District with Virginia, his wife, and two young children born in Pennsylvania. City directories contained varying listings for him:

in 1859 he was listed as "W. V." Conover, a watchmaker, working at 41 Union Street with a residence in Edgefield; in 1860 he was shown as "W. G." Canoven, a watchmaker, again working at 41 Union Street with a residence in Edgefield.[72]

COOK, Mat. Watchmaker. Shelby County, 1860.

Mat Cook, who was born about 1838 in Germany, was working as a watchmaker and living in the Fourteenth District of Shelby County at the time of the 1860 census. He and his German-born wife, Anna, lived in the residence of Jacob Sorge (q.v.).

COOKE, G. E. Silversmith. Clarksville, Montgomery County, 1859–60.

G. E. Cooke worked in Clarksville during 1859–60. In 1860 the twenty-four-year-old Pennsylvania native identified himself as a silversmith to the census taker working "north and east of the Cumberland River." An advertisement in the 1859–60 *Williams' Clarksville Directory* noted Cooke's establishment: "G. E. Cooke, Wholesale and Retail Dealer in WATCHES, CLOCKS, JEWELRY, Silver and Plated Wares, and Fancy Goods . . . ALL KINDS OF JOBBING NEATLY AND PROMPTLY DONE." The *State Gazetteer* for 1860 listed Cooke under "Jewelry, Watches, Clocks, Etc." on the east side of the public square in Clarksville.[73]

The "T E & Co." mark (fig. 56) found on silver with Cooke's mark indicates that during the 1850s Cooke purchased at least some of his silverware from T. Evans and Company (Theodore Evans and John Cook) of New York City.[74]

CORY (CORREY), Charles. Silversmith. Pulaski, Giles County, 1850; Lynnville, Giles County, 1860.

Charles Córy was born about 1822 in New Jersey. At the time of the 1850 census, he was working in Pulaski as a silversmith and living in the household of John N. Patterson. He had $1,200 invested in his one-man business that annually produced $1,000 worth of jewelry and "other miscellaneous articles."[75]

By 1860 Cory owned his residence in Lynnville; also listed in his household were Rachael "Correy," forty-two, also born in New Jersey; Henry "Correy," a fourteen-year-old born in Ohio; and Harry Bishop, an eight-year-old native of Tennessee. At that time Cory identified himself as a watchmaker and estimated the value of his real property at $3,000 and his personal property at $4,000.[76]

COYORT (COZART), William P. Silversmith, watch and clock repairer. Jonesboro, Washington County, 1845; Knoxville, Knox County, 1850.

William Coyort was born in Tennessee about 1820. A March 1845 advertisement informed Jonesboro citizens that he was prepared to repair clocks and watches or manufacture jewelry. At the time of the 1850 census he was living in Knox County, with his wife and two children, and was continuing his work as a silvermsith.[77]

CRANE, Ezra. Silver and brass plater. Winchester, Franklin County, 1850–60.

Ezra Crane was born in New Jersey about 1820. By 1850 he was working in Winchester as a brass and silver plater and living in the household of Mary Nerrinan, a

56. "G. E. COOKE COIN" mark used by wholesaler and retailer G. E. Cooke, 1859–60, Clarksville. The marks "TE & Co." and "NY" in a lozenge to the right of Cooke's is identified in Beldon's Marks of American Silversmiths *as the mark of Theodore Evans and John Cook (T. Evans & Co.) who worked in New York City from 1856–64.*

57. Mark attributed to Ezra Crane of Winchester, Franklin County, 1855–60.

58. Mark used by J. S. Curtis of Memphis, c. 1850. Courtesy of the Tennessee State Museum, photograph by Stephen D. Cox.

tavern keeper. His estate at the time was valued at $400. Crane remained in Winchester at least through 1860 when the *State Gazetteer* for that year listed him as a silver plater with a shop on Main Street.[78]

The 1860 Franklin County federal census noted that Crane was forty-four years of age and that the value of his real estate was $3,500; his personal property was valued at $2,260. He lived in a boarding house with Noah Crane, twenty-nine, a cigar maker.

A "CRANE" mark (fig. 57) struck with an intaglio die is attributed to Ezra Crane.

CRESSY, (....?). Silversmith. Columbia, Maury County, 1814.

According to Goodspeed's *History of Tennessee*, a man named Cressy was the first silversmith in Columbia; it was reported that he began working there as early as 1814.[79]

CUNNINGHAM, E. B. Silversmith. Pikeville, Bledsoe County, 1850.

E. B. Cunningham was born about 1797 in Connecticut. He married a Connecticut woman, and after the 1840 birth of their last child in Connecticut, he moved his family to Tennessee. The 1850 census listed Cunningham as a silversmith in Pikeville. His assets were valued at $250.[80]

CURTIS, J. S. Silversmith. Memphis, Shelby County, 1850.

J. S. Curtis was born in South Carolina about 1830; by 1838 he had arrived in Tennessee with his parents, brothers, and sister. By 1850 the family had settled in Memphis where Curtis continued to live in his father's household, working as a silversmith.[81]

DALEY, Edwin B. Silversmith. Nashville, Davidson County, 1860.

Edwin B. Daley, a twenty-five-year old silversmith from Pennsylvania, listed his personal and real property at $100 each in the 1860 census for Nashville. At that time Daley was living in the Third Ward household of Joshua Flowers (q.v.).

DANIEL, George C. Silversmith, watch and clockmaker. Henry County, 1840; Jackson, Madison County, 1843.

George C. Daniel was working in Elizabeth City, North Carolina, as early as 1829. By 1830 he had moved to Halifax in the same state where he carried on the clock and watch business and both mended and manufactured silver goods and jewelry; Daniel employed a London watchmaker.[1]

By January 1832 Daniel had left Halifax and moved to Henry County, Tennessee, where an 1840 census listed George C. Daniel, his wife, two children, and two slaves but failed to mention a township location. Thereafter, he apparently lived in Jackson, Madison County; an 1843 advertisement in the *Jackson Republican* noted that Daniel had vacated the brick building he had formerly occupied as a "jeweller's shop".[2]

DANIELS, S. T. Jeweler. Somerville, Fayette County, 1860.

S. T. Daniels worked as a jeweler in Somerville, Fayette County, at the time the 1860 census was taken. The twenty-two-year-old North Carolinian evaluated his personal estate at $2,500.

DANNER, William C. Watch and clockmaker, jeweler. Knoxville, Knox County, 1857, 1859–60.

William C. Danner and G. W. McFarlane (q.v.) operated a jewelry business on Gay Street in Knoxville in 1857. Two years later Danner and a man named Miller formed the partnership of Danner and Miller (q.v.), a watchmaking and jewelry business also located on Gay Street. This partnership lasted at least through 1860.[3]

William C. Danner may have been related to Jacob Danner (1763–1850), a silversmith of Middletown, Virginia. An Edinburgh, Virginia, newspaper account of Jacob Danner's death revealed he did have a son, although the article failed to supply his name.[4]

DANNER and MILLER. Watch and clockmakers, jewelers. Knoxville, Knox County, 1859–60.

William C. Danner (q.v.) and Miller (perhaps John Miller, q.v.), had joined forces by 1859 to form the partnership of Danner and Miller, watchmakers and jewel-

NOTICE.
THE SUBSCRIBER
Has commenced the
WATCH-MAKING
OR
REPAIRING BUSINESS.

IN the white frame house in market street, first door east of Montgomery & Nelson's store, lately occupied by Samuel F. Adams as a watch making shop, and is prepared to repair watches and clocks of all descriptions on the shortest notice and in the neatest manner. Not having any inexperienced hand in the shop, he hopes to be able to give entire satisfaction to those who may favour him with their custom. Travellers and those living at a distance will be promptly attended to. D W. DAVIS.

N. B. Gold and silver ware of any required Patterns on hand, and for sale on the most moderate terms going in the western country, watch rigging of all description, fancy articles, &c.

Knoxville, June 8 3t

*59. D. W. Davis's statement that he did not have "any inexperienced hand in the shop," in his "Watch-Making or Repairing Business" announcement of 15 June 1819 indicates that he employed several workmen. (*Knoxville Register, *15 June 1819.)*

ers. Their shop on Gay Street, between Cumberland and Church streets, appeared in the 1860 *State Gazetteer* under "Watchmakers and Jewelers" for Knoxville.[5]

DARNELL, John. Clock repairer. Manchester, Coffee County, 1850.

John Darnell was born about 1808 in Virginia. His wife, Susan, was a Tennessee native; the 1838 birth of the Darnells' eldest child established their residence in Tennessee by that time. At the time of the 1850 census Darnell and his family were living in Manchester where he worked as a clock repairer. His personal estate was valued at $225.

DAVIS, D. W. Watchmaker. Knoxville, Knox County, 1819.

In 1819 D. W. Davis began making and repairing watches on Market Street in Knoxville; he was located in a white frame house previously occupied by silversmith and watchmaker Samuel Adams (q.v.). Davis described the nature of his business in an 1819 advertisement (fig. 59): "*N.B.* Gold and silver ware of any required Patterns on hand, and for sale on the most moderate terms going in the western country, watch rigging of all description, fancy articles, etc."[6]

Davis may also have been one of the principals in the Carthage firm of Davis and Jones (q.v.) in 1808, although no connection has been established.[7]

DAVIS and JONES. Silversmiths. Carthage, Smith County, 1808.

Davis and Jones advertised in a Carthage newspaper for November 1808 that they had "purchased the tools of Mr. Barton, deceased," (Benjamin Barton, q.v.) and intended to carry on the silversmithing business "in all its various branches."[8]

Davis may have been D. W. Davis (q.v.), a silversmith later located in Knoxville; another possibility was W. O. Davis who, although not known to have been a silversmith, appeared in an 1810 Carthage newspaper advertisement for W. O. Davis and Company. Jones may have been G. B. Jones (q.v.), a gold and silversmith and clock and watchmaker, later located in Rogersville, Hawkins County.[9]

DEADERICK, Thomas. Silver and goldsmith, watch and clockmaker. Nashville, Davidson County, 1802–d. 1831.

Thomas Deaderick, the son of David and Rosannah Boucher Deaderick (Dietrick), was born in Winchester, Virginia, in 1765. David Dietrick had emigrated from Wurtemburg, Germany in 1747 and had settled in Philadelphia before moving to Winchester where he married Rosanna Boucher. Thomas Deaderick worked in Winchester for several years as a watch and clockmaker and gold and silversmith. He was a man of property, for in 1799 he offered a house and lot for sale in Winchester, as well as 300 acres "near Opiquan [Opegnan] creek" with the two houses thereon, orchards, and barns. In 1802 he moved to Nashville, apparently to join his brothers, one of whom was George Michael Deaderick, the second son of David and Rosannah Deaderick. In 1802 Thomas advertised a "newly opened copper and tin manufactory" in Nashville. He was in partnership with a man by the name of Sittler.[10]

Upon opening his Nashville shop that year, Deaderick offered (fig. 60) not only the usual gold and silver items, but also a "light stage waggon hung on springs," which probably had brought him along the westward route down the Shenandoah Valley and across the Cumberland Mountains to Nashville. For several years thereafter, Deaderick held lotteries for "the disposal of watches . . . and handsome Gold and Silver work."[11] This custom was popular among men of his trade.

An 1808 notice in the *Impartial Review and Cumberland Repository* listed Deaderick's purchase of a lot in Columbia, Maury County, perhaps an indication of his success in business affairs. In 1812 Thomas Deaderick and Wilkins Tannehill published their need for "100 water proof casks" and offered "a liberal price for clean dry Ashes," another indication of Deaderick's diverse interests, possibly soapmaking or whiskey in this instance. An 1820 report in the *Nashville Gazette* fretted over robberies committed during the "last several months," and warned citizens that the robbers had "aspired to business on a large scale," having stolen several thousand dollars' worth of goods from Deaderick's shop "last Wednesday night." Missing were "cloths, shawls, sewing silk, 'beeds' cotton and other hose. . . ."[12]

Deaderick was a "marrying man," and three of his four wives were Virginians. His 1789 marriage to Nancy Raworth, who may have been the sister of Nashville silversmith Edward Raworth, ended shortly thereafter, probably with her death. The following year Deaderick married Ann Julia Dangerfield, who died in 1808 leaving a family of young children. In 1813 he married Elizabeth Frances Dangerfield, his former wife's sister, also a native of Winchester, Virginia. Through the years Deaderick maintained close ties with Winchester, transacting several real estate sales in the area. His final marriage, which took place sometime before 1818, was to Eliza Frances, a native of Tennessee.[13]

Deaderick died in Nashville on 15 October 1831 at the age of sixty-six. The Deaderick family continued to prosper after his death. Deaderick Street in the central part of modern Nashville is a testimony to their success.[14]

At some point during his career, Deaderick made a spoon (figs. 60a, 60b) for James Robertson, one of Nashville's founders. It is the only known example of Deaderick's work extant.

THOMAS DEADERICK,

ACQUAINTS the citizens of Naſhville, and its vicinity, that he has opened ſhop in Naſhville, where he has for ſale a handſome aſſortment of gold Ear bobs and drops, gold rings, ſet and plain, gold knot claſps for gloves, gold locket's, gold keys, &c. &c.—alſo an aſſortment of ſilver work, ſay table ſpoons, ladles, tea ſpoons, ſugar tongues, with many other articles in the ſilver and gold line, I have ſome faſhionable watches, plain and capt, for ſale, which I will warrant one year—watches repaired on the ſhorteſt notice, warranted one year, alſo all kind of gold and ſilver work, made and repaired by him,—caſh given for old gold and ſilver.

Naſhville, Auguſt 20th, 1802.

N. B. I have a light ſtage waggon, hung on ſprings for ſale. T. D.

60. *Thomas Deaderick announced the commencement of his business in the Nashville* Tennessee Gazette *of 25 August 1802.*

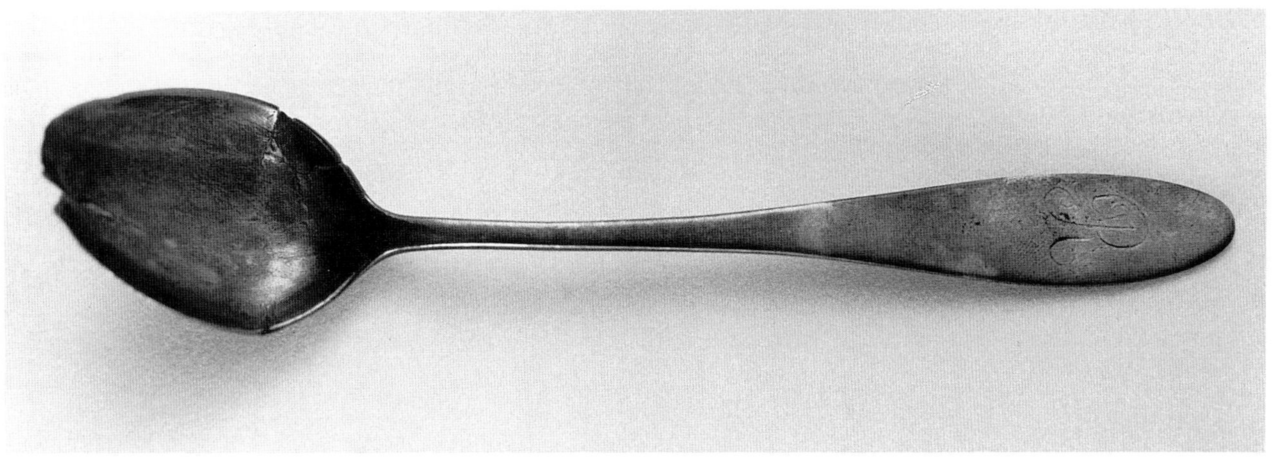

60a, 60b. *Teaspoon marked "TD" on the reverse, attributed to Thomas Deaderick, c. 1810, engraved "R," Nashville. LOA: 5½". Courtesy of the Tennessee State Museum. This spoon belonged to James Robertson, one of Nashville's early residents.*

DELANCY, (....?). Silver and goldsmith, watch and clock repairer. Knoxville, Knox County, 1826–28?.

In 1826 Delancy, whose first name is unknown, formed a partnership with Samuel Bell (q.v.) of Knoxville at Bell's establishment on Gay Street. The firm was known as Bell and Delancy (q.v.). The firm made gold and silver work "to any pattern" and repaired clocks and watches. By 1828 the partnership had been dissolved. Although Bell continued his work in Knoxville, no further reference to Delancy has been found.[15]

In 1804 a John Delancey was listed as a jeweler on Broadway in New York City. No relationship between the two men has been established.[16]

DE YOUNG, Michael. Silversmith, jeweler, watchmaker. Knoxville, Knox County, 1824.

In 1824 Michael De Young, a silversmith, was operating a shop at 198 Market Street in Knoxville. During that year, he advertised a large supply of jewelry, gold and silverware, watches, and "silver spoons of his own manufacture." This is the only known reference to De Young's work in Tennessee.[17] A connection may exist between the Knoxville De Young and a Michael De Young, silversmith, of Baltimore (circa 1816–36). A Ralph De Young is listed in an 1837 Cincinnati directory as a jeweler and a silversmith;[18] however, no link between the Tennessee silversmith and either the Baltimore or Cincinnati De Youngs has been established.

DICKINSON, G. W. Jeweler. Memphis, Shelby County, 1855–59.

In 1855 G. W. Dickinson was working as a jeweler at 31 Front Row in Memphis, the address of J. E. Merriman's (q.v.) shop. An 1859 Memphis directory lists him at Union Street, above Bayou Street.[19]

DIETRICH, Julius. Watchmaker, jeweler. Franklin, Williamson County, 1860 and later.

Julius Dietrich, who was born about 1822 in Saxony, and his wife Emelia arrived in Tennessee about 1853; they had been residents of Georgia for a year or more. By 1860 Dietrich was living in Franklin and working as a watchmaker. His "jewelry and fancy store" was opposite the Presbyterian Church. Fifteen years later he was still in Franklin, serving the town in the same capacity.[20]

DONAHOE, Robert. Jeweler. Knoxville, Knox County, 1860.

The 1860 census for Knox County recorded that an eighteen-year-old Irishman, Robert Donahoe, was working in Knoxville's District One as a jeweler.

DONELSON, W. B. Silversmith. Nashville, Davidson County, 1860.

In 1860 W. B. Donelson, aged thirty, was listed as a silversmith in the federal census for Davidson County. Donelson lived in the G. Payne household in the Edgefield area of Nashville; L. Furtwangler (q.v.), a silversmith and watchmaker, was given the same address. The census cryptically recorded Donelson's birthplace as "Ca."

DONIGAN, George Washington. Silversmith, watchmaker, jeweler. Nashville, Davidson County, 1850–d. 1864.

George Washington Donigan was born in New York about 1824. Before moving to Nashville he married Eleanor Elizabeth Chambers, of Staten Island, New York, believed to have been a member of the family for whom Chambers Street was named. The couple moved to Nashville by 1850, where they lived in the household of A. C. Carter, a grocer; Donigan worked as a silversmith.[21]

Success did not evade Donigan in Nashville. From 1853–55 he worked with John Campbell (Campbell and Donigan, q.v.) as "Dealers in Watches, Jewelry, Silverware, Etc." at the corner of College and Union streets. Following the dissolution of that partnership, Donigan remained at the same location until the mid-1860s.[22] Donigan, a "staunch Presbyterian" and a thirty-third degree Mason, had four children: Anna, a member of the first graduating class of Ward's Seminary, a precursor of Ward-Belmont College; George Washington Donigan, Jr.; Medera; and Clara. At the time of the 1860 census for Davidson County, which listed "Donegan's" birthplace as Virginia, the children ranged in age from one (Clara) to eleven (Anna).[23]

61. *George Washington Donigan (b. 1824-d. 1864), 1855–64. Private collection, photograph by J. Curney & Son.*

61a. *Pair of beakers marked "G. W. DONIGAN" on the bottom, c. 1850, engraved "Presented to/ MEB/ by/ Mother," Nashville. HOA: 3⅜", width across rim: 2⅞". Courtesy of the Tennessee State Museum and a private collection, photograph by Helga Photo Studio, Inc. for* Antiques.

61b, 61c. *Two marks used by George Washington Donigan, 1850–60 and 1850–64, respectively.*

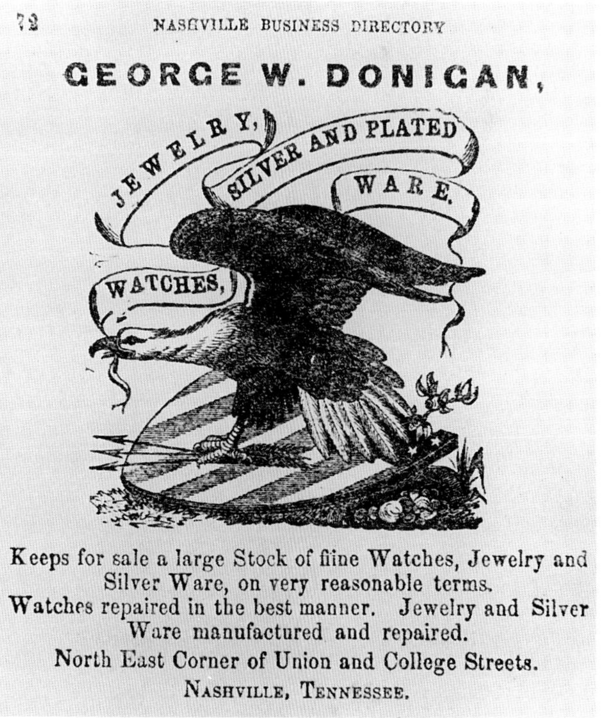

72 NASHVILLE BUSINESS DIRECTORY

GEORGE W. DONIGAN,

Keeps for sale a large Stock of fine Watches, Jewelry and Silver Ware, on very reasonable terms.
Watches repaired in the best manner. Jewelry and Silver Ware manufactured and repaired.
North East Corner of Union and College Streets.
NASHVILLE, TENNESSEE.

61d. *George W. Donigan's advertisement in the* Nashville Business Directory, *1860? Courtesy of the Tennessee State Museum.*

Although Donigan survived the turmoil of the Civil War, his last days reflect the unsettled times that followed. Imprisoned during the war for unknown reasons, he was released only to be wounded on the streets of Nashville by a stray bullet. He died on 15 January 1864 of tetanus, which was related to his injury, and was buried in Mount Olivet Cemetery in Nashville.[24]

The names in the firm's "Accounts Receivable" listed in Donigan's 12 April 1864 inventory revealed that the silversmith's patrons were among the wealthiest and most influential people in Middle Tennessee. A later Nashville firm, Gates (q.v.) and Pohlman, paid tribute to Donigan's successful silversmithing business when it advertised in 1865 as "successors to George W. Donigan."[25]

Donigan apparently retailed imported silver. Although there are pieces of silver that have only his mark (figs. 61a, 61b, and 61c), a set of forks has been recorded that bears not only his, but that of "W. H. & H."[26]

DRAPER, T. Watchmaker. Knoxville, Knox County, 1859–60.

During 1859–60, T. Draper was working in Knoxville as a watchmaker. According to the *Knoxville Directory* for that year, he kept shop on southeast Gay Street, between Cumberland and Church streets.[27]

A John Draper was working as a silversmith in Cincinnati, Ohio, in 1844, and a Joseph Draper was located in Wilmington, Delaware, circa 1816–32 as well as in Cincinnati, Ohio, circa 1849. Boultinghouse noted another Joseph Draper in Marshall County, Kentucky, circa 1850.[28]

DUTOLT, H. Watchmaker. Nashville, Davidson County, 1860.

In 1860 H. Dutolt was working as a watchmaker at 30 South Market Street in Nashville. He probably was employed at that address by I. M. Sobel (q.v.) and Company, clock and watchmakers, silversmiths, silver platers, and jewelers.[29]

DYER, Edmund B. Watch and clockmaker, silversmith, gilder, jeweler. Knoxville, Knox County, 1819–20.

In 1819 Edmund B. Dyer, Samuel Bell (q.v.), and James Simpson (q.v.) were working together under the firm name of Bell, Dyer and Simpson (q.v.) on Gay Street in Knoxville, where they offered their services as watch and clockmakers, jewelers, gilders and silversmiths. The firm was dissolved in 1820.[3]

EARNEST, Elijah E. Watchmaker. Knoxville, Knox County, 1859–60.

Elijah E. Earnest worked as a watchmaker on East Jacksboro Road between Coffin and Bellevue Roads, Knoxville, during 1859–60.[1]

EDMOND, (....?). Silversmith. Nashville, Davidson County, 1810.

A Nashville newspaper account of 25 May 1810 revealed that "Mr. Edmond," a silversmith "of this city," identified ore discovered in the lower end of Davidson County as "lead and antimony." The paper noted how much in demand these materials were because "intercourse with Europe" was forbidden.[2]

It is conceivable that Edmond was related to the Edinburgh (Scotland) and Petersboro (probably Petersburg, Virginia) silversmith Thomas Emond (circa 1802) whom Cutten recorded in *The Silversmiths of Virginia*. Emond, whose name was occasionally misspelled in newspaper ads as "Edmond," also worked in Raleigh, North Carolina, circa 1806–21.[3]

EDMONDS, J. Jeweler. Memphis, Shelby County, 1860.

A nineteen-year-old native of Illinois, J. Edmonds was working as a jeweler and living in the Fifth Ward of Memphis at the time of the 1860 census.

ELLIFF, J. P. Silversmith. Pulaski, Giles County, 1840.

In March 1840 J. P. Elliff was working as silversmith on North Main Street in Pulaski.[4]

ELLIS, Joseph. Silversmith. Stantonville, McNairy County, 1860.

Joseph Ellis, a thirty-four-year-old native of Tennessee, was working as a silversmith in Stantonville, in southwest Tennessee at the time of the 1860 census. He lived in the home of James Ellis, possibly his brother.

Although Kovel noted five silversmiths with the surname Ellis in Philadelphia during the mid-1800s, no connection has been established.[5]

ELLISTON, John. Silversmith, clockmaker. Nashville, Davidson County, 1809–d. 1823.

John Elliston was born in Kentucky on 21 November 1793, the son of Benjamin Elliston and Sarah Hiter. Family tradition records that both John Elliston and his uncle, Joseph Thorpe Elliston (q.v.), were apprenticed to Kentucky silversmith Samuel Ayres. According to Clayton's *History of Davidson County*, in 1809 "John Elliston, a silversmith" had a shop adjoining Bass's Tannery on Market Street at the intersection of Union. Family histories record that John and Joseph Elliston were partners. Their shop is said to have produced movements for tallcase clocks as well as silverware. The ".Elliston" mark (fig. 62b) was a shortened version of Joseph Elliston's old stamp, "J. T. Elliston." The two men met with great success in their business, and although more is known of Joseph Elliston than his nephew, both men invested wisely in Nashville real estate and became wealthy citizens.[6]

John married Ann T. Ridley in 1815 and died eight years later at the age of twenty-nine. John's will directed

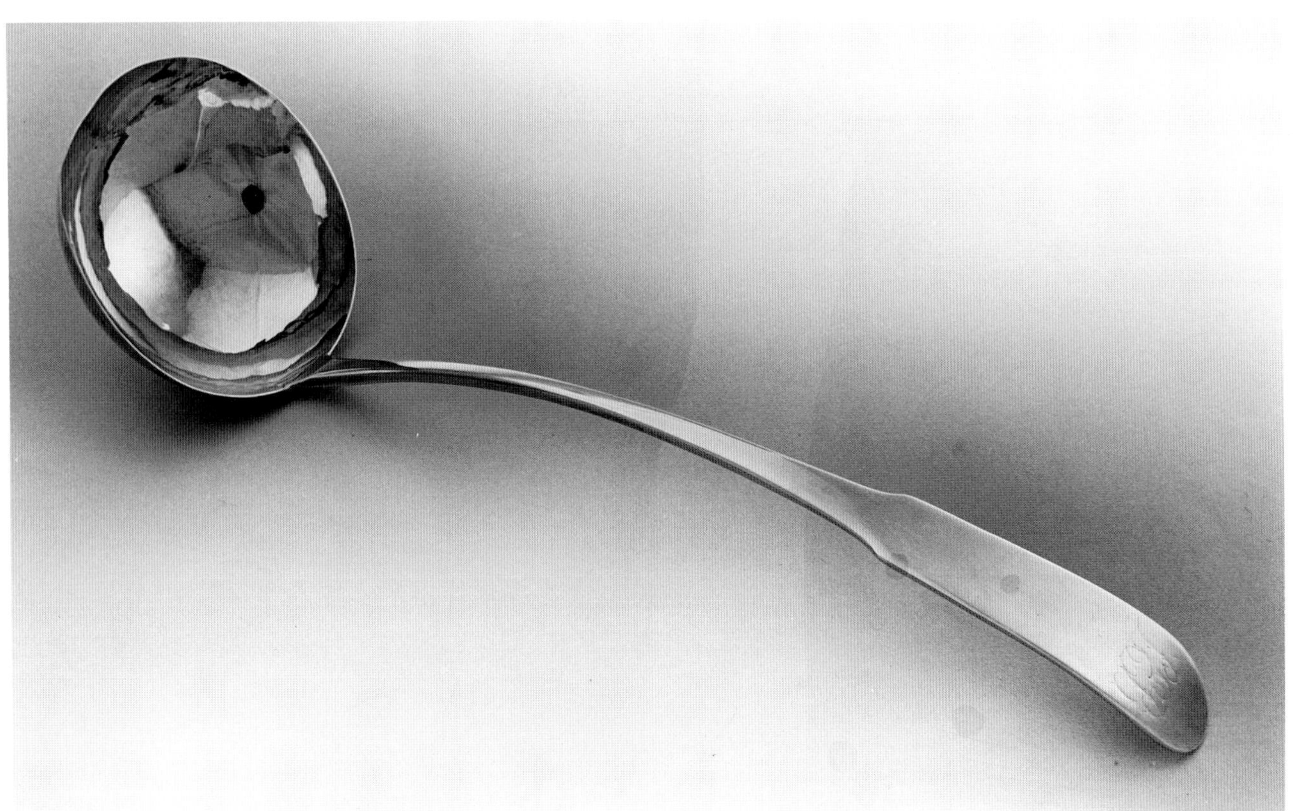

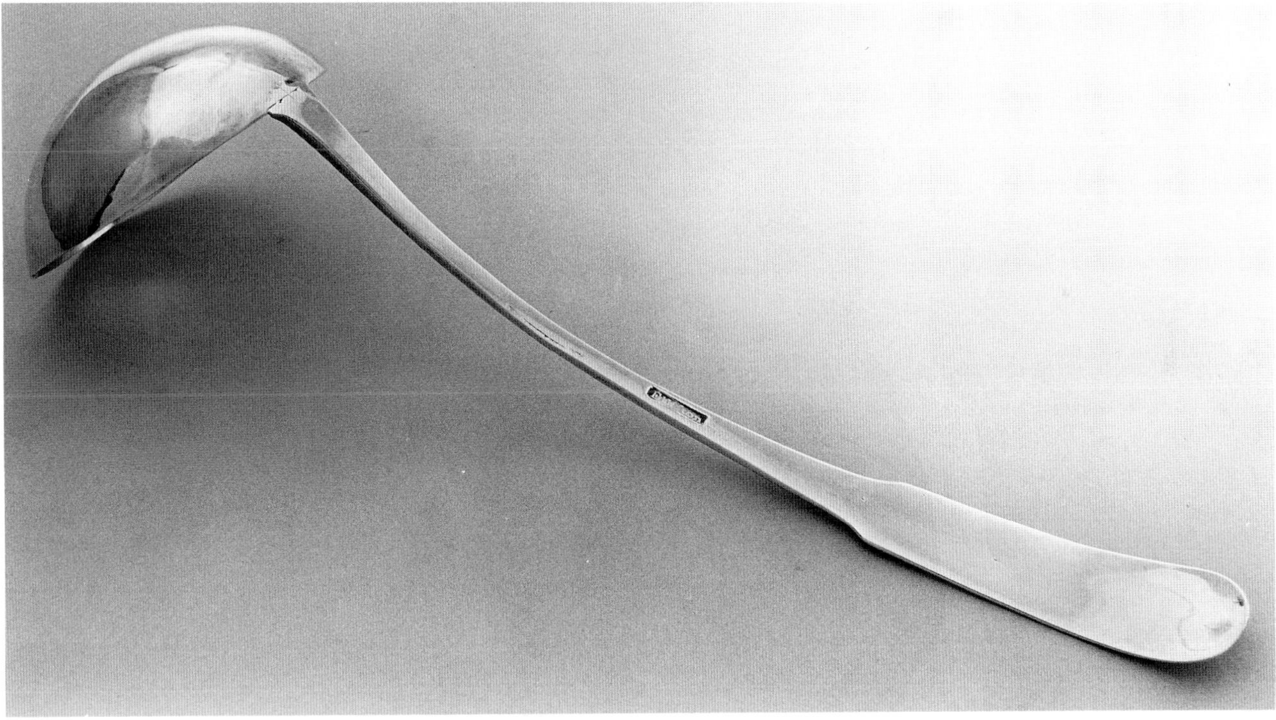

62, 62a. *Punch ladle marked ".Elliston.," attributed to John Elliston, 1810–23, engraved "LEB," Nashville. LOA: 12¼", width across bowl: 3½". Private collection. Although it is not known when John Elliston joined his uncle Joseph Thorp Elliston in the silversmithing business, it is thought that the "J.T." was removed from Joseph's mark when the partnership began.*

that Joseph T. Elliston, executor of the estate and guardian of John's two sons, sell the deceased's tools, materials, and work "that belongs to my shop," and that "the proceeds, the money on hand, with the debts due me, I wish applied to the payment of my debts, and if sufficient I want nothing else sold at this time." Many well-known figures in the area, including Sam Houston, Felix Grundy, and Samuel Driver, patronized the fashionable Elliston shop and owed John money at the time of his death.[7]

The sale of articles in the estate totaled well over $500 and included the following items:[8]

Item	*Buyer*	*Price*
1 watch	Solomon Clerk	7.25
2 watches	John Grundy	8.75
2 watches	Miller & Murrell	27.50
16 gold watch seals	Miller & Murrell	24.00
2 gold watch seals	G. Wharton	4.25
5 gold watch seals	N. H. Robertson	12.87
14 gold watch keys	Miller & Murrell	11.00
3 gold watch chains		
1 pair gold watch chains	Miller & Murrell	24.50
26 gold brest [sic] pins	Miller & Murrell	40.50
6 gold brest [sic] pins	Wilbern	16.00
3 gold brest [sic] pins	Wharton	6.00
9 gold brest [sic] pins	Manchester	15.18
16 pair gold ear rings	Miller & Murrell	29.10
2 pair gold ear rings	Brooks	1.87
2 pair gold ear rings	Clark	2.62
1 pair gold ear rings	Shall	7.25
3 pair silver spectacles	J. Decker	5.00
2 Bretches [sic] Buckles	G. Wharton	8.00
2 shoe buckles	Manchester	.50
1 set of castors	Miller & Murrell	3.00
4 spectakle [sic] cases	Miller & Murrell	.50
1 segar [sic] box	Brooks	1.50
1 lot watch keys common	Richmond	3.75
1 lot watch keys common	Wilbern	3.06
1 lot gilt seals	Miller & Murrell	1.37
1 lot steel chains	Miller & Murrell	
1 pr. gold ear rings	Manchester	2.75
10 gold barrells [sic]	Miller & Murrell	2.50
3 morning necklaces	Miller & Murell	3.00
24 finger rings	Miller & Murell	20.56
2 6/12 thimbles	Miller & Murrell	11.06
2 gold clasps	Miller & Murrell	8.87
1 dozen tea spoons	Thos. Welch	11.00
1 dozen tea spoons	Brooks	10.86
1 3/12 tea spoons	McGavock	5.75
5/12 tea spoons	Crenshaw	3.25
1 pr. tongs & cream spoon	Miller & Murell	5.00
1 pr. tongs & cream spoon	Welch	4.87
2 pr. suspenders buckles	Barrow	3.00
2 pr. suspenders buckles	Miller & Murrell	3.00
1 lot sequar [sic] signs	Crenshaw	1.00
1 lot glass	Miller & Murrell	3.06
1 set smith tools	Miller & Murrell	48.62
1 set of watch tools	Miller & Murrell	23.12
3 gross watch glass		17.25
1 gross watch glass	Richmond	6.24
1 lot of watch springs	Miller & Murell	28.74
2 show cases	Manchester	4.00
2 show cases	Miller & Murrell	4.00
3 desks	Miller & Murrell	4.75
1 table	Miller & Murrell	1.00
2 clocks	Ridley	64.50

ELLISTON, Joseph Thorp. Silversmith, clock and watchmaker, jeweler. Nashville, Davidson County, 1799–d. 1856.

Joseph Thorp Elliston (fig. 63) was born on 15 December 1779 in Culpeper, Virginia. He was one of eleven children. His parents, Robert and Elizabeth Thorp Elliston, moved to Kentucky in 1795; there, at the age of sixteen, Joseph was apprenticed to Samuel Ayres to learn the silversmithing and clockmaking trades.[9]

Two years later Elliston established himself in Nashville as that city's first silversmith, jeweler, clock and watchmaker. An Elliston tallcase clock (figs. 63i, 63j) has a cherry and poplar case probably fashioned by a Nashville cabinetmaker. As Nashville, which at that time was still a frontier town, expanded, Elliston invested in real estate and very quickly became a wealthy man. Indeed, by 1847 he owned over $24,000 in real property and $1,300 in personal property (three slaves).[10]

Elliston was one of Nashville's five incorporators and served for at least three one-year terms as an alderman (1808, 1810, 1820) as well as mayor (1814–16). In 1816 he helped found Nashville Female Academy, which, by the time the Civil War forced its closure, had become the largest school for girls in the world. In 1837 he was active in establishing the House of Industry, a forerunner of the Y.W.C.A.[11] As a member of the commission for building the Tennessee State Capitol in the 1850s, he served on the committee which chose William Strickland as architect. An early capitalist and philanthropist, Elliston was not bound by convention. Although a staunch supporter of the Methodist Church, he owned and raced thoroughbreds.[12]

Elliston married Louise Mullen about 1801; she died shortly after the birth of their sixth child in 1815. Two years later, in 1817, Elliston took a second wife, widow Elizabeth Odom of Sumner County. The couple resided in their Nashville home, "Burlington," where Elliston died in 1856.[13]

Elliston opened his silversmithing shop about 1797 when he arrived in Nashville. He initially worked alone as a watchmaker, silversmith, and jeweler in a shop at the corner of Union and Market streets near the courthouse. In 1801 Elliston advertised his immediate need for an apprentice, ". . . a young man between the age of 13

63. *Portrait of Joseph Thorp Elliston (b. 1779-d. 1856) by Washington Bogart Cooper, 1831, oil on canvas, HOA: 29¼", WOA: ½". Private collection, photograph by Cynthia Stow.*

JOSEPH T. ELLISTON,

WATCH-MAKER, SILVERSMITH & JEWELLER,

INFORMS the public, that he carries on the above buſineſs, in its various branches, in the ſhop formerly occupied by Mr. Rutherford, near the courthouſe, where the ſtricteſt attention will be paid to the orders of thoſe who may employ him in any line of his profeſſion. Watches will be repaired, and work in gold and ſilver executed in the moſt faſhionable manner, on the ſhorteſt notice.

WANTED IMMEDIATELY.

A young man between the age of 13 and 14 as an

APPRDNTICE,

To the Silverſmiths buſineſs, for terms apply to

JOSEPH T. ELLISTON.

Naſhville, June 3d, 1801.

63a, 63b. *On 25 February 1800, Joseph T. Elliston announced that he repaired watches and executed "work in gold and silver . . . in the most fashionable manner." A year later, he was advertising for an apprentice (Nashville* Tennessee Gazette, *25 Feb. 1800; 3 June 1801).*

and 14 (fig. 63b)." The firm of Elliston and Huner (q.v.) was formed in 1802, but by the following year Elliston was again working on his own and advertising the first of many lotteries to be held at his shop. In 1804 he offered a six and one-fourth cents reward for the return of Robert Barret, a runaway apprentice "to the silversmiths business." Barret was not Elliston's only runaway; in 1808 he lost James Young and James Wilkins, and in 1814 William Murrell disappeared.[14]

In early 1808 Elliston enlarged his business as a watchmaker, silver and goldsmith and purchased a new stock of French and English jewelry. Six years later Elliston was forced to move from his house and shop due to a dreadful fire reported in an "extra" of the *Nashville Clarion*, but he quickly reopened in "the yellow house next to Talbot's Tavern on the north side of public square." As mayor that year, Elliston signed a notice for a "fire bucket inspection." From 1816–19 he and Samuel Seay were partners in the firm of Seay and Elliston, but their advertisements gave no indication that theirs was a silversmithing business. In 1820 Elliston moved from a Water

63c, 63d. *Sugar tongs marked "J. T. Elliston.," c. 1810, engraved "C," Nashville. LOA: 6½". Private collection.*

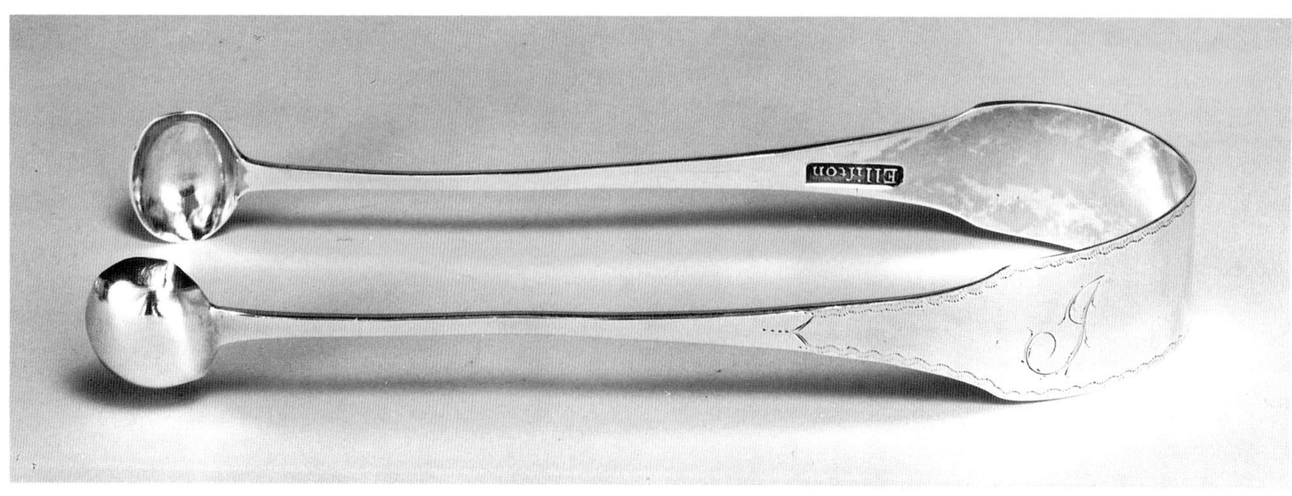

63e. *Sugar tongs marked ".Elliston," c. 1810, engraved "J," Nashville. LOA: 6½". Courtesy of the Ladies' Hermitage Association, photograph by Helga Photo Studio, Inc. These tongs have a history of having been made for Andrew Jackson.*

63f. *".ELLISTON" mark, c. 1810. This mark is the same as that on the sugar tongs illustrated in fig. 63e.*

63g. *Mustard or condiment ladle marked "J. T. Elliston.," 1800–10, engraved "T," Nashville. LOA: 5⅞", width across bowl: 1⅛", rise: 1⅜". Private collection.*

63h. *Pair of teaspoons marked "J. T. Elliston.," 1800–10, engraved "MEK," Nashville. LOA: 5⅜", width across bowl: 1/18". Private collection.*

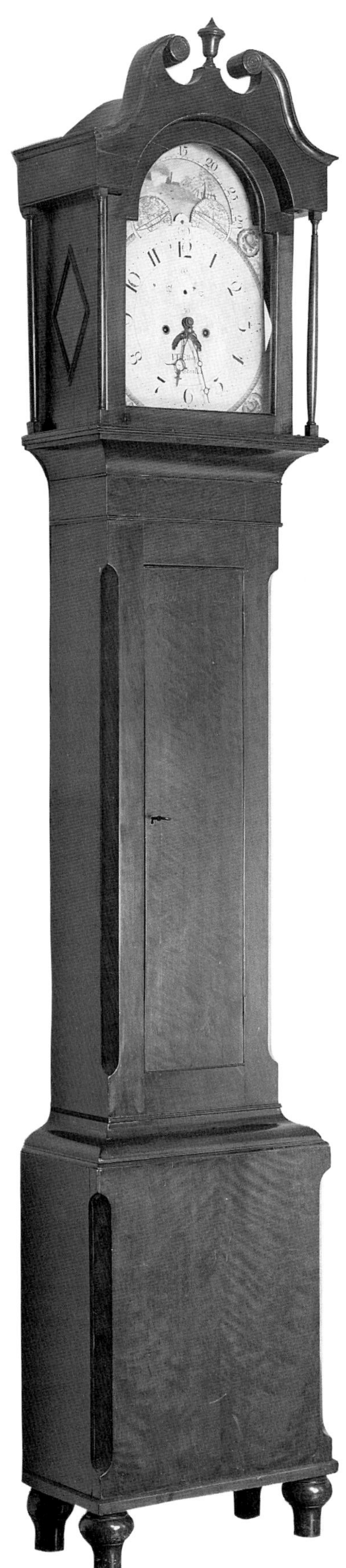

63i, 63j. *Tallcase clock signed on the dial "I. T. Elliston/ Nashvilla," 1810–20. HOA: 112", WOA: 19", DOA: 9½". Private collection, MRF S-11, 672. The case, of cherry and poplar, is probably of local make; the eight-day movement was made in Birmingham, England.*

Street location to a shop on Market Street where he invited the public to inspect a large collection of "Wax Figures."[15]

"J. T. Elliston." (fig. 63d) is believed to have been his first mark. When Elliston's nephew, John Elliston (q.v.) joined the firm, the mark was shortened to ".Elliston" (fig. 63f). This alteration apparently was effected by simply removing the "J. T" from the original die.[16] This theory is further supported by the fact that no separate mark for John Elliston has been recorded. A spoon (fig. 63m) that has descended in the family of the Reverend James Whitsitt, who established the Mill Creek Baptist Church at his home near Nashville about 1796, bears an "ITE" mark (figs. 63n) which may be that of Joseph Elliston, although this attribution is uncertain. Traditionally, the use of initials as a mark preceded the use of a silversmith's full name.[17]

Very little silver made by Joseph Thorp Elliston has

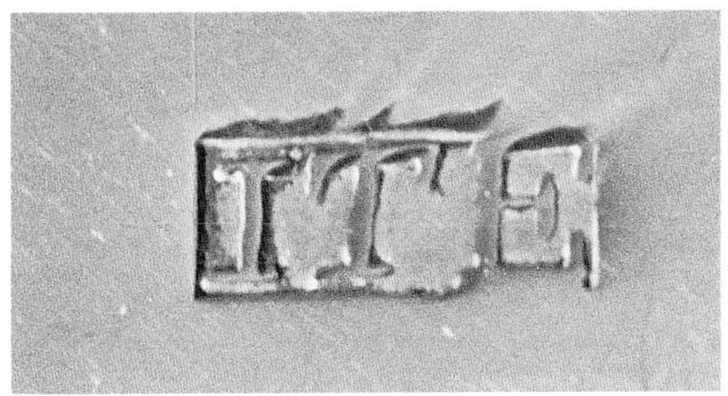

63k, 63l. *Tablespoon marked "ITE," tentatively attributed to Joseph Thorp Elliston, c. 1810, engraved on the obverse "W". LOA: 8½". Private collection.*

been found and none dates later than 1820 stylistically. One ladle could have been made as late as 1820. Presumably, Joseph Elliston's active participation in the trade diminished as he concentrated his effort in other successful investments. Indeed, there were no advertisements for Elliston's silversmithing business beyond 1820, although he lived until 1856.

ELLISTON and HEENER (HUNER). Clock and watchmakers, gold and silversmiths. Nashville, Davidson County, 1802.

Joseph T. Elliston and Heener (q.v.), first name unknown, worked together as "Elliston and Heener, Clock and Watch Makers" in 1802. The firm's advertisements (fig. 64) indicated that the two men were prepared to furnish all kinds of clocks on short notice, in what they believed would be the "first attempt of clock making in the Mero District." Their other services included watch-

3 ELLISTON & HEENER,
Clock & Watch Makers,

INFORMS their friends and the public that they may be furnished with clocks of all descriptions on short notice,—they flatter themselves that this first attempt of Clock making business in Mero district, will merit the encouragement of the public, especially when they will warrant clocks made by them equal to any. Old clocks cleaned and repaired, Watchmaking, Gold and silver work done as usual.

Nashville, July 22d, 1802.

A generous price given for old silver, brass, copper and pewter.

One or two apprentices will be taken to either or all the above branches of business.

64. *In the Nashville* Tennessee Gazette *of 2 August 1802, "Elliston & Heener . . . flatter[ed] themselves that this first attempt of Clock making business in Mero district, will merit the encouragement of the public. . . ."*

making, clock and watch repair, and gold and silver work. Elliston, whose name appears at the end of one advertisement, stated that they were working together not "as copartners, only a division of the profits of the Clock making business." At the time, the two men apparently assumed they would have enough work to warrant the need of "one or two apprentices," although there is no record of the firm's business beyond 1802.[18]

EUBANKS, John. Silversmith. Lebanon, Wilson County, 1860.

John Eubanks, who was born about 1833 in Kentucky, listed his occupation as silversmith in the 1860 census for Wilson County. Eubanks lived with his wife Emma and four-year-old son, Willie, both natives of Kentucky, in the county's Tenth District.

EVERMAN, Lewis (L. B.). Silversmith. Huntingdon, Carroll County, 1850; Jackson, Madison County, 1857–60.

Lewis Everman was born about 1821 in Kentucky. At the time of the 1850 census he was working as a silversmith in Huntingdon and living with a number of others in the household of Young W. Allen, a clerk of the county court.

Seven years later an L. B. Everman, probably the same man, advertised under the sign of a watch in the *Jackson Madisonian*, published in neighboring Madison County. Unlike today's advertisers who use a variety of approaches, Everman ran the same notice from April 1856 through June 1857.[19] At the time of the 1860 census for Madison County, the thirty-nine-year-old L. B. Everman was still working at the silversmith trade in Jackson and living with M. B. Everman, forty-one, probably his wife, and a Mary A. Bell, both natives of North Carolina.

FADLEY, James. Jeweler. Memphis, Shelby County, 1856–57.

The *Memphis City Directory* for 1856–57 listed James Fadley as a dealer in jewelry, clocks, and watches but did not supply an address.[1]

FADLEY, John M. Jeweler. Memphis, Shelby County, 1855.

In 1855 John M. Fadley was working as a jeweler at 217 Main Street, Memphis, probably for A. Linde (q.v.) and Company, also located at that address. At that time he lived at 49 Court Street.[2]

Historian Swannee Bennett recorded a J. M. Fadley working in Helena, Phillips County, Arkansas, as a watch and clockmaker in 1850–51.[3]

FAGAN, Banard. Clock and watchmaker. Athens, McMinn County, 1844.

Banard Fagan worked for an undefined period in Athens as a clock and watchmaker. A 19 January 1844 advertisement in the *Athens Courier* noted that Fagan "continues to carry on business" in the shop formerly occupied by silversmith George Sehorn (q.v.).

Cutten recorded a B. Fagan in Cassville, Georgia, in June 1846; it is possible that he was the same man.[4]

FALLEN, F. Watchmaker, jeweler. Chattanooga, Hamilton County, 1860.

In 1860 F. Fallen was working on Market Street as a watchmaker and jeweler in Chattanooga.[5]

FALLER, Bernhard L. Watchmaker, jeweler. Nashville, Davidson County, 1859–d. 1871.

Bernhard L. Faller, who was born on 7 August 1832 at Lenzkirch in Baden, Germany, was working in Nashville with his brother, Frank A. Faller (q.v.), by 1859. The brothers worked as watchmakers and jewelers until Bernhard's death in 1871.[6]

FALLER, Frank A. Watchmaker, jeweler. Nashville, Davidson County, 1855–60 and later.

Frank A. Faller was born at Lenzkirch in Baden, Germany, 10 September 1830. In 1855, at the age of twenty-five, he opened a watchmaking and jewelry shop at 19 Deaderick Street in Nashville. Four years later he was joined at the same address by his younger brother, Bernhard L. Faller (q.v.), at the same address. An 1869 directory listed the firm as Faller and Brother, still at the same address.[7]

After his brother's death in 1871, Faller continued to operate his Deaderick Street shop as late as 1878; he and his wife Louise lived at 113 North High Street. Faller died on 12 November 1883 and was buried in Mt. Olivet Cemetery, Nashville. He left his "collection of coins, books, and all tools of trade" to his son, L. Albert Faller, "for his sole use."[8]

FALLER (FALLEN), Vincent. Watchmaker, jeweler. Chattanooga, Hamilton County, 1856–60.

In 1856 Vincent Faller informed the citizens of Chattanooga that he had settled in that town permanently and was prepared to repair "Watches, Clocks and Jewelry, Musical Boxes and any other running machinery." He advertised again as a watchmaker during the following year in the Chattanooga listings of the *Nashville Business Directory*.[9]

The 1860 federal census of Hamilton County cited "Fallen's" birthplace as Baden, Germany. His age was given as fifty-three, and his personal estate was valued at $2,500. It is possible that Vincent was related to Bernhard Faller (q.v.) and Frank Faller (q.v.), for they, too, were born in Baden, Germany.

FARRES, Adam R. Silversmith. Pulaski, Giles County, 1818–25.

Goodspeed's *History of Tennessee* listed Adam R. Farres as a silversmith in the town of Pulaski from 1818–25.[10]

FEAREN, J. Clock repairer. Nashville, Davidson County, 1849.

J. Fearen identified himself as a tradesman "always ready to attend to the repairs of his patrons' clocks." His advertisement, published 22 August 1849 in Nashville's *Daily Centre-State American*, promised that orders left at "W. R. Demumbrane's Boarding House on Market Street" in Nashville would be attended to promptly.

FELMER and GRAF. Watchmakers & jewelers. Memphis, Shelby County, 1856.

In 1856 the watchmaking and jewelry firm of Felmer and Graf was operating at 146 Main Street in Memphis.[11]

FELTY (FELTS), James. Silversmith. Knoxville, Knox County, 1850.

James Felty was born in Tennessee in 1831. At the time of the 1850 census he was living in the household of Samuel Bell (q.v.), a Knoxville silversmith, and working for Bell as an assistant.[12]

FIELD (FIELDS), Jeremiah. Clock and watchmaker, gold and silversmith. Carthage, Smith County, 1811?. *Jeweler, clock and watchmaker.* Franklin, Williamson County, 1829–45?; Lawrenceburg, Lawrence County, d. 1853.

As early as 1811, Jeremiah Field may have been working as a partner in the Carthage clock and watchmaking, gold and silversmithing firm of Fields and Garner (q.v.). Evidence for the activities of this partnership is limited to the 1811 announcement of the shop's opening.[13]

In Fayetteville, North Carolina, a Jeremiah Fields was jailed in 1819 for having made counterfeit fifty-dollar notes by altering three-dollar bills from a Fayetteville bank. He did this by pasting a figure "fifty" taken from a fifty-cent North Carolina treasury bill over the figure "three" on the genuine bill. Perhaps this was the same Field who, in 1829, informed the public of Franklin, Tennessee, that he had moved his shop to the white house opposite Mr. Daniel Dwyer's. There he offered a supply of jewelry and dry goods as well as his services as a clock and watchmaker. Three years later, in an enterprising move, he advertised grapevines of wine-making and table quality.[14]

In preparation for his departure from Franklin in 1836, Field requested that all persons having claims against him to present them, all those with watches in his shop to call for them, and all those indebted to him to settle their debts. It appears, however, that he did not leave, for two years later he warned Franklin citizens that he would not pay the debts of John Field, a minor.[15]

Louise G. Lynch's *Miscellaneous Records of Williamson County* revealed that Jeremiah Field was involved in several troublesome court proceedings. He was assaulted, beaten, and "ill treated" by a Thomas Manney in November 1838. In 1845 he deserted his wife, Mary Odom, and children, leaving them with no visible means of support.[16]

Field died on 10 November 1853 in Lawrenceburg, Tennessee, at about seventy years of age, bequeathing property to daughters Mary and Elizabeth, but leaving his son John only ten dollars.[17]

In 1770 a Jeremiah Fields had served as spokesman for fifty Regulators demanding "unprejudiced jurors and the public accounting for taxes by the sheriffs" at the Superior Court of Hillsborough, North Carolina. Perhaps this Fields was in some way related to Tennessee's Jeremiah Field.[18] It is more likely, however, that the Regulator and the counterfeiter were related.

FIELDS and GARNER. Clock and watchmakers, gold and silversmiths. Carthage, Smith County, 1811.

Early in 1811, Fields and Garner opened for business in Carthage as "Clock and Watch Makers, Gold and Silversmiths" opposite Hazen and Company. The firm offered musical and plain clocks, all kinds of watches, the neatest manner of repair work, and "hair work executed with elegance. The highest price given in cash or work for Cut-Money, Old Gold or Silver."[19] The partners may have been Jeremiah Field (q.v.), later of Franklin, Williamson County, and Griffin Garner (q.v.), later of Knoxville.

FLASHMAN, Phillip. Jeweler. Nashville, 1859–60 and later.

Phillip Flashman, who was born in Bavaria, was listed in the 1859 *Nashville Business Directory* as a jeweler at 26 South Market Street. During the same year, he was active in the Young Mens Hebrew Benevolent Society, which was formed to give aid to immigrants.[20] The 1860 *State Gazetteer* listed him under "Jewelry, Watches, Clocks, Etc." at 30 Broad Street in Nashville; he remained active in business and civic life for a number of years later.[21]

FLESHART, Francis I. Gold and silversmith, watch and clockmaker. Knoxville, Knox County, d.1809.

Knox County court records of April 1809 contained an inventory of the estate of Frances Fleshart, which listed the tools of a silversmith, and clock and watchmaker; included were one small bellows, one forging block and hammer, one clock case "and materials to finish," watch chains, springs, crystals, one set of gold scales and weights, five ounces of silver, gold earrings, and silver teaspoons. Elizabeth Fleshart, his widow, acted as administratrix of the estate.[22] The *Knoxville Gazette* for 20 May 1809 contained a notice that the partnership of Garner and Cain (q.v.) "commenced business in the house formerly occupied by Francis Fleshart dec'd."[23]

65, 65a. *Spanish milled dollar, 1807. Courtesy of the Tennessee State Museum. Robert A. Fletcher and other early silversmiths used the Spanish dollar, termed "coin" silver, as "raw material" because of its high silver content (approximately ninety percent).*

FLESHART, Francis II. Silversmith's apprentice. Knoxville, Knox County, 1813.

Knox County court minutes for 6 July 1813 recorded that Francis Fleshart, an orphan, was "bound as an apprentice to Thomas Cain" (q.v.). According to court records dated two years earlier, Francis, his brother Joseph, and sisters Polly, Betsy, Caroline, and Susanna Fleshart had been placed under the guardianship of James Dardis after their mother, Elizabeth, died intestate.[24] It is probable that Francis was the son of the deceased Francis Fleshart I (q.v.).

It is not known whether Francis completed his apprenticeship under Cain.

FLETCHER, Robert A. Silver and goldsmith, watchmaker. Murfreesboro, Rutherford County, 1820.

Robert A. Fletcher, a silversmith, was working in Murfreesboro in 1820. According to the census of manufactures taken that year, his shop consumed about $700 worth of raw material yearly, including gold and silver, chiefly Spanish milled dollars (figs. 65, 65a), and all kinds of gold, with the exception of American coin; these were used in the manufacture of spoons, other plate, watches, and jewelry repair.[25]

Fletcher employed two men and two boys and paid them a total of $300 a year. His costs were about fifty percent above those of Philadelphia silversmiths, but his output was "sufficient to procure meat and bread. . . ." When asked about prospects in the area, he noted that demand was good because the Rutherford population was increasing, as it was in other new counties.[26]

FLINT, F. P. Silversmith. Nashville, Davidson County, 1816–d. 1823.

In 1816 F. P. Flint joined fellow Bostonian and silversmith Barton Richmond (q.v.) in the firm of Richmond and Flint (q.v.) located on Market Street in Nashville. In November 1819 the *Nashville Whig* carried a notice of "T. P." Flint's marriage to Eunice Healey, presumably of Massachusetts, for the wedding took place in that state. Nashville newspapers regularly published the partnership's advertisements until Flint's death in 1823.[27]

FLOWERS, Joshua. Silversmith, watchmaker. Nashville, Davidson County, 1840?–60 and later.

Joshua Flowers was born in Maryland about 1816. Flowers and his Irish-born wife, Eliza, were living in Maryland at the birth of their first child, Jessamin, in 1837, but by 1846 had moved to Tennessee where a second child, Ellen, was born. Flowers presumably was a partner in Calhoun and Flowers (q.v.) of Nashville (circa 1840–44). The firm kept shop on Union Street, next door to H. R. W. Hill's office. Calhoun made and repaired jewelry, and Flowers attended to the watch business. In 1844 they moved to the square and informed the public they had reduced their prices to suit the times.[28]

66, 66a. *Pair of forks marked "J. FLOWERS./NASHVILLE T.," 1845–50, engraved "JHC." LOA: 7". Courtesy of the Tennessee State Museum.*

66b. *Mark, accompanied by a pseudo hallmark, used by Joshua Flowers, 1850–60.*

By 1847 Flowers owned property in Nashville, and by the following year he had opened his own shop at the "sign of the BIG WATCH" on Nashville's Union Street between College and Cherry. There he repaired watches and jewelry and carried an assortment of fancy goods, dental tools, and false teeth.[29] Flowers was listed at the same address in Nashville directories and newspapers through 1860 and beyond; he issued many extensive advertisements detailing his stock.[30] The 1850–60 decade brought Flowers prosperity. In 1850 he identified himself as a silversmith with a value of $900. By 1860 he listed himself as a watchmaker and evaluated his personal property at $9,200 and his real property at $8,000. The last known reference to Flowers was his purchase of a lot on Market Street in Nashville on 18 July 1867.

FOSHEE, J. M. Silversmith. Harrison, Hamilton County, 1860.

J. M. Foshee was born in Tennessee about 1829. By 1860 he was working as a silversmith in Harrison; Foshee and his wife, Martha, lived with R. G. Campbell, a sheriff.[31]

FOWLER, Wells I. Silversmith, watchmaker, jeweler. Clarksville, Montgomery County, 1819–20.

As early as 1819, Wells Fowler had opened a silversmith shop in Clarksville on the east side of the public square "next door to Mayor Fort's house." He offered (fig. 67) his services in the various branches of his trade, carried a large assortment of jewelry and watches, and sought (fig. 67a) the assistance of two journeymen silversmiths. The

JEWELRY,

Silversmithing, &c.

THE subscriber, takes this method of informing the citizens of Clarksville and its vicinity, that he has just established the Watch and Silversmithing business in all its various branches, on the east side of the public square, next door to major Fort's dwelling house; in this place. and is now opening a Large and Elegant assortment of Jewelry and Watches;

CONSISTING OF

Gold and Silver Patent Lever Watches, Do. Horizontal, do Plain; Carrol, Jet, and Amulett Earrings, Gold Breast Pins, and Finger Rings; Ladies' Bracelets, Necklace, redicule clasps & silver Thimbles. Also, ladies' & genlemens' Gold Watch Chains, Seals and Keys, gilt. Together, with many other articles in his line, too numerous to mention. Orders from a distance, will be punctually attended to.

WELLS FOWLER.

June 14—tf

Wanted Immediately

ONE or TWO JOURNEYMEN SILVERSMITHS—apply to

WELLS FOWLER.

Clarksville, Ten. June 28.

Exchange for Cash

A LIKELY NEGRO BOY, about fourteen years of age—apply to

WM. J. LYNES.

June 28

67, 67a. *Wells Fowler announced in the* Clarksville Town Gazette and Farmer *of 28 June 1819 that he had "just established the Watch and Silversmithing business." He also stated that he was looking for "One or Two Journeymen Silversmiths."*

following year he was scheduled to take his turn on night patrol, a duty assigned to the city's responsible citizens at the time.[32]

Wells Fowler I may have been the W. Fowler who dissolved his silversmithing and clockmaking partnership with W. P. Loomis in Frankfort, Kentucky, early in 1819.[33]

FOWLER, Wells II. Silversmith, jeweler. Clarksville, Montgomery County, 1839–60.

In the spring of 1839 the *Clarksville Chronicle* published Wells Fowler's advertisement which implored his customers for cash. "I am compelled to have money . . ." he wrote, and he must have received it, for in late May of the same year he advertised a large selection of jewelry, watches, and pen knives, all received from Philadelphia.[34]

In 1847 Fowler advertised "Something New" in another *Chronicle* notice, offering jewelry, toys, and fancy articles. The 1850 census for Montgomery County revealed that this Wells Fowler was born in Massachusetts in 1808, too late for him to be confused with Wells Fowler I, and was working as a watchmaker and living at the hotel of G. O. Newman. The 1850 census of manufactures for Montgomery County noted that Fowler used $300 worth of gold and silver yearly. He employed one other man; the shop's annual hand production was valued at $1,200. Fowler placed advertisements or was listed in business directories and the *State Gazetteer* through 1860.[35]

FRANK, P. F. L. Watch repairer. Memphis, Shelby County, 1859.

In 1859 P. F. L. Frank was working as a watch repairer at 106 Front Row in Memphis.[36]

FRANSIOLI and WILLIAMSON. Dealers in silver and silverware. Memphis, Shelby County, 1855–60.

At some point after 1850, Stephen Fransioli and Francis H. Williamson formed a partnership in Memphis as dealers in silver, silverware, German silver, cutlery, china, and glass. From 1855–60 their shop was located at 188 Main Street.[37]

FRAZIER, Rodolph. Watchmaker. Memphis, Shelby County, 1856–57.

In 1856 Rodolph Frazier was working in Memphis as a watchmaker; his residence was located at the corner of Pontotoc and Second streets.[38]

Alexander and William Frazer (Frazier) worked as silversmiths in Paris, Kentucky, circa 1799; they were in Lexington during the first half of the nineteenth century.[39] No connection between the Kentucky Fraziers and Tennessee's Rodolph Frazier is known.

FREDRICK, Conrad. Clockmaker. Clarksville, Montgomery County, 1842–50.

Thirty-six year-old German-born Conrad Fredrick was working as a clockmaker in Clarksville at the time of the 1850 census. Frederick and his North Carolina-born wife, Mahala, were living in Tennessee by 1842 when their first child was born.

FREEMAN, A. R. Silver plater. Nashville, Davidson County, 1815–20.

Advertisements in the *Louisville Correspondent* placed during the latter part of 1814 indicated that A. R. Freeman was operating a silver plating business there that year, but by 1815 he was advertising in Nashville as a silver plater at a Water Street house once occupied by Joseph T. Elliston (q.v.). He urged the residents of Nashville to buy goods "manufactured in America" as they were "much lower . . . than imported." Plated bridle bits and stirrup irons "of the most fashionable patterns" as well as carriage and gig mounting were offered for sale by Freeman in addition to replating work.[40] As Electroplating was not invented until 1840 in England and probably was not in use until later in the United States, Freeman very likely was using French or closeplating. However, the possibility of his using the "old" Sheffield technique cannot be ruled out, although no marked examples of Sheffield-type plated ware made in this country have been found.

In 1820 Freeman agreed to handle unfinished business for silversmith Edward Raworth (q.v.) when Raworth left Nashville. Freeman was then located "at Mr. Terris'," opposite the Nashville Bank on College Street.[41]

FREEMAN, Samuel H. Silversmith, watchmaker, jeweler. Trenton, Gibson County, 1858–60 and later.

Samuel H. Freeman, a watchmaker and jeweler, had moved to Trenton by March 1858 when he announced his readiness to "repair watches, clocks and jewelry upon the shortest notice" at his shop on College Street opposite Union Hall. The 1860 census for Gibson County

68, 68a. *Serving spoons marked "S. FREEMAN," c. 1860, engraved "Mary Willard," Trenton. (Right) LOA: 8⅞, (Left) LOA: 8⁹⁄₁₆". Private collection. The mark illustrated in fig. 68a is tentatively attributed to Samuel H. Freeman.*

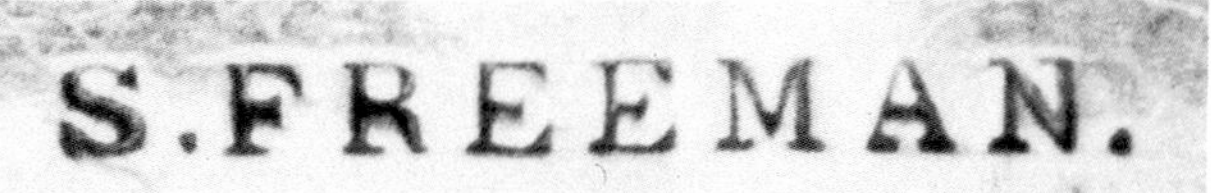

listed the thirty-year-old Kentuckian as a silversmith; his personal estate was valued at $5,000. Freeman later joined T. W. Spencer (q.v.) in the firm of Freeman and Spencer, watchmakers and jewelers, located one door west of Union Hall.[42] Two serving spoons (fig. 68) marked "S. FREEMAN" may be Freeman's work.

FROSE, R. Watchmaker. Memphis, Shelby County, 1856.

In 1856 R. Frose was working as a watchmaker with F. H. Clark (q.v.) and Company on Main Street in Memphis.[43]

FURST, Samuel. Watchmaker. Memphis, Shelby County, 1855.

In 1855 Samuel Furst was working as a watchmaker at F. H. Clark (q.v.) and Company on Main Street in Memphis. A Moritz Furst worked as silversmith in Philadelphia during 1807–33; no connection between the two men has been found.[44]

FURTWRANGLER (FORTWANGLER), Leo. Clock and watchmaker, silversmith. Nashville, Davidson County, 1834–60 and later.

Leo Furtwrangler was born in Germany about 1815. In February 1834 a Nashville newspaper advertised Furtwrangler's "CLOCK FACTORY." The following year, a Franklin newspaper publicized his "Clock and Organ making Business." By 1850 Furtwrangler was living in the Nashville household of Ann E. Lawrence, a school teacher.[45] Furtwrangler, aged forty, was listed as a silversmith in the 1860 census for Davidson County. At that time he was living in the Edgefield area of Nashille in the household of G. Payne, a farmer; another silversmith, W. B. Donelson (q.v.) was also a resident there.

Furtwrangler was working as late as 1865, although he was itinerant much of that time. He had headquarters at the shop of watchmaker Frank A. Faller (q.v.), who was located at 19 Deaderick Street in Nashville. Those requiring Furtwrangler's services could visit Faller's shop and leave word for Furtwrangler to stop by on his next round of travels. Furtwranger's name is penciled on the back of numerous clock dials found in Middle Tennessee, indicating that he repaired the movements.[46]

GARLAND, F. Jeweler. Murfreesboro, Rutherford County, 1837.

According to Goodspeed's *History of Tennessee*, F. Garland was working as a jeweler in Murfreesboro in 1837.[1]

GARLAND, John R. Gold and silversmith, watch repairer. Memphis, Shelby County, 1836–42?; Lebanon, Wilson County, 1850.

Born in Virginia in 1790, John R. Garland established himself in Greenville, South Carolina, but the disappearance of three watches from his shop in 1826 proved a discouragement to his success there. According to Burton's *South Carolina Silversmiths*, Garland's enemies circulated rumors questioning Garland's honesty after the watches were lost. He countered with advertisements denying any wrongdoing. Although the thief was apprehended shortly thereafter with two watches and a key to Garland's shop, the damage was done. By January 1828 Garland had moved to Macon, Georgia, where he first worked as a partner in the firm of Garland and Menard, then independently, and later as a partner in the firm of Rockwell and Garland. The latter partnership was dissolved by December 1829.[2]

Seven years later Garland had moved to Memphis, where he formed a short-lived partnership with William Cissna (q.v.). From 1843–46 Garland worked in North Carolina, repairing watches and manufacturing gold and silver items in Greensboro and Charlotte; however, the 1850 census for Lebanon, Wilson County, recorded that he had returned to Tennessee. The census listed Garland, aged sixty, as a silversmith living in John Baird's inn.[3]

GARLAND and CISSNA. Clock and watch repairers, silversmiths, jewelers. Memphis, Shelby County, 1836.

In April 1836 J. R. Garland (q.v.) and William Cissna (q.v.) formed the partnership of Garland and Cissna, "Clock and Watch Repairers, SILVERSMITHS and JEWELLERS," in Memphis. Their advertisements (fig. 69) in the *Memphis Enquirer* also noted Cissna's skills as a dental surgeon who was prepared "to attend" ladies at their residences if preferred. The partnership had been dissolved by June 1836 when Cissna set up his own shop on Main Street.[4]

Clock and Watch Repairers,
SILVERSMITHS & JEWELLERS.

J. R. GARLAND & W. CISSNA respectfully inform the citizens of Memphis and the public generally, that they have associated themselves for the purpose of carrying on the above business in the town of Memphis: and hope, by strict attention to the same, good workmanship, and moderate charges, to obtain the confidence and patronage of a generous community.

N. B. W. Cissna having acquired the art of Surgeon Dentistry, and being provided with a superior set of instruments, flatters himself that he will afford general satisfaction to all who call on him.—Ladies who may wish his services will be attended to at their residences if preferred.

Memphis, April 20—3t.

69. *The partnership of "J. R. Garland & W. Cissna," advertised in the* Memphis Enquirer *of 20 April 1836, was shortlived; within two months it was dissolved.*

GARNER, Griffin G. Gold and silversmith, clock and watchmaker, jeweler. Knoxville, Knox County, 1816–d. 1821.

Griffin G. Garner, born about 1780, was working in Fincastle, Virginia, in 1808; he had moved to Knoxville by August 1816, when he offered liberal encouragement and constant employ to one or two journeymen in the gold and silver business, and one journeyman in the clock and watch business. He also advertised his need for an apprentice from a good family (see fig. 10). The following March, Garner notified fellow Knoxvillians that in addition to his original establishment on Market Street, he had opened a second store on Cumberland Street that was to be run by Samuel Allen.[5]

Throughout 1818–19, Garner advertised for sale "at reasonable terms" two shops, his house, lot, and all the improvements that stood thereon: kitchen, stable, smokehouse, granary, and garden house, all of which were convenient to the town spring.[6] Although ill health or financial reversals may have been the cause for the series of advertisements, Garner did not abandon his work during that period, for in January of 1819 he promised "good wages and constant employ" to a journeyman, and asked for two watchmakers, two silversmiths, and one jeweler to work "by the piece, month or years." By that time he had moved from his former shop to a "white house on Gay Street" where he was ready for business.[7]

In August of the same year, Garner threatened to turn over to an "officer for collection" all those who had not paid their debts; he observed that he was "driven by necessity (see fig. 15)." By September 1819 he had recovered his health sufficiently "to devote his time and attention to this shop," but warned fellow citizens against removing "wood or sand off my island opposite town."[8]

In October 1820 Garner opened a "House of Entertainment," or tavern, on the corner of Market and Gay Streets "immediately opposite the Bank of the State of Tennessee. . . ."[9] Such business efforts during the 1819–20 period may have reflected Garner's struggle in the midst of a depression.[10]

In an advertisement of November 1820, Garner warned the residents of Knoxville to:

> Beware of the Villain. A man by the name of Wm. P. Davis came to my house . . . he pretends to be deaf and dumb. He can read and write very well, dark skin, cross eyed, 2 fingers lost off of one hand . . . made great pretense of having money. He left . . . without settling off his bill . . . and took a watch out of my shop . . . a reward of $20 to any person who will deliver him to me in Knoxville. . . ."[11]

Griffin G. Garner died in 1821 at the age of forty-one after a "long and lingering illness," leaving a wife and six children. When warned of his approaching death, according to his obituary, "Conviction seized his mind!" Although "because of his education . . . he had professed to disbelieve the Scriptures," he looked to the Saviour until "the hour of his dissolution."[12]

70. *Mark tentatively attributed to either Griffin Garner or John Garner, 1809–13. This mark is probably earlier than that illustrated in fig. 70b, as it is cruder. John Garner's working dates are earlier; it is possible that this is his mark.*

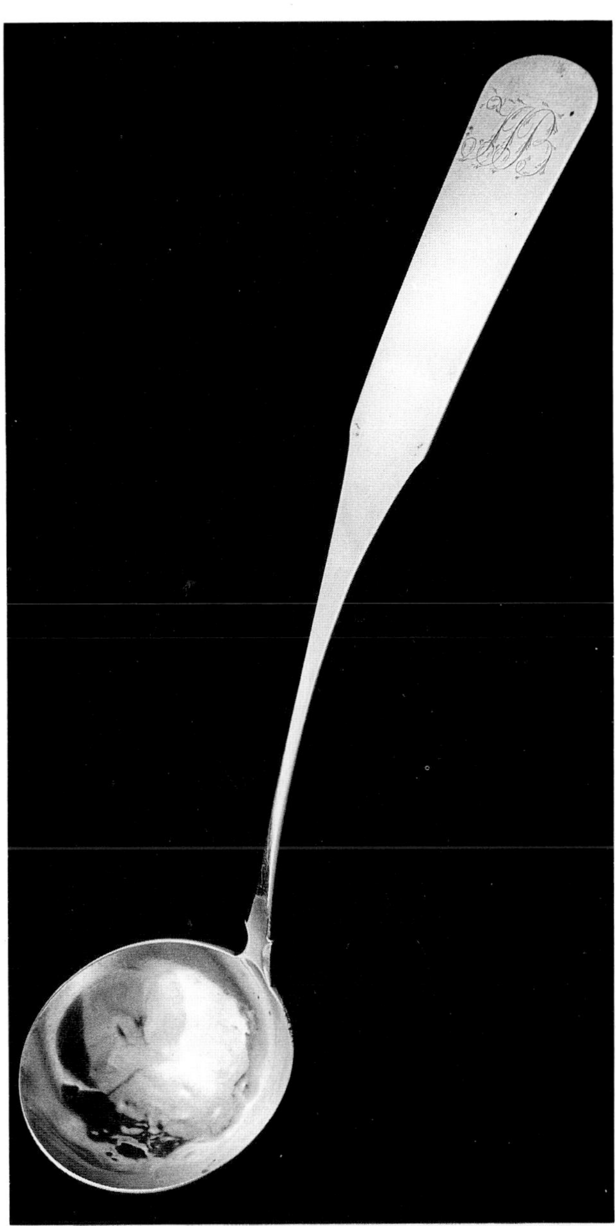

70a, 70b. *Punch ladle marked "GARNER" flanked by eagles, 1810–20, engraved "TJB," Knoxville. LOA: 14⅛", width across bowl 3⁹⁄₁₆". Private collection. The working dates of both John and Griffin Garner fall within the same range as the date of this ladle.*

GARNER, *John. Clock and watchmaker, gold and silversmith, jeweler?.* Knoxville, Knox County, 1809–11; Nashville, Davidson County, 1812–15?.

John Garner first appeared in Knoxville in partnership with silversmith Thomas Cain (q.v.) (Garner and Cain, q.v.) in May 1809. Their joint venture "in the house formerly occupied by Mr. Francis Fleshart, dec'd." (q.v.) was short-lived, dissolving in October of that same year. Garner continued doing business as a watch and clockmaker, and gold and silversmith, at the firm's old shop and sought the help of a journeyman for the gold and silversmith business in a *Knoxville Gazette* advertisement at the time.[13]

In April 1811 Garner moved to a new house between Dr. Strong's brick building and John Anthony's tavern, where he kept on hand an assortment of gold and silver work. In September, because he intended to leave Knoxville, he requested all those indebted to him to pay up and all those with watches or jewelry in his shop to retrieve such items before 30 October of that year. By June 1812 he had moved to Market Street in Nashville, where he took a shop next door to Messrs. Cantrell and Acuff's store. In 1813 his shop was located on the north corner of the public square.[14]

In the spring of 1814, the *Clarion and Tennessee State Gazette* noted that two of John Garner's horses, Dragon and Powhatan, would "stand the ensuing season" at farms within six miles of Nashville.[15] Garner probably remained in Nashville until about 1815 when boot and shoemaker John Larkins advertised his location at the house "formerly occupied by Mr. John Garner. . . ."[16]

Five years later, the *Nashville Clarion* published a summons for John Garner of Bowling Green, Kentucky. A 5 January 1830 advertisement appeared in the *Pittsburgh Gazette* requesting the whereabouts of John Garner. "Mr. Garner was formerly a Jeweller and Silversmith by trade, but subsequently followed merchandising. He is a tolerably tall, fair-skinned, blue-eyed genteel looking man, about 45 years of age . . . believed to have resided latterly in the neighborhood of Pittsburgh, Pennsylvania." Later still, he moved to Ohio where E. D. Beckman, author of *Cincinnati Silversmiths*, found a John Garner working in 1829. He died there in 1832.[17]

GARNER *and* CAIN. *Watchmakers, gold and silversmiths.* Knoxville, Knox County, 1809.

John Garner (q.v.) and Thomas Cain (q.v.) formed a brief partnership in 1809 as Knoxville watchmakers and gold and silversmiths in a house formerly owned by Francis Fleshart (q.v.). The firm was dissolved by mutual consent in October 1809.[18]

71. The Gates & Pohlman shop, at the northeast corner of College and Union streets in Nashville, 1880s. Courtesy of the Tennessee State Library and Archives. The trade sign between the windows advertised music boxes, silver and plated ware, fancy goods, table and pocket cutlery, spectacles, diamonds, watches, clocks, and fine jewelry.

GATES, *W. T. Watchmaker.* Nashville, Davidson County, 1855–d. 1907.

Born about 1829 in Virginia, W. T. Gates worked as a watchmaker from 1855–57 at 32 South High Street in Nashville. By 1859 he was a "watchworkman" at G. W. Donigan's (q.v.) shop at the corner of Union and College streets in Nashville; a year later his work status had changed to "watchmaker." In 1865 William H. Pohlman joined Gates in the partnership Gates and Pohlman), succeeding "Donigin" his old shop (fig. 71). Gates and Pohlman continued to work together for a number of years, apparently retailing imported silver (fig. 71a).[19]

Gates and his Tennessee-born wife, Susan, lived at 523 Woodland Street in the Edgefield section of Nashville with their three children, William H., Robert B, and Eva. Gates died in 1907 and was buried at Nashville's Mt. Olivet Cemetery where earlier he had buried an infant son on G. W. Donigan's plot.[20]

71a. *Mark used by Gates & Pohlman, post-1865. The "W & H" is a mark used by Wood & Hughes (1840–99) of New York City (see figs. 46b, 84, 99h, 121a, and 126a).*

GAYLORD, William. Jeweler. Memphis, Shelby County, 1855–57.

During 1855–57, William Gaylord worked as a jeweler for J. E. Merriman (q.v.) and Company of 253 Main Street in Memphis. The firm dealt in clocks, watches, jewelry, and silverware.[21]

GENNET (JENNET), Lorenso. Watchmaker. Columbia, Maury County, 1860.

Lorenso Gennet was born in New York about 1820. By 1860 he was working as a watchmaker in Columbia, probably at the shop of Joseph H. James (q.v.), for he lived with the James family at that time. He may have been related to Sarah Gennet James, Joseph James's wife. Both Gennet and James's wife had been born in New York, and James's first partner had been Charles Gennet, Sarah's brother, who worked in Richmond, Virginia.[22]

GILKEY, Quincy A. Jeweler. Memphis, Shelby County, 1860.

In 1860 Quincy A. Gilkey was an associate in A. J. Warren and Company (q.v.), a Memphis firm which dealt in watches, jewelry, silverware, and fancy goods at 293 Main Street.[23] According to the census that year, Gilkey lived in the William Archer (q.v.) household in the city's Fifth Ward; he evaluated his personal estate at $8,000.

GILLESPIE, Samuel A. and Company. Retailer of jewelry, silver plate. Columbia, Maury County, 1828.

In 1828 Samuel Gillespie was operating a variety store that supplied its Columbia customers with all manner of jewelry, wines, medicines, shoes and boots, iron castings, clothing, and dry goods. A December 1828 advertisement heralded shipments of dry goods "daily arriving; only from thirty to forty days out of the Cities of PHILADELPHIA, BALTIMORE, PITTSBURGH & WHEELING."[24]

Kovel recorded a Samuel Gillespie working as a silversmith in Louisville, Kentucky (circa 1848–49).[25]

GILLIAM, Edward. Watch and clockmaker and repairer, jeweler? Nashville, Davidson County, 1834.

In September 1834 Edward Gilliam requested citizens of Nashville to try his skills as a watch and clockmaker and repairer. "Lately from Ireland," Gilliam promised moderate charges both for his services and the jewelry he hoped to sell.[26]

GOLTZ, Adolph. Watchmaker, jeweler. Nashville, Davidson County, 1850–57.

The 1850 census for Davidson County listed Adolph Goltz as a twenty-five-year-old watchmaker. Born in Prussia, he lived in the home of a German grocer, A. Leonhard. Nashville directories for 1855 and 1857 cited "A. Goltz's" firm, Goltz and Huellebrand (q.v.), at 4 Union Street; his residence was located in north Nashville. Directories for 1853 ("J. A. Galtz, 3 Union Street"), 1859 and 1860 ("J. A. Goltz, 4 Union") listed a man with a similar name and working address.[27]

GOLTZ, Julius. Watchmaker. Nashville, Davidson County, 1853?, 1859–60.

At the time of the 1860 census for Davidson County, Julius Goltz, a twenty-nine-year-old Prussian, was working as a watchmaker in Nashville. Goltz and his wife Elizabeth lived in the county's Tenth District with three children, all born in Tennessee: Julius, aged seven, Charles, five, and John, one.

An 1853 directory listed a J. A. *Galtz*, jeweler, at 3 Union Street. By 1859–60, J. A. Goltz's jewelry shop was located at 4 Union Street. Whether these brief notations refer to Julius Goltz remains unclear, as does the relationship between Adolph and Julius Goltz. It is likely that they were actually only one man.[28]

GOLTZ and HUELLEBRAND. Watchmakers, jewelers. Nashville, Davidson County, 1855–56.

About 1855 Adolph Goltz (q.v.) and R. Huellebrand (q.v.), a watchmaker, opened a jewelry store (Goltz and

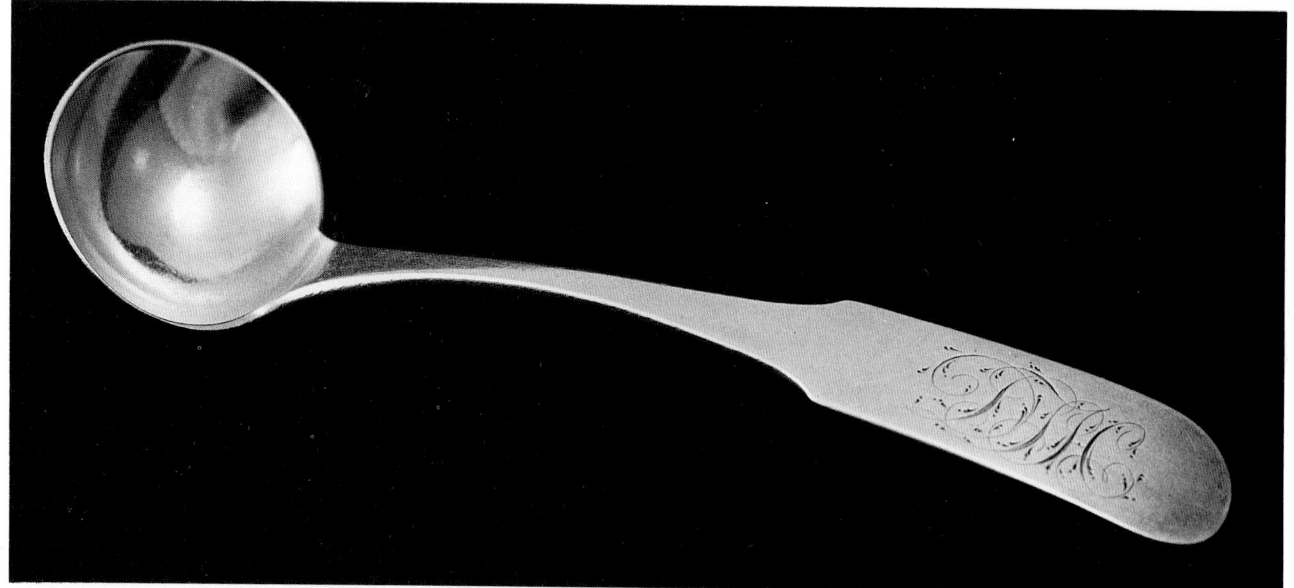

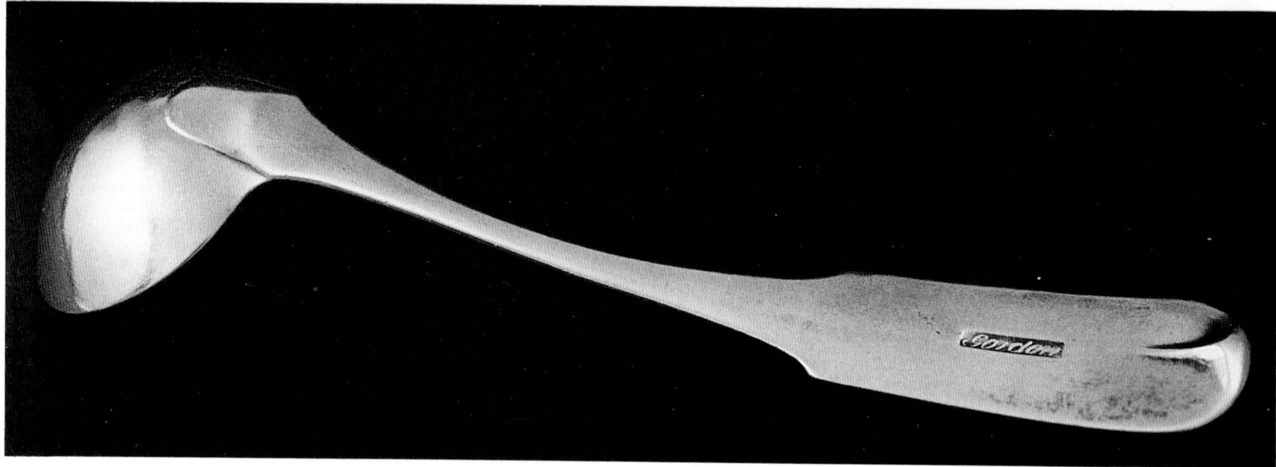

72, 72a, 72b. *Sauce ladle marked "Gordon," 1820, engraved "DLH," Nashville. LOA: 5½", width across bowl: 1¾". Private collection. The date of this ladle and its Nashville provenance led to its attribution as the work of Robert Gordon rather than that of George Gordon of New York City.*

Huellebrand) at 4 Union Street in Nashville. Two years later a directory listed the two men working separately at the same address; by 1859 Huellebrand had opened his own shop at 5 Union Street, while Goltz remained in the orginal shop at 4 Union.[29]

GOODMAN and BRO. Dealers in dry goods, jewelry and watches. Cleveland, Bradley County, 1860.

In 1860 Goodman and Bro. operated a shop in Cleveland. The *State Gazetteer* for that year listed the firm as dealers in dry goods, jewelry, and watches, but failed to record the names of the brothers.[30]

GORDON, L. Retailer of jewelry. Nashville, Davidson County, 1816.

L. Gordon, who evidently was an itinerant retailer, made a brief showing of an assortment of "elegant jewelry and watches" at the Nashville Inn, Nashville, in 1816.[31]

GORDON, Robert. Watch and clockmaker. Nashville, Davidson County, 1817–22.

Robert Gordon opened a shop on Market Street, Nashville, in October 1817, offering his own watches and clocks as well as the repair of timepieces brought to his attention. He had acquired his "complete knowledge" of the business "in several of the largest cities" of Scotland and England.[32]

In November 1817 Gordon apparently formed a partnership with E. Raworth (q.v.), a Nashville silversmith; the firm of Raworth and Gordon (q.v.) was in operation through at least 1818. In February 1822 Gordon announced that he expected to leave the state and requested customers to pick up their "items" at his "silver-smith establishment. . . ."[33]

A Gordon mark (fig. 72b) appears on a ladle (figs. 72, 72a) of an appropriate period for Robert Gordon of Nashville. The ladle exhibits what appears to be a Middle Tennessee style.[34] Belden, in *Marks of American Silversmiths*, illustrated a virtually identical mark attributed to George Gordon, who was listed in New York directories circa 1827–30.

GOWDEY, James F. Silversmith. Nashville, Davidson County, 1860?

Silver (figs. 73, 73a) marked "J. Gowdey" and "J. Gowdey / Nashville Tenn" (fig. 73b) is herein tentatively attributed to James Gowdey, who was born in 1843, the son of leading Nashville jeweler Thomas Gowdey (q.v.). The 1850 census for Davidson County listed a household headed by a James F. Gowdey, born in Ireland in 1795, whose wife was Ann Gowdey; however, this is the same biographical information assigned to Thomas Gowdey in the 1860 census, and that is confirmed by Clayton's *History of Davidson County*. It is possible that the 1850 census-taker mistakenly identified James, rather than Thomas, as the head of the Gowdey household in 1850.[35]

73a. *Cup marked "J. GOWDEY/ NASHVILLE TENN.," 1860–65, engraved "DLR." HOA: 3⅛", width across rim: 3". Courtesy of the Tennessee State Museum.*

73b. *Mark attributed to James F. Gowdey, Nashville, 1860–65. Courtesy of the Tennessee State Museum, photograph by Stephen D. Cox.*

73. *Cup marked "J. GOWDEY/ NASHVILLE TENN.10" with a dog, a profile, and a "G," 1865, Nashville. HOA: 3⅜", with across rim: 2¼". Private collection. Gowdey's mark is struck over the marks of its maker, A. B. Warden of Philadelphia (see fig. 25).*

74. *Thomas Gowdey (b. 1795-d.1863), from W. W. Clayton's* History of Davidson County, Tennessee, *1880, photograph by Jack Shwab.*

GOWDEY, Thomas. Jeweler, retailer. Nashville, Davidson County, 1825–d. 1863.

Thomas Gowdey (fig. 74) was born on 29 August 1795, the son of Dr. John Gowdey and his wife Margaret, in Castlewellan, County Down, Ireland. A lieutenant in the British army, Thomas Gowdey fought under Lord Nelson until a wound disabled him. He emigrated to Charleston, South Carolina, in 1818 and from there moved to Madison, Georgia, where he pursued the mercantile business. In 1823 he married Ann Power, the daughter of Thomas McCarton, and the couple moved to Nashville two years later, where Gowdey opened a jewelry shop and restaurant "on the Square." An extensive advertisement of 1834 listed over two hundred items "just received from New York and Philadelphia" at Gowdey's shop. The obvious misspelling of his name in one mark (fig. 74c) indicates that at least some of his silver was manufactured out of state. One spoon (figs. 74h, 74i) bears marks (fig. 74j) attributed to William Gale and Son of New York.[36] The "T. GOWDEY" and "NASHVILLE TENN." marks may have been struck either by Gale or Gowdey himself. Whether Gowdey ever trained as a silversmith remains in doubt. His advertisements contained many items suggesting that he practiced the trade, but he was not invited to, or perhaps chose not to attend, the organizational meetings of a Nashville association of silversmiths, watchmakers, and clockmakers in 1836. It is possible that Gowdey may have been excluded because he was a retailer.

In 1843 Gowdey and John Peabody established the partnership of Gowdey and Peabody (q.v.), which was located on the public square. By 1847 Gowdey owned $12,000 in real property and one slave valued at $500. Six years later he was again in business for himself as an importer and dealer in watches and jewelry at 25 Public Square. Subsequent directories revealed that Gowdey's business remained at the same address, while his residence changed from South Field to Vauxhall to "Demunbrane" Street. The 1860 census listed Thomas Gowdey and his wife Ann, along with their children Addie, aged thirty, James, seventeen, and a Thomas Cox, aged nine.[37] At that time, Gowdey evaluated his real property at $125,000 and his personal property at $60,000.

Gowdey was a leading citizen and successful businessman in Nashville for over forty years. As president of the Hibernian Society, he assisted fellow Irishmen in establishing themselves in this country; he was also an active Freemason, completing all his degrees. Gowdey died on 27 June 1863. The first sentence of his last will and testament, probated in July 1863, began with the words "I, Thomas Gowdey, Jeweler. . . ."[38]

74a. *Punch ladle marked "T. GOWDY," c. 1855, engraved "From/ Pa & Ma/ to/ Will," Nashville? LOA: 14", width across bowl: 4¼". Courtesy of the Tennessee State Museum.*

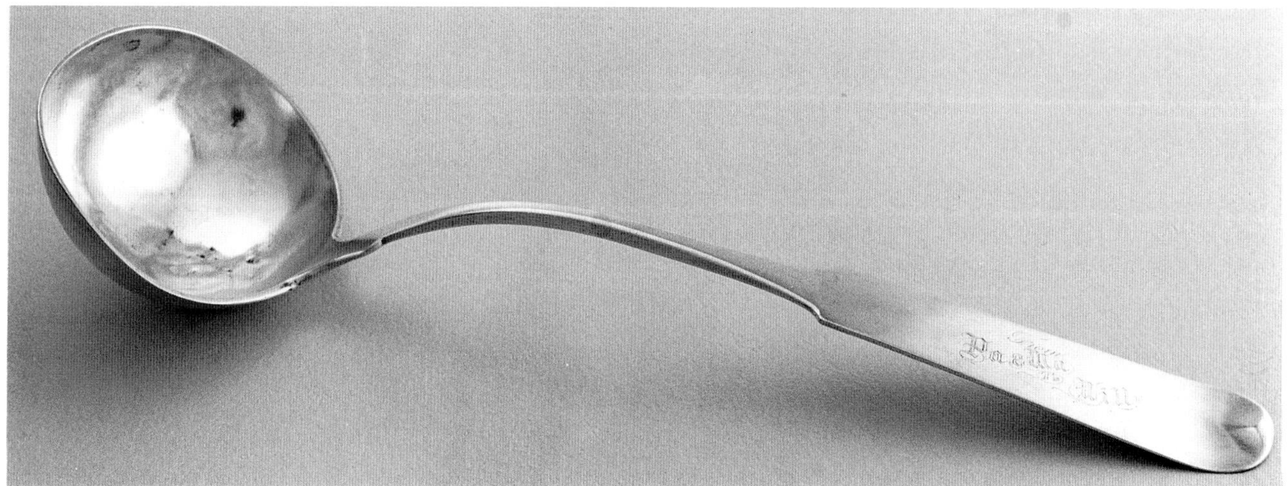

74b, 74c. *Water pitcher marked "T. GOWDY," 1855, engraved "Betty M. Woods./ January 6. 1855.," Nashville?. HOA: 9½", diameter at base: 4¼". Courtesy of the Tennessee State Museum, gift of Dr. and Mrs. Ben Caldwell. Betty Woods was the niece of William Edward West, a Tennessee and Kentucky artist, and a descendant of Benjamin West.*

74d. *Pair of goblets, unmarked, engraved "Betty M. Woods./ January 6. 1855," Nashville. HOA: 6", width across rim: 3⅓". Courtesy of the Tennessee State Museum.*

74e, 74f. *Set of forks marked "T. GOWDEY," c. 1850, engraved "TEN," Nashville?. LOA: 7¾". Courtesy of the Tennessee State Museum.*

74g. *Set of teaspoons marked "T. GOWDEY," c. 1850, engraved AMM," Nashville?. LOA: 5⅜". Private collection.*

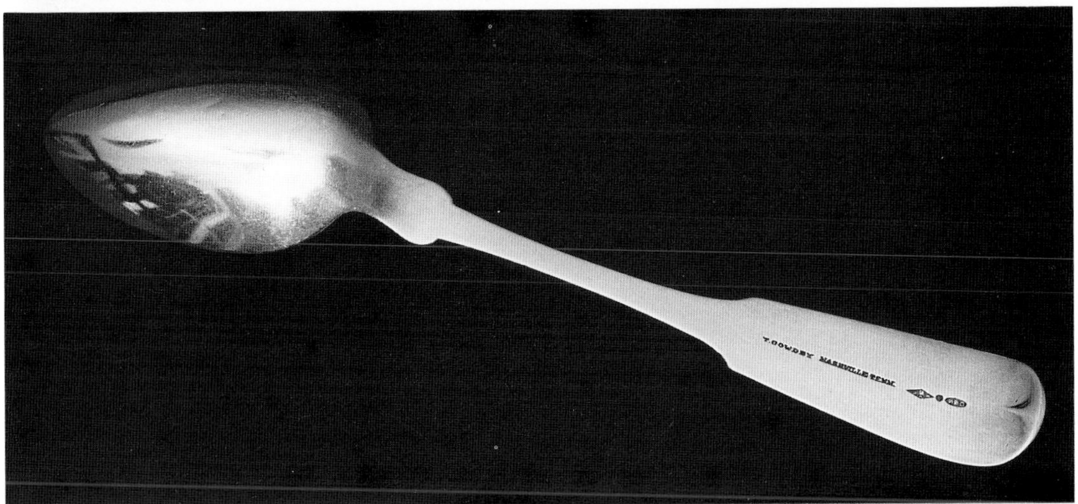

74h, 74i, 74j. *Serving spoon marked "T. GOWDEY NASHVILLE TENN." and "G & S/ 1/ 15/ 8," 1851, engraved "G. D. G." LOA: 8⅝". Private collection. The "G & S" mark illustrated in fig. 74j is attributed to William Gale & Son (1850–54) of New York City.*

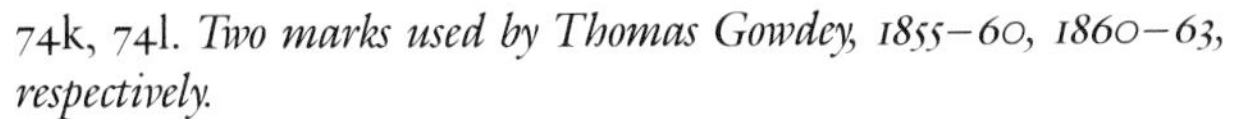

74k, 74l. *Two marks used by Thomas Gowdey, 1855–60, 1860–63, respectively.*

HAVE enlarged their fancy establishment on the Public Square, and now offer to their friends and the public the most extensive stock of Goods in their line ever exhibited in Nashville; consisting of **Clocks, Watches, Jewelry, Silver Plate, Plated, Britania & German Silver Ware.**

Fine Cutlery, Guns, Pistols, Military Goods and Sporting Equipage.

A great variety of Lamps, Tea Trays, Mantle Ornaments and house furnishing articles.

Fine Stationery, Perfumery, and every appendage for the work table, toilet and writing desk.

Surveyors' and Pocket Compasses, Mathematical and Philosophical Instruments.

Watchmaker's Tools and Materials, Fishing Tackle, Walking Canes, Fancy Boxes, Toys, &c., &c.

N. B. Connected with the establishment are superior workmen in the following branches: Clock and Watch makers, Jewelers, Silver Smiths and Engravers. Hair wove for necklaces or bracelets to any pattern.

July 8, 1845—1m

75. *In the* Nashville Union *of 8 July 1845, "Gowdey & Peabody" offered an extensive assortment of goods in "their fancy establishment," adding that "superior workmen" in the "Clock and Watch makers, Jewelers, Silver Smiths and Engravers" businesses were "Connected with the establishment."*

75a. *Urn marked on the base "GALE AND HAYDEN" in a rectangle with truncated corners and "G & H" and "1846"; marked on the bottom "G & H" and "GOWDEY & PEABODY," engraved "Presented to Henry Clay, the gallant champion of the Whig cause by the Whig Ladies of Tennessee./ a testimonial of their respect for his character, of their gratitude for his patriotism, and public services, and their admiration for his talents, and his high and noble bearing under all the trying circumstances of his eventful life./ The historic muse will cherish, defend & perpetuate his reputation./ Detur digniori." HOA: 32". Courtesy of the Tennessee State Museum. Gowdey & Peabody apparently only retailed this urn. The "G & H" and "GALE AND HAYDEN" marks probably represent the firm of Gale and Hayden, working in New York, c. 1846–50 (Belden,* Marks, *181). However, the "G & H" marks as well as the 1846 date mark also have been attributed to the firm of Gale & Hughes, working in New York, 1845–50 (Darling Foundation,* New York State Silversmiths, *Eggertsville, N. Y., 1964, 82). Henry Clay was one of the leaders of the Whig coalition founded in 1836, and he lost the presidential election of 1844 to James K. Polk. The inscription on this urn evinces the loyalty of Clay's supporters despite his defeat.*

GOWDEY and PEABODY. Jewelers, clock and watch repairers, silversmiths. Nashville, Davidson County, 1843–47.

Thomas Gowdey (q.v.) and John Peabody (q.v.) formed the partnership of Gowdey and Peabody in Nashville about 1843 "at the sign of the spectacles and watch on the Public Square". There they offered (fig. 75) an assortment of clocks, watches, silver plate, silver goods, as well as silver and gold plating, clock and watch repair, and the manufacture of jewelry and silver work. In 1845 they enlarged their establishment to include additional workmen and a more extensive stock. At the 1847 listing of taxable property in Nashville, the two men jointly owned property worth $1,500 on Cherry and Line Streets.[39]

Several Gowdey & Peabody marks have been found. Some bear the "G & H" mark (fig. 75b) of Gale and Hayden or Gale and Hughes, New York, circa 1848. An urn (fig. 75a) presented to Henry Clay in 1846 was made for Gowdey and Peabody by Gale and Hayden or Gale and Hughes.

75b, 75c. *Two marks used by the firm of Gowdey and Peabody, 1846 and 1850, respectively. Courtesy of Tennessee State Museum, photographs by Stephen D. Cox. The "G & H/ 1/46/8" mark illustrated in fig. 75b are attributed to "Gale & Hughes" (William Gale and Jasper W. Hughes, c. 1845–50) of New York City.*

76, 76a. *Pair of beakers marked "C. Guiteau.," both engraved "Premium awarded/ by the/ Agricultural Association/ of/ Davidson County Tenn./ 1841," Nashville. HOA: 3¾", width across rim: 2⅞". Courtesy of Belle Meade Mansion. The inscription on the left beaker also reads "To/ W. G. Harding/ For his 2 year old/ Heifer/ Queen of Scots"; the right beaker also is inscribed "To/ W. G. Harding/ For his aged Bull/ Sam Patch,/ Imptd." The bases of both beakers are engraved "William Harding Jackson/ 1906" (Fig. 76a).*

GRANET, P. Jeweler, watch repairer. Nashville, Davidson County, 1849–51.

P. Granet operated a "Nashville Fancy Store" on Union Street and later (1849–51) on College Street. There he repaired watches, jewelry, and silverware, and sold jewelry, silver, and gold laces.[40]

GROVES, John B. Dealer in jewelry. Columbia, Maury County, 1847.

In 1847 John B. Groves offered his customers jewelry and dry goods from his "Grove's Corner" shop in Columbia.[41]

GRUBBS, W. B. Dealer in jewelry, watches, and clocks. Nashville, Davidson County, 1859–60.

W. B. Grubbs first appeared in Nashville in 1853 as a bookkeeper at 54 Public Square. By 1859 he was living in Edgefield District and had opened a wholesale fancy goods store at 4 Public Square, where he remained through 1860.[42]

GUITEAU, C. Watchmaker, silversmith, jeweler, engraver. Nashville, Davidson County, 1836–45?.

C. Guiteau worked in Nashville as a watchmaker, silversmith, jeweler, and engraver. On 25 December 1836 he was elected secretary-treasurer at the first meeting of the association of watchmakers, silversmiths, and jewelers of Nashville. As such, he was to "keep a true account of moneys received for any purpose . . . [and] deliver to each and every watchmaker in this city a regular bill of Prices as established" and inform newcomers in the profession about the association (see Appendix I).[43]

In 1838 Guiteau was operating a shop on Deaderick Street "2nd door from W. H. Hunt Esq." before joining Peabody (q.v.) in the partnership of Peabody and Guiteau [q.v.] and moving to "Peabody's old stand on the Public Square" in 1839. That partnership had been dissolved by 1841 when Peabody advertised on his own.[44] A pair of beakers (fig. 76) marked (fig. 76a) by Guiteau after his association with Peabody are in the collection of the Belle Meade Mansion in Nashville.

76b, 76c. *Beaker marked "C. Guiteau.," 1841, engraved "Heiss," Nashville?. HOA: 3⅜", width across rim: 2⅞". Private collection, photograph by Bradford L. Rauschenberg. The mark illustrated in fig. 76c also has been attributed to Calvin Guiteau (c. 1828–45) of Watertown, New York; however, it is possible that both Guiteaus were the same man.*

76d. *Tongs marked "C. Guiteau.," 1840–45, Nashville. LOA: 6¼". Private collection.*

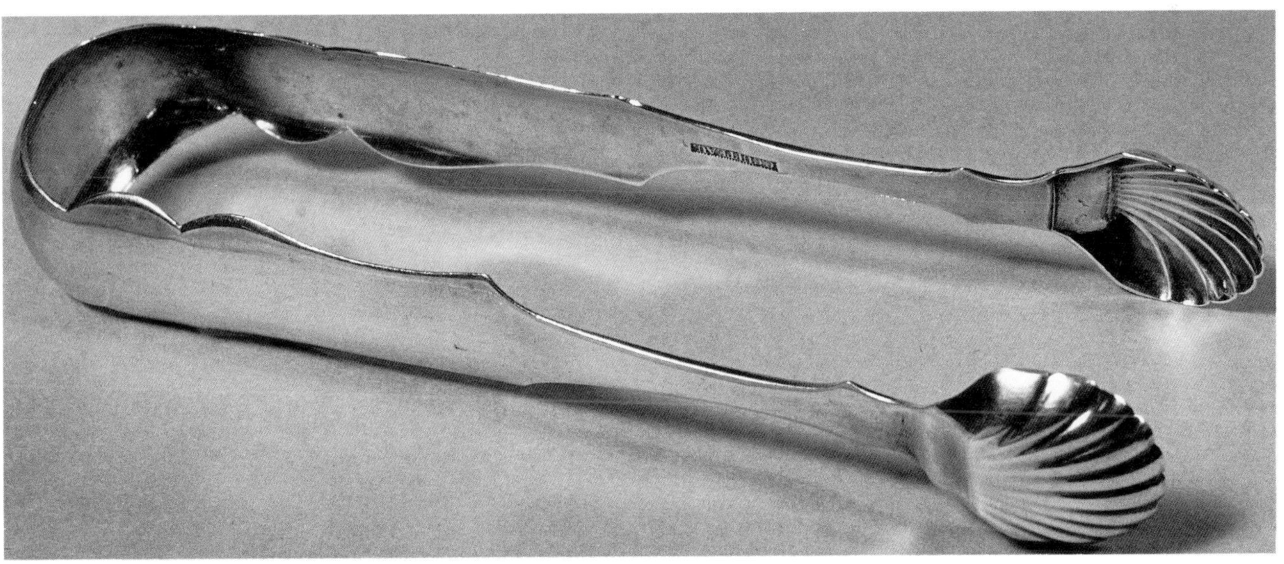

A tax list dated 1 December 1845 indicated that "C. Guiteau" had paid an "overage" of $1.50 to Davidson County. Guiteau may have remained in Nashville at least through that date.[45]

Several sources recorded a Calvin Guiteau in Watertown, New York, circa 1828–45, possibly the same man as the Nashville artisan.[46]

GULLET, Peter. Clock seller. Purdy, McNairy County, 1860.

According to the 1860 census for McNairy County, Peter Gullet was born in Maryland about 1805 but had moved to Tennessee by 1832. Gullet and his wife, a South Carolinian, lived in District Seven of McNairy County, in the town of Purdy, with their five children, all of whom were born in Tennessee. According to the census, he earned his living as a clock seller. Ten years earlier Gullet had been a stage driver; it is doubtful that he ever made a clock.[47]

77, 77a, 77b. *Teaspoon marked "S. P. Hamilton" and "Coin" with a lion, c. 1860, engraved "Kate," Knoxville. LOA: 5 11/16". Courtesy of the Tennessee State Museum, photograph of fig. 77b by Stephen D. Cox.*

HAMILTON, Samuel P. Jeweler. Knoxville, Knox County, 1859–60.

Samuel P. Hamilton was a twenty-five-year-old Virginian who was working as a jeweler in his brother William's Knoxville firm (q.v.) during 1859–60. That year the census for Knox County revealed that Hamilton, a bachelor, lived with his brother.

In the collection of the Tennessee State Museum are several teaspoons (figs. 77, 77a) engraved "Kate" and marked (fig. 77b) "S. P. HAMILTON" that descended in the Heiskell family who "reportedly lived in Knoxville in the 1800s until the Civil War."[1]

Kovel recorded that a Philadelphia silversmith named Samuel Hamilton was working in 1837.[2]

HAMILTON, William F. Jeweler. Knoxville, Knox County, 1859–60.

During 1859–60 William F. Hamilton and his brother, Samuel P. Hamilton, operated the firm of "William F. Hamilton and Brother," a watch and clockmaker's shop and jewelry store on the southwest corner of Gay and Cumberland Streets in Knoxville. In 1860 Hamilton, a native of Virginia, evaluated his real estate at $6000 and his personal property at $12,000.[3]

HARLOW, A. Watchmaker. Nashville, Davidson County, 1860.

A. Harlow appeared in the 1860 *Nashville Directory* as a watchmaker. He boarded at the Sewanee House hotel.[4]

HARMON, John. Clock and watchmaker. Greeneville, Greene County, 1820–30?

In 1820 John Harmon was working as a clock and watchmaker in Greeneville. According to the census of manufactures for that year, he employed one man, manufactured twelve-month clocks, and made watches; he performed $200 worth of clock work and $50 worth of watch work annually. Ten years later, the federal census for Greene County listed three John Harmons; presumably one was the clock and watchmaker.

A spoon with a Tennessee provenance bears an "I. H." mark (fig. 78) and is possibly the work of John Harmon. The letter "I" often was substituted for "J" in the Roman-style lettering of early marks. The serrations that not only surround the rectangle into which the initials were but also separate the "I" and the "H" are unusual.

78. "I H" mark tentatively attributed to John Harmon of Greenville, 1820–30?. Private collection, photograph by Bill Howell.

HARPER, Jesse H. Clocksmith, gunsmith. Jackson, Madison County, 1855?–60 and later.

Described as a "prominent gun and clock smith" of Jackson in Goodspeed's *History of Tennessee*, Jesse H. Harper is said to have devoted a good portion of his life to teaching, believing that "education is the commonest birthright of every child," rich and poor alike.[5]

Born in North Carolina in 1826, the son of a successful artisan/farmer, Harper left home at the age of fifteen to attend school. After several years of education, he worked his way west as a teacher, settling in Jackson during the mid-1850s. There, at his own expense, he established the Harper's Male and Female Institute. Over a period of years, he donated more than $20,000 in tuition, school supplies, and clothing to needy children.[6]

Harper also took an active interest in community affairs and held a number of political positions before becoming mayor in 1860. The following year, he was defeated in the mayoral race because of his political stance as a Unionist. Later Harper held several appointed offices including those of postmaster, county commissioner, city recorder, and justice of the peace.[7]

HARRINGTON, H. G. Silversmith, silver plater. Memphis, Shelby County, 1859–60.

During 1859–60, Harrington was working as a silver plater at the corner of Second and Union Streets in Memphis. He lived on Hernando Street between Vance and Brown's avenues.[8]

HARRINTON, F. Silver plater. Memphis, Shelby County, 1860.

At the time of the 1860 census for Shelby County, F. Harrinton was working as a silver plater in Memphis. The thirty-year-old Tennessee native lived in the city's Seventh Ward with Ann, his wife, and two-year-old Clara.

HARRIS, A. S. Watchmaker, jeweler. Trenton, Gibson County, 1860.

In 1860 A. S. Harris opened a "Watch Making and Jewelry Establishment" in the front room of the Gibson House in Trenton.[9]

HARRIS, George Washington. Silversmith's apprentice. Knoxville, Knox County, 1828?; *Silversmith*, 1842–50.

Born on 20 March 1814, George Washington Harris was the descendant of Sir George Harris, "of Brentwood, near London; his mother was Margaret Glover Bell Harris. . . ." Harris left Allegheny City, Pennsylvania, at an early age to join his half-brother, silversmith Samuel Bell (q.v.), in Knoxville. After serving an apprenticeship in Bell's shop, Harris worked the Knoxville-Decatur steamboat route, attaining the rank of captain on the steam-powered paddle wheeler *Knoxville*, a position he held for three years.[10]

In 1839 Harris tried farming in the foothills of the Smoky Mountains, but by 1842 his debts forced him to return to metalworking in Knoxville. An 1843 *Knoxville Register* announced Harris's "new work shop in metals" with a stock of jewelry, silverware, and racing cups. In 1846 one of his associates at his shop on the corner of Cumberland and Prince streets was David Large Hope (q.v.). Harris continued to pursue silversmithing through 1850 when the federal census for that year recorded that Harris, his Tennessee-born wife, Mary E., and their three children shared their home with a glass blower, a glass cutter, and a cook.[11]

During the 1850s Harris undertook a number of enterprises, including an association with the Holston Glass Works, the establishment of a sawmill, and the geological survey of lower East Tennessee for copper. He received a political appointment as postmaster and was employed with the Nashville and Chattanooga Railroad. During this period Harris also established himself as a writer, a skill for which he is now best remembered.[12] Harris had begun to write while farming, submitting political sketches to the *Knoxville Argus*. Over the years he developed a particularly popular character named Sut Lovingood, an earthy, backwoods Southerner and self-described "nat'ral born durn'd fool." A teller of tall tales full of local East Tennessee color, Sut's hatred of hypocrisy and his insight on the human condition manifested itself in satire on the political situation of that time. First honored as a pioneer in southwestern humor in a 1930 anthology by literary critic Franklin J. Meine, Harris ranks as one of the most gifted writers of the genre. His sketches are now included in many texts on American literature.[13]

Following the fall of Nashville to the Union army in February 1862, Harris moved to Trenton, Georgia, and then to Decatur, Alabama. After the war, he returned to Knoxville and a position with the Wills Valley Railroad.[14]

Harris's death in 1869 was described as "sudden and mysterious." Characterized as a small, unassuming man, a public-spirited citizen, and "upon occasion as full of jokes and tricks as his literary brainchild Sut," he apparently had won the affection of his fellow townsmen. At his demise, Knoxville's *Press and Herald* appealed for facts touching on Harris's mysterious death, so that "the world might know whether Capt. George W. Harris died by the stroke of his God, or the poisoned chalice of a wicked man."[15]

HARRISON, Abner. Silversmith. Knoxville, Knox County, 1813.

The only documentation of Abner Harrison's work was found in *Wilson's Knoxville Gazette* for 25 October 1813, when Harrison and Thomas Cain, advertising as the firm of Cain and Harrison (q.v.), sought a journeyman gold and silversmith who understood watch repair.

A *Nashville Whig* item dated 5 March 1816 mentioned an engraver named Harrison in Pittsburg, Franklin County, but no connection between this man and Abner Harrison has been established.

HASTREITER, Dominick. Gold and silversmith. Nashville, Davidson County, 1850.

Dominick Hastreiter, born in Bavaria about 1810, was working in Nashville by 1850 as a gold and silversmith; he was located on Church Street between College and Market streets. He lived in the household of Joseph Ruohs, cabinetmaker.[16]

By a process "entirely new . . . in this country," using gold or silver, Hastrieter gilded church ornaments, tower balls, or watches, manufactured ornaments of all types, and repaired clocks and watches. The process to which Hastreiter made reference probably was electroplating, which had been patented by George and Henry Elkington in England in 1840.[17]

HEENER (HUNER), (....?). Clock and watchmaker. Nashville, Davidson County, 1802.

Heener, whose first name is unknown, was working with Joseph Thorp Elliston (q.v.) in the clock and watchmaking business in Nashville in the summer of 1802 (Elliston and Heener, q.v.). The firm, which advertised itself as the first clockmaking establishment in the Mero district, was prepared to make and repair all types of clocks and watches on short notice and perform gold and silver work. Elliston, whose name appears at the end of the firm's advertisement, noted the two men were not working "as copartners," but rather had agreed upon a "division of the arising profits of the Clock Making business."[18]

HENDERSON and ADAMS. Merchants. Memphis, Shelby County, 1836.

In March 1836 Henderson and Adams began the "Dry Goods and Fancy Store" business in a house formerly occupied by H. McCallen and Company on the north side of Nelson and Titus's store in Memphis. Their stock included "Spring and Summer Dry Goods, Hats, Shoes, Hardware, Jewelry, Queensware and Groceries" that the partners asserted would rival any in quality, assortment, and cheapness.[19]

HERBRICK (HENBRICK), John. Watchmaker. Nashville, Davidson County, 1860.

John Herbrick, who was born in Austria about 1822, was working in Nashville as a watchmaker at 28 South Market Street in 1860. Herbrick and his wife Jacobenia, a native of Wurttemberg, had three Austrian-born children, a child born in Ohio, and nine-month-old Augustin, born in Tennessee. They lived in the Second Ward on North Market Street in Nashville.[20]

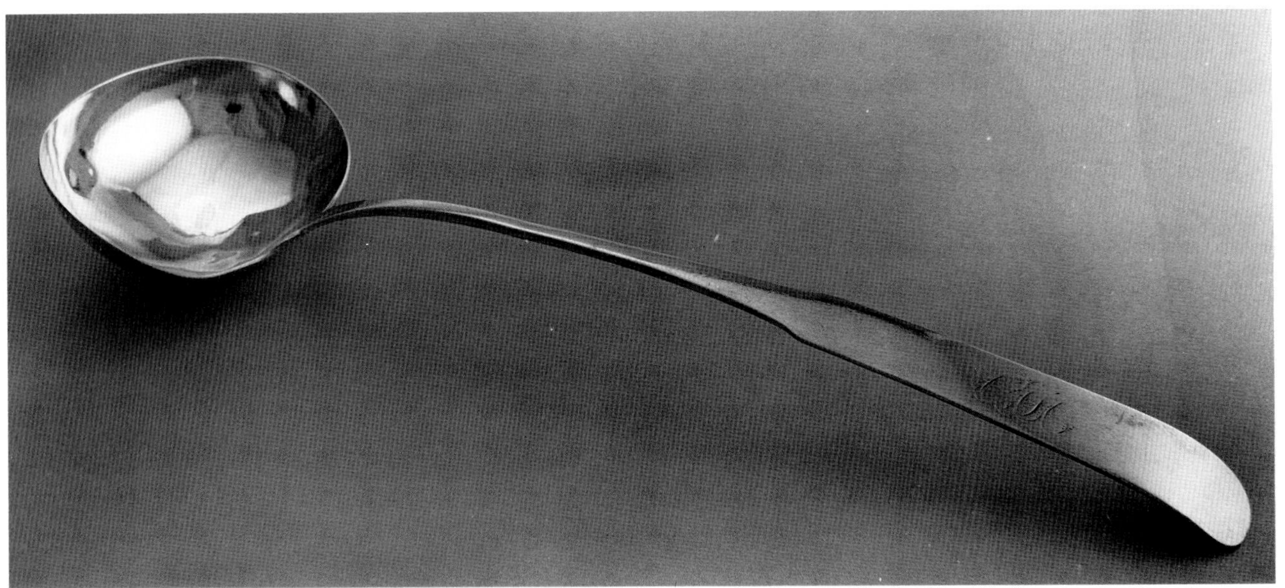

79, 79a. *Punch ladle marked "HILLIARD," 1800–10, engraved "CM," Jonesboro. LOA: 14⅝", width across bowl: 2", rise of shaft: 4¼". Courtesy of the Tennessee State Museum. The mark illustrated in fig. 79a also has been recorded on a serving spoon with a North Carolina history and has been attributed to either William Hilliard or George Hilliard, both of Fayetteville, North Carolina. William Hilliard came to Jonesboro from Fayetteville and returned to North Carolina in 1805.*

HILL, James. Clock and watchmaker, gold and silversmith, jeweler. Knoxville, Knox County, 1816.

In September 1816 James Hill commenced the "CLOCK & WATCH, Gold & Silver Smith Business" on Cumberland Street, one door from Dr. J. C. Strong's in Knoxville.[21]

An engraver named James Hill worked in Boston from 1803 through 1810; no connection has been established.[22]

HILL, Thomas. Jeweler. Memphis, Shelby County, 1856–59.

Thomas Hill was a partner in the Memphis firm of F. H. Clark and Company (q.v.) from 1856–59.[23]

HILLIARD, William. Gold and silversmith, watch repairer. Jonesboro, Washington County, 1804.

In 1801 the Fayetteville, North Carolina, silversmith William Hilliard took William Dye as an apprentice to the silversmith's trade; in February 1804 Hilliard moved into a house "lately occupied by Dr. Chester" in Jonesboro, Tennessee. There he cleaned and repaired watches on moderate terms and sought old gold and silver to carry on his silversmithing business. He advertised his need for two apprentices at the time.[24]

By December 1805, Hilliard had returned to Cumberland County, North Carolina, and had opened a "Watch Maker and Jeweller" shop in Fayetteville, where he remained at least through 1814.[25]

HINE, Charles. Jeweler, engraver. Nashville, Davidson County, 1855–57.

Charles Hine worked in Nashville as a jeweler and engraver from 1855–57. He was listed in the *Nashville Business Directory* for those years, first at 56 North College Street as a jeweler and engraver and then at 77 North High Street as a jeweler.[26]

HINKLIN (HOULIHN), John. Silversmith. Robertson County, 1847?–50.

John Hinklin was born in Ireland about 1810. He married a North Carolina woman and by 1847 had moved to Tennessee where their eldest child was born that year. At the time of the 1850 census, Hinklin and his family were living in Robertson County, where he worked as a silversmith; his personal estate was valued at $100.

HIRSCHFELD, A. Watchmaker, jeweler. Nashville, Davidson County, 1855–57.

A. Hirschfeld worked in Nashville as a watchmaker and jeweler at 99 North Market Street from 1855–57.[27]

THOMAS HITER,
CLOCK & WATCH-MAKER,
SILVERSMITH AND JEWELER;
Begs leave to inform the citizens of Franklin and its vicinity, that he has opened SHOP in the above place, where he intends profecuting the different branches of his trade, he flatters himfelf that his experience in the above bufinefs will enable him to give general fatisfaction to thofe who may confide their work to him.
☞ He will give the higheft price for old Silver.

80. *Thomas Hiter, "CLOCK & WATCH-MAKER, SILVERSMITH AND JEWELER," announced the opening of his shop in Franklin in the Nashville* Democratic Clarion and Tennessee Gazette *of 15 June 1810.*

80a, 80b. 80c. *Sauce ladle marked "T. H.," 1800–10, engraved "Sally Hiter," Franklin. LOA: 8", width across bowl: 2", rise: 3/4". Private collection. Thomas Hiter married Sally M'Crory in 1811.*

HITER, Thomas H. Clock and watchmaker, silversmith, jeweler. Franklin, Williamson County, 1810–11? 1820–24, 1829–40.

Thomas H. Hiter worked in Franklin as a silversmith, clockmaker, watchmaker, and jeweler as early as 1810. On 8 February 1811 he married Sally M'Crory of Williamson County and that same day formed a clock and watchmaking, silversmith, and jeweler firm (Hiter and Raworth) in Nashville, probably with Edward Raworth, a Nashville silversmith. Fourteen days later, the business partnership was dissolved by mutual consent; the Hiters may have moved out of state at that time, for no records of Hiter's presence in Tennessee for a number of years following the dissolution have been found.[28] By 1820, however, Hiter was again in Franklin, detailing losses from a November robbery at his shop and asking citizens to help find the thief "as ruin will be the consequence if he is not detected."[29]

In 1822 Hiter requested payment of debts owed to him ("Pay me what thou Owes") and informed his customers that he had taken Thomas A. Thomson (q.v.) into his business (Hiter and Thomson, q.v.). An announcement that year for the annual session of regimental court martial for the twenty-first regiment of Tennessee militia carries Hiter's name as Judge Advocate.[30] Later in 1822, due to "hard necessity," Hiter turned over the collection of his debts to Eli M'Gau and advertised his property for sale to the highest bidder. Offered were a two-story brick house and storeroom, household furniture, a frame shop, a brick shop, brick smokehouse and dairy, and "a good hewed log kitchen." Also to be sold were "one NEGRO WOMAN, named Polly, about 24 years of age" and "two NEGRO BOYS, children of Polly, one about two years old and the other about four months. . . ."[31]

In 1824, after the Hiter-Thomson partnership was dissolved, Hiter "resumed business on his own footing" in the brick house adjoining the store of J. Dwyer in Franklin. At that time, he intended to devote his time almost exclusively to repairing watches.[32] After 1824 there is a gap in information regarding Hiter's activities until 1829, when he announced his return to Franklin and the resumption of his trade in Dr. Crockett's "small framed house" on the southeast side of the public square. Hiter announced his candidacy for "Register of Williamson County"; he died in 1840.[33]

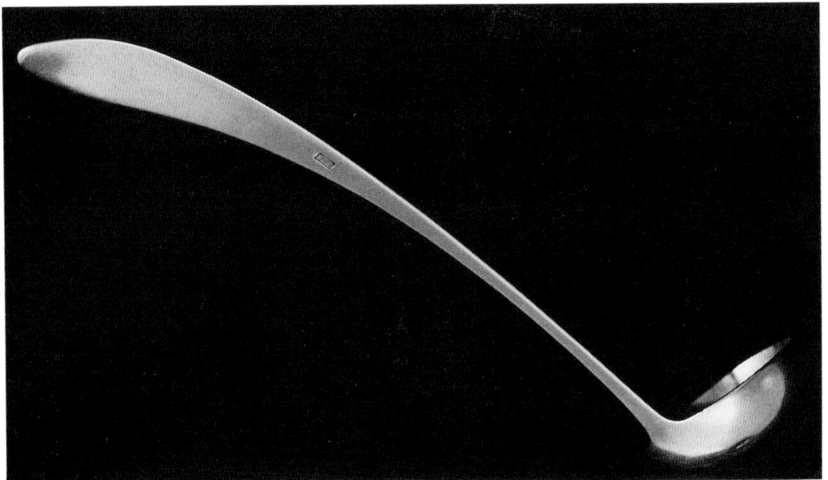

80b

80c

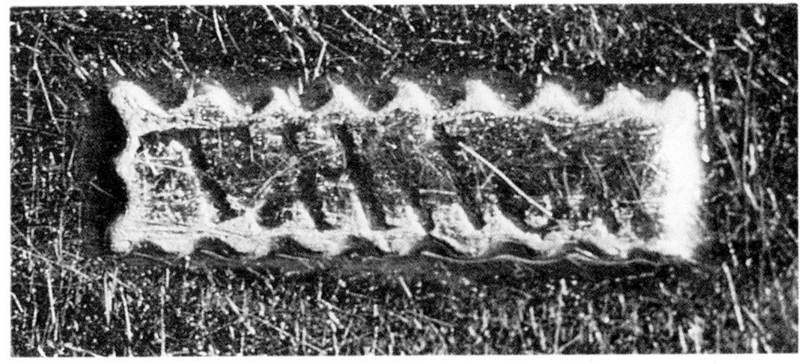

80d. *"T. Hiter" mark attributed to Thomas Hiter, 1815–25.*

HITER & RAWORTH. Clock and watchmakers, silversmiths, jewelers. Nashville, Davidson County, 1811.

Thomas H. Hiter (q.v.) and Edward Raworth (q.v.) formed a clock and watchmaking, silversmith, and jewelry business on 8 February 1811. The men promised to execute promptly any orders for "Court Seals, Gold Cyphers, Hair work and other engraving;" ore and mineral specimens were to be "thankfully received and carefully anlyzed [sic]." The firm was dissolved by mutual consent only two weeks later.[34]

HITER & THOMSON. Silversmiths. Franklin, Williamson County, 1822.

Thomas H. Hiter (q.v.) and Thomas A. Thomson (q.v.) formed the partnership of Hiter and Thomson in early 1822. A single notice in the Franklin *Independent Gazette* is the only known evidence of the firm's existence; by 1824 Hiter had resumed business on his own.[35]

HODGE, James. Silversmith. Columbia, Maury County, 1820–d. 1887.

According to tombstone records, James Hodge was born in Tennessee in 1800; census records, however, listed the year of his birth as 1804. By 1820 he was living in Columbia as an apprentice to the silversmith's trade under his brother-in-law Samuel Northern (q.v.), whose business Hodge took over when Northern returned to Davidson County.[36]

Hodge's first residence was a log house on Pulaski Pike, but by 1850 he had amassed a fortune of $16,000 and built a "substantial brick house (fig. 81c) near the railroad in Columbia." At the time of the 1860 census, Hodge evaluated his real property at $41,800 and his personal property at $17,300. The comparatively large population of Maury County at that date may have accounted for Hodge's financial success.[37] W. S. Fleming's "Historical Sketch of Maury County" suggested that Hodge's diligence was the reason he became one of the county's wealthiest citizens: "For more than fifty years he rarely, if ever, missed a day from his shop; and even after he became independently rich, he continued his business . . . an example of what can be accomplished by close attention to one's vocation in life."[38]

Hodge married Nancy B. Atkinson on 30 October 1832

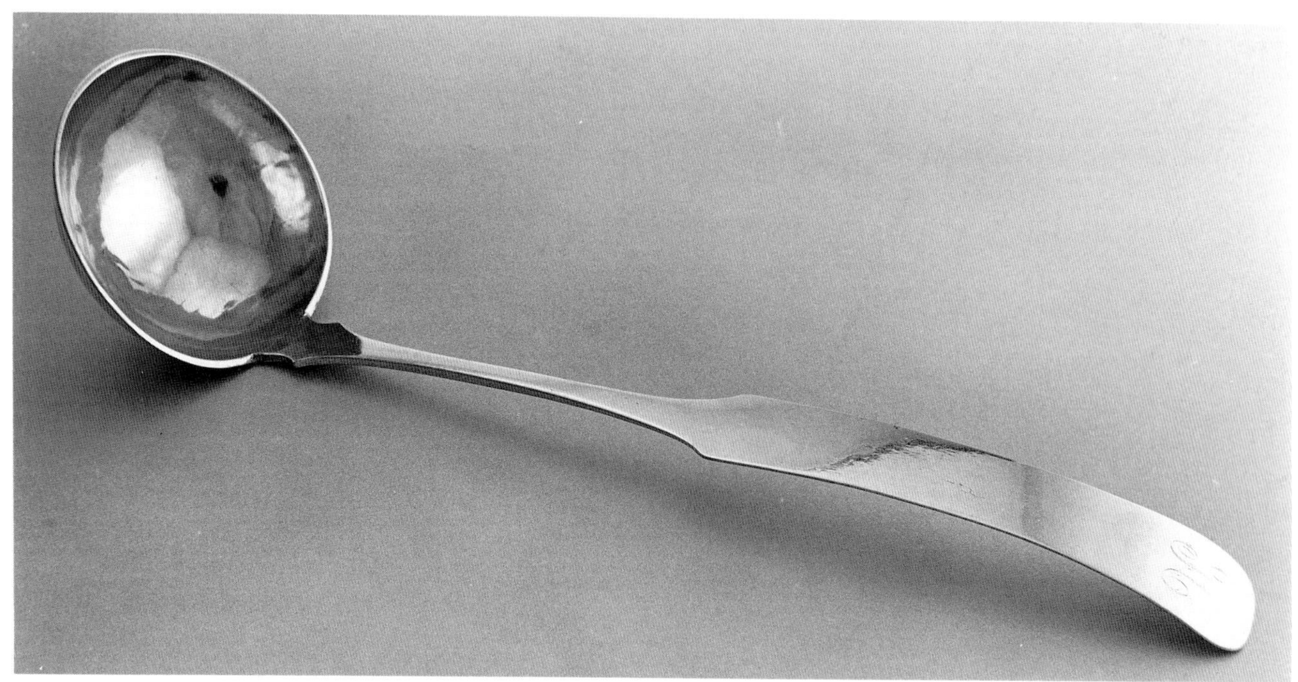

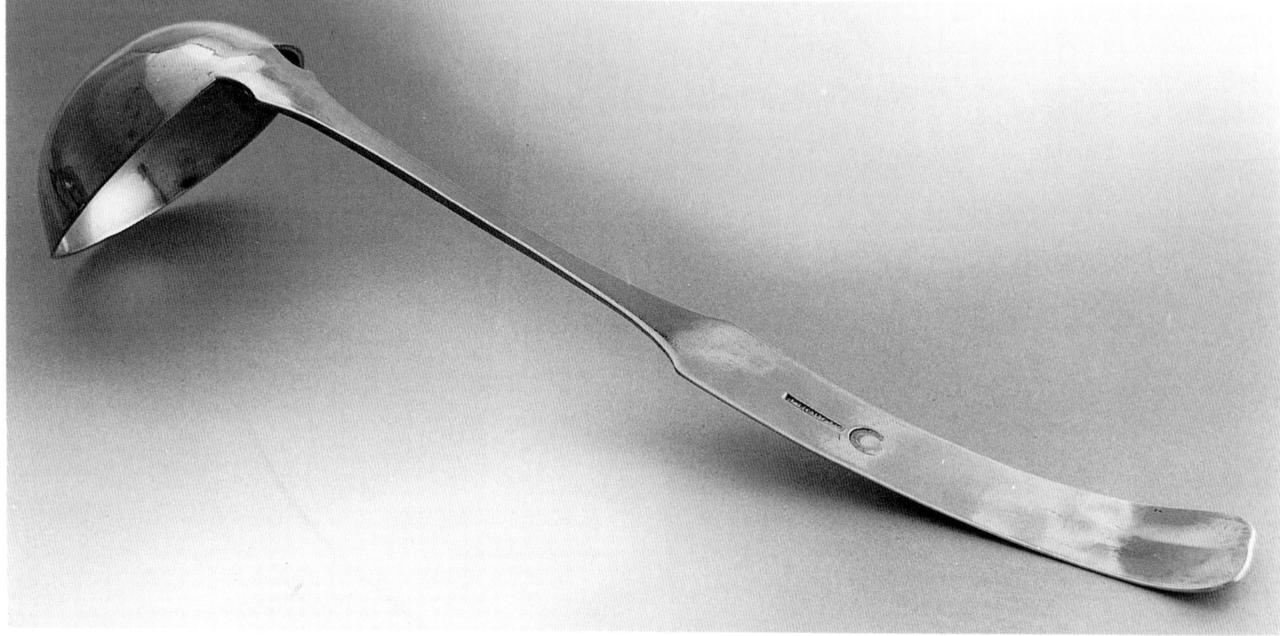

81, 81a, 81b. *Punch ladle marked "J. HODGE" in a rectangle and "CO[LUM]BI[A]T" in a circle stamp, 1825, engraved "H." LOA: 14½", width across bowl: 3⅞", rise: 3⅞". Private collection.*

81c. *This Columbia house was the home of James Hodge in the 1850s; the building is no longer standing. Courtesy of Orman Photo Shop, Columbia, Tenn., photograph by Ray Bent, c. 1935.*

in Williamson County; the couple had two sons, Jesse A. and James S. (q.v.), who pre-deceased their parents. Hodge continued working through 1876, using two dies to mark his silver: "J. HODGE" and a circle inscribed "COLUMBIA T." James Hodge died in 1887 and is buried at Rose Hill in Columbia.[39]

In his later years Hodge returned to the log house built by Nathan Vaught that he had formerly occupied. During the Civil War the house lay between the Confederate and Federal armies, and a tree in the yard was struck by a federal cannon ball. Hodge was known as somewhat of a historian, and his memories were published in local papers during the 1870s. He was a close friend of General Felix Zollicoffer (later editor of the *Republican Daily Banner and Nashville Whig*) when Zollicoffer was a young printer in Columbia. Author Jill Garrett, in her *Obituaries from Tennessee Newspapers*, revealed that she had the Hodges' log house moved to her own property in 1976.[40]

HODGE, James S. Watchmaker. Columbia, Maury County, 1860.

James S. Hodge, son of Nancy and James Hodge (q.v.), was listed as a watchmaker, aged twenty-six, in the Maury County census for 1860. He lived with his parents and brother in Columbia; he probably worked in his father's shop.[41]

HODGE, William R. Silversmith. Columbia, Maury County, 1820?–28.

William R. Hodge (b.1807–d. 1879) was the brother of silversmith James Hodge (q.v.). He arrived in Columbia "soon after 1820," was apprenticed to the silversmith trade under his brother-in-law, Samuel Northern

82. *William R. Hodge (b.1807-d.1879), 1850–60. Courtesy of Orman Photo Shop, Columbia, Tenn.*

(q.v.), and prospered there in the silversmithing business. An 1828 *Western Mercury* notice requested readers to retrieve, before 1 January 1829, watches that had been left in the shop once owned by Samuel Northern. Otherwise, Hodge warned, he would sell the timepieces for expenses.[42]

When William R. Hodge married Frances S. Atkinson on 2 September 1834, Solomon Berson of Franklin (q.v.) was listed as his bondsman in the Williamson County court records.[43]

According to Garrett's *Maury County Newspapers, 1810–1844*, Hodge was appointed mayor of Columbia in 1849. In the federal census for 1850, Hodge was listed as a merchant; there were seven children in his household: William, fourteen; Gustavus, twelve; James, ten; A. B., eight; George, six; Mary, four; Alphose [sic], two. Listings in Nashville directories for the Columbia area through the 1850s indicated that his merchandising featured "staple and fancy dry goods."[44]

HOEPTER, Henry. Watchmaker. McMinn County, 1860.

At the time of the 1860 census for McMinn County, seventeen-year-old Henry Hoepter was working as a watchmaker and living in the residence of W. R. Grubbs. A native of Bavaria, Hoepter estimated the value of his personal estate at $50.

83, 83a. *Set of spoons with various marks used by David L. Hope. Private collections, photograph by Helga Photo Studio, Inc. Left: pair of teaspoons marked with an incised "HOPE," 1850?, engraved "Hope," Knoxville. LOA: 5⅞". Center: pair of tablespoons marked with an incised "HOPE" and a masonic emblem (fig. 83a), 1855?, engraved "Hope," Knoxville. LOA: 8½". Right: Teaspoon marked "HOPE," 1870, engraved "J. W. Hope/ Knoxville Tenn." LOA: 6". Far right: Teaspoon marked "HOPE," engraved "D. L. Hope, 1869," Knoxville. LOA: 5⅞".*

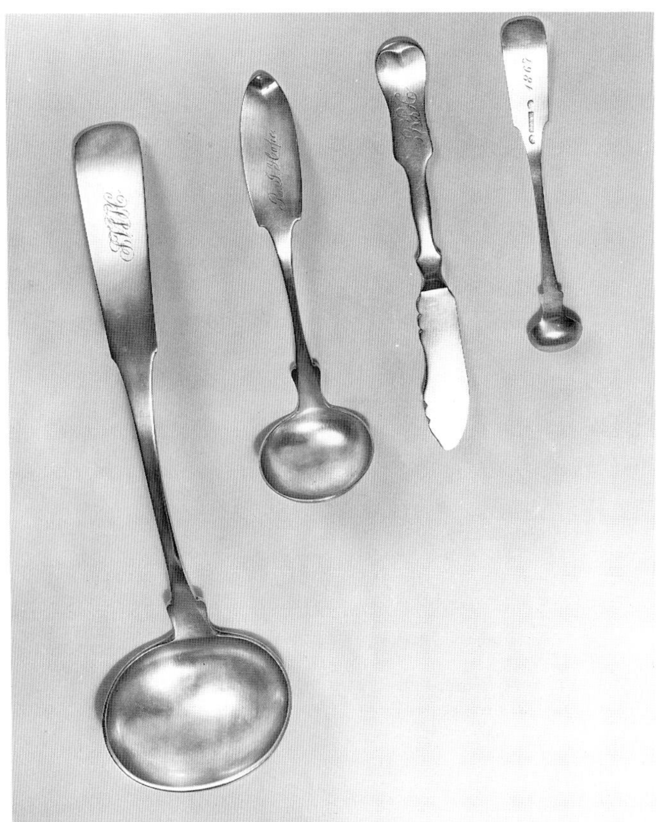

83b, 83c. *Spoon, knife, and ladles marked by David L. Hope. Private collections, photograph by Helga Photo Studio, Inc. Left: mustard spoon marked with a "HOPE" flanked by masonic emblems (fig. 83c), 1867, Knoxville. LOA: 5¾". Center left: butter knife marked "HOPE," 1850–60?, engraved "RJH," Knoxville. LOA: 7¼". Center right: cream ladle marked "HOPE," 1850– 60?, engraved "R. J. Hope," Knoxville. LOA: 7¼", width across bowl: 2⅛", rise: ⅞". Right: punch ladle marked "HOPE," 1850– 60?, engraved "JWH," Knoxville. LOA: 12", width across bowl: 3¾", rise 1⅝". In 1828 Hope became a Master Mason; the mark illustrated in fig. 83c includes a masonic emblem (see fig. 83a).*

HOFFAR, Ancus. Silversmith's apprentice. Knoxville, Knox County, 1827.

Ancus Hoffar was an apprentice of noted Knoxville silversmith Samuel Bell. According to an early 1828 newspaper notice, Hoffar ran away from Bell's establishment on the night of 23 December 1827. Bell offered a six-and-one-quarter cent reward for his return and threatened to enforce the law against any person harboring or employing his runaway apprentice.[45]

HOFMANN, John H. Silver plater. Memphis, Shelby County, 1855–56.

During 1855–56 John H. Hofmann was a silver plater and ornamental brass finisher in Memphis. At his shop on Second Street, one door above Union, he plated all kinds of coach and house hardware, made and repaired ornamental brass work, and offered both fire and galvanic (electroplate) gilding or silvering.[46]

HOPE, David Large. Silversmith. Knoxville, Knox County, 1828–d. 1869.

David Large Hope was born 26 June 1799 at Ramsey Plantation outside Knoxville. His father, Thomas Hope, an English-born architect and builder, worked in South Carolina, Tennessee, and later, Virginia; his mother, Elizabeth Large Hope, was a South Carolinian.[47]

David L. Hope served a silversmithing apprenticeship in Huntsville, Alabama. Research completed by Beverly Burbage, a Knoxville attorney, revealed that Hope was working on his own as early as 1828, and perhaps earlier. Hope had returned to Knoxville by that time, for in June of 1828 he received the degree of Master Mason at Mount Libanus Lodge, No. 59, in Knoxville.[48]

John Trotwood Moore, in *Tennessee, the Volunteer State*, suggested that Hope worked for Knoxville silversmith Samuel Bell (q.v.) for thirty years, but William Beall, a Knoxville historian, located an 1846 advertisement announcing that David L. Hope, a "long time resident here," was then at G. W. Harris's (q.v.) shop on the corner of Cumberland and Prince streets. As Harris's work as a silversmith was intermittent, it is conceivable that Hope worked for both men.[49]

Later, Hope bought the contents of Samuel Bell's silversmithing shop and established his own business. This purchase very likely occurred when Bell moved to Texas about 1852. Hope remained active in the silversmithing and jewelry business until his death in 1869.[50]

A Presbyterian and a Whig according to Moore, Hope married Mary E. Welch in January 1830. The couple had three children, Jane, David James, and John William, before Mary died in 1847. Both sons followed their father's footsteps into the business.[51]

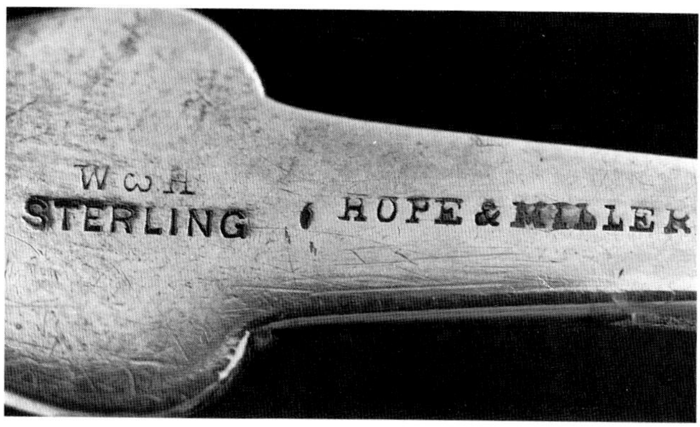

84. *"HOPE & MILLER" mark used by John William Hope and Fred Miller, c. 1869. Courtesy of the Tennessee State Museum, photograph by Stephen D. Cox. Wood & Hughes (1840–99) of New York probably made this piece; the "W & H" is their mark (see figs. 46b, 71a, 99b, 121a, and 126a).*

HOPE, John William. Watchmaker. Knoxville, Knox County, 1860–d. 1914.

John William Hope, the son of Knoxville silversmith David Large Hope (q.v.), was born 27 December 1843. Both John William and his brother, David James, apprenticed to their father; in the *Knoxville Business Directory* of 1859–60, John Hope was identified as a watchmaker boarding in the home of David L. Hope.[52]

Family records suggest that after David Large Hope's death in 1869, his sons formed the partnership of Hope and Miller with Fred Miller (fig. 84). Later, John and his brother worked as "Hope Brothers." John's sons, James David Hope (1846–1923) and Albert Guinn Hope (1869–1955), continued to operate the Hope Brothers firm until Albert's death. Three generations of Hopes worked with silver and jewelry in Knoxville for a total of one hundred and twenty-seven years.[53] John W. Hope died 9 September 1914.[54]

HORNSBY, James H. Silversmith. Athens, McMinn County, 1850?–60 and later.

James H. Hornsby was born in Tennessee about 1821. At the time of the 1850 census, Hornsby and his wife Harriet Coleman were living in the Athens household of William M. Sehorn, a silversmith (q.v.). Sehorn was married to Ann Coleman, the sister of Hornsby's wife. During the 1850s through at least 1860, the firm of Sehorn and Hornsby functioned as dealers in dry goods, watches, and clocks on the north side of the public square.[55]

Chancery Court records for McMinn County reveal that Hornsby continued to live in or near Athens through at least 1890. In 1870 he purchased fifty-one acres one-half mile from Athens and sold seventy-six acres in the town's Seventh District in 1890. An inventory of the personal property of William M. Sehorn recorded in McMinn County on 19 December 1879 listed money paid to the estate by James H. Hornsby, "surviving partner of Sehorn and Hornsby."[56]

HOTCHKISS, Richard L. Jeweler. Brownsville, Haywood County, 1860.

Richard L. Hotchkiss, born about 1837, was listed as a Brownsville jeweler in the 1860 census for Haywood County. The young native of Tennessee evaluated his personal property at $8000 and his real property at the same figure, a large estate for such a young man. Margaret J. Hotchkiss, twenty-three, and Stephen Hotchkiss (q.v.) lived with him at that time.

HOTCHKISS, Stephen. Jeweler. Brownsville, Haywood County, 1860.

At the time of the 1860 census for Haywood County, Stephen Hotchkiss was working as a jeweler in Brownsville. The twenty-two-year-old, a native of Tennessee, estimated the worth of his personal property at $7,000. He lived with Richard L. Hotchkiss (q.v.).

HOUPT, H. Watchmaker. Ripley, Lauderdale County, 1860.

Born in Pennsylvania about 1832, H. Houpt was listed as a watchmaker in Ripley in the 1860 census for Lauderdale County. He estimated the value of his personal estate at $500 at that time.

HOWARD, William H. and Company. Retailer in jewelry. Paris, Henry County, 1835.

William H. Howard and Company advertised jewelry and fancy cutlery "of every description" in the Paris *West Tennessean* for 16 May 1835.

HOYTE, Perkins. Watchmaker, silversmith?. Franklin, Williamson County, 1850.

Perkins Hoyte was born about 1803 in Virginia. At the time of the 1850 census he was working in Franklin, Williamson County, as a watchmaker and living in the household of Michael Custer, a hotel keeper.

According to Cutten's *Silversmiths of Georgia*, a Jonathan Perkins Hoyte, born in 1805 at Rumney, New Hampshire, was doing repair and gold and silver work in Clarksville, Georgia, prior to August 1847. In April 1849 Hoyte published a notice that he defied those who were "trying to drive him away . . . the business of my shop will continue. J. P. Hoyt." In 1852 the same J. P. Hoyte was working in Laurens, South Carolina; he was still there in 1854 when he advertised that he repaired clocks, watches, jewelry.[57]

It is possible that J. P. Hoyte of Georgia and Perkins Hoyte of Tennessee were the same man. Although the places of birth differ, facts recorded in census records were not always accurate. Nothing other than the details recorded in the 1850 census is presently known of Perkins's activities or length of stay in Tennessee; his appar-

85. *Downtown Nashville, 1890s. Courtesy of the Tennessee State Library and Archives. The Huellebrand Brothers' shop can be found in the lower right hand corner.*

ent disappearance from Georgia in 1849 and the record of his activity in South Carolina in 1852 provide a chronological gap of several years which may have been explained by a possible move to Tennessee.

HUELLEBRAND (HILLEBRAND, HULUBRAND, HULLEBRAND), R. Watchmaker, jeweler. Nashville, Davidson County, 1853–60 and later.

R. Huellebrand probably was working in Nashville as early as 1853 as a principal of Hillebrand and Company, a watch and jewelry company located at 42 South Market Street. By 1855 Huellebrand and Adolph Goltz (q.v.) had opened a jewelry store at 4 Union Street; the firm of Goltz and Huellebrand was listed at that address in the 1857 *Nashville Business Directory*. In 1859 Huellebrand moved to 5 Union Street (located at the corner of Union and Market streets) and advertised under his own name as a watchmaker and jeweler. An 1860 directory lists Huellebrand at 3 Union, an 1870 directory at 34 Union, and an 1875 directory at 40 Union.[58] A late nineteenth-century photograph (fig. 85) of Nashville indicates that a brother joined Huellebrand in the jewelry business at some unknown date.

HUGHES, D. W. Watchmaker. Nashville, Davidson County, 1860.

At the time of the 1860 census for Davidson County, a twenty-four-year-old Welshman named D. W. Hughes was working as a watchmaker at 3 Union Street, the same address as R. Huellebrand (q.v.). He lived in Nashville's First Ward and assessed his real property at $300 and his personal property at $500. The 1860 *Nashville Business Directory* and *State Gazetteer* also listed his name.[59]

HUTCHINSON, William. Silversmith?. Nashville, Davidson County, 1847.

In the 1847 listing of taxable property in Nashville, William Hutchinson, born in Kentucky, owned one slave valued at $400 and was "hired to A. Beach, silversmith (q.v.)."[60] Perhaps Hutchinson was in Beach's employ as a silversmith, although this has not been proven.

IRWIN, James A. Apprentice watchmaker. Greene County, 1860.

James A. Irwin was listed as a fourteen-year-old apprentice watchmaker from England in the 1860 census for Greene County. He lived with his fifty-two-year-old father, a carriage maker, three brothers, and three sisters.

JAMES, Joseph Henry. Watchmaker, jeweler. Columbia, Maury County, 1857–95.

Born on 27 April 1823 in Virginia, Joseph Henry James left his widowed mother's farm at the age of fourteen. For a year he tended store for William Butts of Cabin Point, Surry County, Virginia, but soon moved to Petersburg and apprenticed himself to jeweler Charles Lumsden.[1]

In 1841 he moved to Richmond where he worked as a journeyman for jeweler and watchmaker John Hill, then for silversmith Charles Gennet, with whom he formed the partnership of Gennet and James in 1845. James married Gennet's sister, Sarah Maria, in 1848.[2] James later returned to Surry County where he settled near his brother, M. Robert James, and began farming. This occupation and its concomitant rural lifestyle did not suit his wife, however, and in March 1857 the couple moved to Columbia, Maury County, Tennessee, where James once again pursued the silversmith's, jeweler's, and watchmaker's trades after purchasing a stock of jewelry goods in New York City.[3]

In the 1860 census for Maury County, James was listed as a watchmaker; his real property was evaluated at $6,000 and his personal property at $15,000. At that time James and his wife had three sons born in Virginia, Henry, William, and Albert, along with two children born in Tennessee, five-year-old Emma, and two-year-old Edgar. Their home also served as a residence for Lorenso Gennet (q.v.), perhaps a relative of James's wife.

Albert James joined his father's business in 1872; at that time the firm became known as J. H. James and Son. When Joseph Henry retired in 1895, Albert and his younger brother Edgar (b. 27 August 1857) formed the partnership of James Brothers. About 1918 the firm took on the name of W. H. Cotham and Company and remained in business through at least 1960.[4]

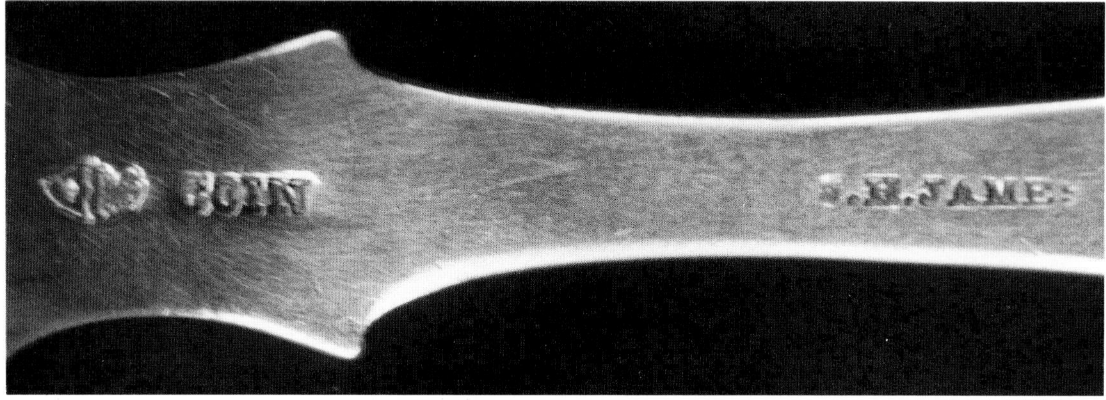

86, 86a, 86b. *Spoons marked by J. H. James, 1860–70, Columbia. Private collections, photographs courtesy of Orman Photo Shop, Columbia, Tenn. Left: teaspoon marked "COIN J. H. JAMES" with manufacturer's pseudo-hallmark. LOA: 5⅞". Right: dessert spoon marked "COIN J. H. JAMES." LOA: 6¾". The mark illustrated in fig. 86b is that of the teaspoon; the manufacturer's mark is indistinguishable.*

86c. *"COIN J. H. JAMES, COL. TENN." mark, c. 1860. Courtesy of the Tennessee State Museum, photograph by Stephen D. Cox.*

Joseph Henry James died in 1901; some of his descendants married into prominent Middle Tennessee families and remain in the area today.[5]

JANNIGAN, Bryant. Clock repairer. Bolivar, Hardeman County, 1850.

Bryant Jannigan was listed as a fifty-one-year old "clock fixer" in the 1850 census. He was working in Bolivar, Hardeman County, where he lived in the household of Solomon Grantha, a farmer. Both Jannigan and Grantha were natives of North Carolina.[6]

JEANMARIE, L. F. Watchmaker, jeweler. Nashville, Davidson County, 1850; Winchester, Franklin County, 1853; McMinnville, Warren County, 1857–60 and later.

The 1850 *Daily Nashville American* announced the opening of L. F. Jeanmarie's watchmaking, watch repair, and jewelry shop on Cedar Street next door to the firm of Clifton and Abbot; this advertisement ran for about a year. By 1853 Jeanmarie was working as a watchmaker and jeweler in Franklin. A directory listing for jewelers placed him in McMinnville by 1857; the 1860 census listed him in that town with Heloise, his wife, and three children: Aline, six, Wallace, three, and Mary, one. According to Goodspeed's *History of Tennessee* he remained in McMinnville through 1887, continuing his work as a jeweler.[7]

JOBE, Samuel M. Watchmaker and jeweler's apprentice. Bolivar, Hardeman County, 1850. Watchmaker. Memphis, Shelby County, 1855–60 and later.

Samuel M. Jobe was born in Tennessee about 1831. According to the 1850 census, he was apprenticed to Daniel J. Wells (q.v.), a watchmaker and jeweler of Hardeman County.[8] By 1855 Jobe had moved to Memphis where he worked as a watchmaker at J. E. Merriman's (q.v.) shop; five years later he became one of Merriman's partners. He lived on Linden Street near St. Martin. At the time of the 1860 census Jobe estimated the worth of his real property to be $10,000, and his personal property, $6,000.[9]

In *Memphis Sketches* Coppack recorded that Jobe was a member of the Howard Association, which was organized in Memphis in 1855 to provide volunteers to tend those sick with yellow fever, thereby enabling healthy citizens to leave the plagued city during epidemics. Coppock revealed that Jobe died in a yellow fever epidemic of 1878; he was reported to have been working as a bookkeeper at that time. His portrait hangs in the Memphis Public Library along with the portraits of others who gave their lives in the same manner.[10]

JOBE, W. L. Jeweler, watchmaker. Memphis, Shelby County, 1856–57.

The 1856–57 *Memphis City Directory* listed W. L. Jobe as a jeweler in J. E. Merriman's shop; Jobe was fifteen at the time. By the time of the 1860 census, he was identified as a watchmaker in Memphis's Second Ward. No relationship between W. L. and Samuel Jobe (q.v.) has been established.[11]

JOHNSON, (....?). Jeweler. McMinnville, Warren County, 1857.

According to the 1857 *Nashville Business Directory*, Johnson, whose first name is unknown, was working in McMinnville, Warren County, as a jeweler. The 1860 *State Gazetteer* listed a Johnson under jewelry, watches, and clocks in Woodbury, Cannon County.[12] As the two counties are contiguous and the towns are no more than twenty miles apart, it is possible that the two listings represent the same man.

JOHNSON, Dan. Jeweler. Memphis, Shelby County, 1860.

Dan Johnson, who was born in Tennessee about 1821, was listed as a "jeweler" in the 1860 census for the First Ward of Memphis. Kovel reported a Daniel B. Johnson working as a silversmith in Utica, New York, circa 1834–58, although no connection with the Memphis jeweler is known.[13]

JOHNSON, J. B. Jeweler. Paris, Henry County, 1856.

The only known reference to J. B. Johnson occurred in a Paris *Patriot* advertisement of 20 March 1856 placed by F. M. Cheek (q.v.), the man who purchased Johnson's "entire WATCH and JEWELRY establishment" in Paris early in 1856.

JOHNSON, Shad B. Jeweler. Memphis, Shelby County, 1860.

Born in Tennessee about 1834, Shad B. Johnson worked as a jeweler and lived in the Second Ward of Memphis at the time of the 1860 census. He evaluated his personal estate at $500.

D.A.JOHNSTON

87. *"D. A. JOHNSTON" mark attributed to Daniel A. Johnston of Nashville, 1853–60.*

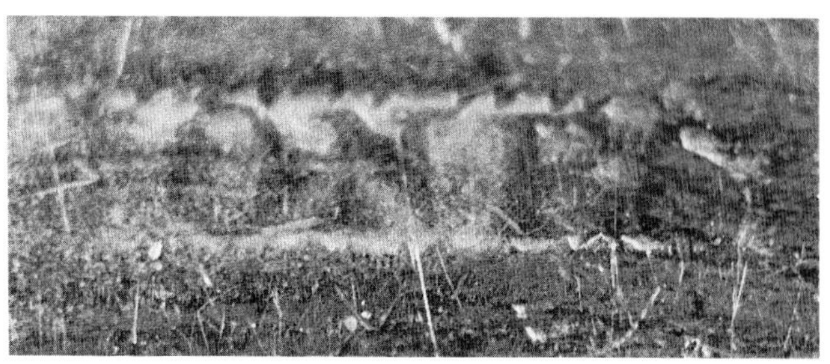

88. *"JONES" mark from a spoon found in Tennessee. Courtesy of the Tennessee State Museum, photograph by Stephen D. Cox. This virtually obliterated mark may represent the work of G. B. Jones of Rogersville.*

JOHNSTON, Daniel A. Watchmaker, jeweler. Nashville, Davidson County, 1853–60.

Daniel A. Johnston, born in Tennessee, was working in Nashville as a watchmaker and jeweler in 1853. He kept shop at 17 Deaderick Street above Nashville silversmith James Shegogg's (q.v.) establishment. By 1855 Johnston had moved to 49 North Cherry Street where he remained at least through 1859. He must have continued his residence in Nashville, for in 1880 he was listed as a patron in the publication of Clayton's *History of Davidson County, Tennessee.*[14]

JONES, A. S. Silversmith. Sullivan County, 1860.

At the time of the 1860 census for Sullivan County, A. S. Jones was working as a silversmith; he was a resident of the the county's Seventeenth District with Virginia, his wife, a native of Virginia, and three young children, all born in Virginia. The twenty-seven-year-old silversmith evaluated his real property at $700 and his personal property at $500.

JONES, G. B. Clock and watchmaker, gold and silversmith. Rogersville, Hawkins County, 1815.

G. B. Jones worked in Rogersville, Hawkins County, as a clock and watchmaker, gold and silversmith. In 1815 he informed the public that he had moved his shop to the former newspaper office of the *Western Pilot* opposite the post office. At that location he made and repaired watches and stocked a large assortment of jewelry and silverware.[15] A well-worn mark (fig. 88) on a spoon found in Tennessee could represent the work of this Rogersville silversmith or perhaps that of J. B. Jones of Boston, circa 1782–1852.

Jones may have been in partnership with a man named Davis in Carthage about 1808, although the documentation of this firm is unclear in regard to the full identity of the partners.[16]

JONES, S. S. Watchmaker, engraver. Memphis, Shelby County, 1849–50.

S. S. Jones was working at 17 Jefferson Street in Memphis as a watchmaker and engraver during 1849–50.[17]

JOSEPHS (JOSEPH), A. (Abraham?, Alexander?). Jeweler. Nashville, Davidson County, 1859–60 and later.

Jewelers named A. Joseph, Alexander Joseph, and Abraham Joseph appeared in city directories for 1859 and 1860 and the census of 1860. Clarification of these surnames has not been possible. However, the 1860 census for Nashville recorded a jeweler named Abraham Josephs who lived with Ellen, his wife, and two-year-old son Alex in the Edgefield section of town. The Josephs shared the home of A. Josephs, a painter, Adalene Josephs, and their son Charles.[18]

JUDD, W. H. Jeweler. Jasper, Marion County, 1860.

W. H. Judd was listed under "Jewelry, Watches, Clocks, Etc." for Jasper, Marion County, in the 1860 *State Gazetteer.*[19]

KAISER, Hamman A. Silversmith, jeweler. Kingston, Roane County, 1857–60.

Hamman A. Kaiser was born in Enliben, Germany, about 1820 and was working as a silversmith in Kingston, Roane County, by 1857. He lived there with his German-born wife Augusta and three young children born in Tennessee. At the time of the 1860 census for Roane County, Kaiser valued his real property at $800 and his personal property at $600. The *State Gazetteer* for the same year listed Kaiser under "Jewelry, Watches & Clocks, Etc.".[1]

KARSNER, B. Watch and clockmaker, gold and silversmith. Kingston, Roane County, 1821.

In 1821 B. Karsner advertised (fig. 89) that he had commenced watch and clockmaking "in its various branches" in the town of Kingston. Although little is known of Karsner's career, his work is documented by a beaker (fig. 89a) of excellent quality that bears an engraved signature (fig. 89b) rather than a stamped touchmark.[2]

KAUFMANN (KAUFFMAN, KAUFMAN), Adolph. Jeweler? watch and clockmaker? Memphis, Shelby County, 1859–60.

Adolph Kaufmann operated a watch and jewelry

March 27, 1821. 4t.

New Establishment.

B. KARSNER, & Co.

RESPECTFULLY inform the citizens of Roane and the adjacent counties, that they have commenced the

WATCH and CLOCK

Making business,

IN ITS VARIOUS BRANCHES,

In the town of

KINGSTON.

East Tennessee.

Where they hope to meet with that encouragement which they may deserve. They will keep constantly on hand an assortment of

Silver and Gold Ware, Watch, Trinkets, &c.

All of which they will sell on very reasonable terms.

N B. Orders from any part of the country, will meet with immediate attention.

March 27, 1821. 6t.

89. *In the* Knoxville Register *of 27 March 1821, "B. KARSNER, & Co." announced the opening of their watch and clock-making business in Kingston, "East Tennessee."*

89a, 89b. *Beaker marked "B. KARSNER & Co.," 1821, engraved "McE," Nashville. HOA: 3 3/8", width across rim: 2 13/16". Courtesy of the Tennessee State Museum, gift of Dr. and Mrs. Ben Caldwell. The mark illustrated in fig. 89b is the only example of an engraved mark found in Tennessee.*

---

establishment in Memphis at 10 Front Row during 1859–60. City directories recorded that an A. Kauffman was the proprietor of a dry goods store on Poplar Street in 1855; in 1857 an individual with the same name was listed as a clothier at 115 Front Row. These directory listings probably represented Adolph Kaufman, indicating that his 1859–60 listing was that of a jewelry merchant rather than a trained jeweler or watchmaker.[3]

KEEN, Henry. Silversmith. Fayetteville, Lincoln County, 1850.

Born in North Carolina about 1818, Henry Keen moved to Tennessee with his wife, Frances, and two children some time during 1839–45. At the time of the 1850 census the couple lived with their growing family of five children in Fayetteville, Lincoln County, where Keen worked as a silversmith.

KELLER, George. Jeweler. Memphis, Shelby County, 1860.

George Keller, a native of Virginia, was a twenty-six-year-old jeweler at the time of the 1860 census. He lived in Memphis's Eighth Ward in the household of James Pooley (q.v.) who also may have been his employer.

Kovel noted a George Keller working as a silversmith in Philadelphia circa 1846.[4] No connection with the Memphis jeweler is known.

KELLY, Edward. Jeweler. Brownsville, Haywood County, 1860.

Eighteen-year-old Tennessee native Edward Kelly lived with and probably worked as a jeweler for his uncle Solomon Berson (q.v.) at the time of the 1860 census for Haywood County. Other household members included his brother, William Kelly (q.v.), and his mother, Juliet Kelly, formerly of Massachusetts.[5]

KELLY, W. O. Retailer. Trenton, Gibson County, 1860.

A spoon marked "W. O. KELLY & BRO. TRENTON TENN" has been recorded in the MESDA files; it also has the mark of a northern manufacturer. The federal census of 1860 for Gibson County listed a W. O. Kelly, carpenter. It is possible that the mark represents the W. O. Kelly mentioned in the census; from the mark it can be assumed that he was a retailer. W. O. Kelly also may have been William Kelly (q.v.), who was working in Trenton after 1860.

KELLY, William. Jeweler. Brownsville, Haywood County, 1860; Trenton, Gibson County, after 1860.

William Kelly, who was born about 1830 in Tennessee, worked as a jeweler in Brownsville in 1860 and lived with the Solomon Berson (q.v.) family. The 1870 census for Gibson County revealed that William Kelly was a resident of Trenton along with his wife, Lucilla, and daughter, Lucy. It is probable he worked there with his brother, Edward, but no documentation, except a mark, supports that supposition.[6]

KENT, Charles. Watchmaker. Alexandria, DeKalb County, 1860; Columbia, Maury County, 1860.

Charles Kent's name appeared in the 1860 *State Gazetteer* listings for "Jewelry, Watches, Clocks, Etc." in Alexandria, DeKalb County. In addition, the 1860 census for Maury County listed a Charles Kent, twenty-six years old, from Switzerland, working as a watchmaker and living in District Nine with his Tennessee-born wife.[7]

KENT, Thomas. Silversmith. Nashville, Davidson County, 1845?–53.

Thomas Kent was born in Cincinnati, Ohio, about 1817. One of seven children of Luke Kent, Sr., an English-born watch and clockmaker, silversmith and jeweler of that city, Thomas Kent worked as a jeweler and watchmaker in Cincinnati from 1836–44. By 1845 he had moved to Tennessee, as the recorded birth of his daughter, Lucy, in that year established. Kent appeared in the 1850 Davidson County census, which also listed his daughter and his Irish wife, Matilda. Kent gave his occupation as a silversmith. Sharing the family's home at the time was Isabel Armitage, a twenty-year-old woman born in Ireland. In 1853 Kent was working at 31 Union Street.[8]

A spoon with the Tennessee look and of an appropriate period found by a Nashville collector bears a "KENT" mark.

90. "KENT" mark, 1850–60. This mark is only tentatively attributed to Thomas Kent as there is the possibility that it was Charles Kent's.

KERLEY, E. R. Watch repairer, jeweler. Gallatin, Sumner County, 1860.

E. R. Kerley was born in Tennessee about 1830 and advertised in January 1860 that he had opened a watchmaking and jewelry shop "at the Book Store of Mr. J. M. Menefee, in Gallatin." He promised prompt and guaranteed repair work on watches, clocks, and musical instruments. Kerley lived with a number of other tradesmen in N. B. Hamilton's Gallatin hotel.[9]

KEYS, W. H. Silver plater. Nashville, Davidson County, 1860.

In 1860 W. H. Keys worked in Nashville as a silver plater at 12½ Deaderick Street, presumably for Henry Parkhurst's (q.v.) silver plating establishment located at the same address.[10]

KILLINGSWORTH, James. Silversmith. Kingston, Roane County, 1825.

James Killingsworth, a silversmith of Kingston, Roane County, informed the public in March 1825 that he had moved his silversmith shop "to the house formerly occupied by Drs. Jordan and Butler and opposite John Loyd's Tavern. . . ." His advertisement promised continued "neatness and dispatch" in the execution of his business.[11] A mark (fig. 91) with the initials "J[?] I[?] K" is attributed to Killingsworth.

KIRTCKNER (KIRCHNER, KERCHNER), John A. Jeweler. Nashville, Davidson County, 1859–60.

John A. Kirtckner, who was born in Bavaria about 1832, worked as a jeweler during 1859–60 with Nashville silversmith, watchmaker, and jeweler George W. Donigan (q.v.), whose shop was located at the corner of College and Union streets.[12]

91. *"[J or I] K" mark attributed to James Killingsworth of Kingston, 1825.*

KNAPP, E. M. Jeweler, watch and clockmaker. Clarksville, Montgomery County, 1860.

E. M. Knapp appeared in the 1860 *State Gazetteer* listings for "Jewelry, Watches, Clocks, Etc." in Clarksville, Montgomery County. He operated a shop on Franklin Street.[13]

KOCH, M. and Company. Watch repairers. Memphis, Shelby County, 1859–60.

In 1859 Matthew Koch and Jacob Sorg were working in Memphis as "M. Koch and Company" on Shelby Street, between Howard's Row and Gayoso Street. Koch, who lived on Winchester Avenue, advertised his services as a watch repairer in the city directory that year. The 1860 *State Gazetteer* listed the firm's address more specifically as 4 Shelby Street.[14]

KUMMER, William F. Jewelry merchant. Nashville, Davidson County, 1814.

William F. Kummer announced in September 1814 that he had just arrived in Nashville with the "richest assortment of jewelry and pearl work ever brought to the western states." He identified Dauce Simon & Co. of Philadelphia as the manufacturers of his jewelry and indicated that he would display his wares at the Bell Tavern for one week only.[15]

LAIRD, D. B. Jeweler, watch and clock repairer. Trenton, Gibson County, 1848–50.

D. B. Laird was born in Pennsylvania about 1812. An advertisement for his watch and jewelry establishment placed him in Trenton, Gibson County, as early as 1848. In that notice, Laird observed that "Watches, Clocks, Music Boxes and Jewelry" would be "carefully repaired." He remained in Trenton at least through 1850; he lived in the household of J. D. Hill, tavern keeper at the Trenton Hotel.[1]

LAND, W. C. Watchmaker, jeweler, engraver. Memphis, Shelby County, 1843–44.

During 1843–44, W. C. Land was working "on Southside Exchange Square" in Memphis as a watchmaker,

W. C. LAND,

Watch Maker,

JEWELLER,

AND,

ENGRAVER,

South side Exch. Square,

Memphis, Ten.

WOULD inform the citizens of Memphis, and the adjacent country, that he has just received a full and complete assortment of *Watch Materials*, and is now fully prepared to execute all orders in the repairing line with neatness and dispatch. He has a small stock of Jewelry on hand, and a few dozen silver Table and Tea Spoons, at unusually low prices.

N. B. The Trade can be supplied with all kinds of Materials, at reasonable prices.

☞ Cash paid for old Gold and Silver.

January 27, 1843. 41-tf

92. *W. C. Land advertised in the* Memphis Weekly Appeal *of 7 July 1843 that he had received a "full and complete assortment of* Watch Materials*" and was "now fully prepared to execute all orders in the repairing line. . . ."*

jeweler, and engraver. In January and July 1843 he informed (fig. 92) the citizens of Memphis that he had received a full and complete assortment of watch materials and was fully prepared to execute "all orders in the repairing line with neatness and dispatch." He offered as well a small stock of jewelry and a few dozen silver tablespoons and teaspoons at "unusually low prices" and proffered cash for old gold and silver. A 15 December 1843 notice in the *Memphis Weekly Appeal* indicated that he intended to leave town,[2] yet he ran virtually the same advertisement in the same newspaper the following March.

LARKEN, John. Silversmith, clock and watchmaker, jeweler. Nashville, Davidson County, 1815.

A 21 September 1814 advertisement in the Louisville *Kentucky Correspondent* indicated that John Larken may have been a principal in the firm of "Tyler and Larkin" that noted experience in the watchmaking and silversmith business of both New York and Philadelphia.

In May 1815 Larken advertised in Nashville that he had served an apprenticeship in "one of the first shops in New York City" and had opened a shop "in the frame building owned by Willie Barrow, Esq., one door below

A Few fine silver lever **Watches** for sale at Lightfort's. As I am about to break and want to run away, I will sell them at cost, if not cheaper. Also, some **Accordeons,** (cheap edition,) on the same terms.

May 25, 1849.—tf

LATEST style (gold chains are out of fashion) **Steel Chains** are now the rage, of which there is plenty, at Lightfort's, also at cost.

May 25, 1849.—tf

93. *Robert L. Lightfort informed the citizens of Jackson that "Steel Chains are now the rage" and that "gold chains are out of fashion" in the Jackson* West Tennessee Whig *of 25 May 1849.*

93b. Bolivar house, built in *1835, that housed Robert Lightfort in the 1860s and served as an inn for stage coach passengers on the route from Memphis to Washington, D. C., 20th cen. Courtesy of A. L. Lightfort.*

93a. *Robert L. Lightfort (b.1828-d.1906) and Ellen Lightfort (b. 1834-d.?), 1895–1905. Private collection.*

R.L.LIGHTFORT STANDARD

93c. *"R. L. Lightfort" mark, 1850–55.*

Leintz's boot and shoe-manufactory" in Nashville. At that location he made and repaired timepieces, sold and repaired jewelry, and kept on hand a large supply of silver work "of the best workmanship."[3] Nothing further is known of his activity in Tennessee.

It appears that Larken later may have moved to Mississippi. A newspaper account listed the names of eleven people killed when a boiler of the steamboat *Constitution* burst near Natchez in May 1817. Among the deceased was an individual identified as John Larken, silversmith, of Natchez, Mississippi.[4]

LATTA, John. Apprentice watchmaker. Columbia, Maury County, 1860.

John Latta was a sixteen-year-old apprentice watchmaker in Columbia at the time of the 1860 census. He lived with his father, mother, two brothers, and two sisters in Columbia's District Nine.

LEDGER, George H. Silversmith. Somerville, Fayette County, 1850.

George H. Ledger was born about 1822 in England and moved to this country, settling in Somerville, Fayette County. In 1850 he was working as a silversmith and living in the household of Thomas Parks of Somerville.[5]

LEFEVER, Isaac. Silversmith. Cherry Valley, Wilson County, 1860.

Twenty-two-year-old Isaac Lefever was working as a silversmith at the time of the 1860 census for Wilson County, possibly for William Raney (q.v.), with whom Lefever lived at that time.

LEONARD, Hardin (Harding). Silver plater. Nashville, Davidson County, 1850–60.

Hardin Leonard was born about 1826 in Alabama; by 1846 he had moved to Tennessee. At the time of the 1850 census he was working in Nashville as a silver plater; his household included Mary, his wife, and their two Tennessee-born children, William, four, and Thomas, two. His estate was valued at $300.[6]

Three years later Leonard appeared in the *Nashville Business Directory* as a silver and brass plater at 71 North College Street. Shortly thereafter he moved to 69 North College Street, where he worked as a silver and brass plater and repairer of locks, keys, pistols, and guns until 1860. He lived on McGavock Street, where another son and three daughters were born.[7] The 1860 census for Davidson County recorded that Leonard estimated the value of his real property at $1,000 and his personal property at $300.

LEVY, Jonas. Silversmith, watchmaker. Memphis, Shelby County, 1855–60.

According to the 1850 census, Jonas Levy was a silversmith and watchmaker in Pulaski County, Arkansas.[8] A native of England, Levy had moved to Tennessee by 1855, the year he was working at 12 Union Street in Memphis.[9] In 1856 he was listed in the city directory as "Levy and Company, Jewelers," still at 12 Union between Main Street and Front Row, and he was similarly listed in the directory through 1860.[10] The 1860 *State Gazetteer* included Levy under "Jewelry, Watches, Clocks, Etc," but listed his address as 4 Union Street. At the time of the 1860 census he was fifty-two and living with his wife Rebecca in the Sixth Ward of Memphis.

LIDDON, A. Jeweler. Murfreesboro, Rutherford County, 1817?.

According to Goodspeed's *History of Tennessee*, a man named A. Liddon was among the earliest merchants in Murfreesboro, Rutherford County, a town incorporated on 17 October 1817. The county was organized by an act of the General Assembly in October 1803; the first county court meeting was held on 3 January 1804. A. Liddon, reported to have made the county seal, was identified as a jeweler and one of the town's earliest citizens.[11]

LIGHTFORT (LIGHTFOOT, LIGHTFORD), Robert L. Silversmith, watchmaker, jeweler. Jackson, Madison County, 1849–55; Bolivar, Hardeman County, 1860 and later.

Robert L. Lightfort (fig. 93a) was born in North Carolina about 1828. An advertisement placed him in Jackson, Madison County, Tennessee, by 1849. At that time he offered for sale a few fine silver lever watches at cost or less "as I am about to break and want to run away." He also advertised accordians and steel watch chains, noting that "gold chains are out of fashion."[12] A year later, however, a listing in the 1850 census indicated that silversmith R. L. "Lightfoot" remained a resident of Madison County and was living in the household of William Alexander. Shortly thereafter, in July 1851, Lightfort married a Scottish-born woman named Ellen "at the old cotton factory, near Whiteville."[13]

The 1853 *Nashville Business Directory* listed a silversmith named Lightfoot working in Madison County, and in 1855 R. L. "Lightford" advertised his services as a jeweler in the *Jackson Madisonian*. According to family history, in 1862 Lightfort and his wife purchased land in Bolivar, Hardeman County, and settled there. "Lightford" is listed as a resident of Hardeman County in the 1860 census, indicating the possibility that the family was living in Bolivar before 1862. At the time the value of Lightfort's personal property was estimated at $500. A 19 May 1876 Hardeman County court record of Daniel I. Well's estate listed R. L. Lightfort as the surviving partner in the firm of D. I. Wells and Company. Lightfort died on 13 November 1906.[14]

LINCH (LINCK), Francis. Merchant? Nashville, Davidson County, 1822.

Francis Linch and Company advertised in Nashville in 1822. The firm stocked gold and silver epaulettes and watch materials. Linch may have moved to Evansville, Indiana, for in March 1838 the *Nashville Daily Republican Banner* printed a notice about the death of Frances "Linck," a resident of Evansville and the daughter of Francis "Linck," Esq., formerly of Nashville.[15]

Watch & Clock Repairing

JAMES L. LINEBAUGH,

FORMERLY of Lexington, Kentucky, and lately of New-Orleans, respectfully informs the citizens of Denmark, and the adjacent counties, that he has commenced the above business, in Dr. Williamson's building, where Patent Lever Watches, Lapine, Duplex, Horizontal and Repeaters, can be carefully repaired and warranted. Also, plain Watches, Clocks, (Yankees excepted)—Silver ware and Jewelry made. Job work of every discription repaired.

Having served a regular apprenticeship of seven years and having worked in the principle cities in the north and south, he hopes to render a general satisfaction to those who may favor him with their custom.

Denmark, sept. 11, 1830.—tf.

☞N. B. The highest prices in work, given for old gold and silver. J. L. L.

94. *On 11 September 1830 "James L. Linebaugh, Formerly of Lexington, Kentucky, and lately of New Orleans," announced the opening of his watch and clock repairing business in Denmark, adding that he had "served a regular apprenticeship of seven years. . . ." (*Jackson Gazette, *11 Sept. 1830).*

LINDE, A. Gunsmith, dealer in watches, clocks, silverware. Memphis, Shelby County, 1850–60.

In 1850 A. Linde was listed in the *Memphis City Directory* as a dealer in guns and pistols, clocks, cutlery, and sporting equipment; it also was noted that Linde did repair work. According to the 1850 census for Shelby County, the German-born craftsman lived with his three children, Albert, aged thirteen, Flora, eleven, and Theo, five, in the city's Third Ward. By 1855 he had moved his shop from 26 Front Row to 217 Main Street opposite the Odd Fellows' Hall. In 1859 the *Memphis City Directory* listed him on Shelby Street near Union Street; he was included in an index entitled "Watches, Jewelry." The 1860 *State Gazetteer* listed him under "Jewelry, Watches, Clocks, Etc." at 8 Shelby Street.[16]

LINEBAUGH, James L. Silversmith, clock and watchmaker, jeweler. Denmark, Madison County, 1830.

According to one researcher, James L. Linebaugh, probably the son of Daniel Linebaugh, an early settler of Bardstown, Kentucky, worked with B. L. Linebaugh in the silversmithing business in Russellville, Kentucky, as early as 1819. The duration of James Linebaugh's residence in Russellville is unknown. In the summer of 1828 Linebaugh was located in Woodville, Mississippi, where he was working as a clock and watchmaker. By 1830 he had moved to Tennessee, and he advertised as a clock and watchmaker, jeweler, and silversmith in Denmark, Madison County. At that time he stated that he was "formerly of Lexington, Kentucky, and lately of New Orleans," and had served a "regular apprenticeship of seven years." The presence of other Linebaughs working in the same trade in Lexington was revealed in an 1808 advertisement by Robert Frazer, a clockmaker in that city, who offered a reward for runaway apprentice Samuel Linebaugh.[17]

LIVELY, William T. Silversmith. Chattanooga, Hamilton County, 1860.

William T. Lively was born in South Carolina about 1816. At the time of the 1860 census, Lively, his wife, and five children were living in Chattanooga, where he was working as a silversmith and owned personal property valued at $200.

LOVE, Daniel W. Watch and clockmaker. Knoxville, Knox County, 1826–27.

In 1813 Daniel Love, an orphan, was apprenticed to Thomas Cohen, a Lynchburg, Virginia, clockmaker and silversmith. Two years later the indenture was canceled when Cohen "removed to distant parts." By 1817 Love was working in Liberty (now Bedford), Virginia, as a watch and clockmaker.[18] In late 1826 and early 1827 he advertised in Knoxville that he was a former resident of Lynchburg, Virginia, and that he would make clocks and watches in a shop one door west of J. and W. Park's Store, immediately opposite the Knoxville Hotel. In addition, he offered his services as a "WHITE-SMITH." Love returned to Lynchburg about 1840.[19]

LUKINS, J. Jeweler. Murfreesboro, Rutherford County, 1837.

In 1837 J. Lukins was working as a jeweler in Murfreesboro, Rutherford County. Kovel noted a J. Lukens in Philadelphia during the same year. No relationship between Lukins and Lukens has been found.[20]

M'BURNEY, (....?). Clockmaker. Nashville, Davidson County, 1853.

In 1853 M'Burney, whose first name is unknown, was working in Nashville as a clockmaker and repairer of timepieces at "24 Deaderick st.—up Stairs."[1]

McCORMICK (McCORMACK), N. (M.) P. Watchmaker. Memphis, Shelby County, 1859–60.

By 1859 N. P. McCormick was working as a watchmaker at 139 Main Street in Memphis. The 1860 *State Gazetteer* listed "McCormack" at the same address.[2] The Shelby County census for that year listed a watchmaker, "M. P." McCormick, presumably the same man. He was born in Prussia about 1829 and lived in Memphis's First Ward.

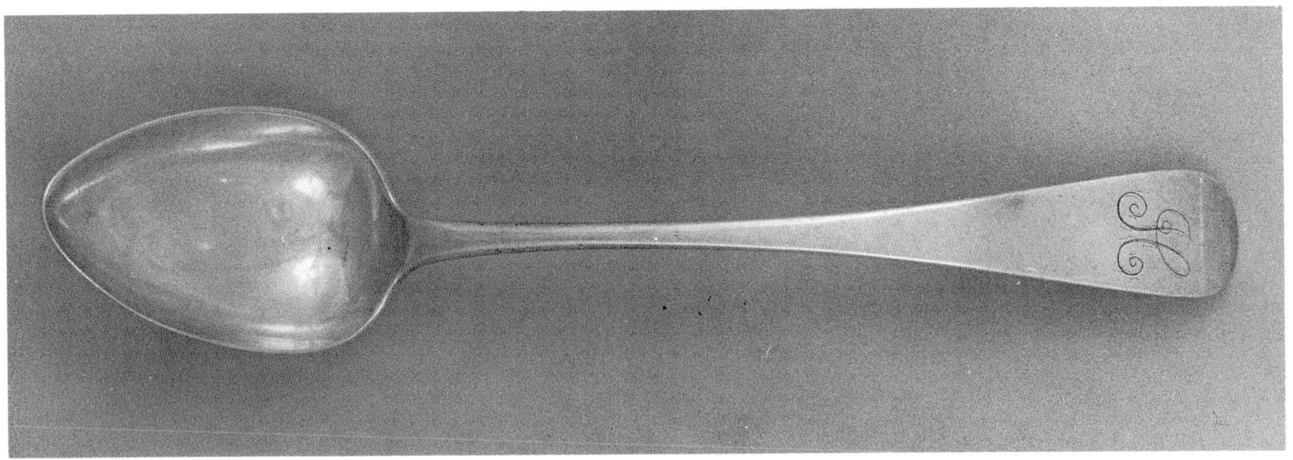

95, 95a. Serving spoon marked "MC COWAT," 1810, engraved "H," Jackson. LOA: 9 1/8". Private collection. The mark illustrated in fig. 95a is attributed to Thomas McCowat. McCowat apparently marked this spoon while he was working in Leesburg, Virginia.

McCOWAT (M'COWATT), Thomas. Silversmith. Nashville, Davidson County, 1823. Watchmaker, jeweler, Jackson, Madison County, 1838–53.

Thomas McCowat was born in Virginia about 1783. In 1811 he was working as a silversmith in Leesburg, Virginia, and looking for "an apprentice, a boy of mechanical genius and good morals." A spoon (fig. 95) is thought to represent McCowat's early nineteenth-century work in Leesburg. He and his family had moved to Tennessee by 1823 when their daughter, Malissa, was born.[3] On 19 July 1824 Thomas "M'Cowatt" advertised in the *Nashville Whig*, describing himself as a silversmith, formerly of Frankfort, Kentucky.

In an 1838 advertisement McCowat promised "assiduous attention" to watch repair and silversmithing at his shop on Market Street, one door north of the post office in Jackson. Appearing just below this advertisement was that of Elizabeth McCowat, the silversmith's wife, who announced that she intended to open a school for "girls and small boys" where she would teach grammar, geography, and needlework.[4]

McCowat remained in Jackson for more than a decade, expanding his stock to include "Brandeth's Pills,"[5] "Dr. Simmons' Vegetable Liver Medicine," and "Southern Tonic. A safe and certain cure for all kinds of Female disorder, and weakness. . . ."[6] At the time of the 1850 Madison County census, his household included his wife Elizabeth, four children, and B. J. Sneed (q.v.), another silversmith. He continued to work in Jackson through at least 1853.[7]

McCRACKEN, (McCRACKIN), William L.(S.) Jeweler, watch and clockmaker. Huntingdon, Carroll County, 1860.

William McCracken, born about 1841 in Tennessee, was listed as a watchmaker in the 1860 census for District Eleven of Huntingdon, Carroll County. He lived with his father, Robert McCrackin, who was the mayor of Huntingdon, his mother, and a brother. The 1860 *State Gazetteer* listed him under "Jewelry, Watches, Clocks, Etc."[8]

McDERMATE, C. Jeweler. Knoxville, Knox County, 1860.

Born in New York about 1833, C. McDermate was working as a jeweler in Knoxville at the time of the 1860 census.

McDOWEL, A. C. Silversmith. Hartsville, Sumner County, 1860.

A. C. McDowel, born about 1834 in Pennsylvania, was living in the Hartsville household of John Touson and working as a silversmith at the time of the 1860 census for Sumner County.

McFARLAND (McFARLANE), George W. Clock and watchmaker. Knoxville, Knox County, 1850–60.

George W. McFarland was born in Virginia about 1800. In 1822 a clockmaker named George McFarlane, perhaps the same man, advertised in the Fredericksburg *Virginia Herald*: "Should there be a sufficient number of

96. *McKiernan and Stout advertised in the Nashville* Clarion and Tennessee Gazette *of 4 November 1817 that they had added silver plating to their coach and harness making business.*

clocks in the neighborhood to make it a matter of consideration, he will make a yearly circuit, for the purpose of repairing them." His base of operations for this service was a tavern in Middlesex County.

McFarland and his Virginia-born wife, Matilda, arrived in Tennessee about 1840. By 1850 they were living in Knox County, where McFarland worked as a watchmaker.[9] Allowing for the various spellings of his name, McFarland may have been W. C. Danner's (q.v.) partner in the Knoxville firm of McFarlane and Danner (q.v.).[10]

By 1860 McFarland operated his own shop on Gay Street between Main and Cumberland streets in Knoxville; his residence was located at the corner of Church and Walnut streets.[11]

McFARLANE and DANNER. Jewelers. Knoxville, Knox County, 1857.

In 1857 the Gay Street jewelry firm of McFarlane and Danner offered its services to the citizens of Knoxville. The two partners were probably George W. McFarland (q.v.) and W. C. Danner (q.v.).[12]

McGUIRE, John M. Jeweler, watch and clockmaker. Dandridge, Jefferson County, 1860.

John M. McGuire, a native of Tennessee, was thirty-eight at the time of the 1860 census for Jefferson County, when his occupation was listed as farmer and silversmith. He appeared in the 1860 *State Gazetteer* listing under "Jewelry, Watches, Clocks, Etc."[13]

Cutten recorded Robert McGuire, a Martinsburg, Virginia silversmith who was working in 1803; no connection with John McGuire is known.[14]

McKENNY, John. Clockmaker. Memphis, Shelby County, 1860.

John McKenny, a seventy-year-old clockmaker from Scotland, was living in the First Ward of Memphis at the time of the 1860 census.

McKENZIE, J. G. Jeweler. Chattanooga, Hamilton County, 1857.

J. G. McKenzie was working as a jeweler in Chattanooga in 1857.[15]

McKIERNAN and STOUT. Coach makers, silver platers. Nashville, Davidson County, 1812?–19.

Bernard McKiernan and S. V. D. Stout (q.v.) were working together as early as 1812 when they announced their services as coachmakers to the readers of the *Nashville Whig*. An 1812 advertisement offered "CASH for old COPPER, BRASS and PEWTER" and sought a well-recommended blacksmith. The principal business of the firm lay in carriage making, and the partners regularly employed apprentice blacksmiths and harness makers. In 1814 they promised to finish both two-and-four-wheeled carriages "in a style equal to any in the eastern cities." In 1815 they added a "hack" or carriage service to Robertson and Sanders's Springs from Nashville on Mondays, returning on Tuesdays. An 1817 advertisement informed "their friends and the public" that they had added silver plating to their business.[16]

In January 1819 the firm was dissolved by mutual consent. Stout then joined with Henry Long "under the style of S. V. D. Stout & Co." (see Stout, Samuel Van Dyke) intending to devote his "whole attention" to the coach and harness making business. In August of that year, McKiernan offered for sale the silver plating establishment occupied by Stout.[17]

An 1820 notice of property for sale in Humphreys County owned by the two men is the last notice that has been found concerning their joint venture.[18]

McLAIN, R. Watchmaker, jeweler. Murfreesboro, Rutherford County, 1853.

In 1853 R. McLain was working in Murfreesboro, Rutherford County, as a watchmaker and jeweler. His shop was located on the east side of the square.[19]

McMURRAY (McMURRY, McMURREY), Thomas. Silversmith, clock and watchmaker. Maryville, Blount County, 1820.

In 1810 Thomas "M'Murray," advertised his need for a journeyman in a Frankfort, Kentucky, newspaper. His advertisement also stated that

> . . . as his affairs begin to wear a more favorable aspect, he conceives it necessary to inform the public, that the two grand evils which have prevented the Clock and Watch-Making business from flourishing in this place, have been want of abilities and extravagant [sic] charges—the former of which the subscriber will endeavor to overcome—and he pledges himself to the public, that the latter will be banished from his shop. The knowledge he has acquired of the business in some of the best shops in Pennsylvania, Ohio, and Kentucky, induces him to entertain the fond hope of giving general satisfaction to those who favor him with their custom.[20]

A year later he was working in Louisville, Georgia. By 1820 he was in Maryville, Blount County, where, according to the census of manufactures, his shop employed one assistant. During the year preceding the census, the shop had used three-and- one-half pounds of silver at $50 per pound, producing fourteen sets of spoons at $6 per set, and ten sets of gun mountings at $5 per set. McMurray's outlay for labor in 1820 totalled $325.[21]

MANCHESTER, Willard. Jeweler. Murfreesboro, Rutherford County, 1817. *Clock and watchmaker*, Nashville, Davidson County, 1822.

A list of the earliest merchants in Murfreesboro, Rutherford County, incorporated in 1817, was published in Goodspeed's *History of Tennessee*; among these individuals was W. Manchester, identified as a jeweler.[1] Manchester probably moved to Nashville shortly thereafter, for a "Will'd." Manchester was operating a clock and watchmaking shop there in 1822. In July of that year he announced that he had moved his store to College Street, nearly opposite the "Bank of the State," where he offered an assortment of jewelry and other goods "For Sale Cheap."[2]

MANNING, Benjamin. Watch and clockmaker, Nashville, Davidson County, 1822–24. *Jeweler*, Murfreesboro, Rutherford County, 1838. *Silversmith*, Pulaski, Giles County, 1850–60.

Benjamin Manning was born in Virginia about 1800. By July 1822 he had moved to Nashville, where he advertised his services as a watch and clockmaker. A year later he married Lucretia Anthony of the Nashville area.[3]

Manning eventually moved to Murfreesboro, where

CHEAPER! & CHEAPER!!

THE Subscriber would present his most grateful acknowledgments to his friends and the public generally, for past favors—and would inform them, that he has changed his business to that of a

CASH BUSINESS ONLY!

and feels no hesitation in saying he will be enabled, not only to sell his Jewelry, of which he has a very neat assortment, at prices much lower than has been known heretofore in this place, and will also, be enabled to execute all Jobs of work at a reduced price. He therefore would solicit a call and examination for a proof of the CASH SYSTEM.

BENJAMIN MANNING.

Murfreesboro, Feb'y 28, 1838.—3tf.

97. *"CHEAPER! & CHEAPER!!" announced Benjamin Manning in his notice of 28 February 1838; his business had become "CASH BUSINESS ONLY" (Murfreesboro* Tennessee Telegraph, *14 Mar. 1838, advertisement dated 28 Feb. 1838).*

in 1838 he announced that he would work only for cash, thereby enabling him to charge lower prices for his work and jewelry. At the time of the 1850 census Manning was working as a silversmith in Lynnville (now Pulaski), Giles County, where he lived with his wife and six children.[4] Ten years later he listed his occupation as watchmaker in the Giles County census and evaluated his real property at $1,500; his personal property was estimated at $1,800.

MANNING, William. Clock repairer. Lynnville, Giles County, 1860.

William Manning, twenty-five years old in 1860, worked as a clock repairer in Lynnville, Giles County, possibly for his father, Benjamin Manning (q.v.), with whom William lived. A native of Tennessee, the younger Manning evaluated his personal estate at $300.[5]

MARCUS, S. Watchmaker. Nashville, Davidson County, 1860.

In 1860 S. Marcus was working in Nashville as a watchmaker at 36 South Market Street.[6]

MARETO and ROJOUX. Watchmaker, jewelers. Memphis, Shelby County, 1859.

Mareto and Rojoux appeared at 180 Main Street, Memphis, in an 1859 city directory listing under "Watches and Jewelry." Mareto probably was A. Mereto (q.v.), a Memphis silversmith and watchmaker who was located at 179 Main Street from 1855–60.[6] Rojoux presumably was M. Rojoux (q.v.), a jeweler who apparently maintained a shop under his own name at 178 Main Street in 1859 in addition to working in partnership with Mareto at 180 Main.[7]

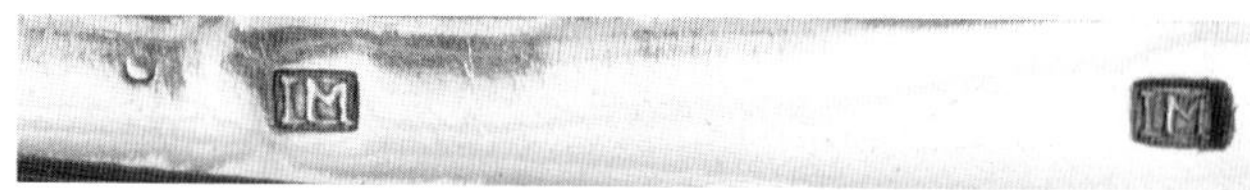

98. "I M" mark from a ladle found in Tennessee, 1805–25. Private collection, photograph by Bill Howell. It is possible that this mark was used by Isaac Martin; the mark is similar to that of Jacob Mohler (d.1773) of Boston, but the ladle dates later than 1773. It also is possible that either J. Miller or Joseph Mount used this mark.

MARTIN, Edwin. Silversmith, watch repairer. Winchester, Franklin County, 1853–60.

In 1853 Edwin Martin was working as a silversmith in Winchester, Franklin County. He operated a shop "near Mowdain house" at least through 1860 when the census of that year evaluated his personal estate at $9,000.[8] A native of South Carolina, Martin's household consisted of his Virginia-born wife and their three children.

An Edward Martin was listed in the Franklin County censuses for 1820 and 1830. It is possible that they were references to Edwin Martin.

MARTIN, Isaac. Jeweler. Nashville, Davidson County, 1808.

In August 1808 Isaac Martin offered for sale an assortment of jewelry and spectacles "at the cheapest rates" at Winn's Inn, Nashville. In the same month, Martin sold tickets for a lottery in which he intended to dispose of watches and jewelry.[9] An "IM" mark (fig. 98) on a Nashville ladle could represent Martin's signature. It also is possible that the mark is either that of J. Miller (q.v.) or Joseph Mount (q.v.).

MARTIN, Joseph. Silversmith. Memphis, Shelby County, 1860.

Joseph Martin, born about 1838 in New York, was working as a silversmith in the Seventh Ward of Memphis at the time of the 1860 census. Susan Martin, eighteen, also a New Yorker, lived with him.

MARTTERER, Andrew. Watchmaker. Nashville, Davidson County, 1860.

Andrew Martterer was nineteen at the time of the 1860 census for Nashville, Davidson County. He was listed as a watchmaker in the household of Frank A. and Bernhard L. Faller (q.q.v.); like the Fallers, Martterer was a native of Baden, Germany.

MASON, William J. Silversmith. McMinnville, Warren County, 1850.

William J. Mason was born in Georgia about 1821. He was in Tennessee by 1829; by 1850 he was a resident of McMinnville, Warren County, where he lived with his parents and sisters and was listed as a silversmith in the census for that year.[10]

MERETO (MARETO), A. Silversmith, clock and watchmaker, jeweler. Memphis, Shelby County, 1855–60.

In 1855 A. Mereto informed his friends "and the public generally" that he had moved to an elegant new store at 179 Main Street, at the corner of Adams and Main streets, in Memphis. He sold and repaired watches, clocks, and jewelry in that city at various addresses through 1860 when the *State Gazetteer* listed an "A. Mereto & Co." at 177 Main.[11] The federal census of that year listed Mereto, thirty-nine, a native of Italy, as a silversmith with personal property valued at $1,000. Mereto, Mary, his Irish wife, and their three-year-old son lived in Ward Two of Memphis.

MERRIMAN, Charles G. Jeweler. Memphis, Shelby County, 1850–59.

Charles G. Merriman was born in Connecticut in 1823. By 1850 he had moved to Memphis, where he was working as a jeweler and living in the household of William H. Batesman.[12] Charles Merriman was the brother of James E. Merriman (q.v.) and became a partner in the firm of J. E. Merriman and Company, which dealt in watches, jewelry, silverware, guns, and cutlery from 1847–60.[13] In the 1850 census of manufactures for Shelby County, Charles Merriman reported he had $500 invested in the "jewelry store." At that time, he was using $200 worth of gold annually, $100 worth of silver, and he employed three people. Merriman estimated the value and nature of his annual production: jewelry, $1,500; repair of watches, $1,400; clocks, $300; other work, $500.

The 1860 *Memphis City Directory* listed Merriman's residence as New Haven, Connecticut. There were a number of Merrimans in the New York and Connecticut silversmithing trade at the time.[14]

MERRIMAN, James E. Jeweler, watchmaker. Memphis, Shelby County, 1841–60 and later.

James E. Merriman was born in Connecticut in 1815, but by 1841 he had moved to Memphis, where he and Frederick H. Clark (q.v.) formed the jewelry, clockmaking, and silversmithing firm of Merriman and Clark.[15]

After the dissolution of that partnership in 1847, Merriman established the firm of J. E. Merriman and Company at 32 Front Row. His brother Charles (q.v.)

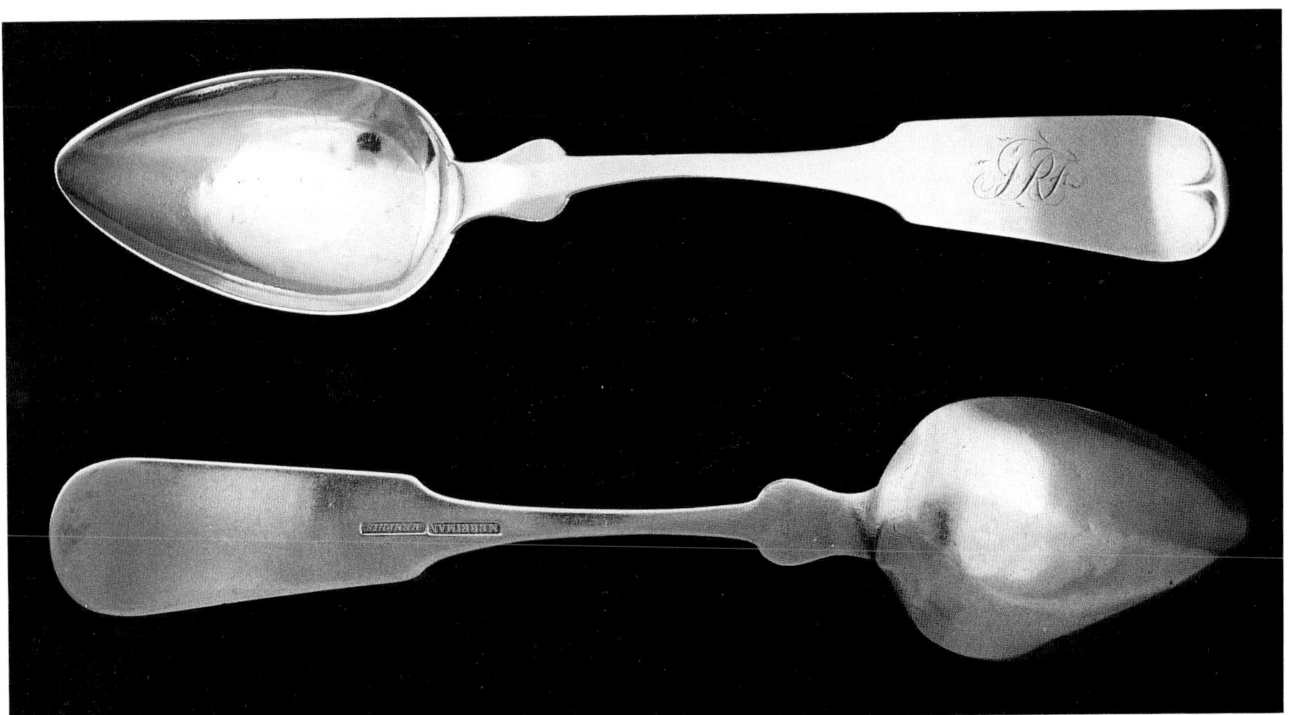

99a. Pair of teaspoons marked "MERRIMAN" and "MEMPHIS," 1841–47, engraved "JRF." LOA: 5⅞". Private collection.

99. "MERRIMAN" attributed to James Merriman; this mark may have been Merriman's earliest.

99b, 99c. Punch ladle marked "MERRIMAN MEMPHIS," 1841–47, engraved "M. E. G. Price." LOA: 13 13/16", width across bowl: 4 1/16", rise: 1⅞". Private collection. The "MEMPHIS" of the mark illustrated in fig. 99c has also been found on silver marked by F. H. Clark & Company and James Pooley (see figs. 54b, 54e, and 105a).

99d, 99e. *Pocket watch marked on enamel dial "J. E. MERRIMAN & CO./ MEMPHIS" and engraved on backplate of works "J. E. MERRIMAN / MEMPHIS," 1850–60.* 1$^{13}/_{16}$". *Private collection. It is probable that the watch works were of English manufacture.*

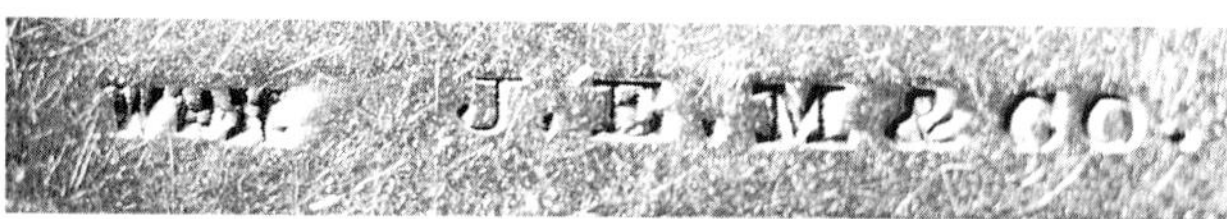

99h, 99i. *Two marks used by James Merriman, 1855–60. The mark illustrated in fig. 99h is from a spoon that also bears the "W & H" mark of Wood & Hughes (1840–99) of New York City. Merriman was one of several Tennessee silversmiths whose silver was manufactured in New York by Wood & Hughes (see also figs. 46b, 78a, 84, 121a, and 126a).*

99f, 99g. *Child's cup marked "MERRIMAN" on the bottom, 1850–55?, Memphis. HOA: 3⅜", width at rim: 2¾". Private collection. The inscription on the cup is not original. The mark illustrated in fig. 99g is incised.*

later became a partner in the firm. In a "public spirited" move, the brothers installed a stone sidewalk for the convenience of their customers in 1852, a refined feature contrasting with the usual plank walks that were subject to decay through weather and usage. The firm advertised "Watches, Clocks, Jewelry, Silverware, Gold Pens, Etc., Etc." at the Front Row address. By 1856 the firm had moved to 253 Main Street, where it remained through 1860.[16] At the time of the Shelby County census for 1865, Merriman, aged forty-five, listed the value of his real property at $50,000 and his personal property at $1000. Other members of his household included four Merriman children ranging in age from three to thirteen; R. H. Wilcox (q.v.), another jeweler, was also a resident in the household.

During the 1850s, M. Rojoux, Samuel M. Jobe, R. F. Wilcox, William Gaylord, W. C. Byrd, and W. L. Jobe (q.q.v.) all worked for J. E. Merriman and Company.[17] During this period the firm evidently imported finished wares from northern shops and produced work of its own. One spoon bears the marks (fig. 99h) of both the Merriman firm and that of Wood and Hughes of New York, working 1840–49. The Merriman firm was not the only Tennessee shop to handle the work of Wood and Hughes; B. H. Stief (q.v.) of Nashville was another (see fig. 121a).

By 1860 Frank G. Bingham had joined the firm, and soon after this the firm's name was changed to Merriman, Byrd and Company, when W. C. Byrd became elevated to a partner.[18] The nature of Frank G. Bingham's service to the firm remains uncertain.

Paul R. Coppock noted in a Memphis newpaper article written more than one hundred years later that during the Reconstruction period following the Civil War, James E. Merriman joined interests with certain "carpetbaggers and scalawags" who ruled Memphis. After their fall from power about 1870, Merriman's success allegedly faltered. Byrd took over the jewelry business, and Merriman, along with R. F. Wilcox, opened another Main Street store that retailed pianos, organs, and sewing machines.[19]

MERRIMAN and CLARK. Watchmakers, jewelers. Memphis, Shelby County, 1841–47.

James E. Merriman (q.v.) and Frederick H. Clark (q.v.) formed a partnership in 1841 that was one of the earliest businesses in Memphis and thus profited from the first real spurt of growth in the city's population.[20] The partners maintained their jewelry and watch and clockmaking firm on Exchange Square, where they advertised "an utter dislike for everything false or 'sham' in its nature." They asserted that they were "careful to deal in nothing that has not the indelible stamp of sterling worth upon it." Their use of the term "sterling" during this period was unusual. The firm also stocked Willard clocks and Colt revolvers.[21] These gun sales probably served as a convenience to those heading into the undeveloped territories of Arkansas, Texas and beyond.[22] An 1844 advertisement offered even more diverse services from the firm: daguerreotypes guaranteed to represent "a perfect facsimile of your face with all the natural colors" at the cost of five dollars.[23]

In 1847 the partnership was dissolved and Clark established the competing firm of F. H. Clark and Company (q.v.); Merriman opened his own establishment, J. E. Merriman and Company.[24]

MILLER, B. (A. B.) Jeweler. Memphis, Shelby County, 1855–60?.

In 1855 B. Miller was working as a jeweler for Frederick H. Clark (q.v.) in Memphis and living on Shelby

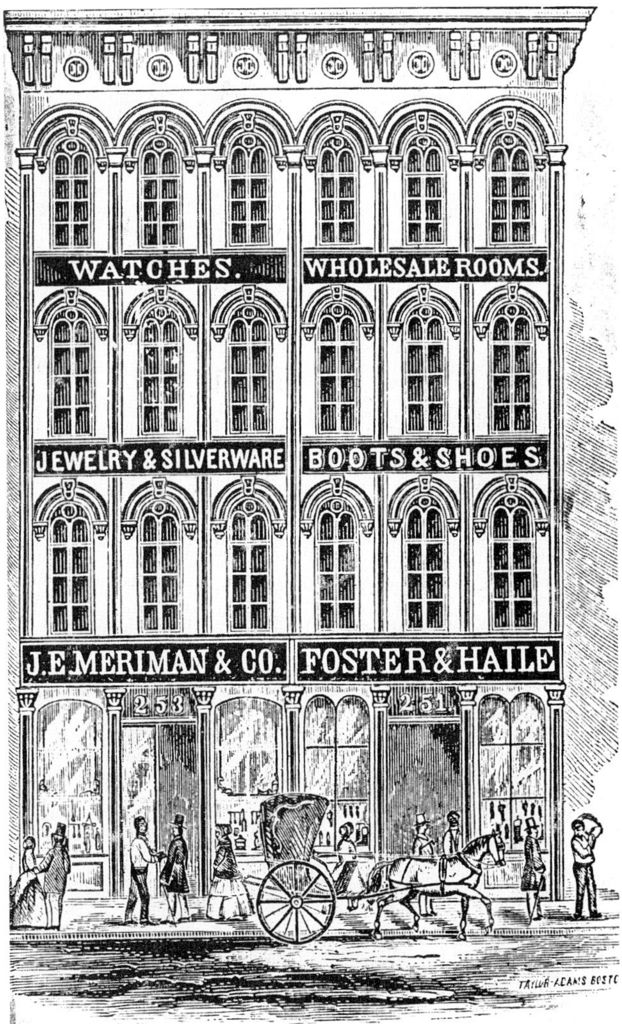

99j. *The James E. Merriman firm at 263 Main Street as it appeared in the Memphis city directory for 1859.*

99k, 99l. *Marks used by James E. Merriman and W. C. Byrd, 1860–70. Courtesy of the Tennessee State Museum, photographs by Stephen D. Cox. Byrd's name is misspelled on the mark illustrated in fig. 99l, an indication that the silver was manufactured elsewhere.*

Street between Linden and McCall streets. An "A. B." Miller, probably the same man, was a partner in the firm of Miller and Leptien (q.v.), which was listed in the 1856–57 *Memphis City Directory*.[25] A. B. Miller, aged thirty-three, was also listed as a jeweler in the 1860 census for Ward Two of Memphis; Miller was recorded as a native of Prussia.

MILLER, Charles. Jeweler. Memphis, Shelby County, 1860.

In the 1860 census for Memphis, Charles Miller stated that his occupation was that of a jeweler and estimated the value of his real property at $7,000 and his personal property at $1,000. Miller, born about 1825 in Germany, lived with Dolley, also a native of Germany, and four children ranging in age from one to ten, all born in Tennessee.

MILLER, J. Clock and watchmaker, silversmith. Nashville, Davidson County, 1823.

J. Miller apparently was associated with William Murrell (q.v.) in the firm of Miller and Murrell early in 1823. Later that same year, Miller briefly worked in partnership with Joseph Mount at J. Elliston's (probably John Elliston's [q.v.]) former shop in Nashville.[26]

Miller may have been related to J. D. Miller, a blacksmith and whitesmith of Nashville (working circa 1817–20).[27] An "IM" mark (see fig. 98) on a Nashville ladle may have been Miller's.

MILLER, John. Silversmith. Rogersville, Hawkins County, 1850.

John Miller was born in Tennessee about 1811 and was working as a silversmith in East Tennessee at the time of the 1850 census for Hawkins County.

MILLER, John. Watchmaker. Knoxville, Knox County, 1859?–60.

John Miller, born about 1828 in Kentucky, was working as a watchmaker in Knoxville at the time of the 1860 census. This man may have been a principal in the firm of Danner and Miller (q.v.).[28]

MILLER, Willie B. Retailer of jewelry. Bolivar, Hardeman County, 1835.

Willie B. Miller of Bolivar, Hardeman County, in an advertisement in the 14 January 1835 *Bolivar Free Press*, thanked his customers for their patronage during the preceding year and announced the arrival of a new shipment of goods. His stock included clothing, jewelry, saddles, books, and groceries.

A silversmith named William Miller was working in Charleston, South Carolina, about 1819; no connection with Tennessee's Willie Miller has been established.[29]

MILLER and LEPTIEN. Watchmakers. Memphis, Shelby County, 1856–57.

In 1856 A. B. Miller (Miller, B. [A. B.], q.v.) and F. Leptien organized the firm of Miller and Leptien, dealers in watches, clocks, and jewelry in a shop on Shelby Street near Union Street in Memphis. Their establishment offered silver plating, silvering, "fire and galvanic gilding," and all kinds of metal work.[30]

MILLER and MOUNT. Clock and watchmakers, silversmiths. Nashville, Davidson County, 1823.

In the fall of 1823, J. Miller (q.v.) and Joseph Mount (q.v.) formed a partnership that lasted for one month. They made and repaired all kinds of clocks, watches, jewelry, and silverware; they were located in J. Elliston's former shop. When the two men discontinued their association, Mount remained at the same location.[31]

MILLER and MURRELL. Clock and watchmakers, silversmiths. Nashville, Davidson County, 1823.

At the March 1823 sale of articles from the estate of deceased Nashville silversmith John Elliston (q.v.), one of the major purchasers was the firm of Miller and Murrell. The firm appears to have been engaged in the sale of jewelry, watchmaking, and silversmithing in view of the articles purchased: "16 pair Gold Ear rings . . . 10 Gold Barrells . . . 24 Finger Rings . . . 1 set of Smith Tools . . . three Gross [450] Watch Glass . . . 2 Show Case."[32]

Murrell probably was silversmith William Murrell (q.v.) who had once been Joseph T. Elliston's (q.v.) apprentice; Miller may have been J. Miller (q.v.) of Nashville.[33]

MITCHELL, Morris. Watchmaker. Memphis, Shelby County, 1849?–50.

Morris Mitchell was born in England about 1821. Mitchell and Mary, his Irish wife, had moved to Tennessee by 1849 when a son, Charles, was born. They probably were living in Memphis at the time, for Mitchell appeared shortly thereafter in the 1850 Shelby County census as a watchmaker. There is an 1860 Memphis listing for a Morris Mitchell in the cotton business; he worked for Sample Mitchell and Company, cotton brokers.[34]

MOORE, Andrew. Jeweler, watch and clockmaker. Columbia, Maury County, 1857–60.

Andrew Moore worked as a jeweler and watch and clockmaker at William R. Hodge's (q.v.) "old stand" in Columbia some time during 1846–50. Presumably he was the same "A. Moore" listed in the 1857 *Nashville Business Directory* as a silversmith in Columbia.[35]

In the 1860 census for Maury County, Andrew Moore listed his occupation as watchmaker and estimated his real property and personal property at $500 respectively.

MORGAN, E. O. Watchmaker. Jackson, Madison County, 1860.

In 1860 twenty-five-year-old E. O. Morgan was working as a watchmaker in Jackson, Madison County, and living in the household of "And. Coller" who, according to the census taken that year, was a "car builder."

MORGAN, J. B. Silversmith. Jefferson County, 1860.

At the time of the 1860 census for Jefferson County, J. B. Morgan, aged thirty-one, was working as a silversmith and living with "A. [Morgan]," his North Carolina-born wife. The couple had six children ranging in age from five months to eight years. Morgan and the children were all natives of Tennessee. Morgan estimated the value of his personal property at $500.

MORROW, George D. Jeweler, watch and clockmaker? Savannah, Hardin County, 1860.

George D. Morrow was listed in the 1860 *State Gazetteer* under "Jewelry, Watches, Clocks, Etc." for Savannah, Hardin County.[36] At the time of the Hardin County census for that year Morrow, aged sixty-two, listed his occupation as "physician." Morrow, his wife, and six children ranging in age from six months to seventeen, were all born in Tennessee.

MORTON, T. D. Dealer in watches, clocks, jewelry, and silver-plated ware. Nashville, Davidson County, 1860.

T. D. Morton advertised in the 1860 *Nashville Business Directory* as a wholesale dealer in watches, clocks, jewelry, and silver-plated ware. His shop was located at the corner of Cedar and Cherry streets and his residence was at 28 Spruce Street.[37]

MOSES, O. H. Watchmaker, dealer in watches, clocks, jewelry. Clarksville, Montgomery County, 1860.

O. H. Moses, born about 1830, was working as a watchmaker in Clarksville, Montgomery County, at the time of the 1860 census. He lived "north and east of the Cumberland River" with Margaret, his New-York-born wife, and two young sons. His name appeared in the 1860 *State Gazetteer* under "Watchmaker and Jewelers" in Clarksville; his shop was located on the "East Side [of the] Public Square." Moses further identified himself in a second listing in the same Gazetteer as a "Watchmaker & Dealer in Watches, Clocks and Jewelry."[38]

MOUNT, Joseph. Clock and watchmaker, silversmith. Nashville, Davidson County, 1823–26.

In October 1823 Joseph Mount, a Nashville silversmith, joined J. Miller (q.v.) in the partnership of Miller and Mount (q.v.) at the "well known stand of J. Elliston [q.v.], dec'd." The partnership was dissolved a month later, but Mount remained at the same location, where he made and repaired clocks, watches, jewelry, and silverware.[39]

At some point Mount temporarily moved out of his shop while it was under repair, but by April 1826 he had resumed business at the same place, which was located next door to the firm of Stewart and Charter on the south side of the square.[40] A Nashville ladle marked "IM" (see fig. 98) may be Mount's work.

MOWELL, W. Watchmaker, jeweler. Nashville, Davidson County, 1860.

W. Mowell appeared in the 1860 *State Gazetteer* under "Watchmakers and Jewelers" for Nashville, Davidson County.[41]

MULKEY, James J. Watchmaker, silversmith?. Chattanooga, Hamilton County, 1849?–50.

James J. Mulkey was born in Georgia about 1819. He married Margaret (....?), a South Carolina woman, and by about 1849, had moved his family to Tennessee. At the time of the 1850 census, Mulkey was living in Chattanooga, where he worked as a watchmaker. At the time, another jeweler, Henry M. Collins (q.v.), and a laborer, George Ca[m]ren, lived with the Mulkeys and their three children.[42] The mark "J. J. M" (fig. 100a) on spoons (fig. 100) found in Tennessee may represent the work of Mulkey.

By 1855 Mulkey had moved to Little Rock, Arkansas, where he remained through 1860.[43]

MULLER, Christian. Jeweler. Memphis, Shelby County, 1857–59.

In 1857 Christian Muller was working as a jeweler on Madison Street in Memphis. By 1859 he had moved to 341 Main Street in the same city, where he offered his services as both jeweler and optician.[44]

MURRELL, William. Silversmith's apprentice. Nashville, Davidson County, 1814. *Clock and watchmaker, silversmith*, 1823.

Joseph T. Elliston (q.v.), the Nashville silversmith, offered a $10 reward for William Murrell when his young apprentice ran away in January 1814. Elliston described Murrell as "about 16 years old, well made, blue eyes, down look when spoken to."[45]

At the sale of the estate of John Elliston (q.v.) in 1823, the firm of Miller and Murrell (q.v.), one partner of which is thought to have been Murrell, was a principal purchaser of tools and goods.[46]

MUSGROVE, J. D. Gold & silver manufacturer. Nashville, Davidson County, 1860.

According to the 1860 *Nashville City and Business Directory*, J. D. Musgrove worked in Nashville as a gold and silver manufacturer. The same directory carried an "S. Musgrove," gold and silver manufacturer, who was certainly the silversmith Samuel Musgrove (q.v), at 20 Deaderick Street. The two men may have been related.[47]

100, 100a. *Pair of tablespoons marked "J J. M.," 1849–55, engraved "ET," Tennessee. LOA: 7⅝". Private collection. The mark illustrated in fig. 100a may be that of James J. Mulkey.*

MUSGROVE, Samuel. Silversmith. Nashville, Davidson County, 1853–60.

Samuel Musgrove was born in Kentucky in 1800, one of ten children of Cuthbert Musgrove, a Scotsman, and Elizabeth Moore Musgrove. In March 1820, at the age of twenty, Musgrove entered into partnership with Cincinnati, Ohio, silversmith Abner Scotcher; the duration of this partnership was only one month. Musgrove apparently continued working in Cincinnati, for in 1827 a "James Phillips returned to set in again to work with Samuel Musgrove to learn the silversmithing business."[48]

An 1831 entry in the Cincinnati diary of J. Deterly noted that a silver breastplate, which had been on a David Kilgour's coffin at the time of his burial, had "turned up" for sale at S. Musgrove's shop. In *Silversmiths of Kentucky*, Boultinghouse suggested that "there was certainly one nefarious hand" involved in the removal of the breastplate from the coffin, but it was not necessarily Musgrove's.[49]

Musgrove appeared in Cincinnati directories through 1840, but by the time of the 1850 census he had moved to Larue County, Kentucky. By 1853 he was located at 188 North Cherry Street in Nashville. Subsequent Nashville directories placed him at 25 Public Square in 1855, 20 Deaderick Street in 1857, 20 South Cherry Street in 1859, and again at 20 Deaderick in 1860. The 1860 *State Gazetteer* included him in its Nashville listings for "Silversmiths and Platers" and "Watchmakers and Jewelers," and a Nashville directory for the same year listed an "S. Musgrove" as a "gold and silver manufacturer."[50]

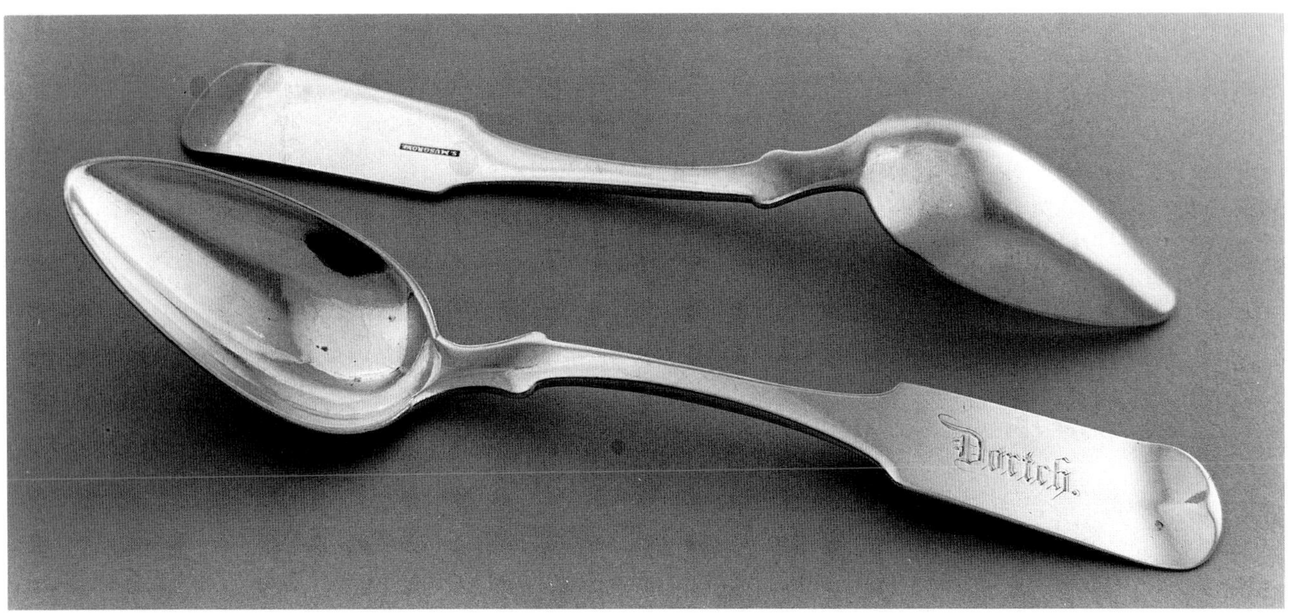

101, 101a. *Pair of serving spoons marked "S. MUSGROVE" in a rectangle, 1850–60, engraved "Dortch," Nashville. LOA: 8", width across bowl: 1¼". Courtesy of the Tennessee State Museum. The mark illustrated in 101a is attributed to Samuel Musgrove.*

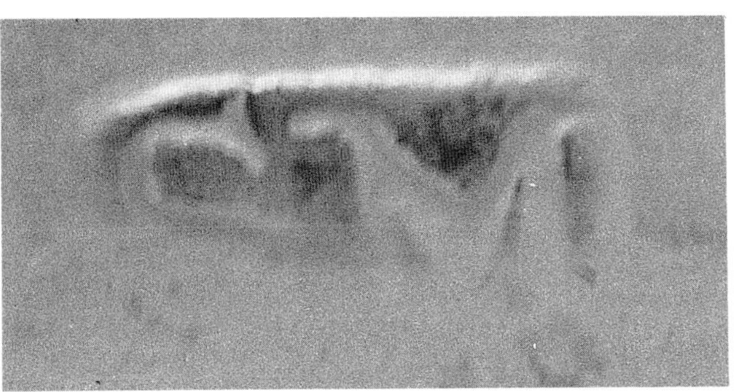

101b, 101c. *Two marks attributed to Samuel Musgrove, 1850–60.*

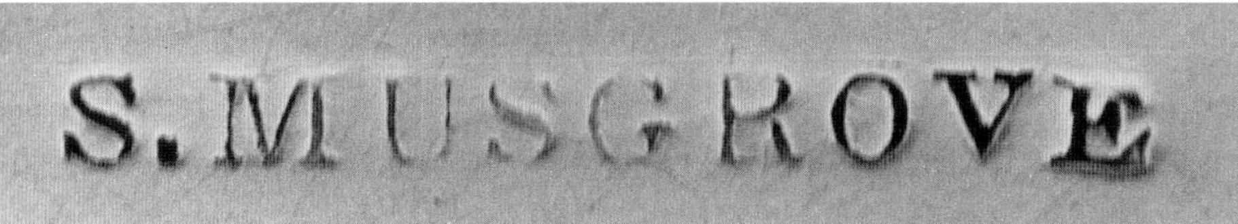

An "SM" mark (fig. 101b) possibly may be the early touch of Samuel Musgrove; the spoon on which it appears was found in Tennessee. A positive attribution cannot be made, although the style of the Roman letters compare favorably with those of a documented mark (fig. 101a).

MYER, L. Watchmaker. Memphis, Shelby County, 1860.

L. Myer, who was born in France about 1815, was working as a watchmaker and living in the Fifth Ward of Memphis at the time of the 1860 census.

NANCE (NANCER), William. Silversmith. Smith County, 1860.

In the 1860 census for Smith County, nineteen-year-old William Nance was listed as a silversmith with a personal estate of $100. He lived with his father, mother, and seven brothers and sisters, all natives of Tennessee, in the Twelfth District of Smith County. His shop was located in District One of the same county, probably in the town of Carthage.

Watches and Jewelry.

PAUL NEGRIN,

WATCH MAKER & JEWELLER.

(FROM FRANCE)

HAS the honor to inform the inhabitants of Nashville and its vicinity, that he has opened his shop at the Office lately occupied by Doctor Roane, near the Branch Bank; and offers for sale a variety of articles in his line of busines. He also repairs Watches and Jewelry, in the best manner, and on reasonable terms.

Nashville, Dec. 8th, 1823.—tf

102. *On 8 December 1823 Paul Negrin, "WATCHMAKER & JEWELLER (From France)" announced the opening of his shop in Nashville (*Nashville Whig, *8 Dec. 1823).*

102a, 102b. *Serving spoon marked "P. NEGRIN" in a rectangle with trimmed corners, 1830–40, engraved "Southall," Nashville. LOA: 8¾". Courtesy of Belle Meade Mansion.*

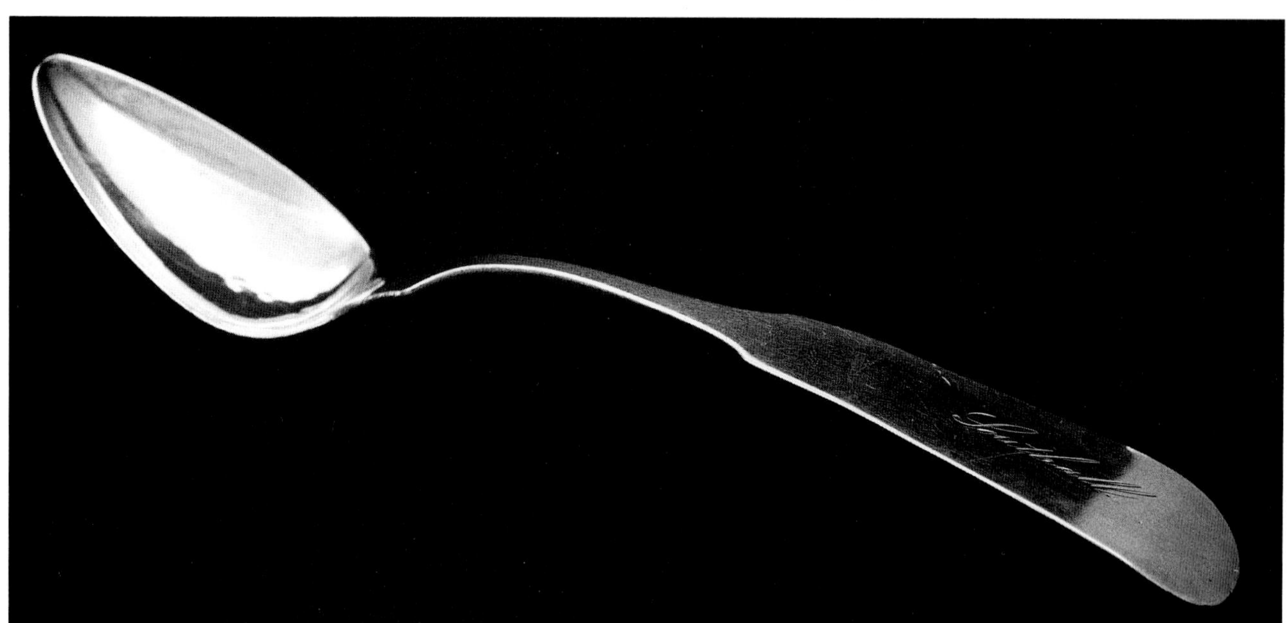

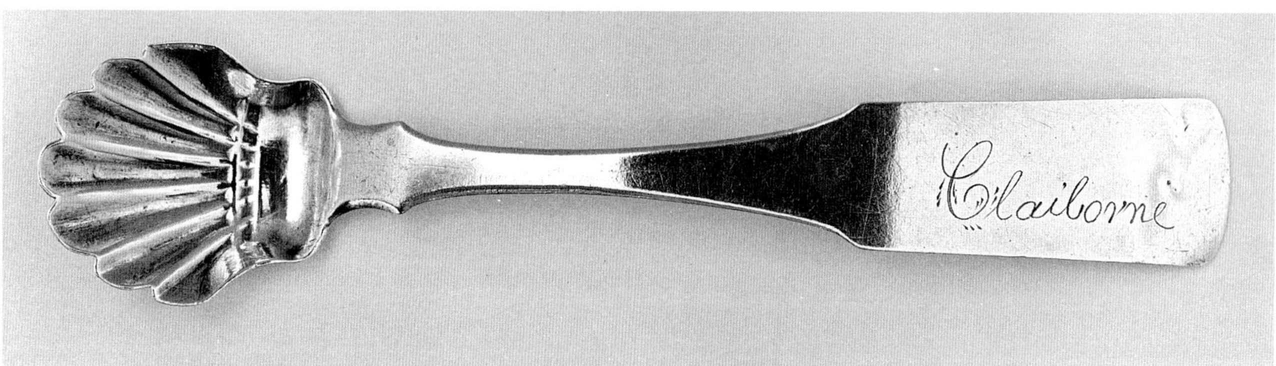

102c. *Salt spoon marked "P. NEGRIN" in a serrated rectangle, 1830–40, engraved "Claiborne," Nashville. LOA: 4 1/16". Private collection, MRF S-13,433.*

102d, 102e. *Two marks used by Paul Negrin, 1830–40. The mark illustrated in fig. 102d was struck by the same die as that of the salt spoon in fig. 102c.*

NEGRIN, Paul. Watchmaker, jeweler, silversmith, retailer. Nashville, Davidson County, 1823–44.

Paul Negrin was born in France and arrived in Nashville via Charlottesville, Virginia, where he operated a watch and jewelry shop. Cutten, in *Silversmiths of Virginia*, confirmed Negrin's presence there from 1820–23.[1]

In a December 1823 advertisement (fig. 102) "PAUL NEGRIN, WATCHMAKER & JEWELLER (From France)" informed the citizens of Nashville that he had opened a shop at an office near the "Branch Bank" formerly occupied by Dr. Roane.[2] Negrin's advertisements appeared regularly in the Nashville newspapers and reflected a growing business. In 1825 he offered gold and silversmithing services as well as jewelry, cut-glass lamps, plated china, sheet music, perfumes, buttons, and military goods.[3] By 1826 he had moved to a presumably larger shop on College Street next door to the "New State Bank." There he exhibited samples of work by T. V. Peticolas, who taught "young ladies" painting and music.[4]

In 1836 Negrin signed an agreement with eight other men in the trade to set prices on silver and repair work, thus forming the "Association of the Watch-Makers, Silversmiths & Jewellers of Nashville (see Appendix I)."[5] The formation of the group may have reflected the economic instability of those years.

Negrin apparently kept abreast of the fluctuation between the values of gold and silver and paper money. In May 1837 an advertisement signed by Paul Negrin sought gold and silver in return for bank notes, promising to accept the notes of both Yeatman, Woods and Company, and Union and Planters' banks of Tennessee as payment for work.[6] National bank policy increasingly drained the frontier of gold and silver specie through 1837.[7] A January 1838 advertisement asked for $10,000 in gold and silver bullion, offering a liberal premium for the exchange. By May 1838 Negrin promised gold and silver for Mississippi bank notes.[8]

A 24 December 1844 advertisement in the *Nashville Union* stated that P. Negrin, who was located on Union Street, had "just received, per steamboat *China*, a new addition to his large variety consisting in part of Gold Pencils; Dolls and a great variety of Children's toys—all suitable for Christmas Presents."

NIX, Samuel T. Watchmaker. Lebanon, Wilson County, 1860.

In 1860 thirty-eight-year-old Samuel T. Nix was working as a "watch smith" in Lebanon. He lived with Levina, his wife, and two children, all natives of Tennessee. In the 1860 census for Wilson County, he evaluated his real property at $4,200 and his personal property at $1,400.

NOEL, Ben C. Jeweler, watchmaker. Nashville, Davidson County, 1860.

Nineteen-year-old Ben C. Noel identified himself as a jeweler in the 1860 census for Nashville, Davidson County. Born in Arkansas, Noel lived in the same household as Joshua Flowers (q.v.) and Edwin B. Daley (q.v.). He worked as a watchmaker in the firm of W. Noel (q.v.) at 20 Deaderick Street, Nashville.[9] A Beverly Noel, jeweler, worked in Frankfort and Louisville, Kentucky (circa 1826–44);[10] it is possible that the Noels working in the trade in Kentucky may have been related to those in Tennessee (see Noel, Theodore; Noel, W.).

NOEL, Theodore. Watchmaker, silversmith. Memphis, Shelby County, 1849–60.

Theodore Noel was born in Kentucky about 1814. He married a Louisiana-born woman named Eugenia Dillard; their first child was born in Mississippi in 1842, their second in Tennessee about 1844. By 1849, according to a city directory, Noel was working as a silversmith in Memphis. In the 1850 census for Shelby County, he gave his occupation as watchmaker, and the 1850 census of manufactures for that county revealed that Noel's firm grossed $550 for the year, mostly in charges for the repair of watches. The 1856–57 *Memphis City Directory* listed him as a watchmaker at the corner of Main and Union Streets, with a residence on Shelby Street. W. Noel (q.v.), later of Nashville, also worked at the same address; it is probable that the two men were related.[11]

By 1859 Theodore Noel's business had moved to 15 Court Street. He appeared in both the 1860 *Memphis City Directory* and the 1860 *State Gazetteer* under jewelry, watches and clocks, still at 15 Court Street.[12] By the time of the 1860 census, Noel, his wife, and five children lived in the Sixth Ward of Memphis. He gave his occupation as jeweler, and he valued his real and personal property at $8,000 each.

A Theodore Noel, watchmaker and jeweler, was working in Frankfort, Kentucky, about 1830; he may have been the same man as the Memphis artisan.[13]

NOEL, W. (M.). Watchmaker. Nashville, Davidson County, 1853, 1859; Memphis, Shelby County, 1856–57.

W. Noel is believed to have been in Nashville in 1853; a business directory of that year listed "W. M. Noel" at 75 North Cherry Street. Noel moved to Memphis for a short period; the *Memphis City Directory* for 1856–57 noted his presence there, as did the 1857 *Nashville Business Directory* under its Memphis listings which included "Noel, W., watchmaker, northwest corner of Main and Union." At the time, he lived on Shelby Street between Linden and Beal streets in Memphis. Theodore Noel (q.v.), also a watchmaker, shared the same business and residence addresses.[14]

Having returned to Nashville by 1859, Noel, who referred to himself as a "scientific and practical watchmaker," advertised that he repaired watches at 47 Cherry Street and that he had "thirty-four years' experience in the business." By 1860 Noel had moved to 20 Deaderick Street; his residence was located on Mulberry Street. Ben C. Noel (q.v.), also a watchmaker, worked at the same location during the same year.[15]

It seems likely that a Washington Noel, who was working in Louisville, Kentucky, about 1836, as well as a W. Noel, watchmaker, working in Arkansas about 1843, were the same man as W. Noel of Nashville and Memphis.[16]

NORTHERN, Samuel. Silversmith. Columbia, Maury County, 1817–28?; Davidson County, 1829?–60 and later; Williamson County, d. 1871.

Samuel Northern arrived in Columbia in 1817, according to Nathan Vaught, a contemporary. Northern and his wife, Polly Hodge Northern, with their "young and growing family" remained in Maury County for about ten years; during that time, Northern taught his brothers-in-law, James and William R. Hodge (q.q.v), the silversmithing trade.[17] The Hodges eventually took over the shop when the Northern family moved back to Davidson County.[18] Northern apparently continued working in that county through at least 1863, for an inventory of T. C. White's estate recorded in the Davidson County clerk's office on 4 September 1863 revealed that White's estate owed Samuel Northern $15.75. White's inventory contained silver spoons, goblets, a pitcher, and a waiter.[19]

According to Garrett's *Obituaries from Tennessee Newspapers*, Samuel Northern died in 1871 at the age of 81; he was in Williamson County at the time of his death.[20]

NUCKOLLS, John. Gold and silversmith, watchmaker, jeweler. Jackson, Madison County, 1824.

John Nuckolls advertised in May 1824 that he had commenced business as a gold and silversmith, watchmaker, and jeweler in Jackson, Madison County.[21]

O'HARA, John P. Silver plater. Memphis, Shelby County, 1855–59.

In 1855 John P. O'Hara was working as a silver plater at 201 Second Street in Memphis; he lived at 29 Third Street. The 1859 *Memphis City Directory* listed a James P. O'Hara, silver plater, on Beale Street;[22] he probably was the same man.

PAILLARD, Ed. Watchmaker. Nashville, Davidson County, 1859.

Ed. Paillard appeared in the 1859 *Nashville City Directory* as a watchmaker at 16 Public Square, the address of William Henry Calhoun's (q.v.) shop. E. Raby (q.v.), another watchmaker, worked at the same address.[1] It is probable that both men were Calhoun's employees.

PARKES, Thomas. Dealer in jewelry. Franklin, Williamson County, 1860.

Thomas Parkes of Franklin, Williamson County, described himself as a "Dealer in books, stationery, watches, jewelry" in the 1860 *State Gazetteer* and appeared in that volume's listing for jewelry, watches, and clocks.[2]

PARKHURST, Henry. Silver plater. Nashville, Davidson County, 1855–60.

In 1855 Henry Parkhurst was working in Nashville as a silver and brass plater; he was in partnership with A. B. Williams (q.v.) in the firm of Williams and Parkhurst (q.v.), a silver plating firm, at 6 Deaderick Street. Both men lived at 74 Union Street.[3]

By 1857 Parkhurst had moved into his own establishment at 12½ Deaderick Street, between the square and Cherry Street. There he stocked harness mountings and "all kinds of house and number Plating, Bell Pulls, and Door Knobs." He remained "upstairs" at 12½ Deaderick through at least 1860, when the census of that year listed him as a forty-five-year-old silver plater from New Jersey.[4]

PARMAN, E. Watchmaker. Memphis, Shelby County, 1860.

At the time of the 1860 census, E. Parman, a twenty-year-old watchmaker born in Ohio, was living in the same household in the Second Ward of Memphis with watchmakers F. H. Trudeau (q.v.), W. L. Jobe (q.v.), and jeweler William Todd (q.v.).

PARROT, Alfred M. Silversmith's apprentice. Nashville, Davidson County, 1817. *Silversmith*, Cairo, Sumner County, 1820.

Alfred M. Parrot, an apprentice with the Nashville silversmithing firm of Richmond and Flint (q.v.), ran away in 1817, and the partners offered a twenty-dollar reward for his return. Parrot was described as "about 18 years of age, stout made . . ." wearing a ". . . dark woollen coat, vest, pantaloons & fur hat." The public was advised that he might have "secreted about some boat, with an intention of going down to New Orleans, where he has a brother, or may have gone to his father who lives in Jackson County."[5]

Whether Parrot ever returned to complete his apprenticeship is not known, but three years after the runaway notice appeared, an A. M. Parrot advertised his intention to "commence the manufacturing of Silver Table and Tea Spoons, Ladles, &c." in Cairo, which lies about thirty miles up the Cumberland River from Nashville.[6] Oral tradition had long suggested the existence of a silversmith in early nineteenth-century Cairo, but only this advertisement identified him by name.

$ 20 Reward.

RANAWAY from the subscribers on Sunday last, an indented apprentice to the Silver smith business by the name of

Alfred M. Parrot;

about 18 years of age, stout made; his cloths are a dark woollen coat, vest, pantaloons & fur hat—he may be secreted about some boat, with an intention of going down to New Orleans, where he has a brother, or may have gone to his father, who lives in Jackson county. All persons are cautioned against harboring, trusting or employing said apprentice, as they would avoid the penalty of the law. The above reward and all reasonable charges will be paid to any person who will deliver him to the subscribers in Nashville, or ten dollars if secured in any jail in West Tennessee.

Richmond & Flint.

Nov. 11th, 1817. 37—3t.

103. *Indented apprentice Alfred M. Parrot, "about 18 years of age, stout made" ran away from silversmiths Richmond & Flint in 1817 (Nashville* Clarion and Tennessee Gazette, *11 Nov. 1817).*

PEABODY, Charles H. Silversmith. Nashville, Davidson County, 1850–51.

Charles H. Peabody was born in 1827 in North Carolina. He had moved to Nashville by 1850 when he succeeded his father, John Peabody (q.v.), in the clock and watch, jewelry, and silversmith business at a shop on Union Street between Cherry and College streets. He warranted his work to be as "fine as silver dollars" and offered a wide variety of goods from guns and pistols to "etherial" gas lamps and table cutlery. His estate at the time was valued at $20,000.[7]

The following year, 1851, Peabody notified the public he would "positively close up business in Nashville by the end of the year" and was, consequently, announcing a "closing sale." This advertisement is the last known of him.[8]

It is possible that Charles Peabody may have been the grandson of John Tyng Peabody, a silversmith working in Wilmington, North Carolina, from 1787-circa 1822.[9] This is based on the likelihood that Charles's father, John (q.v.), who was in Nashville by 1836,[10] may have been John Peabody, the watchmaker, clockmaker, and silversmith of Fayetteville, North Carolina, who was working in that city at least during 1823–27.[11] John Peabody is thought to have been the son of John Tyng Peabody.

PEABODY, John. Silversmith, jeweler, clock and watchmaker. Nashville, Davidson County, 1836–d. 1850.

John Peabody was working Nashville by 1836; he was in partnership with John Campbell in the firm of Peabody and Campbell (q.v.). In December of that year, Peabody and eight others met for the first time as the "Association of the Watch-Makers, Silversmiths & Jewellers of Nashville." They resolved that the association "meet annually in the month of December for the purpose of revising, correcting and establishing rules and regulations for our mutual interest." The resolution passed,[12] although no evidence exists to prove that the association continued to meet.

In 1839 Peabody worked with C. Guiteau (q.v.), but by 1841 he was working alone, advertising himself as a "Dealer in Watches, Jewelry. Fancy Hardware & Silver Plate." According to his advertisements, Peabody also employed workmen in various branches of watch and clock repair, jewelry, and silversmithing.[13]

By 1843 Peabody was a principal in the firm of Gowdey and Peabody (q.v.), along with Thomas Gowdey (q.v.). The firm was located at the sign of the "Spectacles and Watch" on the public square. Peabody continued in this partnership through at least 1845 when an advertisement announced the enlarging of their establishment.[14] In 1849 Peabody was again working independently, having "re-established himself" and opened a store on Union Street between College and Cherry streets. Peabody died on 4 July 1850; an inventory of his estate in Davidson County court records revealed that prominent citizens William Strickland, David McGavock, and Thomas Gowdey were listed on his books. Peabody's stock at his death contained German silverware, a great deal of plated ware, and a large silver plate inventory. Charles H. Peabody (q.v.) succeeded his father in the Nashville shop at least until the fall of 1851.[15]

Cutten's *Silversmiths of North Carolina* recorded a John Peabody, watchmaker, clockmaker, jeweler, and silversmith, in Fayetteville, North Carolina, circa 1823–27.[16] He may have been the same man as John Peabody of Nashville, although the Nashville silversmith used at least one mark (fig. 104a) that differs from the "J. PEABODY" mark of the Fayetteville silver. The mark had no period following the "J."

PEABODY and CAMPBELL. Retailers of jewelry, watches, silver. Nashville, Davidson County, 1836–37.

John Peabody (q.v.), the Nashville silversmith, announced the enlargement of his business on 12 August 1836 and took John Campbell (q.v.) as a partner in the firm of Peabody and Campbell. That advertisement ran at least through January 1837.[17]

104, 104a. *Pair of dessert spoons marked "J. PEABODY" in rectangle, 1840–50, engraved "F E C," Nashville. LOA: 6¾". Courtesy of the Tennessee State Museum, on loan from the author.*

PEABODY and GUITEAU. Watchmakers, silversmiths, jewelers, engravers. Nashville, Davidson County, 1839–43.

In 1839 Calvin Guiteau (q.v.) and John Peabody (q.v.) established the partnership of Peabody and Guiteau, "Watch Makers, Silversmiths, Jewelers, and Engravers," in Nashville. In a move that represented a "union of skill, and a valuable acquisition of firstrate workmen from the east," Guiteau left his Deaderick Street shop to join Peabody at a location on the public square. By 1843 the partnership had been dissolved.[18]

PEABODY, William. Watchmaker. Trenton, Gibson County, 1860.

According to the Federal census for Gibson County in 1860, William Peabody was born about 1810 in Virginia. He was working as a watchmaker and living with a Trenton banker, J. A. Zollicoffer.

PETTIBONE, Samuel. Clock repairer. Rogersville, Hawkins County, 1860.

Born in Connecticut about 1807, Samuel Pettibone had emigrated to Tennessee by 1857 when his daughter, Kate, was born. Pettibone listed his occupation as a "mender of clocks" in the 1860 census for Rogersville in Hawkins County. At that time, he estimated the value of his real property at $1,000 and his personal property at $200.

PFLUG, E. Watchmaker. Memphis, Shelby County, 1850.

E. Pflug was born in Prussia about 1827. By 1850 he had moved to Memphis, where he worked as a watchmaker. At the time of the census for that year he was one of several artisans living in the household of James S. Wilkins (q.v.).[19] Wilkins was a watchmaker and later a partner in the firm of F. H. Clark and Company (q.v.).[20] Pflug probably worked for Wilkins and perhaps later for F. H. Clark and Company.

PHOEBUS, Edward. Silversmith. Memphis, Shelby County, 1850.

At the time of the 1850 census, sixteen-year-old Edward Phoebus, born in Tennessee, identified himself as a silversmith; he boarded in the Memphis home of W. B. Means.[21]

PHOELINS, E. H. Apprentice watchmaker. Memphis, Shelby County, 1850.

E. H. Phoelins was born in Tennessee in 1832. By 1850 he was working as an apprentice watchmaker in Memphis and living in the household of watchmaker James S. Wilkins (q.v.). A number of other watchmakers also boarded with Wilkins.[22]

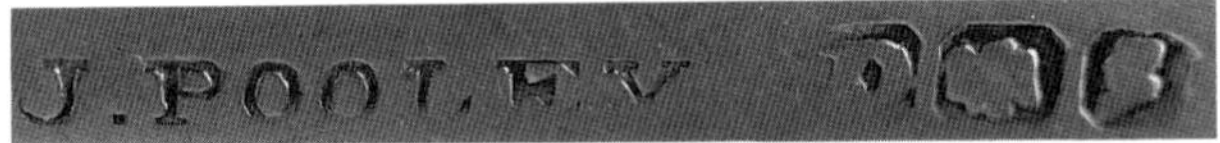

105, 105a. *Two marks used by James Pooley, 1859–60. Courtesy of the Tennessee State Museum, photographs by Stephen D. Cox. The "MEMPHIS" in a rectangle also appears on silver marked by F. H. Clark & Company and James Merriman (see figs. 54b, 54e, and 99c).*

PILE, A. N. Jeweler, watch and clockmaker. Springfield, Robertson County, 1860.

A. N. Pile was working in Springfield, Robertson County, in 1860. The *State Gazetteer* for that year listed him under "Jewelry, Watches, Clocks, Etc."[23]

PIMMER, F. Jeweler, watch and clockmaker. Cornersville, Giles County, 1860.

F. Pimmer appeared in the 1860 *State Gazetteer* under "Jewelry, Watches, Clocks, Etc." for Cornersville, Giles (now Marshall) County. At the time of the listing, the town of Cornersville was in Giles County; it was made a part of Marshall County during the Civil War.[24]

PLENELL, Richard A. Silversmith's apprentice. Bolivar, Hardeman County, 1850.

Richard A. Plenell was an eighteen-year-old North Carolina-born apprentice to silversmith Daniel Wells (q.v.) in Bolivar, Hardeman County, according to the 1850 census. Plenell and his fellow apprentice, Samuel Jobe (q.v.), also boarded with Wells and his wife, Mary.[25]

POOLEY, James. Jeweler. Memphis, Shelby County, 1859–60 and later.

James Pooley worked in New Albany, Indiana (circa 1858–59), before moving to Memphis. There he advertised as a watchmaker, clockmaker, and silver plater during 1859–60, and later. At the time of the 1860 census Pooley lived in the Eighth Ward of Memphis with Augusta, his twenty-nine-year-old wife, a Connecticut native. Two other jewelers, Edward Boskern (q.v.) and George Keller (q.v.), shared the Pooley home. The birthplaces of the Pooley children reflect the family's various moves: William, eight, born in New York; James, six, and "E.," four, Indiana; George, one, Tennessee.

The 1866 *Memphis City Directory* listed the firm of Pooley and Barnum at 265 Main Street in Memphis as "successors to James Pooley."[26]

PORTER, George E. Watch repairer. Nashville, Davidson County, 1839.

In 1839 George E. Porter, who had recently moved to Nashville from New Orleans, was in charge of watch repairing at Henry E. Thomas's (q.v.) new "fancy store" in Nashville. The shop's owner declared that Porter was a "superior workman."[27]

Kovel noted a George E. Porter working in Utica, New York (circa 1834–40), and in Syracuse, New York (circa 1841). No connection is known.[28]

PRICE, Andrew G. Silversmith. Clarksville, Montgomery County, 1859–60.

Andrew G. Price worked in Clarksville as a silversmith. According to that city's 1859–60 directory, he operated a shop on the north side of College Street between Seventh and Eighth streets. During the same year another silversmith, Richard T. Rice (q.v.), was working at the same address.[29] At the time of the 1860 census, the forty-three-year-old silversmith lived with his wife, Mary E., and son in Clarksville next to the residence of Samuel Simpson (q.v.).

PRYOR and BARBEE. Retailer of jewelry. Paris, Henry County, 1849–50.

From October 1849 to January 1850 Pryor and Barbee offered to the readers of Paris, Tennessee's *Republic* a "new and splendid assortment of JEWELRY" as well as a variety of foodstuffs and general household goods.[30]

PYLE, Benjamin. Watchmaker, jeweler. Jackson, Madison County, 1838.

In 1837 Benjamin Pyle became a partner in the Fayetteville, North Carolina, silversmithing firm of Selph and Pyle. After the death of John Selph, Pyle advertised in September 1838 that he was disposing of the remaining stock on hand, as he intended to move west.[31] He evidently already had moved, for an advertisement in Jackson of March 1838 offered a line of fancy goods as well as "particular attention to clock and watch repair," at a shop "just below the printing office." However, in July of that year the Jackson newspaper announced the sale of Pyle's business, setting the date for 2 September 1838.[32] Other than a Jackson notice dated the following month informing readers that a letter was waiting for Benjamin "Pile" at the Jackson post office, nothing further is known of his activity there. Because Pyle had sold his stock in Jackson at the same time that he was offering his remaining inventory in Fayetteville, it is possible that he returned to North Carolina immediately. It was not until November 1841, however, that he announced that he had again begun clock and watch repair in Fayetteville.[33]

Pyle probably was the son of Benjamin Pyle, a silversmith, in Washington, North Carolina, who died in 1812.

106. *"J PYLE" mark attributed to Joshua Pyle, 1830–35, Gallatin. Private collection.*

A public sale of the elder Pyle's goods in February 1813 included an "excellent sett of Watch and Clock making tools, also a sett of Silversmiths and Jewellers tools, a variety of Silver Watches, a considerable stock of watchmaking materials. . . ."[34]

PYLE (PILE), Joshua. Silversmith. Gallatin, Sumner County, 1830–60.

Joshua Pyle, born in 1797 in North Carolina, was a Gallatin resident at the time of the 1830 Sumner County census. By 1840 he was located in a shop on "Main Street, West of the Square," and ten years later he reported property valued at $1,000 to the Sumner County census taker. In 1860 "Pile's" real property was valued at $1500 and his personal property at $3,000. Pyle and his wife, Mary B., were still residents of Gallatin at the time.[35]

No relationship between Joshua Pyle and silversmith Benjamin Pyle (q.v.) of Jackson, Madison County, also a native of North Carolina, is known.

RABY, E. Watchmaker. Nashville, Davidson County, 1859.

In 1859 E. Raby was working as a watchmaker at 16 Public Square in Nashville, probably at William Henry Calhoun's (q.v.) store. Another Nashville watchmaker, Ed. Paillard (q.v.), also worked there.[1]

RAGLAND, John. Silversmith. Lebanon, Wilson County, 1850.

Born about 1808 in Virginia, John Ragland had moved to Tennessee by 1831 when his eldest child, Martha, was born. At the time of the 1850 census he was working as a silversmith in Lebanon, Wilson County, and his assets were valued at fifteen hundred dollars. Jane C., his wife, was a native of Tennessee.[2] Ragland's son, William (q.v.), later worked as a silversmith in Wilson County.

RAGLAND, William M. Silversmith. Lebanon, Wilson County, 1860.

William M. Ragland, born about 1836 in Tennessee, was listed as a silversmith in the 1860 census for Wilson County. Ragland and his wife, Mary, and their two-year-old son were residents of Lebanon. William was the son of Jane and John Ragland (q.v.).

RAIMEY, Henry A. Silversmith. Pulaski, Giles County, 1860.

Henry A. Raimey was born in England about 1823. By 1860 he was working as a silversmith in Pulaski, Giles County, and he estimated his personal estate at $300.

RANEY, William. Silversmith. DeKalb County, 1850; Cherry Valley, Wilson County, 1860.

At the time of the 1850 census, William Raney, a native of Kentucky, was a forty-five-year old silversmith working in DeKalb County. His Tennessee-born wife, Kizziah, and five of their children lived with him. The birthplaces of Raney's children indicate that he had arrived in Tennessee in 1832. In 1860 the Wilson County census listed Raney's birthplace as North Carolina, although the information listed regarding his wife and children indicates that this was the same man who was reported as being from Kentucky in 1850. Listed with Raney in 1860 were his wife and two youngest sons; they were residents of Cherry Valley at the time. Isaac Lefever (q.v.), a young silversmith, lived with them.[3]

RAWORTH, Edward. Silversmith. Nashville, Davidson County, 1808–20.

Edward Raworth was one of Davidson County's earliest silversmiths. It is possible that Raworth came from Virginia with his sister, for another Nashville silversmith, Thomas Deaderick (q.v.), married a Nancy Raworth of Virginia in 1789.[4] A pair of silver tongs with an "E. RAWORTH" mark and with an early provenance in Abingdon, Virginia, further support the conjecture regarding Raworth's place of origin.[5]

While the location and date of Raworth's birth remain uncertain, he was known to be working in Nashville as early as 1808 when he advertised for an apprentice; less than a year later he offered the services of a "New York engraver" at his shop.[6] In February 1811, Raworth entered into partnership with Thomas Hiter (q.v.) in the firm of Hiter and Raworth (q.v.); that agreement was dissolved within the month.[7] Apparently undeterred by whatever difficulties he may have encountered with Hiter, Raworth tried partnerships again on two separate occasions. In December 1814 a lengthy advertisement detailed dozens of items that residents of Nashville could purchase from the firm of Raworth and Biddle; that partnership lasted until the fall of 1817 when it was dissolved by mutual consent. Within the month the new partnership of Raworth and Gordon was formed; the duration of that firm is not known.[8] According to Davidson County circuit court minutes, on 15 July 1816 Raworth won a judgment of $378.22 against Felix Robertson; the nature of the debt was not disclosed. In January 1818

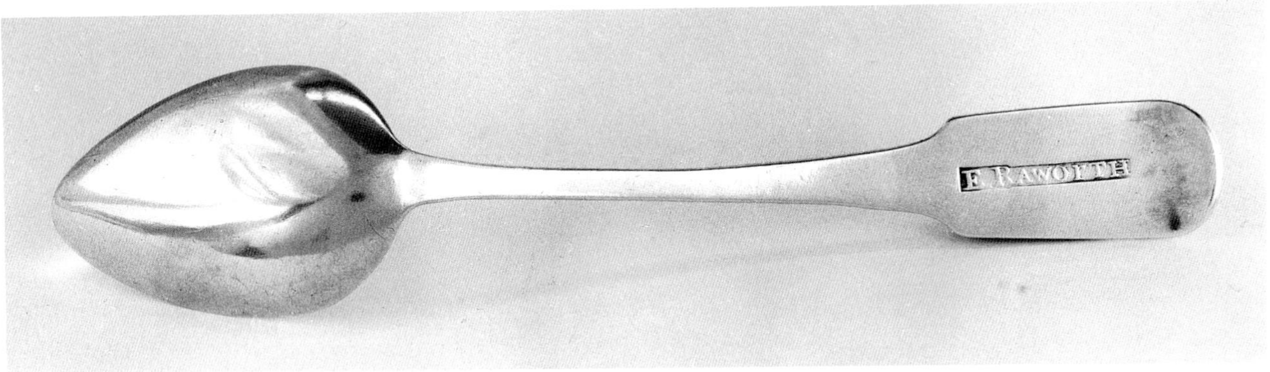

107. *Serving spoon marked "E. RAWORTH," 1810?, engraved "RKEA," Nashville. LOA: 8⅞". Private collection, photograph courtesy of Helga Photo Studio, Inc.*

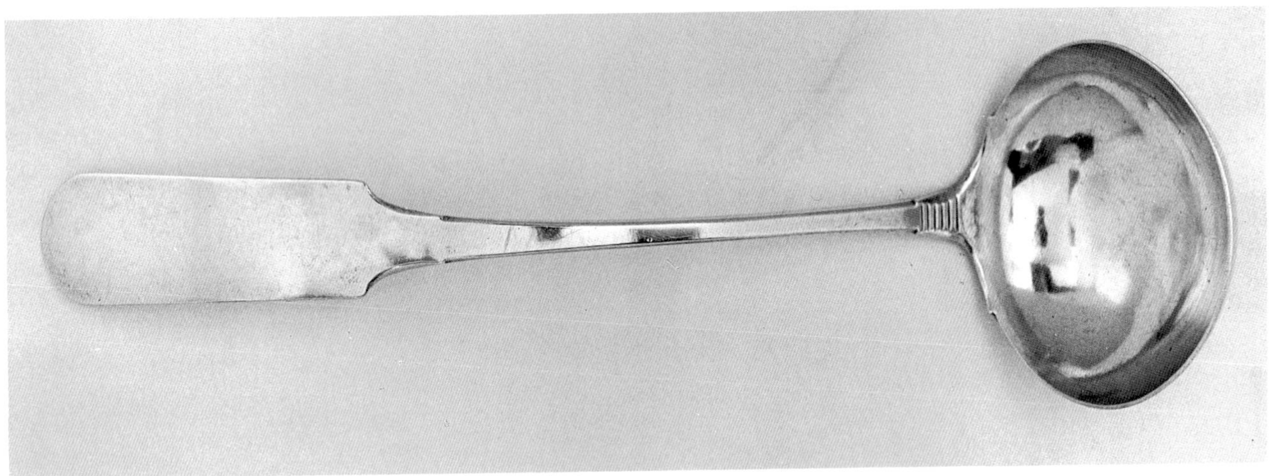

107a, 107b. *Soup ladle marked "E. RAWORTH," 1810–20, Nashville. LOA: 12½". Private collection, MRF S-13,436.*

Raworth's first wife, Priscilla (Brewer?), died and later that year he married Polly Bell.[9]

In March 1820 Raworth warned his customers that he was "removing to the country" and requested that they pick up their orders at his dwelling on Cherry Street. Raworth's final advertisement ran in the Nashville *Clarion and Tennessee Gazette* a month later. In the notice he stated that he had left town and that A. R. Freeman (q.v.) held "watches left with me for repair . . . [as well as] my books and accounts."[10]

A division of property recorded at the January 1836 sessions of the Davidson County Court revealed that Edward Raworth's only legal heirs were his widow, Mary Raworth, and two sons, George F. and Edward (who is later identified as "Egbert A." in the same document). George received a lot which fronted Cherry Street and ran halfway to Summer Street, perhaps the site of his parents' house and shop. Egbert inherited "Lot No. 78" fronting on Summer Street "and running back halfway to Cherry Street and valued at three thousand dollars." An inventory recorded 17 April 1836 listed some silverware but no tools or other evidence that Edward was still engaged in the silversmithing business at the time of his death in the fall of 1835.

E. Raworth & R. Gordon,

HAVE entered into partnership for the purpose of carrying on the

Silver Smith Business,

which they will conduct in all its various— They have on hand an elegant assortment of Jewelry, Watches and Clocks, Silver plate, &c. which they will sell low for cash; the highest price given for old gold & silver.

N. B. A steady man who is a good hand at watch work would be employed, and a youth about fifteen, if well recommended, would be taken as an apprentice.

Nov. 9 —tf

107c. *The announcement of the dissolution of the partnership of Raworth & Biddle appeared on the same day as that of the formation of E. Raworth & R. Gordon (Nashville* Clarion and Tennessee Gazette, *11 Nov. 1817).*

108, 108a. *Two marks attributed to James Reed, 1830–40 and 1840–50, respectively.*

RAWORTH and BIDDLE. Silversmiths. Nashville, Davidson County, 1814–17.

E. Raworth (q.v.) and Biddle (q.v.), first name unknown, both Nashville silversmiths, established the firm of Raworth and Biddle about 1814.[11] An 1815 advertisement in the *Nashville Whig* stated that the partners had received

> from Philadelphia, an elegant assortment of JEWELRY . . . gold, elastic and plain watch chains; ditto seals, keys, and trinkets; Philagree [sic], topez [sic], pearl-set jetten and plain earrings . . . breastpins, elastic and plain hair braceletts [sic] six with clasps, gold and silver lace, and cord assorted, gold and silver epauletts [sic]; fancy stars and buttons for military coats: Ladies long tucking and side-combs, ornaments and plain; Jetten and Cornelion necklaces, ornamented and plain; gold, silver and shell sleeve buttons; Ladies gilt and silver clasps, glass and plain, sleeve and neck clasps; Pencil cases, thimbles and fruit knives; Knee and shoe buckles; A few good clocks, with or without cases. They now have and will constantly keep a constant supply of Table, Tea, Soup and Cream spoons—and other table furniture. WATCHES & CLOCKS carefully repaired, warranted to perform twelve months. The highest price in CASH, given for old GOLD & SILVER.

The partnership was dissolved 28 October 1817, by mutual consent.[12]

RAWORTH and GORDON. Silversmiths, jewelers, watch and clockmakers? Nashville, Davidson County, 1817–18.

Edward Raworth (q.v.) and Robert Gordon (q.v.), Nashville silversmiths, formed the partnership of Raworth and Gordon in 1817. The notice of their new firm adjoined the same advertisement (fig. 107c) as that announcing the dissolution of Raworth's previous partnership with Biddle (q.v.). Raworth and Gordon offered jewelry, watches, and clocks in their shop on the public square. They were still working together in 1818, when "Trim Myers" advertised that his barber shop was "next door to Messrs. Raworth and Gordon's silversmith shop." As late as 1823 the firm owed eight dollars to the estate of silversmith John Elliston (q.v.). As Raworth left Nashville in 1820, the amount probably indicated an uncollected debt.[13]

REAVES, R. R. Jeweler, watch and clockmaker. Terry, Carroll County, 1860.

In 1860 R. R. Reaves was working in Terry, Carroll County. The 1860 *State Gazetteer* listed him under "Jewelry, Watches, Clocks, Etc."[14]

REED, James. Silversmith. Murfreesboro, Rutherford County, 1832–50.

James Reed was born in North Carolina about 1793; he was probably working in Rutherford County, Tennessee, as early as 1830, or at least by the 1832 birth of his eldest son. In the 1850 census his assets were valued at $3,000; he was married to Ellen A., a North Carolinian, and the Murfreesboro couple had one son, Robert D., who worked as a book merchant.[15]

REED, R. D. Jeweler. Murfreesboro, Rutherford County, 1837.

In 1837 R. D. Reed was working as a jeweler in Murfreesboro, Rutherford County, according to Goodspeed's *History of Tennessee.*[16]

REEVES, D. S. Watchmaker, silversmith, jeweler. Nashville, Davidson County, 1836.

D. S. Reeves was one of the founding members of the "Association of the Watch-Makers, Silversmiths & Jewellers of Nashville." The group first met on Christmas Day in 1836, when all present, except Reeves, signed an agreement to exchange information and set guidelines on pricing for the mutual benefit of members.[17] No marked work by Reeves is known.

A David S. Reeves was working in Philadelphia, circa 1830–35.[18] His relationship to the Nashville man, if any, is unknown.

REEVES, T. W. Watchmaker. Somerville, Fayette County, 1860.

In 1860 the Fayette County census listed T. W. Reeves, a female aged twenty-six, as a watchmaker born in Tennessee. If this identification of sex was not a clerical error, Reeves was the only woman found working as a watchmaker in Tennessee. It is possible that the notation was an error, for other members of the household listed suggest a typical family group: "Magrt., 26," and three young children, all born in Tennessee.

RICE, Richard T. Silversmith. Clarksville, Montgomery County, 1859–60.

During 1859–60, Richard T. Rice was working as a silversmith in Clarksville. Rice and Andrew G. Price (q.v.), another silversmith, were located at the same address on the north side of College Street between Seventh and Eighth streets.[19]

RICHLESS, William M. Jeweler. Nashville, Davidson County, 1860.

The 1860 census for Davidson County listed thirty-year-old William M. Richless as a "jeweler merchant" working with W. L. Atkinson (q.v.), J. W. Ruggles (q.v.), and George Calhoun (q.v.) in Nashville's First Ward, probably at William Henry Calhoun's shop. Richless, a native of Pennsylvania, listed his real property at $1,000 and his personal property at $5,000.

Ten years earlier, an eighteen-year-old woman, A. M. Richless, also a native of Pennsylvania, had been listed in the 1850 census for Davidson County as a member of the William Henry Calhoun household.

RICHMOND, Barton. Silversmith. Nashville, Davidson County, 1816–40. *Gold and silver merchant.* Memphis, Shelby County, 1844–59?

In 1816 Barton Richmond, a Bostonian, opened a shop with F. P. Flint (q.v.) in Nashville on Market Street; the firm was advertised as "Richmond and Flint" (q.v.). No connection between Barton Richmond and the Richmond family of silversmiths working in Providence, Rhode Island, about the same time is known.[20]

Davidson County censuses listed Richmond in 1820, 1830, and 1840; however, he was in Memphis by 1844, where he worked as a gold and silver broker, buying and selling specie at a shop on Exchange Square. He may have remained in Shelby County at least through 1859, for in September of that year he received, as executor, all of his wife Catherine's real and personal property.[21]

RICHMOND and FLINT. Silversmiths. Nashville, Davidson County, 1816–23.

Barton Richmond (q.v.) and F. P. Flint (q.v.), Nashville silversmiths, established the firm of Richmond and Flint in 1816. According to one source, both moved from Boston to Nashville as young men. Their shop on Market Street carried watches, jewelry, silver spoons, and military goods that included swords, epaulettes, and plumes.[22]

In November 1817 the firm's apprentice, Alfred M. Parrot (q.v.), ran away, "clothed in a dark woolen coat, vest, pantaloons and fur hat," prompting a $20 reward offer for his return or $10 if he was apprehended and secured in any West Tennessee jail. The partners suspected that he might have sought out his brother in New Orleans or fled to his father's home in Jackson County.[23]

A Richmond and Flint advertisement of 1817 announced that a ". . . great variety of gold Seals, Keys and Chains . . . Silver-ware, plated candlesticks, plated snuffers and trays; a few elegant sets of Britainiaware; plated and gilt mounted swords, epaulettes [sic], plumes and lace" were availabe form their firm. Later that year they received "from BOSTON, PROVIDENCE AND BALTIMORE" a number of similar items. In 1820 the partners announced their interest in buying and selling gold, silver, and all good foreign bank notes, a practice they continued until the partnership ended in 1823 with Flint's death. Richmond later moved to Memphis, where he specialized in buying and selling specie.[24]

A ladle (fig. 109), with the firm's mark, used in the Hermitage by President Andrew Jackson, was sold in 1927 when his great-grandson's effects were auctioned.[25]

109. *Punch ladle marked "RICHMOND & FLINT," 1816–23, engraved "A. J.," Nashville. LOA: 15¼", width across bowl: 4". Courtesy of the Western Reserve Historical Society.*

109a. *"RICHMOND & FLINT" mark, 1816–23. Private collection. This mark is from a ladle engraved "W. D." for William Donelson.*

109b. *Serving spoon marked "RICHMOND & FLINT", 1816–23, engraved "BV," Nashville. LOA: 9⅝". Private collection.*

109c. *Beaker marked "RICHMOND & FLINT", 1816–23, engraved "RCN," Nashville. HOA: 3¼", width across rim: 3¼". Courtesy of the Tennessee State Museum.*

REMOVAL.

Richmond & Flint,

HAVE removed their shop near the square, on market street—They have just received a few

Ladies Watches,

and have on hand a large assortment of articles in their line of business.

May 26——tf.

N. B. For rent a store room & cellar on Market street.

109d. *Richmond & Flint moved to Market Street in Nashville in 1818 (Nashville* Clarion and Tennessee State Gazette, *26 May 1818).*

E. M. Ringo

HAS just received at his Clock & Watch maker's shop, south side of the square, a quantity of Green

Spectacle Glasses,

which he will sell or set to order on moderate terms.

Fayetteville, Sept. 28, 1824.

110. *Elijah M. Ringo sold "Green Spectacle Glasses" at his clock and watchmaker's shop (Fayetteville* Village Messenger, *29 Sept. 1824).*

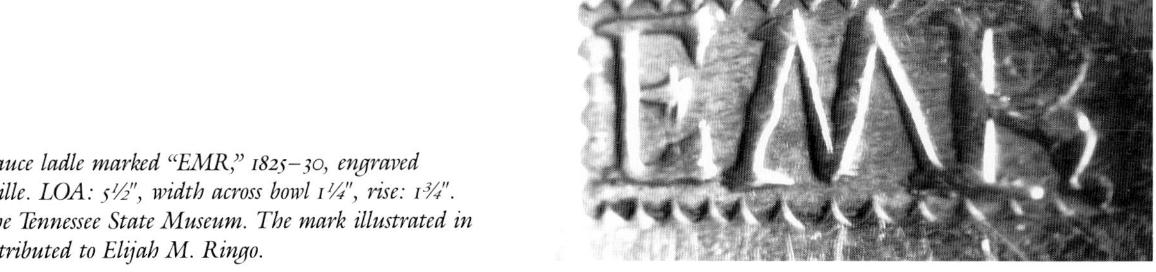

110a, 110b. *Sauce ladle marked "EMR," 1825–30, engraved "SM," Nashville. LOA: 5½", width across bowl 1¼", rise: 1¾". Courtesy of the Tennessee State Museum. The mark illustrated in fig. 110b is attributed to Elijah M. Ringo.*

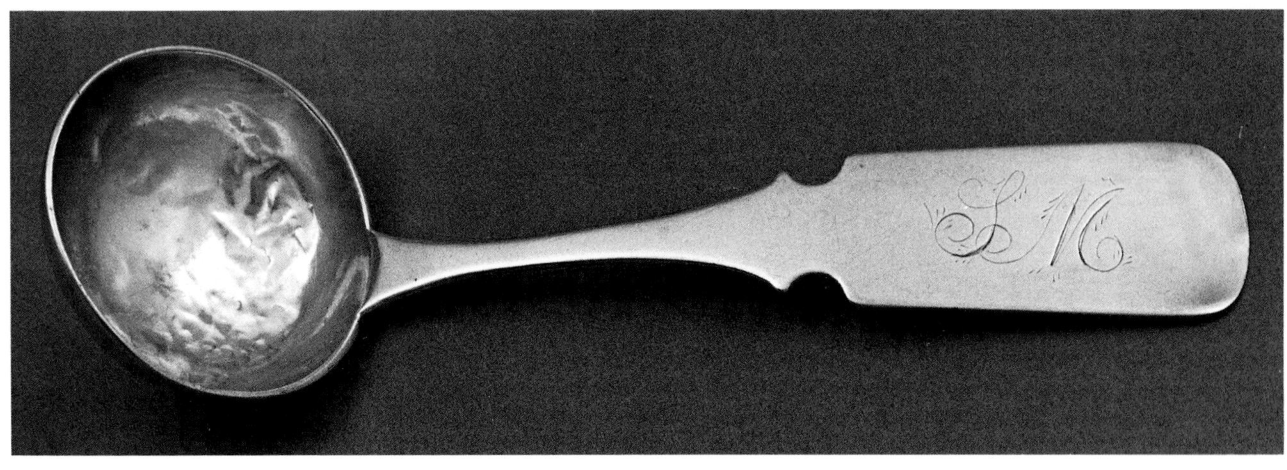

RINGO, Elijah M. Clock and watchmaker; silversmith. Fayetteville, Lincoln County, 1824–50.

Elijah M. Ringo was born in Kentucky about 1798. By September 1824 he was working in Fayetteville, Lincoln County, where he operated a "Clock and Watch maker's shop, south side of the square." Ringo published notices regularly through 1827 requesting that customers settle their accounts.[26]

In 1836 and again in 1844, Ringo served as a trustee of Lincoln County, where he remained at least through 1850. The census for manufacturers for Lincoln County that year reported that Ringo had $700 invested in his one-man business; he used two tons of wood and four bushels of coal in fashioning an annual product valued at $600.[27]

III, IIIa. *Forks marked "A. J. ROBERT," 1835–40, engraved "Dortch," Nashville. LOA: 6 13/16". Private collection.*

ROBERT (ROBERTS), A. J. Jeweler, silversmith, watchmaker. Memphis, Shelby County 1837; Nashville, Davidson County, 1850, 1880; Murfreesboro, Rutherford County, 1860.

The first recorded mention of Roberts appeared in an 1837 *Memphis Enquirer* when his firm, Cissna and Robert (q.v.), advertised rifles and watches.[28] The 1850 census for Davidson County listed "A. Roberts, jeweler," in Nashville. At the time, the thirty-six-year-old native of Kentucky lived with his wife, Mary, and two young sons, Charles and James. At the time of the census ten years later, Robert's family included an additional three children in their Murfreesboro, Rutherford County home. Robert continued to work as a jeweler in Murfreesboro, verified by the listing of "A. J. Robert" in the 1860 *State Gazetteer*.[29] Twenty years later, Clayton's *History of Davidson County* included jeweler A. J. Robert among its Nashville subscribers.[30]

A James Robert was working in Frankfort and Lexington, Kentucky, during 1806–10. No connection with the Tennessee man has been established.[31]

ROBESON, Isaac D. Silversmith, watchmaker, jeweler. Nashville, Davidson County, 1836–40.

Isaac Robeson was one of the men present at the first meeting of the "Association of Watch-Makers, Silversmiths & Jewellers of Nashville" held 25 December 1836. The men signed an agreement to exchange information and establish price guidelines for men of their profession. Robeson was still a resident of Nashville at the time of the 1840 census.[32]

Kovel listed an Isaac Robeson in Philadelphia (circa 1843–46), but no connection with the Nashville Robeson is known.[33]

ROJOUX, M. Jeweler. Memphis, Shelby County, 1855–59.

M. Rojoux first worked for Memphis jewelers J. E. Merriman and C. G. Merriman in 1855. By 1859 he not only maintained his own shop at 178 Main Street but also appears to have been in partnership with A. Mareto (q.v.) (Mereto and Rojoux, q.v.) nearby at 180 Main.[34]

ROSE, William S. Dealer in jewelry, watches, and clocks. Sneedville, Hancock County, 1860.

At the time of the 1860 census for Hancock County, William S. Rose was a successful merchant with real estate valued at $4,200 and a personal estate worth $8,000. Rose and his Irish wife, Mary, had nine children; living with the family was John Atkins (q.v.), a twenty-nine-year-old silversmith from Virginia, presumably Rose's partner in the firm of Rose and Atkins (q.v.).[35]

A William E. Rose was working as a silversmith in New York City c. 1844.[36] No connection with the Tennessee Rose has been established.

ROSE and ATKINS (ADKINS). Retailers of silver, jewelry, watches. Sneedville, Hancock County, 1860.

A listing for the firm of Rose and Atkins appeared in the 1860 *State Gazeteer* under "Jewelry, Watches, Clocks, Etc." for Sneedville. John Atkins (Adkins, q.v.) was listed as a silversmith in the 1860 federal census; William Rose apparently was no more than a merchant.[37]

ROSS, John. Silver plater. Memphis, Shelby County, 1860.

At the time of the 1860 census, John Ross, a twenty-two-year old native of Indiana, was working as a silver plater and living in a boarding house in the Seventh Ward of Memphis.

ROSSANIA, W. H. Watchmaker. La Grange, Fayette County, 1860.

W. H. Rossania, born about 1823 in Germany, was working as a watchmaker in La Grange, Fayette County, at the time of the 1860 census. He and Georgianna Rossania, a twenty-four-year-old Virginian, lived in the county's Thirteenth District. At the time, Rossania evaluated his real property at $1,000 and his personal property at the same figure.

ROULET, M. Silversmith, jeweler. Murfreesboro, Rutherford County, 1854–60 and later.

M. Roulet, a Frenchman, was in Murfreesboro by 1854 when he established a jewelry and silversmith shop that he operated until the 1870s. William R. Bell, an apprentice of Roulet, bought the shop when Roulet went to Chicago to enter the wholesale jewelry business.[39]

ROULET, William. Jeweler. Murfreesboro, Rutherford County, 1838–70.

In 1838 William Roulet was a jeweler in Murfreesboro. No connection has been established between William and "M" Roulet, but it is possible that they were the same man. Goodspeed's *History of Tennessee* indicates William Roulet was still at work as a jeweler in Murfreesboro in 1870.[39]

ROWELL, A. D. Silversmith. Greeneville, Greene County, 1860.

According to the 1860 census for Greene County, A. D. Rowell, a "master silversmith" and native of New Hampshire, was living in John Maloney's hotel. Rowell estimated the value of his personal property at $700. That same year "A. D. Rowell and Company" appeared in the *State Gazetteer* under the "Jewelry, Watches, Clocks, Etc." listings for Greeneville.[40]

ROWELL, C. C. Jeweler. Greeneville, Greene County, 1857.

The *Nashville Directory* listed a C. C. Rowell, who was working as a jeweler, in Greeneville in 1857.[41]

RUDEZINSKI, J. (I.) E. Silversmith, jeweler, watch and clockmaker. Dandridge, Jefferson County, 1860.

In the 1860 census for Jefferson County, Rudezinski, a forty-two-year-old native of Poland, identified himself as a silversmith and valued his real property at $2,200 and his personal property at $200. Also listed were Rudezinski's wife, forty-five, and their sixteen-year-old daughter, both natives of Switzerland. The 1860 *State Gazetteer* revealed that Rudezinski was located in Dandridge, and his business was concerned with "Jewelry, Watches, Clocks, Etc."[42]

RUDISELL, A. W. Apprentice watchmaker. Memphis, Shelby County, 1850.

Nineteen-year-old A. W. Rudisell, a native of North Carolina, was living in the home of James S. Wilkins (q.v.) of Memphis at the time of the 1850 census. Rudisell was listed as an apprentice watchmaker.

RUDISILL, John. Clockmaker. Jackson, Madison County, 1826.

John Rudisill's presence in Tennessee is evinced by a newspaper notice of 1826, wherein the Madison County clockmaker politely asked his customers to "settle up," as he was leaving for New Orleans. He eventually may have settled in Arkansas where a John Rudisell, a native of Mississippi, worked as a silversmith in Phillips County.[43]

RUDISILL (RUDISSILE), John Hamilton. Apprentice silversmith. Raleigh, Shelby County, 1850.

John Hamilton Rudisill was born in Tennessee in 1832. At the time of the 1850 census for Shelby County, he was working as an apprentice silversmith and living with his mother, Melissa Rudisill, in the community of Raleigh, outside Memphis. His father, another John Rudisill (b. 1796), had died in November 1846 leaving his wife head of the household.[44]

RUFFINS, William. Silversmith. Dresden, Weakley County, 1860.

At the time of the 1860 census for Weakley County,

NOTICE.

THE subscriber wishes those that have accompts with him to call and close the same, with Cash or Note—and by complying with this notice, they would do him a favour, and themselves tow, as he is compeled to have money. He takes this course of informing them through the columns of this paper, & therefore hopes they will read and pity his situation.

G. W. RUTH.

Shelbyville Sept. 5th 1828. tf.

112. *In the Shelbyville* Western Intelligencer *of 12 September 1828, George Washington Ruth asked those who had accounts with him to settle them in cash.*

112a. *Mark attributed to George Washington Ruth, c. 1835.*

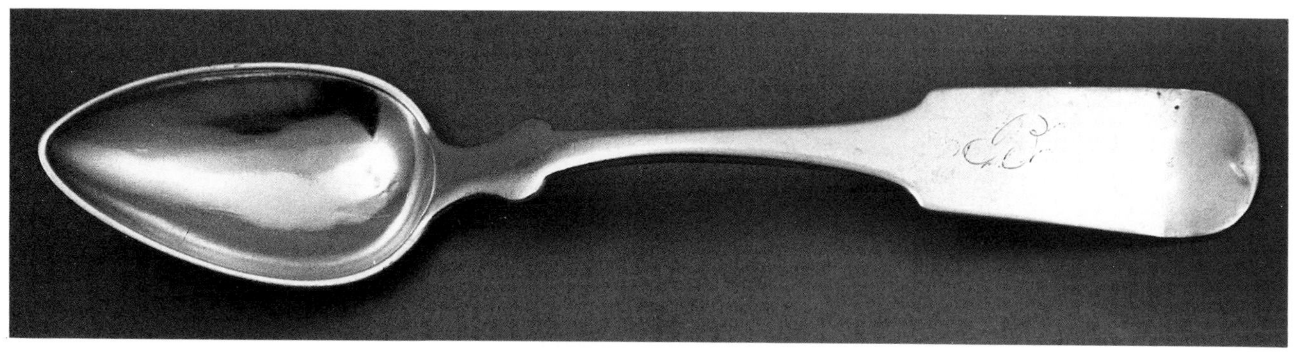

112b, 112c. *Dessert spoon marked "G. W. RUTH," 1850–60, engraved "S," Shelbyville. LOA: 7". Courtesy of the Tennessee State Museum, fig. 112c, photograph by Stephen D. Cox. It should be observed that Ruth struck the die (fig. 112c) too hard, causing the entire face of the die to imprint, rather than simply the letters.*

twenty-one-year-old William Ruffins was working as a silversmith in Dresden. A native of Pennsylvania, Ruffins valued his personal property at $1,200; he was living in a hotel operated by S. Anderson.

RUGGLES, J. H. Watchmaker. Nashville, Davidson County, 1857–60.

J. H. Ruggles, a native of New York, worked as a watchmaker in William H. Calhoun's (q.v.) shop in Nashville from 1857–60. Calhoun's establishment was located at 16 Public Square in 1857, and at the corner of College Street and Public Square in 1860.[45]

RUTH, Charles Leonidas. Silversmith. Shelbyville, Bedford County, 1856?–60 and later.

Born about 1832, Charles Leonidas Ruth worked in Shelbyville, Bedford County, until the outbreak of the Civil War. He was apprenticed to his father, George Washington Ruth (q.v.). In 1873 Ruth established his own firm in Montgomery, Alabama. His younger brother, Ambrose, eventually "followed the trade of watchmaker and jeweler" in the Tennessee towns of Fayetteville and Winchester.[46]

RUTH, George Washington. Silversmith. Shelbyville, Bedford County, 1822–34? 1853–d. 1858; Nashville, Davidson County, 1835–52?

George Washington Ruth was born 6 October 1799 in Granville County, North Carolina. At the age of seventeen, he was apprenticed to John Scott, a well-known silversmith and watchmaker in Raleigh, North Carolina.[47] At the end of his apprenticeship four years later, Ruth left for the "Southwest Territory," now Tennessee, with the clothes he wore and a set of tools Scott had given him. In October 1822 after stopping in Mobile and Huntsville, Alabama, and Fayetteville, North Carolina, Ruth arrived in Shelbyville, Tennessee. He began work in the shop of Daniel Turrentine (q.v.) and shortly thereafter, on 30 May 1824, married Anne Downs. By September 1828 Ruth was operating on his own, for at that

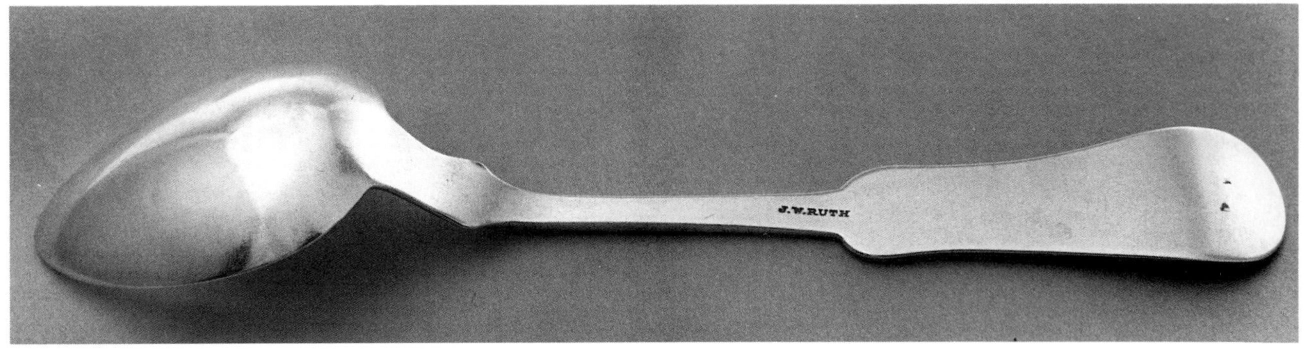

113, 113a. *Tablespoon marked "J. W. RUTH," 1860, engraved "W. F. O.," Shelbyville. LOA: 8 5/16". Courtesy of the Tennessee State Museum. John Wesley Ruth was the eldest son of George Washington Ruth.*

time he pleaded with his customers to settle their accounts as he was in need of money. A year later, the partnership of Turrentine and Ruth (q.v.) was formed. Although their shop was destroyed in the storm of 1830, the two men rebuilt and prospered until the dissolution of their partnership in January 1833.[48]

In March 1835 Ruth asked his Shelbyville patrons to pay their debts as he had "removed to Nashville." By 1853 he had returned to Bedford County, where he was listed as a "Dealer in Watches and Jewelry." Ruth was active in Shelbyville community affairs, serving both as mayor and as magistrate for the city.[49]

Three of the Ruth's seven children died of Asiatic cholera in 1833, but sons John Wesley (q.v.), Charles Leonidas (q.v.), Ambrose D., and Samuel M. learned the trade in their father's shop. When Ruth died on 20 August 1858, John assumed control of the growing business. The Ruth establishment continued to operate in Shelbyville for over one hundred years. It closed in the 1950s.[50]

RUTH, John Wesley. Silversmith, jeweler. Shelbyville, Bedford County, 1856?–d. 1906.

John Wesley Ruth, the eldest son of George Washington Ruth (q.v.), was born on 22 February 1839 in Shelbyville. He learned the silversmithing trade in his father's shop and ran the family business after his father's death in 1858. At the time of the 1860 census the twenty-one-year-old silversmith lived with his mother, brothers, and sister in Shelbyville.[51]

During the Civil War, Ruth and his three brothers fought in the Confederate army. After the war, John resumed his business in Shelbyville and employed his brother Samuel. John's brother Charles (q.v.) moved to Montgomery, Alabama, where he established a shop. Another brother, Ambrose, pursued the trade of watchmaker and jeweler, first in Fayetteville and then in Winchester. John's sons, Albert and Weakley, later joined the firm.[52]

Like his father, John Wesley Ruth was a public-spirited citizen and served two terms as mayor (1873, 1885). He became a Freemason, attaining the level of Knight Templar and receiving as well the honorary degree of Knight of Honor. Ruth died on 14 May 1906.[53]

RYAN, C. B. Merchant. Travisville, Fentress County, 1860.

C. B. Ryan appeared under "Jewelry, Watches, Clocks, Etc." for Travisville in the 1860 *State Gazetteer*. He advertised in that same *Gazetteer* as a "Dealer in Dry Goods, Queensware, Glassware, Hardware, Ready-Made Clothing, Drugs, Medicines, Boots, Shoes, Hats and Caps, Jewelry, Watches, Clocks, and Fancy Goods generally." Ryan obviously was a retailer; he listed himself in the census as a merchant.[54]

RYAN, Job. Silver plater. Nashville, Davidson County, 1860.

Job Ryan was a Nashville silver plater in 1860. He worked at Henry Parkhurst's (q.v.) silver and brass plating establishment at 12½ Deaderick Street.[55]

SALMON, S. Jeweler. Sewanee, Franklin County, 1859.

In 1859 S. Salmon owned a "jeweler Store" at 36 South Market Street in Sewanee.[1]

An Alfred Salmon worked in Cincinnati, Ohio, circa 1825–44, as a silversmith, and a William H. Salmon, worked in Cazenovia, Morrisville and Troy, New York, circa 1830–50. No connection with the Sewanee jeweler is known.[2]

SCHELL (SHELL), S. F. Silversmith. Gallatin, Sumner County, 1838?–60.

S. F. Schell was born in Pennsylvania about 1804. His second child was born in Tennessee some time between 1834 and 1838, documenting Schell's presence in the state by that time. By 1840 he was working in Gallatin as a

"SILVERSMITH, East side of the Square." At the time of the 1850 census, Schell and his family were still residents of Sumner County; he identified himself as a "watchmaker." He remained in Gallatin on the public square through 1860, when he reported his occupation as "jeweller." At that time, he valued his personal property at $500 and his real property at $800.[3]

In *American Silver, Pewter and Silver Plate*, the Kovels noted a Samuel F. Schell (circa 1829–35) in Philadelphia; this may have been the same man, although no connection has been documented.[4]

SCHLEITER, J. S. Jeweler, watch and clockmaker. Gallatin, Sumner County, 1860.

J. S. Schleiter was working in Gallatin in 1860. His name appeared in that year's *State Gazetteer* under listings for "Jewelry, Watches, Clocks, Etc."[5]

SCHMIDT, Fred. Watchmaker. Memphis, Shelby County, 1860.

Born in Prussia, Fred Schmidt was working as a watchmaker and living in the Second Ward of Memphis in 1860. His age was not recorded.

SCHNELLBACHER (SCHNELLBACKER), J. P. Watchmaker. Nashville, Davidson County, 1859–60.

In 1859 J.P. Schnellbacher, born about 1831 in Hessen, Germany, was working as a watchmaker in a Nashville residence and store. The following year the *Nashville Business Directory* listed a Paul Schnellbacker, watchmaker, at G. W. Donigan's (q.v.) a shop at the corner of College and Union streets.[6] The two listings probably represent the same man.

SEHORN, A. O. H. P. Jeweler, watchmaker. Murfreesboro, Rutherford County, 1837–48? 1869; Nashville, Davidson County, 1849–50.

A. O. H. P. Sehorn was born in Tennessee about 1817. As a young man of twenty, he established himself as a jeweler in Murfreesboro. By 10 December 1849 he was operating in "the shop late occupied by John Campbell" (q.v.) in Nashville. On 8 August 1837 Sehorn published a notice in the *Daily Centre-State American* offering a $300 reward for the recovery of gold and silver goods, Nashville Gas Light Company stock, railroad company stock, and cash stolen from his store in a "bold and daring robbery" the preceding night.[7] The *Nashville Business Directory* for 1869 revealed that he was active in the trade in Murfreesboro.[8]

An incised "SEHORN" has been attributed to this man based on the provenance of the silver on which the mark appears.

SEHORN, George. Silversmith. Athens, McMinn County, 1823–43?.

George Sehorn operated one of the first silversmithing shops in Athens, opening his business soon after the town was established in 1823. According to an 1834 *State Gazetteer*, this county seat contained "500 inhabitants, four lawyers, four divines, two churches, four doctors . . . and two silversmiths. . . ." Six years later a local paper advertised "COMBS REPAIRED, D. L. BOOKER and D. S. LEMAN . . . in Athens, at G. Sehorn's silversmith shop. . . ."[9] In 1844 Banard Fagan (q.v.) announced he was "still carrying on business in the shop formerly occupied by George Sehorn."[10] Whether Sehorn had left Athens or merely changed locations is not known.

Two of Sehorn's brothers worked as silversmiths. William Monroe Sehorn (q.v.) was located in Athens, and John Sehorn (q.v.) worked in Shelbyville.[11]

$300 REWARD.

BOLD AND DARING ROBBERY.—My Jewelry Store was entered last night, and Robbed of the following

GOLD WATCHES:

One Diamond set enameled Hunting-case Watch,..............................No 1882
One Gold Lever full jewelled,
(D. B. Adams & Co.)......................" 462
One Gold Hunting Lever, (Johnson)" 1401
One Gold Lepine, (Tobias,)........" 1085
One Gold Hunting Lever (Harrison)" full jewelled and hard dial............" 2688

One Gold Hunting Anchor, (Tobias & Co.) without number

One second hand Gold Anchor, name and number not known.

Also, one Silver Lever and two Silver Anchor Watches.

Together with—3 Fob Chains, 3 pair of Gold Spectacles, 2 Gold Guards, 2 Vest Chains, 7 dozen plain Gold Rings, [12 caret gold,] 4 Gold Thimbles, Breast Pins, &c. &c.

Also—$330 in Money, one Ten Dollar note of which was on the Valley Bank of Virginia.

Receipts for $100 worth of Stock in the Nashville Gas Light Co., and $375 worth of Railroad Stock.

☞ I will give the [illegible] reward for the apprehension of the [illegible] recovery of the Goods, or a [illegible] rewa[illegible] for the Goods or thief. Nashville, [illegible]dnesday, [illegible]ugust 7, 1850.

A.O. H. [illegible] SEHORN.

Aug. 8.—tf

114. *On the night before 7 August 1850, A. O. H. P. Sehorn's store was robbed of several gold watches and other gold and silver items (Madisonville* Hiwassee Patriot, *8 Sept. 1840).*

115, 115a, 115b. *Three marks tentatively attributed to George Sehorn, 1825–40 (figs. 115, 115a), 1840–60 (fig. 115b). The mark illustrated in fig. 115 is from a spoon found in Bedford County. The mark illustrated in fig. 115a is the same mark with the addition of the flowers or sunbursts that flank it; it also has been attributed to William M. Sehorn. The fact that the die was shortened by one letter indicates that it was originally the mark of either George or William Sehorn later modified for use by John Sehorn. The mark illustrated in fig. 115b is similar to those attributed to William Sehorn (see figs. 116b, 116c).*

116. *Cup with "WMS" scratched on the bottom, 1842, engraved "Andrew and Mary Hutsell/ 1842," Shelbyville. HOA: 3⅛", width across rim: 2½". Private collection. This cup is attributed to William Monroe Sehorn.*

It is possible that the ".SEHORN" marks (figs. 115, 115a) on a spoon with a Bedford County provenance may be that of George Sehorn. The period in front of "SEHORN" may indicate that the die was shortened, removing one or more initials. If that is true, the mark may have been used by more than one of the Sehorn brothers, perhaps even two working in partnership.

SEHORN, John M. Silversmith. Shelbyville, Bedford County, 1853–60 and later.

John M. Sehorn worked in Shelbyville as a silversmith from at least 1853–69 or later. The 1853 *Nashville Business Directory* listed "J. N. Sehorn," probably the same man, as a "Dealer in Watches and Jewelry" in Bedford County. The 1860 *State Gazetteer* identified him as "John M." on the east side of the public square in Shelbyville, as did an 1869 notation in Nashville's city directory.[12] Sehorn's brothers, William Monroe (q.v.) and George (q.v.), were also silversmiths.[13]

SEHORN, William Monroe. Silversmith, jeweler, watchmaker. Athens, McMinn County, 1842–d. 1876.

William Monroe Sehorn, the second child of George and Frances Haskins Sehorn, was born in Jefferson County, Tennessee, on 29 December 1817. He was working in McMinn County as early as 1842 when a family history recorded that he made a cup from silver premiums presented at the county fair.[14]

He married Ann Eliza Coleman; the couple had six children: Norah, May, John Oliver, William, Jr., Emma, and George Covington. At the time of the 1850 census, Sehorn was living with his mother, his wife, and four children in Athens. Merchant James H. Hornsby (q.v.) and Harriet, his wife, lived in Sehorn's household as well; Harriet Hornsby was Ann Eliza Sehorn's sister. In the census, Sehorn was identified as a silversmith.[15]

The 1853 *Nashville Business Directory* listed Sehorn as a jeweler and watchmaker under the heading of "principal business houses and professional men" in Athens. According to local tradition, he was a prominent citizen with a large house and shop on the square.[16] When Athens reached the zenith of its prosperity during the 1850s, the firm of Sehorn and Hornsby (q.v.) dealt in dry goods, watches, and clocks on the north side of the square.[17] It is not known when Sehorn formed a partnership with James Hornsby. Sehorn was a trustee of Tennessee Wesleyan at the time of its founding in 1857 and was one of the incorporators of the Franklin Banking Association.[18] Sehorn died in 1876 and was buried in Cedar Grove Cemetery in Athens.[19]

John M. Sehorn (q.v.), a Shelbyville silversmith, and silversmith George Sehorn (q.v.) of Athens were William Monroe Sehorn's brothers.[20]

Athens historian William M. Selden attributed the "SEHORN" mark (fig. 116b) with an eagle and the

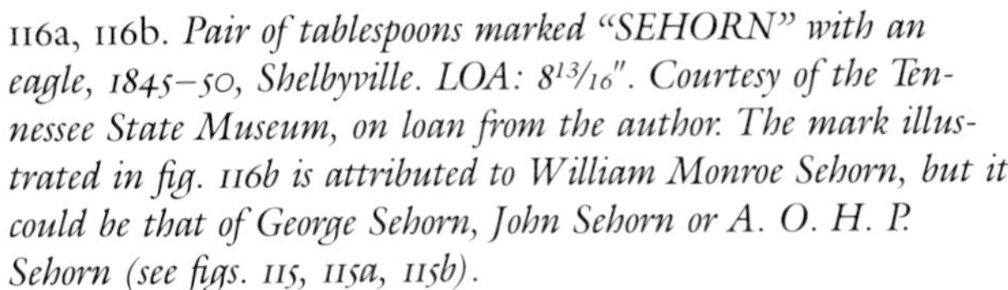

116a, 116b. *Pair of tablespoons marked "SEHORN" with an eagle, 1845–50, Shelbyville. LOA: 8 13/16". Courtesy of the Tennessee State Museum, on loan from the author. The mark illustrated in fig. 116b is attributed to William Monroe Sehorn, but it could be that of George Sehorn, John Sehorn or A. O. H. P. Sehorn (see figs. 115, 115a, 115b).*

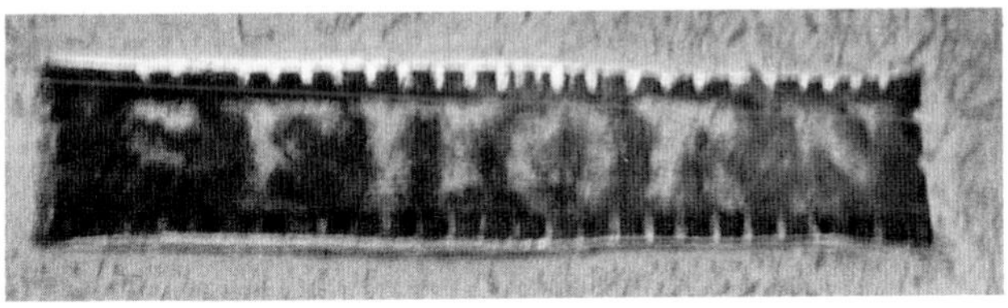

116c. *"SEHORN" mark attributed to William Monroe Sehorn, 1845–50. The similarity of the "SEHORN" of this mark to that of the "SEHORN" in fig. 116b has led to this attribution.*

"SEHORN" mark (see fig. 115a) with sunbursts to William M. Sehorn. Because of its similarity to the mark that is accompanied by an eagle, the "SEHORN" mark (fig. 116c) with serrated edges, but without an eagle, also has been attributed to William M. Sehorn.

SEHORN and HORNSBY. *Dealers in dry goods, watches, clocks.* Athens, McMinn County, 1850s-60.

Sehorn and Hornsby was a jewelry and clock and watchmaking firm in Athens, operating on the north side of Public Square from the 1850s-60. Sehorn was William M. Sehorn (q.v.), with whom James H. Hornsby (q.v.) and his wife boarded. An inventory of the personal property of William M. Sehorn recorded in McMinn County, 19 December 1879, listed a set of jeweler's tools and materials as well as money paid to the estate by James H. Hornsby, "surviving partner of Sehorn and Hornsby."[21]

SEHORNE, Alexander. *Silversmith.* Shelbyville, Bedford County, 1860.

Born in Tennessee about 1820, Alexander Sehorne was working as a silversmith at time of the 1860 census for Bedford County. Sehorne and Catherine, his wife, lived in Shelbyville with four children: Ema, Kate, Oliver, and Mary C. The children were all born in Tennessee and ranged in age from one month to nine years. In 1860 Sehorne estimated the value of his real property at $3,000 and his personal property at $200. It is not known what relation this man was, if any, to the Sehorn family.

SEWELL, Jonathan A. Silversmith. Olympus, Overton County, 1850–60.

Jonathan A. Sewell was born in Tennessee about 1804. At the time of the 1850 census, Sewell and his family were living in Olympus, where he worked as a silversmith. The census listed the value of his assets at $300. Sewell remained in Olympus until at least 1860.[22]

SHEEGOG, Edward. Jeweler. Columbia, Maury County, 1847.

Edward Sheegog's advertisements in *The Columbia Beacon* during 1847 indicate that he operated a variety store that stocked "Fine New-style Jewelry" as well as ready-made clothing and dry goods. Cash buyers were "offered every inducement."[23]

SHEEGOG, James H. Silversmith. Nashville, Davidson County, 1853–55.

James H. Sheegog worked as a silversmith at 17 Deaderick Street in Nashville from 1853–55.[24]

SHIRLEY, George Y. Clock and watchmaker. Sparta, White County, 1825.

George Y. Shirley opened his business in a room adjoining the Washington Hotel in Sparta in May 1825. He identified himself as a clock and watchmaker.[25]

The Nashville *Clarion and Tennessee State Gazette* for 21 July 1818 recounted the following story of a counterfeiter named George Shirley. Although no connection has been established between the Shirleys, it is possible that they were one in the same, as a counterfeiter required engraving skills related to those of silversmithing.

> A man who is called Col. Dixon was some days ago apprehended in Franklin county . . . on a suspicion of having been engaged in counterfeiting. He made some confessions, but was afterwards liberated. He was taken a second time and brought into Lawrence county, Ten. where he made the same confession on oath; he states that himself and George Shirley has been at work in a cave in the aforesaid county of Franklin, near the waters of Little Bear creek, ever since last winter —that they have counterfeited upwards of $60,000 on the State Bank of North Carolina, on the Bank of New York, and on the Potommac Bank, that they gave $5000 to two men who furnished them with provisions and rags to make their paper, that George Shirley took $5000 to himself.

SHOEMAKE, Landay. Watchmaker, silversmith, jeweler. Smith County, 1848? Nashville, Davidson County, 1849.

In 1849 Landay Shoemake, "formerly of Smith County," was working in Nashville as a silversmith with E. K. Burke (q.v.) in the firm of Burke and Shoemake (q.v.), watchmakers, silversmiths, and jewelers located at a shop on College Street next door to the Nashville Insurance office.[26]

SHULER, J. W. Watchmaker. Jackson, Madison County, 1860.

J. W. Shuler, a twenty-two-year-old Pennsylvanian, was working as a watchmaker in Jackson at the time of the 1860 Madison County census. He lived in the home of B. J. Sneed (q.v.).

SIMPKINS, James. Silver plater. Nashville, Davidson County, 1860.

James Simpkins, born in Pennsylvania about 1813, was listed in the 1860 census for Nashville as a silver plater. He lived in the same household as Henry Parkhurst (q.v.) and may have been one of Parkhurst's employees.

SIMPSON, James. Silversmith. Knoxville, Knox County, 1818–d. 1821.

James Simpson was born near Belfast, Ireland, about 1797. In about 1818, presumably not long after his arrival in America, Simpson joined Samuel Bell (q.v.) and Edmund Dyer (q.v.) in the firm of Bell, Dyer and Simpson (q.v.), watch and clockmakers, silversmiths, and jewelers in Knoxville. When the firm was dissolved two years later, Bell and Simpson (q.v.) formed a short-lived partnership that ended in 1821 with Simpson's death of a "pulmonary complaint."[27]

James Simpson's estate inventory, recorded during the April 1823 sessions of the Knox County court, revealed that he owned an eagle punch, the mark used "by a number of Baltimore silversmiths before the Assay Office came into existence." Martha Gandy Fales, in *Early American Silver*, noted that its use became popular after the Revolutionary War.[28] William M. Sehorn (q.v.) in nearby Athens later used an eagle punch with his mark.

SIMPSON, Samuel. Silversmith. Clarksville, Montgomery County, 1837?–48; 1860.

Samuel Simpson was born in Maine about 1807. An 1823 Portland city directory listed a Samuel Simpson, clockmaker, at "No. 8, Jones' Row exchange" in that city, but no documentation has been found to indicate that the Tennessee silversmith by the same name was a resident of Portland; in 1823 he would have been only sixteen years of age. Tennessee's Samuel Simpson was living in the state by 1837 when his oldest son, Alfred, was born. A newspaper notice (fig. 118) revealed that by 1840 Simpson was working as a silversmith in Clarksville.[29]

Simpson evidently maintained his business in Clarksville through 1858 when he sold his property there. Simpson may then have moved to Hopkinsville, Christian County, Kentucky, less than thirty miles from Clarksville, for an S. Simpson advertisement appeared in the 1859–60 Kentucky *State Gazetteer and Business Directory* listing for Hopkinsville.[30] Correspondence with a Trigg County (once part of Christian County), Kentucky, family that has owned several S. Simpson spoons revealed that many of neighboring Trigg County's citizens originally came from the Clarksville area.[31]

117. *"J. SIMPSON" mark, 1818–21. This mark is attributed to James Simpson.*

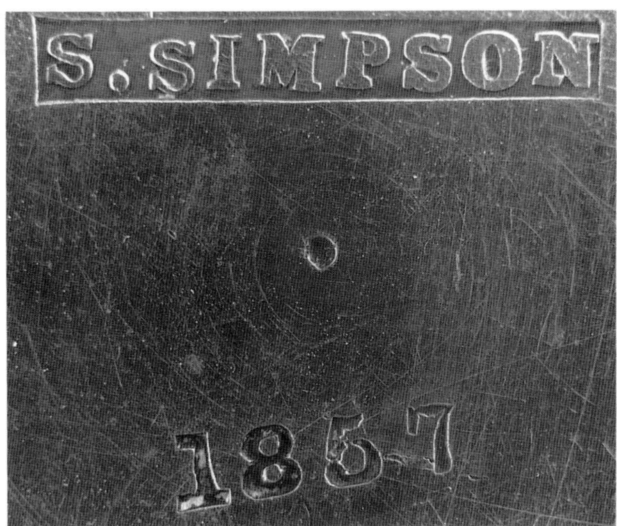

118a, 118b. *Beaker marked "S. SIMPSON" and "1857," engraved "Made by/ S. Simpson/ for/ Christian Co. A. and M. Association/ 1857," Clarksville. HOA: $4\frac{9}{16}$", Width across rim: $3\frac{1}{8}$". Courtesy of the Tennessee State Museum, photographs by Stephen D. Cox.*

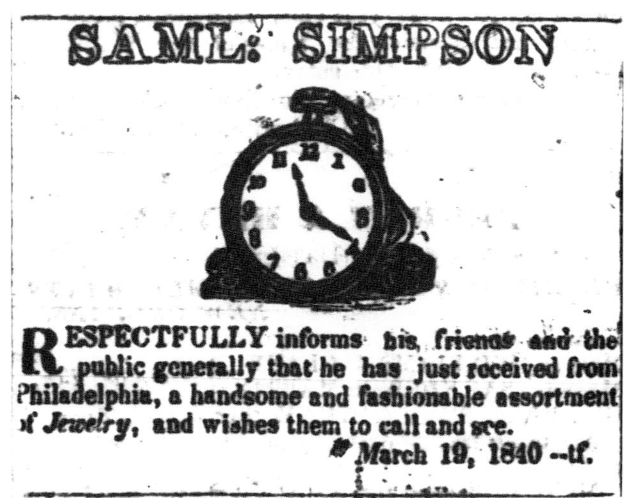

SAML: SIMPSON

RESPECTFULLY informs his friends and the public generally that he has just received from Philadelphia, a handsome and fashionable assortment of *Jewelry*, and wishes them to call and see.

March 19, 1840 --tf.

118. *Samuel Simpson announced in the* Clarksville Chronicle *of 13 February 1840 that he had jewelry from Philadelphia for sale.*

118c. *Goblet marked "S. SIMPSON," engraved "Made by S. Simpson/ For Christian County Agricultural & Mechanical/ Association/ 1857," Clarksville. HOA: $7\frac{3}{8}$", width across rim: $4\frac{1}{8}$". Private collection.*

Simpson returned to Tennessee, for an 1860 census for Montgomery County recorded his presence in Clarksville with his wife and family; his six children ranged in age from three to nineteen. Three additional adults lived in the Simpson household at the time.

SLAYTON, S. G. Gold and silversmith. Jackson, Madison County, 1826–28; 1838.

In 1826 S. G. Slayton established himself in Jackson as a gold and silversmith; the town had been laid out in 1822. In his Market Street shop he offered an assortment of jewelry, repaired clocks and watches, and both made and repaired silver objects. He remained in Jackson through 1828, apparently leaving thereafter. The town prospered, growing to a population of 695 in 1830 and "near 900" in 1833. Slayton returned to Jackson in 1838, informing the "citizens of Madison and surrounding Counties" that he had again commenced business in the shop formerly occupied by Jacob Sossaman (q.v.), another silversmith, on Main Street in Jackson.[32]

SMITH, Huineston. Silversmith. Rogersville, Hawkins County, 1820.

Huineston Smith was working in Rogersville, Hawkins County, as a silversmith in 1820. As noted in the 1820 census of manufactures, his shop annually used $200 worth of silver and $50 worth of gold making "spoons." He employed one man, owned one set of tools, had $600 capital invested, and estimated $200 in contingent expenses.[33]

SMITH, Joel B. Silversmith. Carthage, Smith County, 1820.

In the 1820 census of manufactures for Smith County, Joel B. Smith revealed that his silversmithing trade was a profitable one. He reported an annual use of $100 worth of gold and $900 worth of silver in his one-man shop; his production consisted of tablespoons, teaspoons, spurs, finger rings, watch chains, and seals.[34]

SMITH, John M. Jeweler, watchmaker. Nashville, Davidson County, 1835.

John M. Smith's advertisement in the 19 June 1835 *Nashville Union* announced the sale of his jewelry store to Daniel Webb (q.v.) and John S. Britain (q.v.). He requested that his customers pick up their repaired watches and pay the charges in cash. Although the evolving form of Smith's mark (figs. 119a, 119c, 119d, 119e) seems to indicate an artisan who worked over a number of years, the only documentation of his trade history lies in one advertisement and in his silver.

SNEED, B. J. Silversmith. Jackson, Madison County, 1850, 1860 and later.

Born in North Carolina about 1817, B. J. Sneed was working as a silversmith in Jackson by 1850. He lived in the household of Thomas McCowat (q.v.), another Madison County silversmith.[35] Sometime after 1850 he married a Tennessee woman and moved to Texas where two daughters were born between 1854–56. By 1860 Sneed had returned to Jackson where he listed his occupation as that of a watchmaker. At that time he estimated his personal estate to be worth $900. Another watchmaker, J. W. Shuler (q.v.), lived with the Sneeds.[36]

SOBEL, D. L. Jeweler. Nashville, Davidson County, 1860 and later.

D. L. Sobel, who was born in Austria about 1833, was working as a jeweler at the time of the 1860 census for Davidson County; he was living with Isaac Sobel (q.v.) in Nashville's First Ward. The 1869 *Nashville Business Directory* for 1869 indicated that he was still in business at that time.[37]

SOBEL, Isaac M. Jeweler. Nashville, Davidson County, 1856?–60 and later.

Isaac M. Sobel was born about 1824 and arrived in Nashville with Yette, his wife, and children Leopold and Rebecca some time after 1855. The 1860 federal census for Davidson County listed Sobel's birthplace and that of his wife and firstborn child as Austria; however, Fedora Frank in *Five Families and Eight Young Men* recorded his birthplace as Krakow, Poland.[38] The 1859 *Nashville Business Directory* reported that I. M. Sobel and Company was performing the services of watch and clockmakers, silversmiths, silver platers, and jewelers. In 1860 Sobel lived with his wife and four children in Nashville's First Ward. D. L. Sobel (q.v.) also was a member of the household and probably a partner in the firm of I. M. Sobel and Company. Directories listed varying street numbers for his shop on Market Street, but all of these addresses apparently represent the same location at the corner of Market and Broad. The firm continued its operation well beyond 1860.[39] Sobel's will was probated in Nashville during the February 1883 court term.[40]

SORGE (SORG), Jacob. Watchmaker. Memphis, Shelby County, 1860.

Jacob Sorge, a partner in the firm of M. Koch and Company (q.v.), was living in the Fourteenth District of Shelby County and working as a watchmaker for Koch at the time of the 1860 census. The twenty-seven-year-old German valued his personal estate at $100. Sorge and Ann, his German-born wife, shared their home with Mat Cook (q.v.), another watchmaker.

SOSSAMAN, Jacob. Silversmith. Jackson, Madison County, 1837–38.

Jacob Sossaman was working as a silversmith in Jackson in 1837. Later that year he may have made preparations to vacate his shop, for his 15 December 1837 newspaper notice requested all those indebted to him to pay up, and all those with jewelry or watches in his shop to claim them. Sossaman remained in Jackson through Jan-

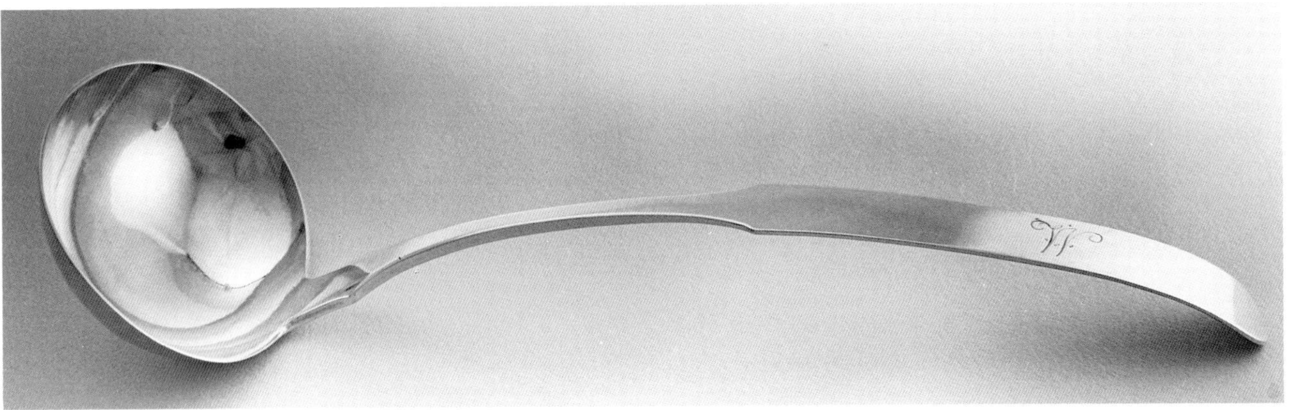

119, 119a. *Punch ladle marked "J. M. SMITH," 1830, engraved "W," Nashville. LOA 13½", width across bowl: 4⅝", rise: 1 1/2. Private collection. The mark is attributed to John M. Smith.*

119b, 119c. *Child's cup marked "J. M. Smith," 1840–45, Nashville. HOA: 3³⁄₁₆", width across rim: 2¾". Private collection.*

119d, 119e. *Two marks attributed to John M. Smith, 1840–50. Fig. 119e, courtesy of the Tennessee State Museum, photograph by Stephen D. Cox.*

---

uary 1838, when his home, shop, and several acres of land adjoining Jackson were sold at auction. By February, silversmith S. G. Slayton (q.v.) had moved into Sossaman's Main Street shop.[41]

A John F. Sossaman, silversmith, was a resident of Mobile, Alabama, about 1820; it is possible that the two men were related.[42]

SPENCER, T. W. Watchmaker, jeweler. Trenton, Gibson County, 1860 and later.

According to an 1861 newspaper story, T. W. Spencer was a "well and favorably known" workman in Gibson County; his workmanship as a watchmaker and jeweler was said to be "of the first water." Spencer and Samuel H. Freeman (q.v.), another Trenton jeweler, formed a partnership during January 1861.[43]

STALLINGS, Zachariah. Clock repairer. Columbia, Maury County, 1850.

Zachariah Stallings was born in Kentucky about 1806. The record of the birth of Mary, his eldest child, placed him in Tennessee by 1840. At the time of the 1850 census for Maury County he was living with his wife Prudence and three children in Columbia and working as a "Clock Repairer."

STANFIELD, John. Watchmaker. Murfreesboro, Rutherford County, 1860.

John Stanfield, who was born about 1839 in North Carolina, was working as a watchmaker in Murfreesboro at the time of the 1860 census. He was living in the J. C. Gray household with F. Winship (q.v.), another watchmaker. Nine years later the *Nashville Business Directory* listings for Murfreesboro included the name of "John A. Stangefield" as a "watchmaker/jeweler," probably the same man.[44]

Rutherford and Bedford Counties are contiguous, and it is possible that John A. Stanfield (q.v.) and John Stanfield were related, but no family tie has been documented.

STANFIELD, John A. Silversmith. Shelbyville, Bedford County, 1830–50.

John A. Stanfield was born about 1810, probably in Tennessee. He was practicing his trade in Shelbyville as early as 1830, remaining there through at least 1850. He was living with Acton Young, a hotelkeeper, at the time of the 1850 census.[45]

STANFORD, Steven. Silver plater. Memphis, Shelby County, 1860.

Steven Stanford, a native of Tennessee, was working as a silver plater in Memphis at the time of the 1860 census. Aged twenty-three, he lived in the city's Second Ward.

STAUB, R. Jeweler. Nashville, Davidson County, 1842–43.

For a short time during 1842–43, R. Staub operated a jewelry shop at the Washington Hotel on College Street in Nashville; he had previously done business in New York. Staub informed the citizens of Nashville that he would sell his entire stock of fine jewelry, watches, chains, spoons, music boxes, and "Breastpins" at cost. In payment, he was willing to accept cotton, feathers, beeswax, furs, dried peaches and apples, old gold and silver, or cash.[46]

STEINDLER, M. Jeweler. Memphis, Shelby County, 1856–60.

In 1856 M. Steindler was working as a jeweler on Jefferson Street, between Main Street and Front Row, in Memphis. At the time of the 1860 census, Steindler, aged thirty-five, and his wife Rosetta, both natives of Bavaria, lived with their five children in the city's First Ward.[47]

W. R. STEWART,
WATCH & CLOCL MAKER, GOLD & SIL, VER SMITH.

He has located himself in M'Minnville, Ten. where he respectfully tenders his services to the citizens of the Mountain District. He hopes to receive the patronage of the adjacent counties, as many facilities are offered by the stage and mail-riders, to convey watches, &c.— No pains or attention on his part wi'l be spared to return watches and other articles sent for repairs, with the greatest safety and despatch. His terms will be reasonable, and he flatters himself none will have reason to complain of the execution of any business with which he may be favored.

Sept. 8, 1831—3t.

120. *William R. Stewart advertised the opening of his establishment in McMinnville for the purpose of serving "the citizens of the Mountain District" in the* Sparta Recorder and Law Journal *of 8 October 1831.*

STEINHARDT, M. Jeweler. Memphis, Shelby County, 1855.

In 1855 M. Steinhardt operated a jewelry shop at 179 Main Street in Memphis; he lived at 106 Front Row.[48]

STEVENS, (....?). Watchmaker, jeweler, silversmith. Nashville, Davidson County, 1849–50.

Stevens, whose first name is unknown, joined Nashville silversmith John Campbell (q.v.) in the partnership of Campbell and Stevens (q.v.) that lasted during circa 1849–50. Their establishment at the corner of Union and College streets in Nashville offered jewelry, watches, and fancy goods. By 1853 the partnership had been dissolved, and Campbell became George W. Donigan's (q.v.) partner.[49]

STEWART, William R. Silversmith. McMinnville, Warren County, 1831; Sparta, White County, 1850–60.

William R. Stewart was born in Kentucky about 1806. In October 1831 he introduced himself as a gold and silversmith to the "citizens of the Mountain District" in McMinnville, offering his services as well to adjacent counties "as many facilities are offered by the stage and mail-riders. . . ." He flattered himself that no one would "have reason to complain" about the quality of his work. By 1850 Stewart was living in Sparta; his household included his wife Mary Ann, the couple's seven children, and L. G. Patterson, a daguerreotype artist and his wife.[50] Stewart was still in Sparta at the time of the 1860 census; he estimated the value of his real property at $1,500 and his personal property at $400.

In *American Silver, Pewter and Silver Plate*, the Kovels noted two William Stewarts: one in Russellville, Kentucky (circa 1790–1851), and another in St. Louis, Missouri (circa 1845).[51] No relationship with the Tennessee silversmith has been established.

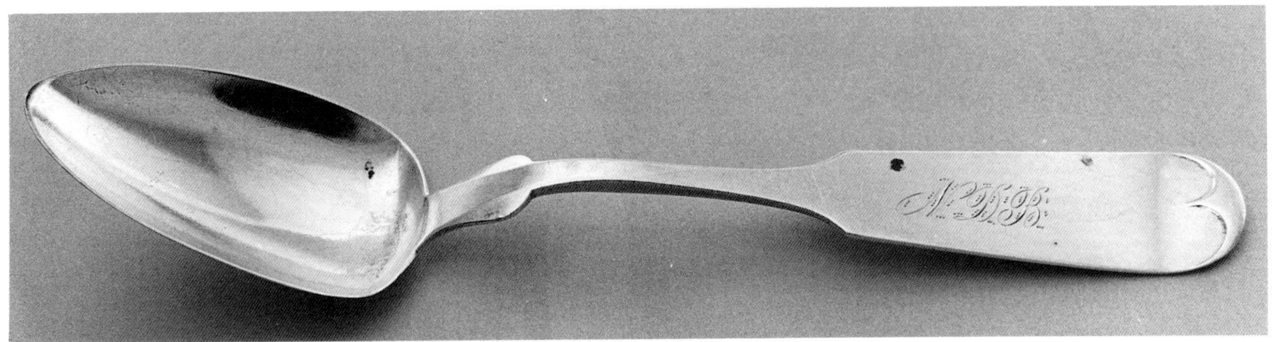

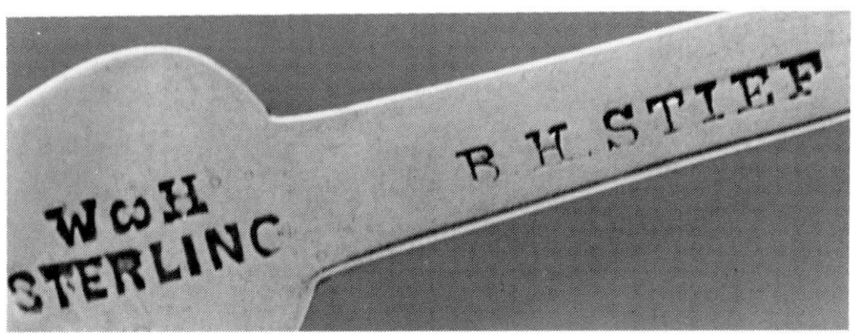

121, 121a. *Tablespoon marked "B. H. STIEF," and "W & H STERLING," 1860–65, engraved "NDB," Nashville. LOA: 7 13/16. Courtesy of the Tennessee State Museum, on loan from the author. The "W & H Sterling" illustrated in fig. 121a indicates that Wood & Hughes (1840–99) of New York made this spoon for Bruno Hugo Stief; several other Tennessee firms imported their silver from Woods & Hughes (see figs. 46b, 71a, 84, 99b, and 126a).*

121b. *Mark used by Bruno Hugo Stief, 1865–70?.*

STIEF, Bruno Hugo. Apprentice watchmaker. Nashville, Davidson County, 1860 and later.

Born the son of Franz and Susan Stief in 1847 in Prussia, Bruno Stief, according to tradition, was apprenticed to Nashville silversmith George Washington Donigan (q.v.). If that is true, he was with Donigan at the time of the 1860 census for Davidson County, which recorded that fifteen-year-old "Bruno W. R." and his brother Oscar (q.v.) were apprentice watchmakers.[52] By 1866 Bruno Stief was working independently as a jeweler at 4 Union Street in Nashville; he remained in the trade for many years.[53]

STIEF, Oscar. Apprentice watchmaker. Nashville, Davidson County, 1860 and later.

Oscar Stief was born in Prussia about 1843 to Susan and Franz Stief. At the time of the 1860 census, the family lived at 22 North Front Street in Nashville's First Ward. Stief was an apprentice watchmaker at 4 Union Street, perhaps in G. W. Donigan's shop located at the corner of Union and Front streets. An 1866 directory noted that Stief was located at 3 South Cherry Street.[54]

STOUT, B. Francis. Silversmith. Cleveland, Bradley County, 1850–60.

B. Francis Stout was born in Tennessee about 1818. At the time of the 1850 census he was living in the Cleveland household of James and Elizabeth Berry and working as a silversmith. Ten years later the census reported his presence in Cleveland, this time listing him as "B. T." Stout.

STOUT, Samuel Van Dyke. Silver plater. Nashville, Davidson County, 1812–19.

As early as 1812, Samuel V. D. Stout was working with B. McKiernan in the firm of McKiernan and Stout (q.v.). The following year he married Catharine Tannehill of Nashville. In 1817 McKiernan and Stout added silver plating to the various services offered by their coach-and-carriage-making firm. With the dissolution of that partnership in early 1819, Stout and Henry Long formed a partnership devoted to coach and harness making. In August 1819 McKiernan offered for sale the two-story wooden building "now occupied by S. V. D. Stout & Co. as a silver plating establishment."[55]

In 1841 Stout served a term as mayor of Nashville.[56] In the 1847 Corporation of Nashville taxable property enumeration, Stout was listed with assets of $15,650: four pieces of real estate valued at $13,100, seven slaves valued at $2,500, and one carriage worth $50.[57] An advertisement in the 30 November 1850 *Daily Nashville American* revealed that Ira Stout, formerly of the late Samuel V. D. Stout's coach manufactory and repair shop on Water Street, had taken over the firm.

STROCK (STRUCKE), D. H. Silversmith, jeweler. Paris, Henry County, 1853; Jackson, Madison County, 1860.

In 1853 D. H. Strock, born about 1823 in Ohio, was working as a silversmith and jeweler in Paris. By 1860, he had moved his business to Jackson, Madison County, where Strock, his wife, and three young children shared their home with August Bailey of Ohio and Phillip McKall, a laborer from Indiana. L. B. Everman's (q.v.) residence was next door to Strock's.[58]

Kovel listed a silversmith named Edmund Strock in Philadelphia, circa 1850. No connection with the Tennessee silversmith is known.[59]

STUMPH, John W. Silversmith, jeweler. Savannah, Hardin County, 1860; Purdy, McNairy County, 1860 and later.

The 1860 census for McNairy County listed John Stumph as a silversmith in Purdy, McNairy County; aged twenty-two, Stumph, a native of Ohio, estimated the value of his personal property at $500. Although the 1860 *State Gazetteer* listed him under "Jewelry, watches, clocks, etc." in Savannah in neighboring Hardin County, Stumph appears to have been a resident of Purdy. The *State Gazetteer* recorded that he was working there as a jeweler as late as 1876.[60]

SWORD, William. Apprentice silversmith. Bean Station, Grainger County, 1826.

William Sword, an apprentice to silversmith William L. Atkinson (q.v.) of Bean Station, ran away 2 April 1826; Atkinson offered a one-cent reward, stating that he would pay the reward and nothing else for Sword's return. Atkinson believed that a "degraded person in the neighborhood" had persuaded Sword to leave, and therefore Atkinson would neither pay charges nor give thanks. It appears that Sword made a successful escape, for nothing further is known of him.[61]

TATE, Philip. Silversmith. Memphis, Shelby County, 1858?–60.

Philip Tate, a forty-seven-year-old silversmith from Germany, apparently had arrived in Tennessee about 1858. At the time of the 1860 census he was living in the Seventh Ward of Memphis with his wife, Louisa, son John, nine, both natives of Germany, and his daughter Louisa, aged two, born in Tennessee.

THOMAS, B. L. Silversmith, jeweler, watch and clockmaker. Dyersburg, Dyer County, 1860.

B. L. Thomas, a native of Kentucky, appeared in the 1860 *State Gazetteer* under "Jewelry, Watches, Clocks, Etc." in Dyersburg. At the time of the Dyer County census for 1860 the twenty-two-year-old silversmith estimated his real property at $4,400 and his personal property at $6,900.[1]

122. *"H. E. Thomas" mark attributed to Henry E. Thomas, 1839–40.*

THOMAS, Charles. Watchmaker. Memphis, Shelby County, 1860.

Charles Thomas was born in Pennsylvania about 1836. By 1860 he was working as a watchmaker. He and his wife, aged twenty-four, a native of Ireland, lived near J. E. Merriman (q.v.) and William C. Byrd (q.v.).

THOMAS, Henry E. Silversmith, jeweler. Nashville, Davidson County, 1839–40.

In 1839 Henry E. Thomas purchased the stock of silversmith Henry Cargill (q.v.) and opened a "New Fancy Store" on the corner of Public Square and Deaderick Street in Nashville. He replenished the old stock with new purchases "from the North" and offered for sale watches, silver spoons, forks, cups, and ladles. Thomas also employed "George E. Porter, recently of New Orleans," to repair watches. An advertisement the following year indicated that Thomas remained at the same location.[2] On one spoon Thomas's mark (fig. 122) appears to have been stamped next to the pseudo hallmarks of another silversmith. The primary mark contains a "G," possibly indicating Gorham, but absent is the anchor used by Gorham in its early pseudo hallmarks.[3]

THOMPSON, J. S. Clock and watchmaker, jeweler. Randolph, Tipton County, 1835.

In 1835 J. S. Thompson was working as a clockmaker, watchmaker, and jeweler in Randolph. At the time, Randolph, a post town established in 1827 on the east bank of the Mississippi River, was a community of twenty or thirty families. The town was "an excellent harbor for steam and flat boats at all stages of water" and convenient for shipping produce from the adjoining counties of Fayette, Haywood, Madison, and Hardeman. Thompson informed the citizens of Randolph that he had permanently located in their town to clean and repair in the best manner all descriptions of watches, clocks, musical boxes, and jewelry.[4]

Silversmith Joseph S. Thompson, who in 1832 was working in Louisville, Kentucky, may have been the same man.[5]

THOMSON, Thomas A. Gold and silversmith, watch and clock repairer, jeweler. Franklin, Williamson County, 1822–30.

In January 1822 Thomas A. Thomson entered a part-

THOMAS A. THOMSON,
Clock & Watch Maker, Gold & Silversmith,

HAS purchased the entire interest in the shop of Hiter & Thomson, and will carry on business in the same shop. All calls in his line of business will be promptly attended to for CASH.

Franklin, Jan. 26th, 1822. n't—jt

123. *In 1822 Thomas A. Thomson of Franklin purchased the entire interest in his former shop, Hiter and Thomson (Franklin* Independent Gazette, *26 Jan. 1822).*

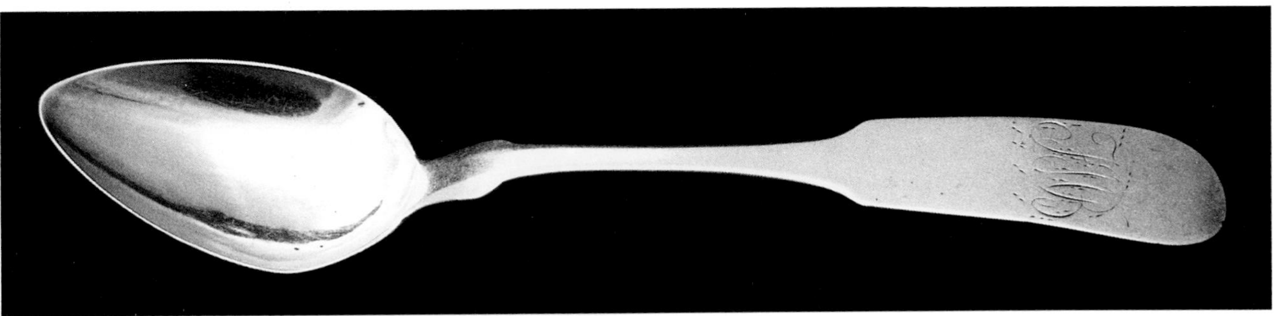

124, 124a. *Tablespoon marked "R. T," 1825?, engraved "TWB," Knoxville. LOA: 7⅝". Private collection. This tablespoon was found in eastern Tennessee; its mark, illustrated in fig. 124a, may have been that of Robert Titus.*

---

nership in Franklin with Thomas Hiter (q.v.); this arrangement lasted less than a month. Thomson purchased the entire interest in the shop and continued to work at the same location as a clock and watchmaker, gold and silversmith.[6] In July 1823 two of Thomson's apprentices ran away; he derisively advertised for the return of his two "STRAY DOGS," one "big dog" named Aaron Winslow, nearly six feet tall, and a smaller one named Trip. He offered a "reward of one cent and no thanks . . . for the big dog—fifty cents and all reasonable expences paid for the little one." He cautioned against anyone harboring the dogs, "particularly the dog Aaron as a body is very apt to smell bad after being in his company. The little fellar Trip 'never hurts nobody'."[7] Later in 1823 Thomson moved his silversmith shop from the east corner of the public square to the white frame house that had been occupied by S. Holland and before that by L. and J. Thompson, saddlers. At that time he advertised for an apprentice, a "smart, active boy of a good family, between 14 and 17 years of age. . . ."[8]

A Thomas Thomson, believed to be the same man, was listed in the Williamson County census of 1830.

TITUS, R. Watchmaker. Knoxville, Knox County, 1826–27.

R. Titus had appeared in Knoxville by December of 1825, when he offered to paint portraits. By February 1826 Titus was advertising his skills as a watchmaker on Cumberland Street. He remained at that address through August 1827.[9]

Cutten recorded a Robert Titus, watchmaker, working in Petersburg, Virginia, circa 1817, possibly the same man.[10]

A spoon (fig. 124) found in eastern Tennessee bears an "R. T." mark (fig. 124a), which may be that of Titus.

125. *"S. T. TONCRAY" mark attributed to Silas T. Toncray, 1829–47. Courtesy of Swannee Bennet, photograph by William B. Worthen.*

TODD, William. Jeweler. Memphis, Shelby County, 1860.

Born in Scotland about 1834, William Todd was working as a jeweler in Memphis by 1860. At that time he lived in the same household as watchmakers E. Parman (q.v.), F. H. Trudeau (q.v.), and W. L. Jobe (q.v.).

TOMKINS, John. Watchmaker. Memphis, Shelby County, 1860.

John Tomkins, born about 1803 in South Carolina, was a watchmaker who in 1860 was living in the Seventh Ward of Memphis with his Louisiana-born wife Mary. The ages given for his daughters Mollie, sixteen, and Eda, nine, along with the notation that they were born in Tennessee, indicated that Tomkins was present in the state by 1844.

TONCRAY, Daniel. Silversmith. Memphis, Shelby County, 1829.

Daniel Toncray worked as a silversmith in Martinsburg, Virginia (circa 1799), Allegheny County, Maryland (circa 1800), and Nelson County, Kentucky (circa 1808–20). He also worked in Memphis, where he died in 1829 at the age of sixty-four. He was silversmith Silas T. Toncray's (q.v.) older brother.[11]

TONCRAY, Silas T. Silversmith. Memphis, Shelby County, 1829–d. 1847.

Silas T. Toncray, born in 1795, was the youngest son of Daniel and Huldah Toncray of Allegheny County, Maryland. About 1812, he was working as a silversmith and engraver in Shelbyville, Kentucky, and he was in Arkansas by about 1821. He moved to Memphis in 1829, the year his brother, Daniel Toncray (q.v.), died in that city.[12]

In Memphis, Toncray worked as a watchmaker, sign painter, doctor, dentist, druggist, and minister. Described as a "hard-side Baptist," he built a small church at his own expense and served as pastor to its largely black congregation for a number of years. He also was a city alderman during 1835–36.[13] J. M. Keating noted in History of the City of Memphis and *Shelby County* that, although Toncray lived in humble circumstances and occupied "a comparatively small space in the public eye, he was one of the most estimable and useful members of the community."[14] Another Memphis historian called him "a mechanical genius," one of the city's "few prominent citizens."[15]

TOURNER, Henry. Watch and clockmaker, jeweler. Somerville, Fayette County, 1840.

Henry Tourner worked in Somerville as a jeweler and clock and watchmaker. He had received his training "at one of the best houses in Liverpool" and in May 1840 opened a "New Watch Establishment" on the public square adjoining Mr. Becker's hotel.[16]

TRABUE and WEST. Dealers in watches, silverware, jewelry. Nashville, Davidson County, 1834–37.

In 1834, the firm of Trabue and West was operating in Nashville next to Yeatman and Woods Bank, where they offered jewelry, gold and silver plated watches, earrings, breast pins, seals, keys, and charms, both at wholesale and retail prices. In an 1837 advertisement that is the last known reference to their partnership, the list of their stock included knives and forks, mahogany boxes with silver handles, a silver plated soup tureen, two sauce tureens, four vegetable dishes, one set of silver-mounted cake plates, and various types of candlesticks.[17]

TRUDEAU, F. H. Watchmaker. Memphis, Shelby County, 1860.

According to the 1860 census for Memphis, thirty-year-old F. H. Trudeau was born in "Canaday." He worked as a watchmaker for James Pooley and lived in the Second Ward of Memphis in the same household as watchmakers E. Parman and W. L. Jobe, as well as jeweler William Todd (qq.v.).[18]

TUNCK, Frederick. Watchmaker. Memphis, Shelby County, 1855–56?

In 1855 Frederick Tunck was employed as a watchmaker at F. H. Clark's (q.v.) shop in Memphis. The 1856 *Memphis City Directory* listed an F. Funck, watchmaker, also at F. H. Clark's; the two listings probably represent the same man.[19]

TURNER, Benjamin. Silversmith. Lebanon, Wilson County, 1850.

Benjamin Turner was born in Tennessee about 1825; at the time of the 1850 census he was working as a silversmith in Lebanon. His household included his Tennessee-born wife Amanda, Sarah Wrore, aged ninety, Catharine Pride, forty-two, and William B. Pride, eighteen.

TURRENTINE (TORENTINE, TORINTINE), Daniel. Silversmith. Shelbyville, Bedford County, 1820–d. 1833.

The Turrentine family were early settlers of Bedford County which was formed in 1807.[20] By 1820 Daniel Turrentine, a silversmith of Shelbyville in that county, was successful enough to employ three men, two boys and one girl; the total annual wages for the employees amounted to $100. Turrentine and his workers used gold, silver, and steel in their production of rings, spoons, and other objects; the total output was worth $500. His assets in 1820 included one set of silversmithing tools, and his capital investment totalled $90. When asked by the census taker about the supply and demand for goods, Turrentine reported, "This is a profitable business in this place."[21]

Turrentine's shop was located on the east side of the public square. In 1822 Turrentine hired silversmith George W. Ruth (q.v.), who later became his partner in the firm of Turrentine and Ruth (q.v.).[22] Turrentine may have left Shelbyville briefly, for in 1828 a local newspaper announced his return to a location on the south side of public square "in the room of the Brick house, between the stores of Messrs. R. Stevenson & Co., and Brittain & Escue."[23] Whether the Turrentine and Ruth partnership had lapsed during Turrentine's absence is not clear. According to the *Shelbyville Sesquicentennial Gazette*, the two men were still partners when the "Great Storm of 1830" struck the town.[24] The storm destroyed the firm's shop, scattered its merchandise, and destroyed Turrentine's house, severely injuring him. Although Turrentine did not fully recover from his injuries, the two men rebuilt their shop and continued working together until January 1833, when their partnership was dissolved. Turrentine died later that year of the Asiatic cholera that swept the area.[25]

A spoon found in Tennessee bears the mark "DT," which may have belonged to Daniel Turrentine; another possibility, however, is that this mark represents David Tyler of Boston, working circa 1760–1804.[26]

TURRENTINE and RUTH. Silversmiths, watchmakers. Shelbyville, Bedford County, 1824–33.

See Turrentine, Daniel; Ruth, George W.

VIAL, Louis. Watchmaker. Clarksville, Montgomery County, 1859, 1869 and later.

In 1859 Louis Vial was working in Clarksville as a watchmaker and dealer in watches, clocks, jewelry, silver, and silver plated ware. After an indeterminate absence, he returned ten years later to re-establish his business there.[27]

WADE, Terence P. Apprentice silver plater, apprentice silversmith. Nashville, Davidson County, 1860 and later.

The 1860 census for Davidson County contained two listings for Wade. One identified "Terry Wade, seventeen, app. silverplater," as a member of the Nashville household shared by Bruno and Oscar Stief (q.q.v.). The second entry listed "Terrance P. Wade," as an "app. silversmith" born in Ohio and living in the Fourth Ward of Nashville in the household of James Moore; his age was given as eighteen. The 1860 *Nashville Business Directory* recorded Wade's working address at that of Henry Parkhurst's (q.v.) silver plating firm at 12½ Deaderick Street. The 1875 *Nashville Business Directory* listed "Terrance P. Wade, bell hanger."[1]

WAGNER, Henry. Watchmaker, jeweler. Nashville, Davidson County, 1853–55.

In 1853 Henry Wagner was working as a watchmaker and jeweler at 5 South Market Street in Nashville. By 1855 he had moved his shop to 26 South Market.[2]

WALK (WOLK), Julius. Watchmaker. Nashville, Davidson County, 1860.

At the time of the 1860 census for Davidson County, Julius Walk, a twenty-three-year-old watchmaker from Indiana, was living with his wife, Zeffronia, a native of France, in the household of Henry Cohen (q.v.) in Nashville. No relationship between this man and Julius Walk, an Indiana jeweler (b. 1841), is known.[3]

WAMBELE, W. W. Silversmith. Kenton, Obion County, 1860.

Silversmith W. W. Wambele, born in Tennessee about 1829, was working in Kenton at the time of the 1860 census for Obion County. He lived with his wife Mary E. and two infants in the county's Eighth District.

WAMBLE, John W. Silversmith. Loudon, Roane County, 1860.

At time of the 1860 census for Roane County, thirty-two-year-old John Wamble was listed as a silversmith in Loudon. The 1860 *State Gazetteer* published his name under "Jewelry, Watches, Clocks, &tc." The Wambles' household included four children: George W., nine; Margaret, eight; James, six; and Lafayette, four.[4]

WARD, J. A. P. Silversmith. Dresden, Weakley County, 1850–60.

Born in North Carolina about 1815, J. A. P. Ward was in Weakley County by 1840. At the time of the 1850 census he and his wife Telitha (Tabitha?) lived in Dresden with their four children; Ward listed his occupation as that of a farmer and valued his real property at $500. By the time of the 1860 census, however, Ward was identified as a silversmith, perhaps indicating an increase in the amount of time he spent at that trade. Ward valued his real property at $1,500 and his personal property at $2,500.

WARNER, John. Watchmaker. Nashville, Davidson County, 1811.

In an 1811 advertisement, John Warner requested that his Nashville customers pick up their watches, for he planned to leave the city.[5]

A John Warner, clock and watchmaker, operated a shop at 66 Chatham Street in New York City during 1790–91. A J. Warner worked as a watchmaker in Norfolk, Virginia circa 1794–1801, and Richmond, Virginia circa 1803. No connection between these artisans and the Nashville man is known.[6]

WARREN, A. J. Dealer in watches, clocks, jewelry. Memphis, Shelby County, 1860.

A. J. Warren, Q. A. Gilkey (q.v.), and William T. Archer (q.v.) were partners in A. J. Warren and Company, a Memphis firm located at the corner of Main and Monroe Streets in 1860. The shop sold and repaired watches, jewelry, silverware, pistols, and canes and engraved "wedding and visiting cards."[7] At the time of the 1860 census, Warren, a native of New York, estimated the value of his personal property at $8,000. He was twenty-eight years old, apparently unmarried, and lived in the city's Fifth Ward, sharing the household with his partners.

Like many other Tennessee jewelers, Warren ordered silver from northern firms; one spoon bears a mark (fig. 126a) which is that of Wood and Hughes of New York.

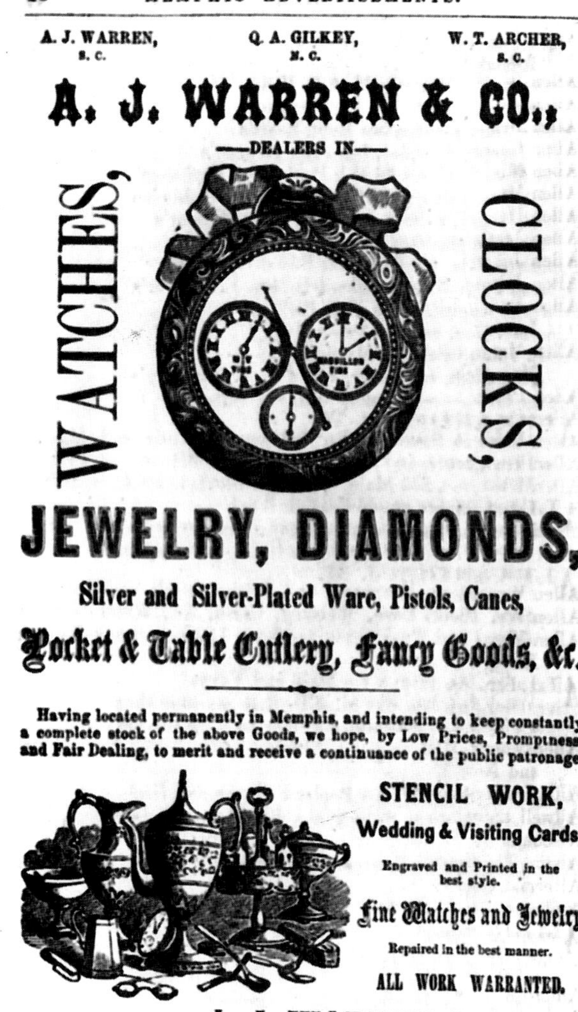

126. *A. J. Warren & Co. advertised in the 1860 Memphis city directory that they were dealers in watches, clocks, jewelry and diamonds.*

WATSON, E. Jeweler. Memphis, Shelby County, 1850.

E. Watson was born in England about 1827. By 1850 he had emigrated to Memphis, where he worked for F. H. Clark (q.v.) and boarded with several other young tradesmen in the household of James S. Wilkins (q.v.), a watchmaker.[8] No further information has been found regarding E. Watson, jeweler, but "Edward" Watson was listed as a painter in the 1860 *Memphis City Directory*; this may have been the same man.[9]

WATSON, William M. Silver plater. Nashville, Davidson County, 1820.

The 15 March 1820 *Nashville Whig* informed its subscribers that William M. Watson, silver plater, had opened a shop on Water Street, three doors above S. V. D. Stout's (q.v.). At that location, Watson sold coach and gig harness mounting, carriage mounting, and all kinds of saddlery. He also repaired and replated old bells and stirrup irons "on the shortest notice."

WEAVER, Charles. Silversmith, watchmaker, jeweler. Nashville, Davidson County, 1846–50.

Charles Weaver, a Nashville watchmaker, jeweler and silversmith, was born in Pennsylvania about 1818. In 1846

126a. *"W & H" and "A. J. WARREN" marks, c. 1860. A. J. Warren and Co. apparently sold silver made by Wood & Hughes (1840–99); several other Tennessee firms sold silver with a "W & H" mark attributed to the New York City firm (see figs. 46b, 71a, 84, 99h, 121a).*

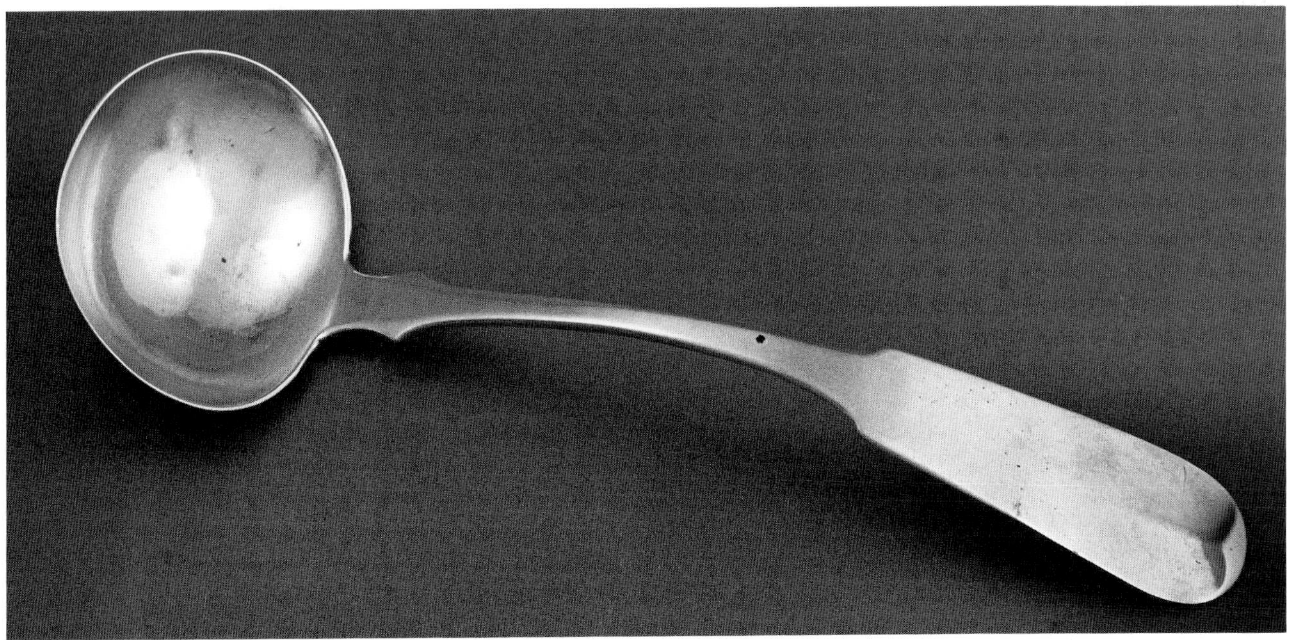

127, 127a. *Sauce ladle marked "E. Watson," 1850?, engraved "W" (adjacent to the bowl), Memphis? LOA: 7½". Courtesy of the Tennessee State Museum.*

he opened a shop on the north side of Broad Street, one door east of College Street, in Nashville. Weaver remained in Nashville at least through 1850; he probably was a partner in the firm of Connely and Weaver (q.v.), a Nashville clock, watch and jewelry firm establishment of the mid-nineteenth century.[10]

Several silversmiths with the Weaver surname worked in Pennsylvania during the eighteenth and nineteenth centuries. Charles Weaver may have been related to one or more of them.[11]

WEBB, Daniel A. Silversmith. Nashville, Davidson County, 1835; Cross Plains, Robertson County, 1850–60.

Daniel A. Webb was born in 1810 in North Carolina. He worked in Indianapolis before moving to Nashville by 1835, where he is believed to have been a partner in the firm of Webb and Britain (q.v.), a silversmith, clock and watchmaking establishment located in a shop on College Street formerly owned by J. M. Smith (q.v.).[12] By time of the 1850 census, Webb and his wife Frances, a native of Tennessee, had moved to Cross Plains, Robertson County, with their four children; his assets were estimated at $75. Webb remained in Cross Plains at least through 1860.[13]

WEBB and BRITAIN. Silversmiths, watch and clock repairers, jewelers. Nashville, Davidson County, 1835.

In 1835 D. A. Webb (q.v.) and Britain (q.v.), whose first name is unknown, established the partnership of Webb and Britain in a Nashville shop on College Street formerly owned by J. M. Smith (q.v.). Watches and clocks were repaired at the shop, and it stocked an as-

128. *"WEBB & BRITAIN" mark, c. 1835. The "WEBB" of this mark, attributed to the Nashville firm of Webb and Britain, is barely distinguishable.*

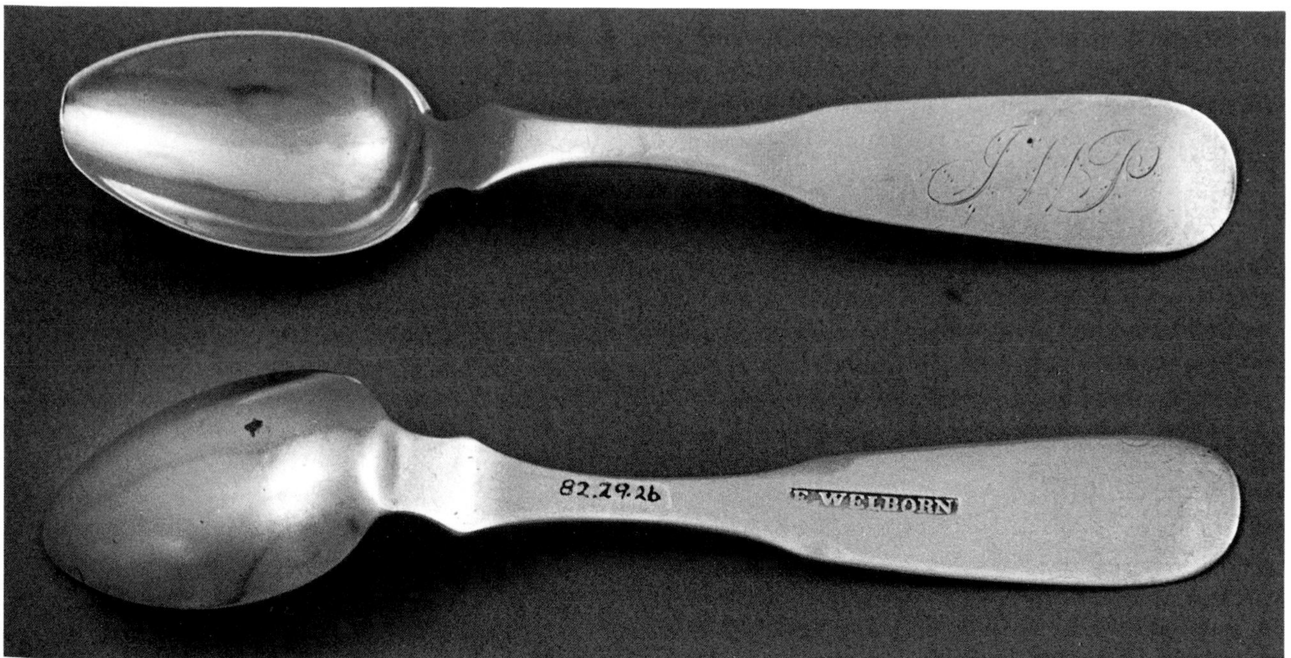

129, 129a. *Pair of tablespoons marked "E. WELBORN," 1835–40, engraved "JHP," Nashville. LOA: 5 1/16". Courtesy of the Tennessee State Museum, fig. 129a, photograph by Stephen D. Cox. These tablespoons are attributed to Enoch Welborn of Nashville.*

---

sortment of watches, jewelry, and silver work.[14] A mark (fig. 128) has been attributed to this firm; the "WEBB" is virtually obliterated.

WEINSTEIN, J. Jeweler, watch and clockmaker. Gallatin, Sumner County, 1860.

In 1860 J. Weinstein was working as a jeweler, and watch and clockmaker in Gallatin. His shop was located on Main Street opposite the public square.[15]

WELBORN, Chesterfield. Watch and clock repairer, jeweler. Nashville, Davidson County, 1848.

In the spring of 1848, Chesterfield Welborn informed "those who might be disposed to patronize him" that he had moved his shop to a house "adjoining the Union Hall" on Market Street in Nashville, where he would repair watches, clocks, and jewelry. He noted that he was particularly experienced in the repair of accordians.[16]

WELBORN, Enoch. Silversmith, watch and clockmaker, jeweler. Gallatin, Sumner County, 1820; Nashville, Davidson County, 1823–47; Memphis, Shelby County, 1853?

Although Enoch Welborn was a Gallatin resident in 1820, by 1823 he had moved to Nashville, where he worked as a watch and clockmaker in a shop formerly occupied by silversmith R. Gordon (q.v.), silversmith. An Enoch "Welbourne," possibly the same man, married Jane Baker in Davidson County on 25 October 1824. Welborn advertised fairly regularly during 1826–29, emphasizing fine jewelry imported from Philadelphia.[17] On 25 December 1836, he joined eight other men for the first meeting of the "Association of Watch-Makers, Silversmiths & Jewellers of Nashville" and was chosen chairman. His duties were to call and preside at all meetings, "explain the needs as understood, [and] define any doubts," that might arise among association members.[18] In 1841 an Enoch Welborn married Mary Ashbridge in

J. K. & D. J. WELLS,

HAVING located themselves in the town of Bolivar, respectfully offer their services to the citizens of the town and the public generally, as **SILVER SMITHS,** and hope by strict attention to business, to merit a share of public patronage. They will repair **CLOCKS & WATCHES,** in the neatest manner, and promise that their charges shall be moderate.

Bolivar, February 20, 1333.

130. *J. K. & D. J. Wells advertised in the Jackson* Southern Statesman *of 23 February 1833 that they had located in Bolivar.*

Davidson County. Welborn was still a resident of Nashville in 1847, for his name appeared on a list of property owners that year; he owned two slaves and additional assets valued at $800.

In 1853 an E. Welborn was working in Memphis as a jeweler on Shelby Street;[19] whether this was the same man or perhaps a son is not known.

WELLS, Daniel Ivy. Silversmith, clock and watch repairer, jeweler. Bolivar, Hardeman County, 1833–d. 1876; Chattanooga, Hamilton County, 1860?

Daniel Wells was born in South Carolina about 1810. By 1833 he had moved to Bolivar, where he (D. "J.") and J. K. Wells (q.v.) advertised (fig. 130) their services as silversmiths and clock and watch repairers. Eastin Morris's *State Gazetteer* for 1834 described Bolivar as a "flourishing post town . . . at the head of a steam boat navigation on the Hatchee, it must become a place of commercial importance." Also in 1834, D. "I." Wells and K. W. Wells (q.v.) advertised that they had moved to a new brick shop in Bolivar on Main Street one door south of Gridley Pynchon and Company. By January 1835, either the partnership had been dissolved or the firm had moved, for at that time a tailor occupied the Wells' shop.[20] The 1850 census for Hardeman County listed two apprentices, Samuel M. Jobe (q.v) and Richard A. Plenell (q.v.) as members of Daniel Wells's household in Bolivar; also listed was Wells's Virginia-born wife, Mary. During that year Wells used five-and-a-half pounds of gold and silver worth $300 to produce $1,500 worth of finished work, according to the census of manufactures for Hardeman County. By 1860 Wells and his family may have moved or purchased land in Chattanooga; the Hamilton County census listed an "A. J." Wells, who was born in 1810 in South Carolina, living with Mary, his Virginia-born wife, and a son, Edgar. Daniel J. Wells, however, was also listed in the 1860 census for Hardeman County with identical information regarding age, birthplace, wife, and son. According to the order of the Hardeman County listings, D. I. Wells may have lived next to the residence of R. L. "Lighford" (Robert Lightfort, q.v.).[21]

Daniel Ivy Wells was described as having served as "a longtime senior warden, lay reader and Sunday school superintendent" in St. James Parish, Bolivar. Hardeman County court records contained an account of the 19 May 1876 sale of Daniel I. Wells's estate documenting R. L. Lightfort as the surviving partner in the firm of "Daniel I. Wells and Company." Wells's widow appears to have remained in Bolivar until her death in 1892.[22]

Although the information regarding Daniel Wells is somewhat confused by differing locations and the inconsistent recording of initials, it is probable that "Daniel Ivy," "Daniel J." and "A. J." Wells were the same man.

WELLS, J. K. Silversmith, clock and watch repairer. Bolivar, Hardeman County, 1833.

In 1833 J. K. Wells was working in Bolivar, where he advertised with "D. J." Wells (Daniel Ivy Wells, q.v.) in the 23 January 1833 Jackson *Southern Statesman*. The partners offered their services as silversmiths, clock and watch repairers.

WELLS, James B. Gold and silversmith. Maryville, Blount County, 1859–60.

James B. Wells was born in North Carolina about 1807. He married a Tennessee woman; the birth of their eldest child placed Wells in Tennessee by 1839. By 1859 he was working in Maryville as a gold and silversmith; at that time, his assets were valued at $1,000.[23] In 1860 he reported in the Blount County census that he owned $4,000 worth of real property and personal property valued at $3,000.

WELLS, K. W. Silversmith. Bolivar, Hardeman County, 1833–35.

As early as January 1833, K. W. Wells was working as a silversmith in Bolivar. In March 1834 K. W. and D. "I." Wells (Daniel Ivy Wells, q.v.) announced that they had moved into a new shop on Main Street in Bolivar, where they performed all kinds of clock, watch and silver work. By January 1835 the partners had vacated their shop. Whether K. W. Wells remained a resident of Bolivar is not known.[24]

WHIPPLE, D. H. Silversmith, clock and watchmaker. Gallatin, Sumner County, 1811.

In April 1811 D. H. Whipple announced that he had equipped himself with "all the necessary apparatus" to carry on the work of a silversmith and clock and watchmaker and was ready to receive business in his Gallatin shop.[25]

Caswell County, North Carolina, court records recorded the presence of a David Whipple in 1780; no connection with the Tennessee man is known.[26]

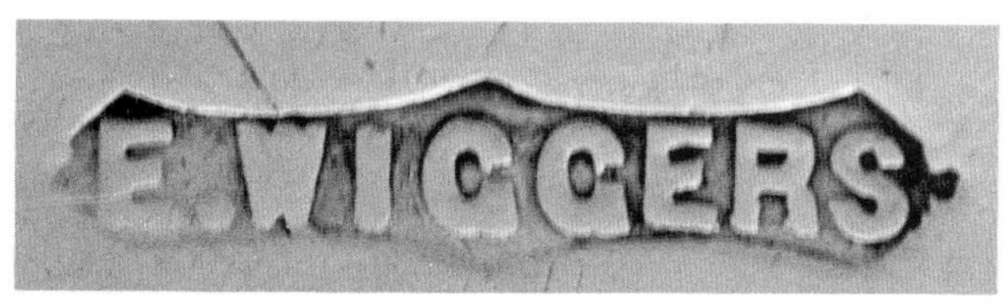

131, 131a. *Two "E. WIGGERS" marks attributed to Ernest Wiggers, c. 1860.*

WHITE, Samuel B. Clock and watchmaker, gold and silversmith. Carthage, Smith County, 1812.

On 8 July 1812 Samuel B. White respectfully informed the readers of the *Carthage Gazette* that he had commenced the "Clock and Watch-Maker, Gold & Silver-Smith" business in "the house adjoining the printing office," where he repaired clocks and watches, performed gold and silver work "on the shortest notice" and offered to purchase old gold and silver.

WHITING, A. Dealer in silver plated ware, jewelry. Nashville, Davidson County, 1825.

A. Whiting advertised in the *Nashville Gazette* of 18 February 1825 that he had "just opened in the store recently occupied by Doctor Hayes. . . ." and that some of his stock came from New York.

WIGGERS, Ernest. Silversmith. Nashville, Davidson County, 1866.

Documentation of Ernest Wiggers's presence in Nashville before 1866 has not been found.[27] However, his surviving work (figs. 131, 131a) appears to be hand made, and it is possible that he may have been working in Tennessee prior to 1860. The 1870 federal census revealed that Wiggers was born in "Hanover Kingdom" (Germany) about 1836.

WILCOX, N. P. Jeweler. Memphis, Shelby County, 1850–55.

N. P. Wilcox was born about 1829 in Connecticut. By 1850 he was living in Memphis in the household of John H. Krafft and working as a jeweler in the shop of J. E. Merriman and Company (q.v.) at 31 Front Row. Five years later Wilcox was still employed by Merriman and had become a boarder in the Merriman household on the corner of St. Patrick and Pontotoc streets. Another Memphis jeweler, Robert F. Wilcox (q.v.), also worked for J. E. Merriman and boarded at the Merriman residence.[28]

WILCOX, Robert F. (H.) Jeweler. Memphis, Shelby County, 1855–60 and later.

Robert F. Wilcox, born about 1833 in Connecticut, first appeared in Memphis as a jeweler in 1855. According to the 1855 *Memphis Directory*, he was employed by J. E. Merriman and Company (q.v.) and boarded at Merriman's home on the corner of St. Patrick and Pontotoc streets. City directories continued to list Wilcox at the Merriman firm until 1872, when separate listings were published for Merriman and "Willcox." The 1860 census also documented that he was a member of the J. E. Merriman household; Merriman evidently was located next door to William C. "Bird," (q.v.) in Ward Six of Memphis. In 1860 Wilcox evaluated his real property at $2000 and his personal property at $100.[29]

WILHOITE and BROTHERS. Dealers in jewelry, watches and clocks. Shelbyville, Bedford County, 1850–60.

Wilhoite and Brothers were retailers in jewelry, watches, and clocks on the south side of the public square in Shelbyville during 1850–60.[30]

WILKINS, James. Apprentice silversmith. Nashville, Davidson County, 1808. *Gold and silversmith*, Columbia, Maury County, 1820–d. 1876.

James Wilkins, born about 1788 in North Carolina, was apprenticed to Nashville silversmith Joseph T. Elliston (q.v.). In 1808 Wilkins and another apprentice ran away, and Elliston offered (fig. 132) a $60 reward for their return to Nashville. Elliston described Wilkins as a stout five-foot-four-inch-tall nineteen-year-old, with dark complexion and hair, and a round full face "much marked with an eruption."[31]

Goodspeed's *History of Tennessee* identified James Wilkins as the second silversmith to set up shop in the town of Columbia. A gold and silversmith, presumably the same James Wilkins, was listed in the 1820 census of manufactures for Maury County; Wilkins's shop used $500 worth of gold and silver annually and employed two men and one boy. Wilkins's total annual expenditure for wages amounted to $340, and he commented that demand for goods was "dull and slow." In 1844 he was still in business in Columbia, offering jewelry, spoons, rings, and silver watches. In the 1860 census, Wilkins, aged seventy-two, valued his real property at $5,000 and his personal property at $4,000.[32]

Wilkins died on 17 April 1876, and his obituary revealed that he had run away from his uncle, "James Ellison." He married Susan "Reaves" in Danville, Virginia in 1811. The couple later moved to Columbia, where they lived for fifty years. Wilkins's will identified his "aged and beloved wife" as Susan Reeves Dix; he left his wife and estate in the care of his niece, Eudora A. Peoples, providing $1,080 for Susan's upkeep. The will also conveyed stock in the Nashville and Decatur Railroad to his son, Marcuis R. Wilkins, and property to his daughter, Martha J. Welch. "Caroline Martin (colored) [received] the house and lot on which S. B. Parrish now lives."[33]

WILKINS, James S. Jeweler, watchmaker. Memphis, Shelby County, 1850–60.

James S. Wilkins was born in New York in 1822. By 1850 he had moved to Memphis where he worked as a jeweler and watchmaker; he shared quarters with jewelers and watchmakers A. C. Wursbach (q.v.) and F. H. Clark (q.v.).[34] By 1856 Wilkins, Clark, and Thomas Hill (q.v.) were all partners in the firm of F. H. Clark and Company, importers and dealers in watches, jewelry, silver and plated wares, fancy goods, cutlery, lamps guns and pistols. They also did engraving and manufactured seals and presses.[35] Wilkins remained a partner in the company through at least 1872.[36]

WILKINS, W. R. Silversmith. Columbia, Maury County, 1860.

W. R. Wilkins, a forty-five year-old Virginian, was working as a silversmith in Columbia at the time of the 1860 census for Maury County; he was a resident of the F. W. Welch household.

WILLIAMS, A. B. Silversmith. Nashville, Davidson County, 1844?-59; Murfreesboro, Rutherford County, 1860.

A. B. Williams was born in North Carolina about 1815. By 1844 he had moved to Tennessee where his daughter, Sarah, was born. At the time of the 1850 census he was living in Nashville, working as a silversmith.[37] In 1853 he was plating silver in a shop at 75 North Market Street; by 1855 he and Henry Parkhurst (q.v.) had established the partnership of Williams and Parkhurst (q.v.). Parkhurst eventually moved to 12½ Deaderick Street, but Williams remained at 6 Deaderick through 1859. He plated all kinds of harness mountings, house and door numbers, bell pulls, and door knobs. His residence was located at 74 Union Street.[38]

In the 1860 census for Murfreesboro, Rutherford County, A. B. Williams, a North Carolina native and probably the same man, was listed as a silversmith and a resident of the household of J. Stewart. He evaluated his personal estate at $200; no spouse or child was listed.

WILLIAMS, Daniel M. Watchmaker, jeweler. Winchester, Franklin County, 1860.

In 1860 Daniel M. Williams was operating a watchmaking and jewelry shop on the southwest side of the public square in Winchester.[39]

WILLIAMS and PARKHURST. Silver platers. Nashville, Davidson County, 1855.

A. B. Williams and Henry Parkhurst formed a silver plating firm about 1855; the shop was located at 6 Deaderick Street in Nashville. By 1857 Parkhurst had opened his own silver and brass plating establishment at 12½ Deaderick Street. Williams remained at the former location.[40]

JAMES WILKINS,
is about 19 years of age, dark complexion, and dark hair, ſtout made, about 5 feet 4 or 5 inches high, round full face, much marked with an eruption —I will pay 15 dollars each for ſecuring them in any jail within 500 miles of Naſhville, and giving me ſuch information that I can get them, or 30 dollars each for delivering them to me in Naſhville—I only will be liable for the above reward if taken in the year 1808.

J. T. ELLISTON.

Naſhville, Sep. 17.

132. *In the* Nashville Clarion *of 27 September 1808, James Wilkins announced that his apprentice, James Young, "about 19 years of age, dark complexion, and dark hair . . . round full face, much marked with an eruption. . . ." had run away.*

133. *"J. S. WILKINS" mark attributed to James S. Wilkins, 1850–60. Courtesy of the Tennessee State Museum, photograph by Stephen D. Cox.*

134. *"D. WILLIAMS" mark attributed to Daniel M. Williams, 1860.*

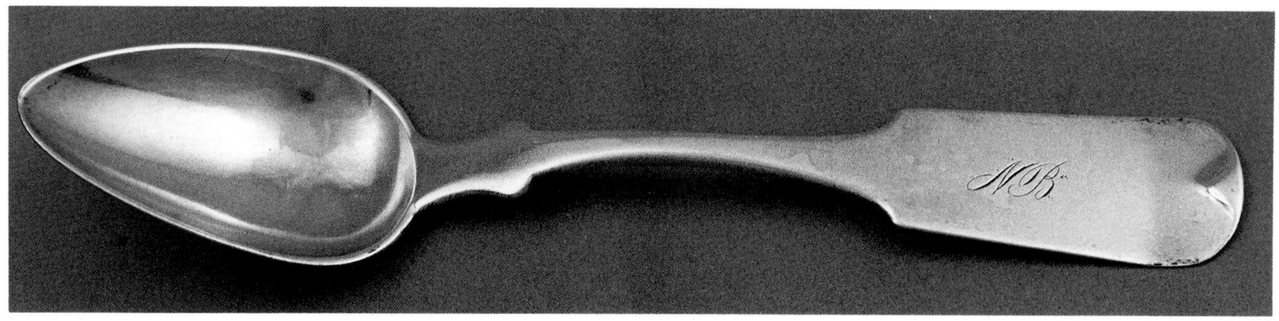

135, 135a. *Tablespoon marked "WINSHIP," 1860?, engraved "NB," Murfreesboro. LOA: 7¼". Courtesy of the Tennessee State Museum, fig. 135a, photograph by Stephen D. Cox. This teaspoon and its mark (fig. 135a) are attributed to F(rank) Winship.*

WILLIAMSON, Francis H. Dealer in silver and silver plated ware. Memphis, Shelby County, 1855–59.

In 1855 Francis H. Williamson was working in a shop at 188 Main Street in Memphis. The firm of Fransioli and Williamson (q.v.), dealers in china, glass, silver, and earthenware, was located at the same address in 1859.[41]

WILLS, Joseph. Silversmith. Rogersville, Hawkins County, 1860.

At the time of the 1860 census for Hawkins County, Joseph Wills was working as a silversmith in Rogersville and living A. R. Edmonds's hotel. The thirty-four-year-old native of Tennessee valued his real property at $1,500 and his personal estate at $3,000.

WILSON, Wallace. Silver plater. Nashville, Davidson County, 1860.

At the time of the 1860 census, Wallace Wilson, a twenty-year-old native of Tennessee, was working as a silver plater at 12½ Deaderick Street in Nashville; this was the address of Henry Parkhurst's (q.v.) silver plating shop. Working there with Wilson were Job Ryan (q.v.) and W. H. Keys (q.v.). Wilson lived at 114 South Cherry Street.[42]

WINSHIP, Frank. Watchmaker, jeweler. Murfreesboro, Rutherford County, 1860 and later; Pulaski, Giles County, 1870.

In the 1860 *State Gazetteer*, "F." Winship was listed as a Murfreesboro watchmaker and jeweler in 1860 at a stand one door above city hall. In the 1860 census for Rutherford County, the thirty-two-year-old Connecticut native estimated the value of his personal estate at $1800. Winship and his wife, listed only as "S.", lived in the residence of J. C. Gray. Two years later the 24 August 1862 *Nashville Dispatch* of 24 August 1862 noted the death of "Susan A. Winship, consort of Frank Winship."[43] By 1870 Winship apparently had moved to Pulaski, where the *Nashville Directory* listed him as a maker of watches and jewelry.[44]

Although Winship was listed only as a watchmaker and jeweler, silver (fig. 135) with both a Winship mark (fig. 135a) and a Tennessee provenance is extant.

WINSLOW, Aaron. Apprentice silversmith. Franklin, Davidson County, 1823.

In 1823 Aaron Winslow ran away from his apprenticeship to Franklin silversmith Thomas Thomson (q.v.), who offered a one-cent reward for Winslow's return in the 4 July 1823 Franklin *Independent Gazette.*

WOLFE (Woffe), Thomas E. Silversmith. Nashville, Davidson County, 1850.

Thomas E. Wolfe was born in England about 1819. By 1850 he was living in the Nashville household of James Moore, an English-born merchant and working as a silversmith.

A Francis H. Wolfe worked as a silversmith in Philadelphia circa 1829–49; no connection between him and the Nashville artisan is known.[45]

WOLFE and BAILEY. Clock and watch repairers, jewelers. Nashville, Davidson County, 1850.

In 1850 Wolfe and Bailey, "from London and Paris," purchased E. K. Burke's (q.v.) tools and advertised their readiness to serve the Nashville public as clock and watch repairers, jewelers, and suppliers of "Masons', Old Fellows' and Temperance Jewels." Wolfe may have been Emmanuel Wolfe, a twenty-five-year-old German merchant listed in the 1850 census with Gertrude, his French wife. Francis M. Bailey, a Tennessee "smith" listed in the Davidson County 1850 census, may have been the other partner although this has not been documented.[46]

WURSBACH (WURSBACK, WURZBACH), Albert C. Watchmaker. Memphis, Shelby County, 1850–55.

Albert C. Wursbach was born in New York about 1823, but by 1850 he had moved to Memphis where he worked as a watchmaker. Wursbach, his wife, and his three-year-old daughter, Julia, lived in the residence of silversmith James S. Wilkins (q.v.). By 1855 Wursbach had joined fellow boarder F. H. Clark (q.v.) as a partner in F. H. Clark and Company (q.v.), which was located on Main Street in Memphis. The firm, which dealt in silver, watches, guns, and fancy goods, remained in business through at least 1860, although Wursbach had left the company by that date.[47]

XERKIN, Peter. Watchmaker, jeweler. Nashville, Davidson County, 1860.

Peter Xerkin appeared in the 1860 *Nashville Directory* as a watchmaker and "pedlar of jewelry, fancy articles, etc."[48]

YARBROUGH, Edwin. Clock and watchmaker, jeweler. Big Rock, Stewart County, 1860.

The 1860 *State Gazetteer* listed Edwin Yarbrough in Big Rock under "Clocks and Jewelry."[49]

YORK, William. Silver and brass plater. Nashville, Davidson County, 1833–34.

William York, silver and brass plater, informed the citizens of Nashville and Huntsville in November 1833 and January and February of 1834 that he had commenced business at Samuel V. D. Stout's (q.v.) coach shop. At that location he offered to plate "carriage work, door plates, knobs, bell pullies and house work generally, bridle bits, [and] stirrup irons. . . ."[50]

YOUNG, James. Apprentice silversmith. Nashville, Davidson County, 1808.

James Young was apprenticed to Nashville silversmith J. T. Elliston (q.v.). In September 1808 Young and a fellow apprentice ran away; Elliston offered a $60 reward for their return to Nashville. He described Young as "about 20 years of age, fair complexion, sandy hair, about 5 feet eight inches high, stout made, his left arm about 3 inches shorter than the right. . . ."[51]

Philadelphia directories of 1817–20 listed an engraver, James H. Young; no connection is known.[52]

136, 136a. *One of William H. Calhoun's advertisements illustrates a pile of silver; another pile of unmarked silver, 1800–60, most of it probably made in Tennessee, is illustrated in fig. 136a. Fig. 136, courtesy of the Tennessee State Museum; fig. 136a, private collection.*

Appendix I

"The book of the Association of the Watch-Makers, Silversmiths & Jewellers of Nashville," 1836. Enoch Welborn, Paul Negrin, John Peabody, John Britton (Britain), Isaac Robeson, John Campbell, C. Guiteau, and D. S. Reeves met on Christmas Day to form this association, the object of which was to set price guidelines and prevent competition. Interestingly enough, D. S. Reeves's signature did not appear on the price agreement; however, Henry A. Cargill signed it.

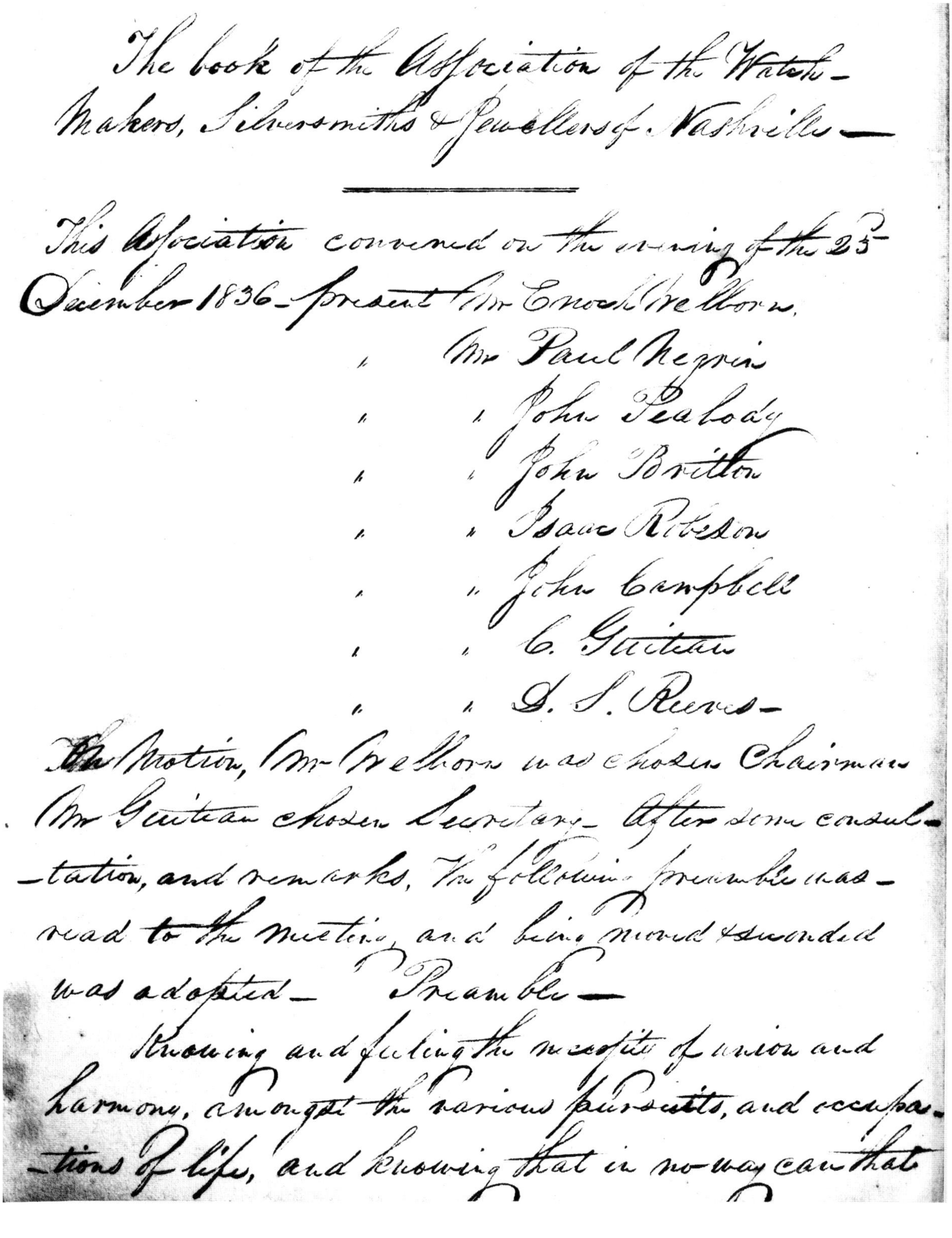

The book of the Association of the Watch-Makers, Silversmiths & Jewellers of Nashville —

This Association convened on the evening of the 25 December 1836 — present Mr Enoch Welborn,

" Mr Paul Negrin

" " John Peabody

" " John Britton

" " Isaac Robeson

" " John Campbell

" " C. Guiteau

" " D. S. Reeves —

On Motion, Mr Welborn was chosen Chairman Mr Guiteau chosen Secretary — After some consultation, and remarks, the following preamble was read to the meeting, and being moved & seconded was adopted — Preamble —

Knowing and feeling the necessity of union and harmony, amongst the various pursuits, and occupations of life, and knowing that in no way can that object be attained, but by a primary meeting of of all concerned in those objects, and various purposes, in which we are engaged, We the undersigned Mutually and individually, and in body agree to abide such rules and regulations as the majority of of the Association present may decide upon by vote, the Majority of two thirds present ruling, each Shop being entitled to one vote—

The following resolution was offered by Mr Peabody Resolved that we meet Annually in the month of December for the purpose of revising, correcting, and establishing, rules and regulations for our mutual interests— Which was adopted—

Resolved that this Association have for its officers one President who shall act as Chairman, and one Secretary who shall also act as Treasurer, both of which shall be chosen Annually at the regular Annual Meetings—

The Chairman shall preside ~~as such~~ at all meetings called, shall explain the rules as understood, define any doubts that arise, call meetings &c &c

The Secretary shall also preside to keep a regular proceeding of the meeting, and shall also act as Treasurer who shall keep a regular book of record, and shall keep a true account of Moneys received for any purpose and also money paid out by him for the use of the Association He shall enter the proceedings of any meeting in this book as record, and shall also deliver to each and every Watch Maker in this city a regular bill of Prices as established, shall also on any New Watch Maker, Silversmith, or Jeweller coming into this city to establish business, present him with a regular bill, and also show him the rules and regulations of this Association and endeavour to have him abide the same as a member, and upon getting his signature, enter it upon records of this book and report the same to the next regular Meeting —

Resolved That no price shall be set for the repairs of any Clock, Watch, or Timepiece before the work is executed, and which price shall conform ~~to~~ strictly to the bill of rates established by this Association, with the addition of Fifty cents for setting up said clock or Timepiece and Twenty five cents for each mile off of the corporation —

2 Resolved, Clocks, Watches, and Timepieces shall be reduced to the following 4 classes — and repairs charged accordingly, —

The Meeting then adjourned to Meet again on Wednesday evening 27th inst —

Met again Wednesday evening 28th Decr 1836 —
The former Officers presiding,

It was then moved to proceed for examining the bill of rates, upon being read over and amended — they were afterwards read and each item acted upon seperately —

1st Class are Clocks or Watches of three parts or powers, 2d Class are Clocks or Watches of two parts or powers — 3 Class are Horizontal Watches and Timepieces of one part or power — 4th Class are common verge or verticle Watches — of one part or power —

The following shall the rates of charges for all clock, or Watch work, and Manufacturing silver Spoons from and after the 1st day of January 1837 — untill otherwise amend by a Meeting of all

A	1st class		2d class		3d class		4th class	
Arbor Fuzee —	$ 3	50	$ 3	00	2	50	2	00
" Barrell	3	50	3	00	2	50	2	00
" to Pallets or Anchor for Lever	3	00	2	50	2	00	"	"
B. —								
Barrell or Mainspring box —	5	00	4	50	4.	00	3	50
Bushing holes —	1	50	1	25	1	00	.	75
Ballance, Brass or Steel —	4	"	3	50	3	"	2	50
C —								
Cleaning	6	00	4	00	2	00	1	00
Click or Click spring	1	50	1	25	1	00	.	75
Click Wheel or rachet —	2	00	1	75	1	50	1	25
Cylinders -	14	00	12	00	10.	00	"	"
Chain Fuzee —	2	75	2	50	2	25	2	00
" Mending or Hook	1	25	1	00	"	75	.	50
" Splicing or piecing	1	75	1	50	1	25	1	00
Clock Cord	1	"		75		50		
D.								
dials, enamled with seconds —	4	00	3	75	3	50	3.	00
" French with Key hole	3	25	3	00	2	75	2	50

	1 Class $		2d Class $		3 Class $		4 Class $	
D—								
English without Seconds	2	75	2	50	2	25	2	00
Dial, Clock with Moon	6	00	5	00	4	00		
" Plain	5	00	4	00	3	00		
E–F–								
Fuzee—New	6	00	5	50	5	00	5	00
Follower	1	25	1	00				75
G—								
Guard—Fuzee	3	00	2	75	2	50	2	25
H—								
Hands Long Second for centre	1	50	1	50	1	50	1	50
do Short Sec, gold centre fine		75		75		75		75
" Common Steel or Gilt		50		50		50		50
Hour & Minute or pair Gold	1	50	1	50	1	50	1	50
" Common Steel fine	1	00	1	00	1	00	1	00
" Common gilt or brass		75		75		75		75
Hook to Mainspring	2	00	1	75	1	50	1	25
" to Chain	1	25	1	00		75		50

J. K.—	1 Class		2 Class		3 Class		4 class	
Jewels diamond cap	3	00	3	00	3	00	3	00
" Cock & foot	4	50	4	00	3	50	3	00
" Slide	4	00	3	50	3	00	2	00
" Pin & Collet to Lever	5	00	4	50	4	00		
" Pin or ruby, only	2	00	2	00	2	00		
Steel pin instead of ruby	1	00	1	00	1	00		
L. M. N. O.								
Lever— Steel	4	00	3	50	3	00		
P—								
Pottence— Main	5	00	4	50	4	00	3	50
" Counter	3	00	2	75			2	00
" Slide	2	50	2	25	2	00	1	75
Pinions— Ballance	5	00	4	50	4	00		
" each common wheel	4	00	3	75	3	50	3	00
Pivots setting & bushing	2	00	1	75	1	50	1	25
Q. R.—								
Regulator or Curb	1	00	1	00	1	00		75
" Wheel	1	00	1	00	1	00	1	00
Rachet, for Click in fusee	2	00	1	75	1	50	1	25

S. T.—	1 Class	2 Class	3 Class	4 Class
Springs Main	3 50	3 00	2 50	2 00
" " Hook	2 00	1 75	1 50	1 25
" Hair ——	1 50	1 50	1 25	1 00
" " Reducing	75	75	75	50
" " Altering	50	50	37½	37½
" To back stop ——	1 50	1 50	1 00	75
Stop or back stop ——	2 00	1 75	1 50	1 00
Staff – Lever, or pinion	5 00	4 50	4 00	
Spring to Music Box $1.00 turn				
U. V.—				
Verge	4 00	3 50		3 00
W. X.—				
Wheels Main	5 00	4 50	4 00	3 50
" Horizontal or duplex —	12 00	12 00	10 00	— "
" Scape ~~to~~ Levers Brass	4 50	4 00	3 50	3 00
" All others dial, & ~~Canon~~	4 00	3 75	3 50	3 00
Canon pinion ——	2 00	2 50	2 00	2 00
~~Setting teeth~~				

After adopting the above bill we then proceed-ed to make a bill of prices for Silver Work-as follows

Making Table spoons plain pr doz	18	00
do Dessart do - -	12	
do Tea do - -	8	
do Salt or Mustard - -	6	
do Soup Ladles - each	6	
do Gravy do - do	4	
do Cream do - do	2	
Sugar Tongs double weight —		

Watch Glasses

Lunetts	75
Patent or flint	63
Flatt —	50
Common —	37½

The above prices being agreed upon—
we then proceeded to vote by ballot for officers
for the ensuing year— Whereupon—
Mr Enoch Welborn was chosen President
" C. Guitean — " — " Secretary—
J. D. Hopkins
J. Peabody—

John. S. Britain
J. J. Robeson
Henry. A. Cargill
Jno Campbell"

Appendix II

Excerpts from John Campbell's stock inventories, 1843 and 1845. The page from Campbell's 1843 stock inventory is a list of the flat and hollow ware he had on hand; no tools were listed in this inventory. The pages from the 1845 inventory list the English origins of his watches, watch parts, items such as counters, cases, and shelves used to store and display his ware, and his tools. Very little silver was listed in this inventory.

Amt Watches & Jewelry — —	6088	89
Silver ware &c		
42 oz 15 dwt Silver tumblers at $1½ p oz —	64	12
36 oz 5 Sil Soup Ladles 1.20 Making $12 —	55	20
26 oz 1½ Doz table Spoons 1.20 making 10 —	41	20
26 „ 6 dwt Desert do 2½ Doz do 11½ —	43	05
37 „ Tea Spoons 5½ Doz 1.20 do 16½ —	50	90
4½ „ 3 cream ladles 1 pr Sugartongs — 3 —	8	40
2½ „ Salt & mustard Spoons 1½ Doz 2½ —	5	40
12¼ „ Forks ½ Doz making 4 —	18	40
2 Silver cups, handles, ea $9.83 — 7.88 —	35	42
3 Small do do — do — 6.50 —	19	50
5 pair Silver butter knives 4½	22	50
4½ do — do — do „ 3½	15	50
2 Silver thimbles — 2½ —	5	00
3 „ nursing tubes — 2 —	6	00
4 pr Sil buckles &c — 5 —	20	00
2 Sil purse clasps 1 at 1.75 1 at 1.50 —	3	25
2 „ Scissors chains — 2.00 —	4	00
2 [illegible] pipes — 50 —	1	00
2 Sil. nut [illegible] — 25 —		50
	6508	23

Amt Brot Ford

C. A. Roberts	Watches	5649	53
T. S. 13037	G. H. Anchor Lever	66	00
Ouchens Registrs 69552	" "	60	00
Wm Robinson Liverpool	" " Lever 10291	78	00
Wm Robinson Liverpool 8489	G. H. Le 5/pr	77	00
E. S. Yeats & Co Liverpool 17382	G. H. Le – 4/pr	88	00
Brown Liverpool 7963	D B G Le	54	00
Geo Simons London 2289	" " " " 5/pr	90	00
Geo Simons London 2314	" " " " 5/pr	90	00
Geo Simons London 1413	" " " " plain	52	00
T. H 8823	G H Lepine	42	00
8328	" " "	40	00
Fred Melly 1646	" " " Sec hand	38	00
		6421	53

	Amt Brot Forward	6421	53
26159	D B G Lepine —	36	00
9866	G H Lever —	75	00
Duchene Giridad 13455	D B G A Lever —	43	00
Josh Johnson Liverpool 3611	D B G Duplex —	70	00
M I Tobias & co 2617 Liverpool	D B G A Le —	50	00
Penlington 6743	D B G A Le —	50	00
13410	D B G A Le —	43	00
Wm Robinson 8313 Liverpool	D B G Le — —	54	00
Josh Johnson 8728 Liverpool	D B S Le —	22	00
Josh Johnson 8732 Liverpool	D B S Le —	22	00
Wm Robison 49505 Liverpool	D B S Le — 5/pr —	31	00
Simons 1405 London	S H Le — —	34	00
Simons 2628 London	S H Le — —	34	00
Mau Hart 10821 London	S H Le — —	33	00
Josh Johnstone 9188 Liverpool	D B S Le — —	16	00
13913	D B S A Le. — 13 jew	18	00
Stauffer Geneva 17025	D B S A Le — 13 jewels	18	00
		7120	53

Am't Bro't fw'd

		$120 53
Stauffer 17026 Geneva	D B S A Le — 13 jewels	18 00
	D B G L — See hand	45 00
	D B G Le — plain case — hard dial	45 00
Wm Robinson 3859 Leiverpool	D C G Le — " " " "	60 00
	9 old Gold watches $6	54 00
	1 clock watch — —	35 00
	2 Silver Horz watches 20 + 15	35 00
Jos & Jno Johnson 5502 Leiverpool	D B S Le — 5/r See hand	25 00
3990	D B S Le — — —	20 00
Josh Johnson 4387 Leiverpool	D B S Le — — —	20 00
Johnson 6736 Leiverpool	D B S Le — — —	15 00
P. Leyland 23768 Leiverpool	D B S Le — — —	12 50
Jno Johnson 3623 Leiverpool	S H L — — —	20 00
Jno Houghton 22623 Leiverpool	D C S Le — — —	25 00
	D. C. S. Le. — — —	25 00
	D B S Le — Black Dial	25 00
B. Erroll 5598 London	S. H. C. W — — —	12 50
	25 old Silver watches — — 3	75 00
		$186 53

Amt Brot Forward

			7686	53
5	Swiss & French watches		45	00
1	fine Large Regulator		150	00
2	" clocks		55	00
1	" Brass Skeleton clock		35	00
1	" Ballance clock		30	00
1	com "		4	00
12	Doz watch jewels ass	9	108	00
2	" table Rollers	12	24	00
1½	" Slide jewels	6	9	00
7	" Eng & French verges	2	14	00
5	verge colletts	25	1	25
1	Lot 69 pieces = Levers. Sep[?]de	25	17	25
11	Gro chain hooks	25	2	75
5¼	Leever hair Springs	75	3	95
7	Doz com " "	50	3	50
10½	" Fuzee chains	1.75	18	37
4⅔	" com watch dials	2½	11	00
8	Lever ~~wat~~ Dials ea 62½		5	00
			8223	60

Qty	Item	Rate	$	¢
	Am^t Bro^t u/p — —		8223	60
1	Gold & Silver Dial —	75 & 1.50	2	25
1	vial Swiss oil — —		"	25
3	Gro watch Screws —	1½	4	50
1	Doz ruby pin jewels —		2	50
½	" Lever chains —	7	3	50
2	Gro key pipes	1.75	3	50
1	Drill Stock for vice		2	00
1	Sett arbors — 25		3	00
7	Drill Stocks with Drills	37½	2	62½
13	Round Burnishes & Gravers		2	25
8	pr tweezers 1.50 5 Screw Drivers	1.25	2	75
2	pivot files .80 3 Dentists	1.50	2	30
7	Doz Small watch files	1.50	10	50
2/3	" fine gold watch hands	3	2	00
6½	" " " " "	2	13	00
4¾	" com " " "	1½	7	13
6½	" Gilt " " "	25	1	62
2	" Steel " " "	2	4	00
			8293	37

Amt brot forward —	8293	37
1 plate ring — —	2	00
6½ gross Lunet glasses 8.50 —	55	25
6½ " Flat do — 5 00	32	50
4 " Com. do 3 50 —	14	00
10 Doz pat do 62½	6	25
old gold & silver on hand	100	00
second handed pins rings &c	25	00
watch work & jobs on hand	50	00
	8578	37
Amt of Dickson & Co bill Due	1015	34
6 Signs Eagle &c —	100	00
side show cases below stairs	150	00
3 counter cases — —	140	00
side cases & shelves 2d story —	75	00
counter drawers &c —	84	00
front Window door & fixtures —	150	00
square show case & looking glass & [illegible] case	20	00
3 chests drawers — —	20	00
	10332	71

furniture &c

Amt brought for $ —	10332 71
Counter 20 oil cloth 9 painting 4 —	33 00
8 drawers 24 & other fixtures to counter	41 00
Matlins bill putting up cases windows door & other fixtures benches &c	70 49
Nelson Turner shelves &c 3d story —	10 00
Lyons bill on paint fixtures glass &c	41 70
work benches & drawers front 3 story	20 00
Beds bedding & other sleeping fixtures	30 00
Large turning Lathe —	40 00
Smaller do —	25 00
draw plates & draw bench	25 00
plating mill & bellows —	35 00
Watch Makers tools in use	50 00
All other tools in use —	100 00
	10853 90
debts payable not yet due	3053 00
	7800 90

Notes

1. Archibald Henderson, *The Conquest of the Old Southwest* (1920, reprint, Spartanburg, S.C., 1974), 4, hereafter cited as Henderson, *Conquest*.

2. Philip M. Hamer, ed., *Tennessee: A History, 1673–1932* (New York, 1933), 13–16, hereafter cited as Hamer, *Tennessee*; Samuel Cole Williams, *Dawn of Tennessee Valley and Tennessee History* (Johnson City, Tenn., 1937), 13–16, 19–29, hereafter cited as Williams, *Dawn*.

3. Williams, *Dawn*, 28–32, 84, 311–12.

4. Couture deserted the interests of France to guide a party of Englishmen down the Tennessee River about 1750. They hoped to establish a trade route to Charleston with the western Indians, thus discouraging Indian trade with the French along the Mississippi to New Orleans. Williams, *Dawn*, 21–3.

Explorers tended to remain aloof from the Indians, while the traders interested in acquiring pelts, lived among, dressed like, and sometimes married the natives. Hamer, *Tennessee*, 20–1. In general, the French traded along the Cumberland river with the Shawnee, while the English traded along the Tennessee River with the Cherokee. When the Cherokee ousted the Shawnee about 1714, however, the Cumberland region remained unoccupied for about sixty years. Williams, *Dawn*, 72–7.

5. Williams, *Dawn*, 18–24; Hamer, *Tennessee*, 61.

6. Williams, *Dawn*, 52–3; Marcus Lewis in *Development of Early Emigrant Trails in the United States East of the Mississippi River* (1933, reprint, Washington, D. C., 1972) and William Myer in "Indian Trails of the Southeast" in the *Forty-Second Annual Report of the Bureau of American Ethnology to the Secretary of the Smithsonian Institution* (Washington, D. C., 1924–25) supply masterly works on this subject. "A Map of the Tennassee Government . . . by Gen'l. D. Smith. . . .", dated 1793, in Mathew Carey, *Carey's General Atlas* (Philadelphia, 1796) provides a good overview.

7. Alternatively, North Carolinians could take a more northerly approach at Rutledge through the Cumberland Gap into Monticello, eventually meeting the Kentucky Road. F. Lucas, Jr., "Geographical, Statistical, and Historical Map of Tennessee, No. 28," in *A Complete Historical, Chronological, and Geographical American Atlas* (Philadelphia, 1822.)

8. Hamer, *Tennessee*, 386–8.

9. Williams, *Dawn*, 120.

10. *Ibid.*, 184–6.

11. *Ibid.*, 154; Hamer, *Tennessee*, 29.

12. Henderson, *Conquest*, 100, 108; Thomas P. Abernethy, *From Frontier to Plantation in Tennessee* (1932, reprint, Memphis, Tenn., 1955), 20, hereafter cited as Abernethy, *Frontier*.

13. Williams, *Dawn*, 272–4.

14. John Haywood, *The Civil and Political History of the State of Tennessee from Its Earliest Settlement up to the Year 1796 including the Boundaries of the State* (1823, reprint, Knoxville, Tenn., 1969), 50–2; Williams, *Dawn*, 34.

15. Abernethy, *Frontier*, 17–18.

16. Henderson, *Conquest*, n.p.

17. Granville's title to the land was not set aside until years after the Revolutionary War, when the Supreme Court finally dismissed his case in 1817. Williams, *Dawn*, 315.

18. *Ibid.*, 312, 401–10.

19. George Bean advertised his skills as goldsmith, jeweler, and gunsmith in the *Knoxville Gazette* for 3 Nov. 1792.

20. In 1780, James Robertson was named to head a committee of representatives to oversee the fulfillment of the Cumberland Compact drawn up by Richard Henderson. Abernethy, *Frontier*, 28–30.

21. Williams, *Dawn*, 338, 348–51.

22. *Ibid.*, 369.

23. Hamer, *Tennessee*, 68; Williams, *Dawn*, 367.

24. Marcus W. Lewis, *Development of Early Emigrant Trails in the United States East of the Mississippi River* (Washington, D. C., 1972), 4, hereafter cited as Lewis, *Early Trails*.

25. Jebidiah Morse, *The American Geography or a View of the Present Situation of the U. S. of America* (London, 1794), 527, hereafter cited as Morse, *American Geography*; Samuel Cole Williams, *Tennessee During the Revolutionary War*, (1944, reprint, Knoxville, 1974), 3; U. S. Bureau of the Census, *A Century of Population Growth . . . 1790–1900* (Washington, D. C., 1909), n. p.

26. Morse, *American Geography*, 527, 532; Abernethy, *Frontier*, 146.

27. Until the Louisiana Purchase, some settlers in the western region favored joining France to safeguard their trade routes, while people on the Cumberland named their district "Mero" after Governor Miro, the Spanish governor of New Orleans. James Phelan, *History of Tennessee: The Making of a State* (Boston and New York, 1889), 165; Morse, *American Geography*, 535; Daniel Smith, *A Short Description of the Tennessee Government, 1793* in *Tennessee Beginnings* (Spartanburg, S. C., 1974), 4, 10.

28. The territory then contained 10 counties: Blount, Davidson, Sullivan, Greene, Jefferson, Sevier, Hawkins, Sumner, Washington, and Tennessee, now Robertson and Montgomery. Eastin Morris, *The Tennessee Gazetteer or Topographical Dictionary*, ed. Robert McBride and Owen Meredith (1834, reprint, Nashville, Tenn., 1971), 34, hereafter cited as Morris, *Tennessee Gazetteer*).

29. *Ibid.*, 7.

30. As early as 1805 Davidson County was larger than any of the earlier East Tennessee counties. Morris, *Tennessee Gazetteer*, 65–6.

31. Marcus Lewis noted that water routes existed "in places contiguous to land trails, sometimes supplementing them, sometimes practically excluding them," yet the early emigrants chose overland trails more often. Lewis, *Early Trails*, 3. Both Samuel Cole Williams in *Dawn of Tennessee Valley and Tennessee History* and Thomas P. Abernethy in *From Frontier to Plantation* wrote fine descriptions of these roads.

32. Samuel Cole Williams, *Tennessee During the Revolutionary War* (Knoxville, Tenn., 1944), 46–7.

33. F. A. Michaux, "Travels West of the Alleghany Mountains," in *Early Western Travels, 1748–1846*, ed. Reuben Gold Thwaites, vol. 3 (Cleveland, Ohio, 1904), 261. In 1804, the legislature authorized counties to lay out roads, build bridges, and establish ferries. All white men had to work on the roads or pay the county 75 cents a day. Hamer, *Tennessee*, 386.

34. An 1802 advertisement by newly arrived Thomas Deaderick offered his services as a silversmith as well as the hire of a "light stage-wagon" that had probably brought him from Virginia. Nashville *Tennessee Gazette*, 22 Sept. 1802.

35. Abernethy, *Frontier*, 155.

36. J. J. B. DeBow, *The Seventh Census of the United States: 1850* (Washington, D. C., 1853), 2, hereafter cited as Debow, *Seventh Census*.

37. Henderson, *Conquest*, xiv.

38. Morse, *American Geography*, 532.

39. One is reminded of Flynt's and Fales's description of New Hampshire's silversmiths at about the same time. "There was not a great demand for the more expensive and elegant articles. Spoons, because of their utility, durability and original demand are the only items which have survived to this day in any quantity." Henry N. Flynt and Martha Gandy Fales, *The Heritage Foundation Collection of Silver with Biographical Sketches of New England Silversmiths, 1625–1825* (Old Deerfield, Mass., 1968), 18.

40. Hamer, *Tennessee*, 186.

41. Graham Hood described apprentices taken at age 14 and bound for at least seven years, forbidden to open their own shops until they reached 21. Graham Hood, *American Silver: A History of Style, 1650–1900* (New York, 1971), 17–18.

42. Perhaps an earlier assumption that the terms "goldsmith and silversmith" are synonymous is mistaken during Tennessee's emerging period of silversmithing. The fine distinctions these men used to describe themselves in their advertisements may be lost to 20th century man.

43. The content of Spanish milled dollars provided .900 parts silver

as raw material. Flynt and Fales, *Heritage Foundation Collection*, 34.

44. *Ibid.*, 20.

45. The Revolutionary War had depleted supplies in English mills. Abernethy, *Frontier*, 225.

46. *Ibid.*

47. *Ibid.*, 226.

48. DeBow, *Seventh Census*, 2; J. Gray Smith, *A Brief Historical, Statistical and Descriptive Review of East Tennessee . . . with Remarks to Emigrants* (1842, reprinted, Spartanburg, S. C., 1974), 20.

49. Abernethy, *Frontier*, 288–90.

50. *Ibid.*, 231–5.

51. Frances Trollope, *Domestic Manners of the Americans*, ed. Donald Smalley (1832, reprint, New York, 1949), 193.

52. Jo C. Guild, *Old Times in Tennessee* (Nashville, Tenn., 1878), 37.

53. Hamer, *Tennessee*, 393.

54. Fewer advertisements from this middle period stated the need for apprentices or described runaways. The apprentice system was still practiced but it was becoming less defined during this period.

55. A Washington family descendant related the story of her ancestor's arrival in Tennessee to the author: Joseph Washington, second cousin of George Washington, moved in 1796 to his land in the vicinity of the Red River near Springfield in Robertson County. He allegedly lived in a cave on the site for about two years until he could raise a log home. His marriage to Mary Cheatham increased his land and holdings, and in 1819 "Wessyngton," a neoclassical manor, was built of bricks made on the place. This plantation, which had grown to 15,000 acres by 1892, remained in the family until 1984. Most of the mansion's hollow ware had been imported from Philadelphia, while the family's flatware had come from Philadelphia, New York, and John Campbell's shop in Nashville.

56. Herschel Gower, ed., *Pen and Sword: The Life and Journals of Randal W. McGavock.* (Nashville, Tenn., 1959), 19.

57. T. Vance Little, letter to the author, n. d.

58. W. W. Clayton, *History of Davidson County, Tennessee* (Philadelphia, 1880), 206.

59. In Portsmouth, New Hampshire, a single notice of a goldsmith's guild meeting appeared in 1762, and in 1786 New York City apparently had a gold and silversmiths society that met regularly. Martha Gandy Fales, *Early American Silver* (New York, 1970. rev. ed., 1973), 193–4.

60. Fedora S. Frank, *Five Families and Eight Young Men* (Nashville, Tenn., 1962), 36.

61. By comparison, Pennsylvania had 64 railroads in operation at that time, Ohio maintained 32, and North Carolina, 13. *Statistical View of the U. S., Embracing Its Territory, Population, Moral and Social Condition, Indicating Property, and Revenue: The Detailed Statistics of Cities, Towns, and Counties* (Washington, D. C., 1854), 189.

62. Tommy W. Rogers, "Origins and Destination of Tennessee Migrants, 1850–1860," *Tennessee Historical Quarterly*, 27(1968): 119.

63. Naomi Hailey, *A Guide to Genealogical Research in Tennessee* (Owensboro, Ky., 1979), 44, 47.

64. A compilation from the returns of the 1850 federal census for Tennessee noted the following: 3 clockmakers, 3 gilders, 23 gold-and-silversmiths, 10 jewelers, and 42 watchmakers. The census of manufactures for the same year, however, recorded only 4 silversmiths (Samuel Bell, Charles Cory, Wells Fowler, and William Sehorn), one silversmith/jeweler/watchmaker (E. M. Ringo), one watchmaker/jeweler (F. H. Clark), and three jewelers (C. G. Merriman, T. Noel, and D. I. Wells). In order to be listed in the census of manufactures, a shop had to produce $500 annually, a fact which may explain the difference in the population census figures and those of the census of manufactures.

65. Stephen G. C. Ensko, *American Silversmiths and Their Marks* (Southampton, N. Y., 1937), 20; Louise Conway Belden, *Marks of Tennessee Silversmiths in the Ineson Bissell Collection* (Charlottesville, Va., 1980), 52; Federal Census for 1850, Davidson County, Tenn.

66. Martha Gandy Fales, *Early American Silver for the Cautious Collector* (New York, 1970), 202–6; Stephen K. Victor, "'From the Shop to the Manufactory,' Silver and Industry, 1970[?]," in *Silver in American Life*, ed. Barbara McLean Ward and Gerald W. R. Ward (Boston, 1979), 23–31.

67. *The Goodspeed Histories of Giles, Lincoln, Franklin and Moore Counties of Tennessee.* 1886, reprint, Columbia, Tenn., 1976), 762, 874.

68. Notes from a file of Rutherford County papers at the Tennessee State Library and Archives confirmed a "low church" plainness. At Fellowship Baptist Church, the amount appropriated annually for the purpose of preparing the elements fo the Lord's Supper in 1844 was 50 cents. "For the first 25 years of its history (1827–52) the estimated amount of money given to the church for all causes is $475.00 exclusive of its building operations." DAR, Robert Cartwright Chapter, *Centennial History of Fellowship Baptist Church*, 5, 10.

(A)

1. Mrs. Elliott Adams, letter to the author, 7 Mar. 1983.

2. Benjamin Sharpe, Commissioner, List of the Taxable Property in the Corporation of Nashville, 1847, ms., Ben West Public Library, Nashville, Tennessee.

3. *Nashville Business Directory*, 1855–56, 57; 1857, 23; 1859, 2; 1860, 116; 1875, 86; 1878, 50. Hereafter cited as *NBD*.

4. Adams to Caldwell, 7 Mar. 1983; Susan Clover Symonds, "Portraits of Andrew Jackson: 1815–1845," (Master's thesis, University of Delaware, 1965), 46.

5. Mt. Olivet Cemetery records, Nashville, Tennessee.

6. Adams to Caldwell, 7 Mar. 1983.

7. *Wilson's Knoxville Gazette*, 13 May 1809; George Barton Cutten, *The Silversmiths of Virginia (Together with Watchmakers and Jewelers) from 1694 to 1850* (Richmond, Va., 1952), 3–4.

8. *Knoxville Register*, 15 June 1819.

9. *National Banner and Nashville Whig*, 28 Nov. 1828; 2 Jan. 1829.

10. *Knox. Reg.*, 27 Mar. 1817.

11. Federal census for 1860, Hamilton County, Tenn.; John L. Mitchell, *Tennessee State Gazetteer, and Business Directory, for 1860–1861* (Nashville, Tenn., 1860), 441.

12. Federal census for 1860, Hamilton Ct., Tenn.; *NBD*, 1857, 309; Mitchell, *State Gazetteer*, 441; *NBD*, 1869, 29; *NBD*, 1875, 306.

13. *Knox. Reg.*, 13 Apr. 1819; 21 Dec. 1819.

14. *Memphis Weekly Appeal*, 28 July 1843.

15. *Memphis City Directory*, 1860, 48, 335, hereafter cited as *MCD*.

16. James H. Craig, *The Arts and Crafts in North Carolina, 1699–1840* (Winston-Salem, N. C., 1965), 166, 182–3.

17. Mitchell, *State Gazetteer*, 441; Federal census for 1860, Hancock County, Tennessee.

18. Federal census for 1850, Davidson County, Tennessee; *NBD*, 1853, 11; *NBD*, 1857, 29; *NBD*, 1860, 122.

19. S. E. Massengill, *The Massengills, Massengales and Variants* (Bristol, Tenn., 1931), 218; *Baltimore Town and Fell's Point Directory* (Baltimore, 1796); *The New Baltimore Directory, and Annual Register: for 1800 and 1801* (Baltimore, 1800); Cornelius William Stafford, comp., *The Baltimore Directory, for 1802* (Baltimore, 1802); 1803 (Baltimore, 1803); James Robinson, comp., *The Baltimore Directory, for 1804* (Baltimore, 1804); James McHenry, comp., *Baltimore Directory, and Citizen's Register, for 1807*, (Baltimore, 1807); William Fry, comp., *Baltimore Directory for 1810* (Baltimore, 1810); James Lakin, comp., *Baltimore Directory and Register for 1814–15* (Baltimore, 1814); Edward Matchett, comp., *Baltimore Directory and Register for the Year 1816* (Baltimore, 1816); James Kennedy, comp., *Baltimore Directory for 1817–18 . . .* (Baltimore, 1817).

20. Massengill, *Massengills*, 218.

21. Paul M. Fink, "The Great Seal of the State of Tennessee. An Inquiry into its Makers," *Tennessee Historical Quarterly* 20, No. 4(Dec. 1961): 381–3.

22. Massengill, *Massengills*, 218; *Baltimore Advertiser*, 18 Sept. 1787.

23. Massengill, *Massengills*, 218.

24. Federal census for 1850, Washington County, Tennessee; Massengill, *Massengills*, 218.

25. Fink, "Great Seal," *THQ* 20, No. 4(Dec. 1961): 381–3.

26. Massengill, *Massengills*, 218; Federal census for 1810, Grainger County, Tennessee; *Knoxville Enquirer*, 3 May 1826.

27. Federal census for 1850, Grainger Ct., Tenn.; Massengill, *Massengills*, 218.

28. *Knox. Enq.*, 3 May 1826.

29. Federal census for 1850, Washington Ct., Tenn.; Massengill, *Massengills*, 218.

30. Fink, "Great Seal," *THQ* 20, No. 4(Dec. 1961): 381–3; Massengill, *Massengills*, 218.

31. Jonesboro(ugh) *Farmer's Journal*, 16 Dec. 1825.

32. Paul M. Fink, *Jonesborough: The First Century of Tennessee's First Town* (Washington County, Tenn., 1972), 122–32.

33. Federal censuses for 1850, 1860, Washington Ct., Tenn.; Fink, "Great Seal," *THQ* 20 No. 4(Dec. 1961): 381–3.

34. Jonesboro(ugh) *Farm. Jour.*, 16 Dec. 1825.

35. Fink, *Jonesborough*, 290.

36. Federal census for 1860, Stewart County, Tennessee; *State Gazetteer*, 1860, 441.

(B)

1. Federal census for 1870, Davidson Ct., Tenn.; *NBD*, 1855, 15; 1857, 30; 1860, 122; 1869, 25.

2. *NBD*, 1855, 15; 1857, 30; 1859, 22, 1870, 267.

3. *Ibid.*, 1855, 15; 1857, 30.

4. Federal census for 1860, Shelby County, Tennessee; *MCD*, 1859–60, 46.

5. *NBD*, 1855–56, 16.

6. Marquis Boultinghouse, *Silversmiths of Kentucky, 1785–1900: Jewelers, Watch and Clock Makers* (Lexington, Ky., 1980), 57.

7. Smith County Court Records, microfilm, Roll 104, Will Book, Tennessee State Libary and Archives, Nashville, Tennessee; Carthage *Western Express*, 21 Nov. 1808.

8. Cutten, *Silversmiths of Virginia*, 4–6.

9. Federal census for 1850, Bradley County, Tennessee; *Goodspeed's History of Tennessee Containing Historical and Biographical Sketches of Thirty East Tennessee Counties. . . .* (1887, reprint, Nashville, Tenn., 1972), 828.

10. Cutten, *Silversmiths of Virginia*, 1.

11. Federal census for 1850, Davidson Ct., Tenn.; Sharpe, List of Taxable Property; *NBD*, 1853, 56; 1855, 2: 1857, 32.

12. Ralph M. and Terry H. Kovel, *American Silver, Pewter and Silver Plate* (New York, 1961), 26; Belden, *Marks*, 52.

13. James Ault Grady, *William Bean, Pioneer of Tennessee and His Descendants* (Knoxville, Tenn., 1973), 58; Jeanette Tillotson Acklen, comp., *Tennessee Tombstone Inscriptions and Manuscripts* (Baltimore, 1976), 441.

14. *Containing Sketches of Thirty East Tennessee Counties*, 853.

15. Grady, *William Bean*, 58.

16. *Nashville Daily True Whig*, 23 Feb. 1850; *Nashville Daily Union*, 5 Mar. 1850.

17. *The Goodspeed Histories of Cannon, Coffee, DeKalb, Warren, and White Counties. . . .* (1887, McMinnville, Tenn., 1972), 851; Mitchell, *State Gazetteer*, 441.

18. Kovel and Kovel, *American Silver*, 28.

19. *MCD*, 1855–56, 97.

20. Federal census for 1850, Knox County, Tennessee; San Antonio Museum Association, *Early Texas Furniture and Decorative Arts* (San Antonio, Tex., 1973), 254.

21. Robert Van Deventer, letter to the author, 15 May 1983; Mary U. Rothrock, ed. *The French Broad-Holston Country: A History of Knox County, Tennessee* (Knoxville, Tenn., 1946), 378–9.

22. Rothrock, *French Broad*, 378–9.

23. *Knox. Reg.*, 21 Dec. 1819.

24. *Ibid.*, 18 Apr. 1820; 16 Oct. 1821; 24 Sept. 1822; 8 Oct. 1822, 21 Mar. 1822.

25. *Ibid.*, 2 July 1824; 9 June 1825.

26. *Ibid.*, 9 Dec. 1825.

27. *Ibid.*, 9 Jan. 1828; 29 Mar. 1826; 31 Dec. 1828; Rothrock, *French Broad*, 378–9.

28. *Knox. Reg.*, 19 Dec. 1832; *Knoxville Republican*, 12 Dec. 1832; *Knoxville Times*, 27 Dec. 1839.

29. *Knox. Rep.*, 12 Dec. 1832; *Knox. Times*, 27 Dec. 1839; Rothrock, *French Broad*, 378–9.

30. Rothrock, *French Broad*, 378–9.

31. *Ibid.*; William P. Beall, Curator of the Armstrong-Lockett House, Knoxville, Tennessee, wrote in "Silversmiths and Goldsmiths of East Tennessee" that Bell was an associate of Samuel Bowie. *Knoxville Journal*, 2 Oct. 1971.

32. San Antonio Museum Association, *Early Texas Furniture*, 157; Rothrock, *French Broad*, 378–9.

33. Rothrock, *French Broad*, 378–9.

34. Walter Nold Mathis, letter to the author, 1 Jan. 1983; *San Antonio Light*, 3 Mar. 1882.

35. Rothrock, *French Broad*, 378–9; *Knox. Reg.*, 18 Apr. 1820.

36. *Knox. Reg.*, 29 Mar. 1826; 27 Feb. 1828.

37. *Ibid.*, 21 Dec. 1812; 18 Apr. 1820.

38. *Ibid.*, 18 Apr. 1820; San Antonio Museum Association, *Early Texas Furniture*, 157.

39. *Knox. Reg.*, 16 Oct. 1820.

40. *Ibid.*, 16 Oct. 1821; Knox County Court Records, microfilm, Roll 155, Book 3, Inventories & Sales, n. p., Tenn. St. Lib. & Arch.

41. Mitchell, *State Gazetteer*, 483; *MCD*, 1860, 77, 366.

42. Clarence Berson, letter to the author, 1 Feb. 1983; Berson family papers courtesy of Mrs. W. G. Berson, Clarence Berson, Southern Historical Collection, University of North Carolina Library, Southern Historical Collection, Chapel Hill, North Carolina.

43. Berson Papers.

44. Franklin *Western Weekly Review*, 11 Aug. 1833; 12 Dec. 1834; 8 May 1835; 22 May 1836; 30 Mar. 1838; 25 May 1838.

45. Henry Van Pelt to Mrs. Lucinda S. Berson, 17 July 1846, Berson Papers.

46. Berson Papers. 47. *Ibid.*

48. Berson to Caldwell, 1 Feb. 1983; Robert Y. Moses, letter to the author, 11 Sept. 1981.

49. Berson Papers.

50. Franklin *West. Wkly. Rev.*, 8 Nov. 1833; 24 Oct. 1834; 12 Dec. 1834; 8 May 1835; 22 Apr. 1836; 17 Feb. 1837; 30 Mar. 1838.

51. *Ibid.*, 25 May 1838.

52. Berson Papers. 53. *Ibid.*

54. *Ibid.* Much of this information was derived from Berson family history and the William Berson papers written to prove Berson's lineage and his right to reimbursement under French law governing those countrymen who had lost property during the insurrections on Santo Domingo.

55. Craig, *Arts and Crafts*, 45; Franklin *West. Wkly. Rev.*, 26 Feb. 1836.

56. Franklin *West. Wkly. Rev.*, 25 Feb. 1838; Berson to Caldwell, 1 Feb. 1983.

57. Franklin *West. Wkly. Rev.*, 25 Feb. 1833.

58. *Ibid.*, 24 Oct. 1834; 12 Dec. 1834; 8 May 1835; 30 Mar. 1838.

59. *Ibid*, 25 May 1838.

60. *Ibid.*, 16 May 1838.

61. Berson to Caldwell, 1 Feb. 1983.

62. *Nashville Whig Banner*, 27 Dec. 1824; *Nashville Clarion and Tennessee Gazette*, 11 Nov. 1817.

63. Cutten, *Silversmiths of Virginia*, 81.

64. Federal census for 1850, Montgomery County, Tennessee.

65. Noble W. and Lucy F. Hiatt, *The Silversmiths of Kentucky* (Louisville, Ky., 1954), 13.

66. Fedora Frank, *Five Families*, 28, 35, 137; *NBD*, 1870, 267.

67. Frank, *Five Families*, 44, 137; Annette Levy, letter to the author, 13 May 1983.

68. Fedora S. Frank, *Beginnings on Market Street* (Nashville, Tenn., 1976), 12, 130.

69. *Paris Sentinel*, 13 Mar. 1857.

70. *NBD*, 1859, 29–30; 1860, 130; 1869, 25.

71. *Ibid.*, 1853, 65, 344; 1859, 29.

72. *Ibid.*, 1859, 29.

73. Federal census for 1850, Shelby Ct., Tenn.

74. Boultinghouse, *Silversmiths*, 76.

75. Jonesboro(ugh) *Farm. Jour.*, 16 Dec. 1825.

76. J. Hall Pleasants and Howard Sill. *Maryland Silversmiths, 1715–1830* (1930, reprint, Harrison, N.Y., 1972), 276.

77. *Nashville Union*, 27 May 1835; The Book of the Association of Watchmakers, Silversmiths, and Jewellers of Nashville, unpublished manuscript in the author's collection (hereafter cited as Appendix I).

78. *NBD*, 1859, 34.

79. Federal census for 1850, Davidson Ct., Tenn., under James Moss; *NBD*, 1855, 22; 1857, 41.

80. Kovel and Kovel, *American Silver*, 280.

81. *NBD*, 1855, 22; 1857, 41; Harriet Chappell Owsley, *Index to Interments, Nashville City Cemetery, 1846–1962* (Nashville, Tenn., 1964), 9; Kovel and Kovel, *American Silver*, 42.

82. *NBD*, 1855, 22; 1857, 41; Kovel and Kovel, *American Silver*, 42.

83. Mitchell, *State Gazetteer*, 441.

84. *Ibid.*

85. Federal census for 1850, Davidson Ct., Tenn.; Boultinghouse, *Silversmiths*, 82; Ruth Hunter Roach, *St. Louis Silversmiths* (St. Louis, Mo., 1967), 90.

86. Nashville *Daily Center-State American*, 4 Mar. 1849; Federal census for 1850, Davidson Ct., Tenn.; *Nash. Daily Union*, 28 July 1850.

87. Nashville *Daily Cent. St. Am.*, 4 Mar. 1849.

88. *MCD*, 1859, 58, 223. 89. *Ibid.*, 58.

90. *Ibid.*, 1865–66, 113; 1867–68, 181; Paul R. Coppock, "Mid-South Memoirs—Wonder of Richness for Citizens of Fashion," Memphis *Commercial Appeal*, 16 Sept. 1979.

91. Coppock, "Mid-South Memoirs," Memphis *Comm. Appeal*, 16 Sept. 1979.

92. Augusta, Georgia, *Southern Sentinel and Gazette of the State*, 11 Feb. 1796; Charleston County, South Carolina, Court Records, microfilm, Land Records Miscellaneous, Part 92, Books E7-H7, 1801–3, 295–300, Museum of Early Southern Decorative Arts, Winston-Salem, North Carolina.

(C)

1. Cutten, *Silversmiths of Virginia*, 109.

2. *Raleigh Register*, 19 Nov. 1807; *Wilson's Knox. Gaz.*, 20 May 1809; 14 Oct. 1809; 7 Oct. 1811; 3 Aug. 1812; 27 Sept. 1813; Knox County Court Records, Minute Book 8, 1813–16, 26, Tenn. St. Lib. & Arch.

3. *Wilson's Knox. Gaz.*, 3 Aug. 1812.

4. Cutten, *Silversmiths of Virginia*, 109.

5. *Wilson's Knox. Gaz.*, 25 Oct. 1813.

6. C. Somers Miller, letter to the author, 22 Sept. 1971.

7. Ida Calhoun Burritt, letter to the author, 17 Jan. 1972.

8. Burritt to Caldwell, 17 Jan. 1972; Federal census for 1850, Davidson Ct., Tenn.

9. Burritt to Caldwell, 17 Jan. 1972; Louise Davis, "Early Silversmiths Left Mark on City," Nashville *Tennessean*, 14 Aug. 1983.

10. Dorothy T. Rainwater, *American Silver Manufacturers* (Hanover, Pa., 1966), 204; Davis, "Early Silversmiths," Nash. *Tenn.*, 14 Aug. 1983.

11. Federal census for 1850, Davidson Ct., Tenn.; Burritt to Caldwell, 17 Jan. 1972.

12. Burritt to Caldwell, 17 Jan. 1972; *Nashville Whig*, 20 Mar. 1840; 16 Jan. 1844.

13. Burritt to Caldwell, 17 Jan. 1972; *Carthage Casket*, 21 July 1848; *Daily Nashville American*, 26 Apr. 1848.

14. *NBD*, 1855, 25; 1857, 48; 1859, 36; 1860, 138; 1870, 267.

15. Burritt to Caldwell, 17 Jan. 1972.

16. *Ibid.*

17. *Nash. Union*, 20 Mar. 1840; *Nash. Whig*, 16 Nov. 1843, 16 Jan. 1844.

18. Mitchell, *State Gazetteer*, 441.

19. *Knox. Reg.*, 15 Sept. 1818.

20. Kovel and Kovel, *American Silver*, 53.

21. Rhea Knittle, *Early Ohio Silversmiths and Pewterers, 1787–1847* (Cleveland, Ohio, 1943), 39.

22. George Barton Cutten, *Silversmiths of North Carolina, 1696–1850* (Raleigh, N. C., 1973), 18; Craig, *Arts and Crafts*, 60, 65.

23. Cutten, *Silversmiths of North Carolina*, 20; E. Milby Burton, *South Carolina Silversmiths* (Charleston, S. C., 1968), 211.

24. *Nash. Union*, 23 Aug. 1836;

25. Appendix I.

26. *Nashville Clarion*, 8 July 1845; *Nash. Whig*, 16 Jan. 1844; "Inventory of Stock of John Campbell," unpublished manuscript in the author's collection (Appendix II); Sharpe, List of Taxable Property.

27. *Nash. Daily Union*, 17 May 1849; 1 Sept. 1850; *NBD*, 1853, 56; 1855, 25; 1857, 25; James R. Crutchfield, *Heritage of Grandeur* (Franklin, Tenn., 1981), 29; Rose A. Robertson, letter to the author, 16 Nov. 1984: Williamson County Court Records, microfilm, Roll 94, Will Book 17, Tenn. St. Lib. & Arch.

28. Mrs. Herbert P. Richards, letter to the author, 2 Feb. 1972.

29. *NBD*, 1853, 56; 1855, 25.

30. *Nash. Daily Union*, 1 Sept. 1850; 17 May 1849.

31. Federal census for 1850, Shelby Ct., Tenn.; *MCD*, 1855–56, 104; 1856–57, 77.

32. *NBD*, 1860, 140.

33. Federal census for 1850, Overton County, Tennessee, under William G. Roberts.

34. Mitchell, *State Gazetteer*, 1860, 441.

35. Federal census for 1850, Warren County, Tennessee.

36. *Nashville Republic*, 18 Oct. 1836; Appendix I.

37. *Nash. Union*, 7 Oct. 1837; *Nash. Whig*, 25 June 1838; 16 Nov. 1838.

38. *Nash. Whig*, 16 Nov. 1838; *Nash. Union*, 25 Sept. 1839.

39. Federal census for 1850, Lauderdale County, Tennessee.

40. Franklin *Williamson County News*, 15 June 1905; Dana C. Brooks, letter to the author, 13 May 1983; 19 June 1983; *NBD*, 1869, 299; 1875, 322.

41. Brooks to Caldwell, 13 May 1983; 19 June 1983.

42. Franklin *Williamson Ct. News*, 12 Apr. 1903; Federal census for 1850, Williamson County, Tennessee.

43. Franklin *Williamson Ct. News*, 12 Apr. 1903.

44. Brooks to Caldwell, 13 May 1983; Franklin *Williamson Ct. News*, 12 Apr. 1903.

45. Nancy A. Parks to the Honorable A. P. McCormick, 1893, Dana C. Brooks collection.

46. Brooks to Caldwell, 13 May 1983; 19 June 1983.

47. *Ibid.* 48. *Ibid.*

49. *Ibid.*

50. Franklin *West. Wkly. Rev.*, 26 Feb. 1831; 14 Apr. 1831; 8 Nov. 1833; 15 Jan. 1836; 29 Jan. 1836.

51. Brooks to Caldwell, 13 May 1983.

52. Federal census for 1850, Williamson Ct., Tenn; Franklin *West. Wkly. Rev.*, 18 Aug. 1854.

53. Funeral notice, 16 Dec. 1878, Dana C. Brooks collection.

54. *NBD*, 1860, 138, 142.

55. Paris *Patriot*, 20 Mar. 1856.

56. *Memphis Enquirer*, 20 Apr. 1836; 22 June 1836.

57. *Ibid.*, 6 May 1837.

58. *Ibid.*, 20 Apr. 1836.

59. *Ibid.*, 6 May 1837.

60. Charles E. Smart, *The Makers of Surveying Instruments in America since 1700*, vol. 2, (Troy, N.Y., 1967), 192; Coppock, "Mid-South Memoirs," Memphis *Comm. Appeal*, 16 Sept. 1979; *Memp. Wkly. Appeal*, 23 Feb. 1843; 15 Mar. 1844; 14 July 1845.

61. *MCD*, 1850, 14; Federal census for 1850, Shelby Ct., Tenn.

62. *MCD*, 1855–56, 44; 1856–57, 212; 1859, 62; Mitchell, *State Gazetteer*, 441.

63. Frank, *Five Families*, 32; Frank, *Market Street*, 204–5.

64. *NBD*, 1855, 29; 1857, 56; 1859, 41, 215; 1860, 144; 1870, 267; 1875, 115; Frank, *Five Families*, 137; Frank, *Market Street*, 29, 61, 115, 204–5.

65. *NBD*, 1855, 30; 1857, 57, Frank, *Five Families*, 134, 137; Levy to Caldwell, 13 May 1983.

66. Federal census for Hamilton Ct., Tenn., under James J. Mulkey; *NBD*, 1853, 186; Mitchell, *State Gazetteer*, 441.

67. *NBD*, 1855, 30; 1857, 59.

68. *Jackson Gazette*, 12 Feb. 1825; 28 Jan. 1826.

69. *NBD*, 1859, 44; 1860, 148.

70. Nashville *Daily Cent. St. Am.*, 28 Feb. 1850.

71. *NBD*, 1859, 44.

72. *Ibid.*, 1859, 44; 1860, 140.

73. *Williams' Clarksville Directory, City Guide and Business Mirror, 1859–1860*, vol. 1 (Clarksville, Tenn., 1859), 34; Mitchell, *State Gazetteer*, 441.

74. Belden, *Marks*, 160.

75. Federal census for 1850, Giles County, Tennessee, under John N. Patterson.

76. Federal census for 1860, Giles Ct., Tenn.; Federal census for 1850, Giles Ct., Tenn., manufacturers schedule.

77. Federal census for 1850, Knox Ct., Tenn.; Jonesboro(ugh) *Whig*, 5 Mar. 1845.

78. Federal census for 1850, Franklin County, Tennessee; Mitchell, *State Gazetteer*, 315, 472.

79. *The Goodspeed Histories of Maury, Williamson, Rutherford, Wilson, Bedford and Marshall Counties of Tennessee* (1886, reprint, Columbia, Tenn., 1971), 768.

80. Federal census for 1850, Bledsoe County, Tennessee.

81. Federal census for 1850, Shelby Ct., Tenn.

(D)

1. Craig, *Arts and Crafts*, 64, 68, 69.

2. *Ibid.*, 71; *Jackson Republican*, 24 Mar. 1843; Federal census for 1850, Henry County, Tennessee.

3. *NBD*, 1857, 268; *Knoxville Business Directory*, 1859–60, 49, hereafter cited as *KBD*; Mitchell, *State Gazetteer*, 441.

4. Jacob Danner's obituary, 1850, n. d., n. p., Winchester, Virginia, courtesy of Mr. Klaus Wust, Edinburg, Virginia.

5. *KBD*, 1859–60, 49; Mitchell, *State Gazetteer*, 483.

6. *Knox. Reg.*, 8 June 1819.

7. Carthage *West. Expr.*, 21 Nov. 1808.

8. *Ibid.*

9. *Carthage Gazette*, 23 Mar. 1810.

10. Zella Armstrong, *Notable Southern Families*, vol. 1 (Chattanooga, Tenn., 1918), 59, 74; *Winchester (Virginia) Gazette*, 12 June 1799; Nash. *Tenn. Gaz.*, 22 Sept. 1802.

11. Nash. *Tenn. Gaz.*, 25 Aug. 1802; 2 Nov. 1803; 4 Jan. 1804; *Nashville Whig*, 13 Mar. 1822; Cutten, *Silversmiths of Virginia*, 211.

12. Nashville *Impartial Review and Cumberland Repository*, 1 Sept. 1808; Nashville *Democratic Clarion and Tennessee Gazette*, 28 Apr. 1812; *Nashville Gazette*, 13 May 1820.

13. Cutten, *Silversmiths of Virginia*, 211; Armstrong, *Notable Southern Families*, 74; Nash. *Impart. Rev. & Cumberland Repos.*, 7 Apr. 1808.

14. Armstrong, *Notable Southern Families*, 74.

15. *Knox. Enq.*, 13 Oct. 1824.

16. David Longworth, comp., *Longworth's American Almanac, New-York Register, and City Directory* (New York, 1804).

17. Pleasants and Sill, *Maryland Silversmiths*, 1972, 114–15.

18. Elizabeth D. Beckman, *Cincinnati Silversmiths, Jewelers, Watch and Clockmakers* (Cincinnati, Ohio, 1975), 44.

19. *MCD*, 1855, 113; 1859, 71.

20. Federal census for 1860, Williamson Ct., Tenn.; Mitchell, *State Gazetteer*, 67, 441; *NBD*, 1875, 322.

21. Federal census for 1850, Davidson Ct., Tenn., under A. C. Carter; James P. Kranz, Jr., letter to the author, 13 Mar. 1981; 8 March 1981.

22. *NBD*, 1853, 56; 1855, 37, 55; 1857, 72; 1859, 52, 216; 1860, 156; 1865, 14.

23. Kranz to Caldwell, 8 Mar. 1981; Federal census for 1860, Davidson Ct., Tenn.

24. Kranz to Caldwell, 13 Mar. 1981; Jill Garrett, *Obituaries from Tennessee Newspapers* (Easley, S. C., 1980), 98; Mt. Olivet Cemetery records.

25. Davidson County Court Records, microfilm, Inventories and Sales, Roll 434, Book 19, 338–49, Tenn. St. Lib. & Arch.; *NBD*, 1865, 14.

26. Derita Coleman Williams, *A View of Tennessee Silversmiths: A Loan Exhibition* (Memphis, Tenn., 1983), 16.

27. *KBD*, 1859–60, 50.

28. Kovel and Kovel, *American Silver*, 85; Boultinghouse, *Silversmiths of Kentucky*, 100.

29. *NBD*, 1860, 160.

30. *Knox. Reg.*, 21 Dec. 1819; 18 Apr. 1820.

(E)

1. *KBD*, 1859–60, 51.

2. Nash. *Dem. Clarion & Tenn. Gaz.*, 25 May 1810.

3. Cutten, *Silversmiths of Virginia*, 111–12.

4. Pulaski *Whig Courier*, 6 Mar. 1840.

5. Kovel and Kovel, *American Silver*, 92.

6. Clayton, *History of Davidson County*, 199–200; Basil Elliston, letter to the author, 17 Mar. 1983, containing a family sketch compiled by Grace B. Paine and Colonel Louis Farrell.

7. Davidson Ct. Court Rec., Wills and Inventories, Book 8, 171, Tenn. St. Lib. & Arch.; Elliston to Caldwell, 17 Mar. 1983; Clayton, *History of Davidson County*, 200.

8. Davidson Ct. Court Rec., Wills & Inv., Bk. 8, 221–4.

9. Elliston to Caldwell, 17 Mar. 1983.

10. Mrs. B. J. Prueher, letter to the author, 1 Feb. 1983; Ellen Beasley, ed., *Made in Tennessee* (Nashville, Tenn, 1971), 23; Ed Huddleston, "Joseph Thorp Elliston—Came to Town with Little But Left City a Great Legacy," *Nashville Banner*, 22 Oct. 1965; Sharpe, List of Taxable Property.

11. Prueher to Caldwell, 1 Feb. 1983.

12. *Ibid.*

13. *Ibid.*

14. *Ibid.*; Nash. *Tenn. Gaz.*, 25 Feb. 1800; 3 June 1801; 28 July 1802; Nashville *Tennessee Gazette and Mero District Advertiser*, 19 Oct. 1803; 4 Jan. 1804; Nash. *Impart. Rev. & Cumberland Repos.*, 29 Sept. 1808; Nashville *Clarion and Tennessee State Gazette*, 1 Feb. 1814.

15. *Nash. Clarion*, 1 Mar. 1808; *Nashville Clarion Extra*, 15 Mar. 1814; *Nash. Clarion*, 15 Mar. 1814; 8 Nov. 1814; *Nash. Whig*, 23 Apr. 1816; 22 May 1819; 27 Oct. 1819; *Nash. Clarion*, 23 May 1820.

16. Elliston to Caldwell, 17 Mar. 1983.

17. Amelia Edwards, telephone conversation with author, 20 Nov. 1984.

18. Nash. *Tenn. Gaz.*, 22 July 1802; 28 July 1802.

19. *Jackson Madisonian*, 20 June 1857.

(F)

1. *MCD*, 1856–57, 99.

2. *Ibid.*, 1855–56, 117.

3. Swannee Bennett, "Arkansas Artists and Artisans of the Nineteenth Century," ms, courtesy of Swannee Bennett.

4. George Barton Cutten, *The Silversmiths of Georgia* (Savannah, Ga., 1958), 40.

5. Mitchell, *State Gazetteer*, 441.

6. Federal census for 1860, Davidson Ct., Tenn.; Mt. Olivet Cemetery records; *NBD*, 1859, 59; 1860–61, 166; 1869, 25; 1870, 267.

7. Mt. Olivet Cemetery records and tombstone; *NBD*, 1855, 42; 1860–61, 166; 1869, 25.

8. Mt. Olivet Cemetery records and tombstone; *NBD*, 1875, 135; 1878, 162.

9. *Chattanooga Gazette*, 12 July 1856; *NBD*, 1857, 304, 309.

10. *The Goodspeed Histories of Giles, Lincoln, Franklin and Moore Counties*, 761.

11. *MCD*, 1856–57, 235.

12. Federal census for 1850, Davidson Ct., Tenn.; Rothrock, *French Broad*, 378–9.

13. *Wilson's Knox. Gaz.*, 22 Apr. 1811.

14. Georgetown, South Carolina *Winyaw Intelligencer*, 23 Jan. 1819; Franklin *Western Balance*, 30 Jan. 1829; Franklin *West. Wkly. Rev.*, 23 Nov. 1832.

15. Franklin *West. Wkly. Rev.*, 22 July 1836; 20 July 1838.

16. Louise Gillespie Lynch, *Miscellaneous Records of Williamson County*, vol. 2 (privately published, 1978), 25, 73.

17. Louise Gillespie Lynch, *Early Obituaries of Williamson County*, (privately published, 1977), 79; Lawrence County Court Records, microfilm, Roll 30, May 1852–55, 172, Tenn. St. Lib. & Arch.

18. Henderson, *Conquest*, 179–81.

19. *Wilson's Knox. Gaz.*, 22 Apr. 1811.

20. Frank, *Five Families*, 24, 47; *NBD*, 1859, 62.

21. Mitchell, *State Gazetteer*, 441, 215; Frank, *Market Street*, 82.

22. Knox Ct. Court Rec., microfilm, Roll 155, Bk. 1, 288–9, 299–300; Knox Ct. Court Min. Bk 8, 1813–16, 26.

23. *Knox. Gaz.*, 20 May 1809.

24. Knox Ct. Court Min. Bk. 8, 1813–16, 26; 7, 1809–12, 159.

25. Federal census of manufactures, 1829, Rutherford County, Tennessee.

26. *Ibid.*

27. *Nash. Whig*, 25 Dec. 1816; *Nash. Clarion*, 12 Aug. 1817; Jane H. Thomas, *Old Days in Nashville: Reminiscences* (1897, reprint, Nashville, Tenn., 1969), 49; *Nash. Clarion*, 19 Dec. 1818; *Nash. Whig*, 17 Nov. 1819; 12 Jan. 1820; 25 July 1823.

28. Federal census for 1850, Davidson Ct., Tenn.; *Nash. Union*, 19 Feb. 1840; *Nash.*, 16 Jan. 1844.

29. Sharpe, List of Taxable Property.

30. *Daily Nash. Am.*, 31 Dec. 1850; *NBD*, 1853, 56, 346; *Daily Nash. Am.*, 31 Dec. 1856; *NBD*, 1860, 169; 1866, 120; 1869, 25.

31. Federal census for 1860, Hamilton Ct., Tenn.

32. Clarksville *Tennessee Weekly Chronicle*, 28 June 1819; Ursula Smith Beach, *Along the Warioto: A History of Montgomery County, Tennessee* (Nashville, Tenn: 1964), 69–71.

33. Frankfurt, Kentucky *Argus of Western America*, 19 Mar. 1819.

34. *Clarksville Chronicle*, 28 Mar. 1839; 30 May 1839.

35. *Ibid.*, 30 May 1847; *NBD*, 1853, 227; 1857; Mitchell, *State Gazetteer*, 380.

36. *MCD*, 1859, 82.

37. *Ibid.*, 1850, 19; 1855, 120; 1856–57, 107; 1859, 208; 1860, 166.

38. *Ibid.*, 1856–57, 107.

39. Kovel and Kovel, *American Silver*, 104.

40. *Nash. Whig*, 26 Sept. 1815; *Louisville Correspondent*, 6 July 1814; 12 Oct. 1814.

41. Nashville *Clarion & Tenn. Gaz.*, 18 Apr. 1820.

42. *Trenton Southern Standard*, 17 Mar. 1858; 12 Jan. 1861.

43. *MCD*, 1856–57, 107.

44. *Ibid.*, 1855, 121; Kovel and Kovel, *American Silver*, 106.

45. Federal census for 1850, Davidson Ct., Tenn; *Nashville Republican*, 19 Feb. 1834; Franklin *West. Wkly. Rev.*, 27 Feb. 1835.

46. J. E. Coleman, letter to the author, 31 Dec. 1971.

(G)

1. *Maury, Williamson, Rutherford, Wilson, Bedford and Marshall Counties*, 828.
2. Burton, *South Carolina Silversmiths*, 241–2; Cutten, *Silversmiths of Georgia*, 53–4.
3. *Memp. Enq.*, 20 Apr. 1836; Cutten, *Silversmiths of North Carolina*, 39–40.
4. *Memp. Enq.*, 20 Apr. 1836; 22 June 1836.
5. *Knox. Reg.*, 27 Mar. 1821; Cutten, *Silversmiths of Virginia*, 350; *Knox. Reg.*, 10 Aug. 1816; 13 Feb. 1818.
6. *Knox. Reg.*, 3 Feb. 1818; 10 Feb. 1818; 17 Feb. 1818; 3 Nov. 1818; 24 Nov. 1818; 5 Jan. 1819.
7. *Ibid.*, 31 Aug. 1819; 21 Sept. 1819.
8. *Ibid.*, 5 Jan. 1819; 12 Jan. 1819.
9. *Ibid.*, 24 Oct. 1820.
10. George D. Free, *History of Tennessee from Its Earliest Discoveries and Settlements* (Nashville, Tenn., 1896), 82–3.
11. *Knox. Reg.*, 28 Nov. 1820.
12. *Ibid.*,, 27 Mar. 1821.
13. *Wilson's Knox. Gaz.*, 20 May 1809; 14 Oct. 1809.
14. *Ibid.*, 22 Apr. 1811; 30 Sept. 1811; *Nash. Clarion*, 16 June 1812; 16 Nov. 1813.
15. Nash. *Clarion & Tenn. St. Gazette*, 8 Mar. 1814.
16. *Nash. Whig*, 28 Feb. 1815.
17. *Nash. Clarion*, 11 Jan. 1820; Beckman, *Cincinnati Silversmiths*, 58.
18. *Wilson's Knox. Gaz.*, 20 May 1809; 14 Oct. 1809.
19. Federal census for 1880, Davidson Ct., Tenn.; *NBD*, 1855–56, 47; 1857, 89; 1859, 67; 1860, 174; 1865, 14, 185; 1868, 125; 1878, 179.
20. Federal census for 1880, Davidson Ct., Tenn.; Mt. Olivet Cemetery records.
21. *MCD*, 1855–56, 122; 1856–57, 109.
22. Federal census for 1860, Maury County, Tennessee; Colin James, Jr., "The James Family of Surry Co., Virginia," John Bennett Boddie, *Historical Southern Families*, vol. 5 Redwood City, Calif., 1960), 99.
23. *MCD*, 1860, 173.
24. Columbia *Western Mercury*, 20 Dec. 1828.
25. Kovel and Kovel, *American Silver*, 112.
26. *Nashville Republican and State Gazette*, 18 Sept. 1834.
27. *NBD*, 1853, 57, 346; 1855–56, 49; 1857, 91, 112; 1859, 68, 84; 1860–61, 178; Mitchell, *State Gazetteer*, 441, 483.
28. *Ibid.*
29. *NBD*, 1855–56, 49; 1857, 91, 112; 1859, 68, 84.
30. Mitchell, *State Gazetteer*, 43, 441.
31. *Nash. Whig*, 4 Dec. 1816.
32. *Nashville Whig and Tennessee Advertiser*, 6 Oct. 1817.
33. *Nash. Clarion*, 11 Nov. 1817; 26 May 1818.
34. Belden, *Marks*, 197.
35. Clayton, *History of Davidson County*, 364.
36. *Ibid.*; Thomas, *Old Days in Nashville*, 69; *Nashville Rep.*, 1 Mar. 1834; Belden, *Marks*, 181.
37. *Nash. Union*, 25 July 1843; Sharpe, List of Taxable Property; *NBD*, 1853, 57; 1855, 50; 1857, 93; 1859, 69; 1860, 178, 255.
38. Clayton, *History of Davidson Co.*, 364; Davidson Ct. Ct. Rec. Wills & Inv., Bk. 19, 198–200.
39. *Nash. Union*, 25 July 1843; 8 July 1845; Sharpe, List of Taxable Property.
40. *Nashville True Whig*, 7 July 1849; 24 Nov. 1849; 28 May 1851.
41. *Columbia Beacon*, 11 June 1847.
42. *NBD*, 1853, 15; 1859, 72; Mitchell, *State Gazetteer*, 217.
43. Appendix I.
44. *Nashville Patriot*, 23 May 1838; *Nash. Union*, 17 May 1839; Nash. *Daily Cen. St. Am.*, 30 Aug. 1841.
45. Davidson Ct. Court Rec., microfilm, Roll 1612, Book C, 352.
46. Darling Foundation of New York State Early American Silversmiths and Silver, *New York State Silversmiths* (Eggertsville, N. Y., 1964), 93; Belden, *Marks*, p. 204.
47. Federal censuses for 1840, 1850, 1860, McNairy County, Tennessee.

(H-I)

1. Federal censuses for 1830, 1840, 1850, 1860, Knox Ct., Tenn.; Robin C. Hale letter to the Tennessee State Museum, 27 Apr. 1982.
2. Kovel and Kovel, *American Silver*, 128.
3. *KBD*, 1859–60, 55, 87; Mitchell, *State Gazetteer*, 441; Federal census for 1860, Knox Ct., Tenn.
4. *NBD*, 1860, 186.
5. *The Goodspeed Histories of Madison County* (1887, reprint, Columbia, Tenn, 1972), 866–8.
6. *Ibid.* Two Chatham County, North Carolina gunsmiths, Edward Harper (b. 1780) and John Harper (b. 1815) are recorded in John Bivins, *Longrifles of North Carolina* (York, Pa., 1969), 156.
7. *Madison County*, 866–8.
8. *MCD*, 1859, 220; 1860, 185.
9. *Trenton South. Standard*, 16 Feb. 1860.
10. Federal census for 1850, Knox Ct., Tenn.; Edd Winfield Parks, *Segments of Southern Thought* (Athens, Ga., 1938), 218–22; George Washington Harris, *Sut Lovingood's Yarns* ed. M. Thomas Inge (New Haven, Conn., 1966), 16–17; Bert Neville, *Directory of Tennessee River Steamboats, 1821–1928* (Selma, Ala., 1963), 20.
11. Harris, *Sut Lovingood*, 16–17; *Knox. Reg.*, 27 Dec. 1843; *Knoxville Standard*, 30 June 1846; Federal census for 1850, Knox Ct., Tenn.
12. Harris, *Sut Lovingood*, 17.
13. *Ibid.*, 17–20.
14. *Ibid.*
15. *Ibid.*
16. Federal census for 1850, Davidson Ct., Tenn.
17. Nashville *Daily Cen. St. Am.*, 19 Feb. 1850; G. Bernard Hughes, *Sheffield Silver Plate* (New York, 1970), 38.
18. *Nash. Clarion*, 22 July 1802; 28 July 1802.
19. *Memp. Enq.*, 19 Mar. 1836.
20. *NBD*, 1860, 190; Federal census for 1860, Davidson Ct., Tenn.
21. *Knox. Reg.*, 21 September 1816.
22. *Boston Directory*, 1803, 66; 1805, 66; 1806, 65; 1807, 87; 1809, 74; 1810, 101.
23. *MCD*, 1856–57, 212; 1859, 73, 97.
24. Craig, *Arts and Crafts*, 35; Jonesboro(ugh) *Washington Advertiser*, 1 Feb. 1804.
25. Craig, *Arts and Crafts*, 36–7; Cutten, *Silversmiths of North Carolina*, 45–6.
26. *NBD*, 1855–56, 58; 1857, 107.
27. *Ibid.*, 1855–56, 59; 1857, 107.
28. Nash. *Dem. Clarion & Tenn. Gaz.*, 15 June 1810; 8 Feb. 1811; 22 Feb. 1811; Boultinghouse, *Silversmiths*, 155.
29. *Nash. Whig*, 8 Nov. 1820.
30. Franklin *Independent Gazette*, 26 Jan. 1822; 8 June 1822.
31. *Ibid.*, 17 July 1822.
32. *Ibid.*, 23 Jan. 1824.
33. Franklin *West. Balance*, 30 Jan. 1829; Franklin *West. Wkly. Rev.*, 20 Nov. 1835; Mrs. Jesse Short, Jr., letter to the author, 10 Jan. 1985.
34. Nash. *Dem. Clarion & Tenn. Gaz.*, 8 Feb. 1811; 22 Feb. 1811.
35. Franklin *Ind. Gaz.*, 26 Jan. 1822; 23 Jan. 1824.
36. Nathan Vaught, "Memoir," ms, Tenn. St. Lib. & Arch., 105–6; Garrett, *Obituaries*, 169.
37. Vaught, "Memoir," ms., 105; Federal census for 1850, Maury Ct., Tenn.; Jill Garrett, letter to the author, 24 Mar. 1983; W. S. Fleming, "Historical Sketch of Maury County," ms, Columbia, Tennessee, Public Library.
38. Fleming, "Historical Sketch," ms.
39. Garrett to Caldwell, 24 Mar. 1983; Garrett, *Obituaries*, 169.
40. *Ibid.*
41. Federal census for 1860, Maury Ct., Tenn.
42. Malcolm Fowler, *They Passed This Way: A Personal Narrative of Harnett County* (Harnett County, N. C., 1955), 69; Vaught, "Memoir," ms., 106; *Maury, Williamson, Rutherford, Wilson, Bedford and Marshall Counties*, 768; Columbia *West. Mercury*, 20 Dec. 1828.
43. Edmond K. Hamilton, comp. *Marriage Records of Williamson County, Tennessee, 1804–50* (Hartford, Ky., 1979), 41.
44. Jill Garrett, *Maury County, Tennessee, Newspapers, 1846–1850* (Columbia, Tenn., 1965), 85–6; *NBD*, 1853, 187; 1857, 295; 1860–61, 286.
45. *Knox. Reg.*, 9 Jan. 1828.
46. *MCD*, 1855–56, 5.
47. Beverly Burbage, letter to the author, 14 Oct. 1981; John Trotwood Moore, *Tennessee, The Volunteer State*, vol. 2 (Nashville, Tenn., 1923), 563–4.
48. Burbage to Caldwell, 14 Oct. 1981.
49. Moore, *Tennessee*, 563–4; William P. Beall, "Silversmiths and Goldsmiths of Tennessee," *Knox. Jour.*, 2 Oct. 1971.
50. *Knoxville Daily Press and Herald*, 20 Apr. 1869.
51. Moore, *Tennessee*, 563–4; Federal census for 1850, Knox Ct., Tenn; Burbage to Caldwell, 14 Oct. 1981.

52. Burbage to Caldwell, 14 Oct. 1981; Moore, *Tennessee*, 563–4; *KBD*, 1859–60, 57.

53. Burbage to Caldwell, 14 Oct. 1981; Beall, "Silversmiths and Goldsmiths," *Knox. Jour.*, 2 Oct. 1971; Moore, *Tennessee*, 563–4.

54. Moore, *Tennessee*, 2: 563–4.

55. William Selden, telephone conversation with author, 24 Mar. 1983; *Containing Sketches of Thirty East Tennessee Counties* (1887, reprint, Nashville, Tenn., 1972), 813; Mitchell, *State Gazetteer*, 441.

56. Chancery Court Records of McMinn County, Tennessee, 1890, 108, 216, Tenn. St. Lib. & Arch.; McMinn County Court Records, microfilm, Roll 65, vol. 1, July 1873–79, 132, 273.

57. Cutten, *Silversmiths of Georgia*, 40–1.

58. *NBD*, 1853, 57; 1855–56, 49; 1857, 91, 112; 1859, 84; 1860, 196; 1870, 267.

59. *Ibid.*, 1860, 198; Mitchell, *State Gazetteer*, 483.

60. Sharpe, List of Taxable Property.

(J)

1. James, "The James Family," *Southern Families*, vol. 5, 99.

2. *Ibid.*

3. *Ibid.*, 100.

4. *Ibid.*

5. *Ibid.*

6. Federal census for 1850, Hardeman County, Tennessee.

7. *Daily Nash. Am.*, 19 Apr. 1850; *NBD*, 1853, 223; 1857, 280; Federal census for 1860, Warren Ct., Tenn; *Cannon, Coffee, DeKalb, Warren, White Counties*, 825.

8. Federal Census for 1850, Hardeman Ct., Tenn.

9. *MCD*, 1855–56, 134; 1856–57, 135; 1860, 205, 248.

10. Paul R. Coppock, *Memphis Sketches* (Memphis, Tenn., 1976), 179–80.

11. *MCD*, 1856–57, 135.

12. *NBD*, 1857, 280; Mitchell, *State Gazetteer*, 441.

13. Kovel and Kovel, *American Silver*, 152.

14. *NBD*, 1853, 55; 1855–56, 65; 1857, 118; 1859, 89; Clayton, *History of Davidson County*, 492.

15. Rogersville *Western Pilot*, 19 Aug. 1815.

16. Carthage *West. Expr.*, 21 Nov. 1808.

17. *MCD*, 1850, 24.

18. *NBD*, 1859, 90; 1860–61, 204.

19. Mitchell, *State Gazetteer*, 441.

(K)

1. *NBD*, 1857, 325; Mitchell, *State Gazetter*, 441.

2. *Knox. Reg.*, 27 Mar. 1821.

3. *MCD*, 1855, 136; 1857, 139; 1859, 106; 1860, 210.

4. Kovel and Kovel, *American Silver*, 156.

5. Berson Papers.

6. *Ibid.*

7. Mitchell, *State Gazetteer*, 441.

8. Beckman, *Cincinnati Silversmiths*, 78–80; *NBD*, 1853, 57.

9. Gallatin *Examiner*, 11 Feb. 1860; Mitchell, *State Gazeteer*, 1860, 441; Federal census for 1860, Sumner County, Tennessee.

10. *NBD*, 1860, 206.

11. *Knox. Enq.*, 14 Mar. 1825.

12. *NBD*, 1859, 94; 1860, 208; Federal census for 1860, Davidson Ct., Tenn.

13. Mitchell, *State Gazetteer*, 39, 441.

14. *MCD*, 1859, 110; 1860, 217; Mitchell, *State Gazetteer*, 1860, 160.

15. *Nash. Whig*, 6 Sept. 1812.

(L)

1. Federal Census for 1850, Gibson County, Tennessee, under J. D. Hill; Trenton, *Star Spangled Banner*, 16 June 1848.

2. *Memp. Wkly. Appeal*, 27 Jan. 1843; 7 July 1843; 15 Mar. 1844.

3. *Nash. Whig*, 9 May 1815.

4. *Petersburg (Virginia) Republican*, 6 June 1817.

5. Federal census for 1850, Fayette County, Tennessee, under Thomas Parks.

6. Federal census for 1850, Davidson Ct., Tenn.

7. *NBD*, 1853, 65, 347; 1855–56, p. 70; 1857, 128; 1859, 97; 1860, 212.

8. Mitchell, *State Gazetteer*, 162, 441.

9. Bennett, "Arkansas Artists," ms.; *MCD*, 1855, 141.

10. *MCD*, 1856–57, 140; 1859, 113; 1860, 224.

11. *Maury, Williamson, Rutherford, Wilson, Bedford, and Marshall Counties*, 813, 826–7.

12. Federal census for 1850, Madison County, Tenness; Jackson *West Tennessee Whig*, 25 May 1849.

13. A. E. Lightfort, letter to the author, ? Jan. 1972.

14. *NBD*, 1853, 235; *Jackson Madisonian*, 7 Nov. 1855; Lightfort to Caldwell, ? Jan. 1972.

15. *Nash. Whig*, 10 Apr. 1822; Silas Emmett Lucas, Jr., *Obituaries from Early Tennessee Newspapers, 1794–1851* (Easley, S. C., 1978), 219.

16. *MCD*, 1850, 75; 1855–56, 18; 1859, 114, 223; 1860, p. 118; Mitchell, *State Gazetteer*, 162, 441.

17. Jerome Redfearn, letter to the author, 16 Feb. 1983; *Jackson Gaz.*, 11 Sept. 1830; Lexington, Kentucky *Reporter*, 5 Dec. 1808.

18. Lynchburg City, Virginia, Court Records, microfilm, Hustings Court Order Book, 1812–17, 163, Virginia State Library; *Lynchburg (Virginia) Press*, 20 June 1817.

19. *Knox. Enq.*, 17 Dec. 1826; *Knox. Reg.*, 17 Jan. 1827; Cutten, *Silversmiths of Virginia*, 59.

20. *Maury, Williamson, Rutherford, Wilson, Bedford and Marshall Counties*, 828; Kovel and Kovel, *American Silver*, 173.

(Mc)

1. *NBD*, 1853, 66.

2. *MCD*, 1859, 224; Mitchell, *State Gazetteer*, 1860, 441, 483.

3. Federal census for 1850, Madison Ct., Tenn.; Leesburg, Virginia *The Washingtonian*, 4 June 1811.

4. Jackson *District Telegraph*, 26 Jan. 1838.

5. Jackson *West Tenn. Whig*, 28 Oct. 1842.

6. *Jackson Rep.*, 28 Feb. 1845.

7. *NBD*, 1853, 235.

8. Mitchell, *State Gazetteer*, 441.

9. Fredericksburg *Virginia Herald*, 28 Dec. 1822; Federal census for 1850, Knox Ct., Tenn.

10. *NBD*, 1857, 268.

11. *KBD*, 1859–60, 64, 87.

12. *NBD*, 1857, 268.

13. Mitchell, *State Gazetteer*, 441.

14. Cutten, *Silversmiths of Virginia*, 76.

15. *NBD*, 1857, 304.

16. *Nash. Whig*, 11 Nov. 1812, 27 July 1813; 7 Jan. 1814; 30 Aug. 1814; 6 June 1815; *Nash. Clarion*, 2 Sept. 1817.

17. *Nash. Whig & Tenn. Adver.*, 9 Jan. 1819.

18. Nash. *Clarion & Tenn. Gaz.*, 8 Feb. 1820.

19. *NBD*, 1853, 222.

20. Frankfort *Palladium*, 23 June 1810.

21. Cutten, *Silversmiths of Georgia*, 50–51; Federal census of manufactures for 1820, Blount County, Tennessee.

(M)

1. *Maury, Williamson, Rutherford, Wilson, Bedford and Marshall Counties*, 826, 827.

2. *Nash. Clarion*, 9 July 1822.

3. Federal census for 1850, Giles Ct., Tenn.; *Nash. Whig*, 31 July 1822; 11 Aug. 1823.

4. Murfreesboro, *Tennessee Telegraph*, 14 Mar. 1838.

5. Federal census for 1860, Giles Ct., Tenn.

6. *NBD*, 1860, 218.

7. *MCD*, 1859, 146, 224; 1855, 206; 1856, 159; 1860, 248.

8. *NBD*, 1853, p. 223; *State Gazetteer*, 1860, p. 316.

9. Nash. *Clarion*, 9 Aug. 1808; 16 Aug. 1808.

10. Federal census for 1850, Warren Ct., Tenn.

11. *MCD*, 1855, 206; 1856–57, 159; *NBD*, 1857, 238, 240; *MCD* 1859, 224; 1860, 248; Mitchell, *State Gazetteer*, 166.

12. Federal census for 1850, Shelby Ct., Tenn., under William H. Batesman.

13. Coppock, "Mid-South Memoirs," Memphis *Comm. Appeal*, 16 Sept. 1979; *MCD*, 1850, 28; 1853, 173; 1855, 148; 1856–57, 159; 1859, 124; 1860, 248.

14. *MCD*, 1860, 248; Kovel and Kovel, *American Silver*, 185.

15. Federal census for 1850, Shelby Ct., Tenn; Coppock, "Mid-South Memoirs," Memphis *Comm. Appeal*, 16 Sept. 1979.

16. Coppock, "Mid-South Memoirs," Memphis *Comm. Appeal*, 16

Sept. 1979; *MCD*, 1850, 28, 1855–56, 201; 1856–57, 159; 1859, 124; 1860, 248.

17. *MCD*, 1850, 42; 1855, 134, 163, 183–4; 1856–57, 109, 135; 1859, 58, 175; Belden, *Marks*, 454.

18. Coppock, "Mid-South Memoirs."

19. *Ibid.* 20. *Ibid.*

21. *Memp. Wkly. Appeal*, 23 Feb. 1843; 14 July 1845.

22. Coppock, "Mid-South Memoirs," Memphis *Comm. Appeal*, 16 Sept. 1979.

23. *Memp. Wkly. Appeal*, 15 Mar. 1844.

24. Coppock, "Mid-South Memoirs," Memphis *Comm. Appeal*, 16 Sept. 1979.

25. *MCD*, 1855, 148; 1856–57, 235.

26. *Nash. Whig*, 20 Oct. 1823; Davidson Ct. Court Rec., Wills & Inv., Bk. 8, 221–4.

27. *Nashville Whig and Advertiser*, 17 Nov. 1817; Nash. *Clarion & Tenn. Gaz.*, 22 Sept. 1818; 18 Apr. 1820.

28. *KBD*, 1859, p. 101.

29. *Directory and Stranger's Guide for the City of Charleston* (Charleston, S. C., 1819), 66.

30. *MCD*, 1856–57, 156; 1855, 148.

31. *Nash. Whig*, 20 Oct. 1823; 17 Nov. 1823.

32. Davidson Ct. Court Rec., Wills & Inv., Bk. 8, 221–4.

33. *Nash. Whig*, 1 Feb. 1814.

34. Federal Census for 1850, Shelby Ct., Tenn.; *MCD*, 1860, 252.

35. Garrett, *Maury County Newspapers*, 8; *NBD*, 1857, 295.

36. Mitchell, *State Gazetteer*, 441.

37. *NBD*, 1860, 177, 226.

38. Mitchell, *State Gazetteer*, 40, 483.

39. *Nash. Whig*, 20 Oct. 1823; 17 Nov. 1823.

40. *Nash. Whig*, 14 Apr. 1826.

41. Mitchell, *State Gazetteer*, 483.

42. Federal census for 1850, Hamilton Ct., Tenn.

43. Swannee Bennett, "Arkansas Silversmiths, Watchmakers, Watch and Clock Repairers," ms., courtesy of Swannee Bennett.

44. *MCD*, 1857, 238; 1859, 128, 224.

45. *Nash. Whig*, 1 Feb. 1814.

46. Davidson Ct. Court Rec., Wills & Inv., Bk. 8, 221–4.

47. *NBD*, 1860, 226.

48. Boultinghouse, *Silversmiths*, 208.

49. *Ibid.*, 209.

50. *Ibid.*; *NBD*, 1853, 57; 1855, 82; 1857, 147; 1859, 110; 1860, 226; Mitchell, *State Gazetteer*, 472, 483; *NBD*, 1860, 226.

(N-O)

1. *Nash. Whig*, 8 Dec. 1823; Cutten, *Silversmiths of Virginia*, 31–2.

2. *Nash. Whig*, 8 Dec. 1823.

3. *Ibid.*, 19 Apr. 1824, 4 Oct. 1824; 20 Dec. 1824; *Nash. Gaz.*, 18 Feb. 1825; 16 Apr. 1825; 15 July 1825; *Nash. Banner*, 17 Sept. 1825.

4. *Nash. Banner*, 27 Jan. 1826; 14 Apr. 1826.

5. Appendix I.

6. *Nash. Rep.*, 9 May 1837.

7. Harold Underwood Faulkner, *America, Its History and People* (New York, 1942), 213, 488, 495–8; *Nash. Patriot*, 16 Jan. 1838.

8. *Nash. Patriot*, 23 May 1838. 9. *NBD*, 1860, 236.

10. Boultinghouse, *Silversmiths*, 211.

11. Federal census for 1850, Shelby Ct., Tenn.; *MCD*, 1850, 31; *MCD* 1856–57, 175.

12. *MCD*, 1859, 131, 224; 1860, 263; Mitchell, *State Gazetteer*, 168, 441.

13. Boultinghouse, *Silversmiths*, 211.

14. *NBD*, 1853, 347; *MCD*, 1856–57, 175; *NBD*, 1857, 240.

15. *NBD*, 1859, 216; 1860, 236.

16. Boultinghouse, *Silversmiths*, 211–12; Bennett, "Arkansas Artists," ms.

17. Vaught, "Memoirs," ms, 105.

18. Columbia *West. Mercury*, 20 Dec. 1828.

19. Davidson Ct. Court Rec., microfilm, Roll 434, Bk. 19, 1861–65, 208, 211.

20. Garrett, *Obituaries*, 276.

21. *Jackson Gaz.*, 29 May 1824.

22. *MCD*, 1855, 154; 1859, 133.

(P)

1. *NBD*, 1859, 36, 120, 128. 2. Mitchell, *State Gazetteer*, 67, 441.

3. *NBD*, 1855, 93, 126. 4. *Ibid.*, 1857, 166; 1860, 240.

5. Nash. *Clarion & Tenn. Gaz.*, 11 Nov. 1817.

6. Unidentified newspaper, 1 Jan. 1820, from a collection of single pages at the Tennessee St. Lib. & Arch.

7. Federal census for 1850, Davidson Ct., Tenn.; Nash. *Daily Cen. St. Am.*, 7 Aug. 1850.

8. *Nashville Daily Gazette*, 22 Oct. 1851.

9. Cutten, *Silversmiths of North Carolina*, 84.

10. Appendix I.

11. Cutten, *Silversmiths of North Carolina*, 84.

12. *Nash. Union*, 23 Aug. 1836; Appendix I.

13. *Nash. Union*, 17 May 1839; Nash. *Daily Cen. St. Am.*, 30 Aug. 1841.

14. *Nash. Union*, 25 July 1843; 8 July 1845.

15. Nash. *Daily Cen. St. Am.*, 24 July 1849; 8 Aug. 1850; Davidson Ct. Court Rec., microfilm, Roll 432, Book 15, 101.

16. Cutten, *Silversmiths of North Carolina*, 84.

17. *Nash. Union*, 23 Aug. 1836, 12 Jan. 1837.

18. *Ibid.*, 17 May 1839, 25 July 1843.

19. Federal census for 1850, Shelby Ct., Tenn., under James S. Wilkins.

20. *Ibid.*; *MCD*, 1856, 212; 1860, 343.

21. Federal census for 1850, Shelby Ct., Tenn., under W. B. Means.

22. Federal census for 1850, Shelby Ct., Tenn., under James S. Wilkins.

23. Mitchell, *State Gazetteer*, 441.

24. *Ibid.*; James McCallum, *A Brief Sketch of the Settlement and Early History of Giles County, Tennessee* (Pulaski, Tenn., 1928), 99.

25. Federal census for 1850, Hardeman Ct., Tenn.

26. Jerome Redfearn, *Indiana Silversmiths, Clock- and Watchmakers, 1729–1900* (Georgetown, Ky., 1984), 71–2; *MCD*, 1859, 139, 224; 1860, 277; *State Gazetteer*, 1860, 168, 441, 472, 483.

27. Nash. *Union*, 25 Sept. 1839.

28. Kovel and Kovel, *American Silver*, 220.

29. *Williams' Clarksville Directory*, 61, 63.

30. Paris *Republic*, 11 Jan. 1850.

31. Craig, *Arts and Crafts*, 80; Cutten, *Silversmiths of North Carolina*, 88.

32. Jackson *District Telegraph and State Sentinel*, 23 Mar. 1838; 13 July 1838.

33. *Ibid.*, 19 Oct. 1838; *Fayetteville Observer*, 10 Nov. 1841.

34. Craig, *Arts and Crafts*, 43; Cutten, *Silversmiths of North Carolina*, 88.

35. Federal censuses for 1830, 1850, 1860, Sumner Ct., Tenn.; Gallatin *Republican Sentinel and Sumner, Smith and Jackson Intelligencer*, 28 Jan. 1840.

(R)

1. *NBD*, 1859, 120, 128.

2. Federal census for 1850, Wilson County, Tennessee.

3. Federal census for 1850, DeKalb County, Tennessee; Federal census for 1860, Wilson Ct., Tenn.

4. Cutten, *Silversmiths of Virginia*, 211.

5. Sam Stuffle, letter to the author, 24 Mar. 1982.

6. Nash. *Impart. Rev. and Cumberland Repos.*, 11 Aug. 1808; Nash. *Dem. Clarion & Tenn. Gaz.*, 3 Jan. 1809.

7. Nash. *Dem. Clarion & Tenn. Gaz.*, 8 Feb. 1811, 22 Feb. 1811.

8. *Nash. Whig*, 27 Dec. 1814; Nash. *Clarion & Tenn. Gaz.*, 11 Nov. 1817.

9. In Jane Thomas, *Old Days in Nashville*, the 94-year-old author recalled a two-room, one-story brick house "built by Mr. Rawworth, a silversmith. He and his wife, who was Priscilla Brewer, lived in the back room and kept a store in the front."; *Nash. Whig & Tenn. Adver.*, 5 Jan. 1818; Nash. *Clarion & Tenn. Gaz.*, 1 Dec. 1818.

10. Nash. *Clarion & Tenn. Gaz.*, 7 Mar. 1820; 18 April 1820.

11. *Nash. Whig*, 27 Dec. 1814; 10 Jan. 1815.

12. *Ibid.*; Nash. *Clarion & Tenn. Gaz.*, 11 Nov. 1817.

13. Nash. *Clarion & Tenn. Gaz.*, 11 Nov. 1817; 26 May 1818; Davidson Ct. Court Rec., Wills & Inv., Bk. 8, 221–4; Nash. *Clarion & Tenn. Gaz.*, 18 Apr. 1820.

14. Mitchell, *State Gazetteer*, 441.

15. Federal censuses for 1830, 1840, 1850, Rutherford Ct., Tenn.

16. *Maury, Williamson, Rutherford, Wilson, Bedford and Marshall Counties*, 828.

17. Appendix I.

18. Kovel and Kovel, *American Silver*, 227.

19. *Williams' Clarksville Directory*, 63.

20. Thomas, *Old Days in Nashville*, 49; *Nash. Whig*, 25 Dec. 1816; *Nash. Clarion*, 12 Aug. 1817; *Nashville Whig*, 25 Aug. 1823.

21. *Memp. Wkly Appeal*, 15 Mar. 1844; Shelby County Court Records, Wills, 3E, 1855–62, 288, Tenn. St. Lib. & Arch.

22. *Nash. Whig*, 25 Dec. 1816; Thomas, *Old Days in Nashville*, 49; Nash. *Clarion & Tenn. Gaz.*, 12 Aug. 1817.

23. Nash. *Clarion & Tenn. Gaz.*, 11 Nov. 1817.

24. *Ibid.*, 3 Mar. 1818; 29 Dec. 1818; 27 Feb. 1819; 3 Apr. 1819; *Nash. Whig*, 12 Jan. 1820; 20 Feb. 1822; 25 July 1823; *Memp. Wkly. Appeal*, 15 Mar. 1844.

25. American Art Association, *Personal Relics: Silver, China, and Glass from The White House, Books from the Hermitage and Other Association Items Once Owned by President Andrew Jackson, Inherited by His Great Grandson, Andrew Jackson IV of Los Angeles, California* (Catalog. New York: 1927), Item 76.

26. Federal census for 1850, Lincoln County, Tennessee; Fayetteville *Village Messenger*, 29 Sept. 1824; 14 Dec. 1827.

27. *Giles, Lincoln, Franklin, and Moore Counties*, 771.

28. *Memp. Enq.*, 6 May 1837.

29. Federal census for 1850, Davidson Ct., Tenn.; 1860, Rutherford Ct., Tenn.; Mitchell, *State Gazetteer*, 194, 483.

30. Clayton, *History of Davidson County*, 496.

31. Frankfort *Palladium*, 19 June 1806; Lexington *Kentucky Gazette and General Advertiser*, 11 Sept. 1806; 20 Oct. 1807; 5 Dec. 1808; 7 Aug. 1810; Boultinghouse, *Silversmiths*, pp. 228–29.

32. Appendix I.

33. Kovel and Kovel, *American Silver*, 233.

34. *MCD*, 1855, 163; 1859, 146, 223.

35. Mitchell, *State Gazetteer*, 441; Federal census for 1860, Hancock Ct., Tenn..

36. Kovel and Kovel, *American Silver*, 234.

37. Mitchell, *State Gazetteer*, 441; Federal census for 1860, Hancock Ct., Tenn.

38. J. E. Coleman, personal communication with the author, 31 Dec. 1971. At that time Coleman revealed he had served a four-year apprenticeship under the William R. Bell who purchased M. Roulet's shop.

39. *Maury, Williamson, Rutherford, Wilson, Bedford and Marshall Counties*, 828–9.

40. Mitchell, *State Gazetteer*, 1860, 441.

41. *NBD*, 1857, 314.

42. Mitchell, *State Gazetteer*, 441.

43. *Jackson Gaz.*, 2 Dec. 1826; Bennett, "Arkansas Artists," ms.

44. Federal census for 1850, Shelby Ct., Tenn., under Melissa Rudissile; Inez Moncrief, letter to the author, 31 Mar. 1983.

45. Federal census for 1860, Davidson Ct., Tenn.; *NBD*, 1857, 181; 1860, 250.

46. Federal censuses for 1850, 1860, Bedford County, Tennessee; *Shelbyville Times Gazette*, Sesquicentennial Issue, 7 Oct. 1969, 58–9.

47. *Ibid*, 58.

48. Morris's *Tennessee Gazetteer* published in 1834 described Shelbyville as the "seat of justice of Bedford County . . . situated on the north-east bank of Duck River, considerably elevated, but on rather an uneven and rocky surface, surrounded by cedar groves. In 1830 this town was almost entirely demolished by a storm. . . . Most of the buildings have been rebuilt which gives the village a very thriving and handsome appearance. In the summer of 1833 the cholera raged with great malignancy, and about one-tenth of the population fell victims to the scourge. It is, however, considered a healthy place, and contains at present about 600 inhabitants. . . "; *Shelbyville Times Gaz.*, Sesquicentennial Issue, 7 Oct. 1969, 58; Shelbyville *Western Intelligencer*, 12 Sept. 1828.

49. Shelbyville *Western Freeman*, 27 Mar. 1835; *NBD*, 1853, 210.

50. *Shelbyville Times Gaz.*, Sesquicentennial Issue, 7 Oct. 1969, 58–9.

51. *Ibid.*, 58.

52. *Ibid.*, 58–9.

53. *Ibid.*, 59; *Maury, Williamson, Rutherford, Wilson, Bedford, and Marshall Counties*, 1171–2.

54. Mitchell, *State Gazetteer*, 441; Federal census for 1860, Fentress County, Tennessee.

55. *NBD*, 1860, 54.

(S)

1. *NBD*, 1859, 133.

2. Beckman, *Cincinnati Silversmiths*, 119; Kovel and Kovel, *American Silver*, 238.

3. Federal census for 1850, Sumner Ct., Tenn.; *Repub. Sent. & Sumner, Smith & Jackson Intell.*, 28 Jan. 1840; Mitchell, *State Gazetteer*, 70, 483.

4. Kovel and Kovel, *American Silver*, 241.

5. Mitchell, *State Gazetteer*, 441.

6. Federal census for 1860, Davidson Ct.; *NBD*, 1859, 134; 1860, 156, 254.

7. Federal census for 1850, Davidson Ct., Tenn.; *Maury, Williamson, Rutherford, Wilson, Bedford and Marshall Counties*, 828; Nash. *Daily Union*, 10 Dec. 1849.

8. *NBD*, 1869, 278.

9. *Containing Sketches of Thirty East Tennessee Counties*, 813; Morris, *Tennessee Gazetteer*, 148; Athens *Hiwassee Patriot*, 8 Sept. 1840.

10. *Athens Courier*, 19 Jan. 1844.

11. W. R. Selden, letter to the author, 23 Feb. 1983; Helen Bryan letter to W. R. Selden, 3 Mar. 1983, courtesy of W. R. Selden.

12. *NBD*, 1853, 210; Mitchel, *State Gazetteer*, 288, 483; *NBD*, 1869, 283.

13. Selden to Caldwell, 23 Feb. 1983; Bryan to Selden, 3 Mar. 1983.

14. Shelbyville Sesquicentennial Exhibit, October 1969, from a card displayed with a spoon at the Tip Thomson exhibit; Bryan to Selden, 3 Mar. 1983.

15. Bryan to Selden, 3 Mar. 1983; Federal census for 1850, McMinn County, Tennessee.

16. *NBD*, 1853, 232; Selden to Caldwell, 23 Feb. 1983.

17. *Containing Sketches of Thirty East Tennessee Counties.*, 813; Mitchell, *State Gazetter*, 10, 441; McMinn Ct. Court Rec., microfilm, Roll 65, vol. 1, 1873–79, 132, 273.

18. Selden to Caldwell, 24 Mar. 1983.

19. Bryan to Selden, 3 Mar. 1983.

20. Selden to Caldwell, 23 Feb. 1983; Bryan to Selden, 3 Mar. 1983.

21. *Containing Sketches of Thirty East Tennessee Counties*, 813; Mitchell, *State Gazetteer*, 1860, 10, 441; Federal census for 1850, McMinn Ct., Tenn.; McMinn Ct. Court Rec., microfilm Roll 65, vol. 1, 1873–79, 132, 273.

22. Federal census for 1850, Overton Ct., Tenn.; Mitchell, *State Gazetteer*, 441.

23. *Columbia Beacon*, 11 June 1847.

24. *NBD*, 1853, 57.

25. *Sparta Review*, 18 May 1825.

26. Nash. *Daily Cen. St. Am.*, 4 Mar. 1849.

27. *Knox. Reg.*, 16 Oct. 1821; 21 Dec. 1819; 18 Apr. 1820; 16 Oct. 1821.

28. Knox Ct. Court Rec., microfilm, Roll 155, Bk 3, Inv. & Sales, n. d.; Pleasants and Sill, *Maryland Silversmiths*, 83–4; Fales, *Early American Silver*, 247.

29. Federal census for 1850, Montgomery Ct., Tenn.; Nathaniel G. Jewett, *The Portland Directory and Register* (Portland, Me., 1823), 51; *Clarksville Chron.*, 13 Feb. 1840.

30. *NBD*, 1853, 227; Ursula Beach, letter to the author, 16 May 1983; Boultinghouse, *Silversmiths*, 250.

31. Mrs. Lewis Clark Wilcoxen, letter to the author, 5 Apr. 1972.

32. *Jackson Gaz.*, 11 Mar. 1826; 8 Nov. 1828; Morris, *Tennessee Gazetteer*, 78; Jackson *Dist. Telegraph*, 2 Feb. 1838.

33. Federal census of manufactures for 1820, Hawkins County, Tennessee.

34. Federal census of manufactures for 1820, Smith County, Tennessee.

35. Federal census for 1850, Madison Ct., Tenn., under Thomas McCowat.

36. Federal census for 1860, Madison Ct., Tenn.

37. *NBD*, 1869, 25.

38. Fedora S. Frank, *Five Families*, 31, 75, 151.

39. *NBD*, 1859, 216; 1860, 171, 260; 1870, 267; 1875, 231; Mitchell, *State Gazetteer*, 233, 441.

40. Davidson Ct. Court Rec., microfilm, Roll 440, Bk. 27, 302–3.

41. Jackson *Dist. Telegraph*, 15 Dec. 1837; 26 Jan. 1838; 2 Feb. 1838.

42. Sidney Adair Smith, "Mobile Silversmiths and Jewelers, 1820–1867," *Antiques* 99(March 1971): 411.

43. *Trenton South. Standard*, 12 Jan. 1861.

44. *NBD*, 1869, 278.

45. Federal censuses for 1830, 1840, 1850, Bedford Ct., Tenn.
46. *Nash. Union*, 9 Dec. 1842; 3 Jan. 1843.
47. *MCD*, 1856–57, 190.
48. *MCD*, 1855, 171.
49. *Nash. Daily Union*, 17 May 1849; 1 Sept. 1850; *NBD*, 1853, 56.
50. Federal census for 1850, White County, Tennessee; *Sparta Recorder and Law Journal*, 8 Oct. 1831.
51. Kovel and Kovel, *American Silver*, 258.
52. Federal census for 1860, Davidson Ct., Tenn.; Kranz to Caldwell, 13 Mar. 1981.
53. *NBD*, 1866, 281; 1870, 267; 1875, 235; 1892, 849.
54. *Ibid.*, 1860, 262; 1866, 286.
55. *Nash. Whig*, 11 Nov. 1812; 12 Oct. 1813; Nash. *Clarion & Tenn. Gaz.*, 2 Sept. 1817; *Nash. Whig & Tenn. Adver.*, 9 Jan. 1819; Nash. *Clarion & Tenn. St. Gaz.*, Nashville, 17 Aug. 1819.
56. Clayton, *History of Davidson County*, 195; Thomas, *Old Days in Nashville*, 43.
57. Sharpe, List of Taxable Property.
58. *NBD*, 1853, 215; Federal census for 1860, Madison Ct., Tenn.
59. Kovel and Kovel, *American Silver*, 262.
60. Mitchell, *State Gazetteer*, 441; John L. Mitchell, *Tennessee State Gazetteer and Business Directory*, (Nashville, Tenn., 1876), 343.
61. *Knox. Enq.*, 3 May 1826.

(T-V)

1. Mitchell, *State Gazetteer*, 62.
2. Nash. *Union*, 25 Sept. 1839; *Nash. Whig*, 20 Mar. 1840.
3. Rainwater, *American Silver Manufacturers*, 59.
4. Morris, *Tennessee Gazetteer*, 137; *Randolph Recorder*, 3 Mar. 1835.
5. Boultinghouse, *Silversmiths*, 270.
6. Franklin *Ind. Gaz.*, Franklin, 26 Jan. 1822.
7. *Ibid.*, 4 July 1823.
8. *Ibid.*, 3 Oct. 1823.
9. *Knox. Enq.*, 15 Dec. 1825; 22 Feb. 1826; 15 Aug. 1827.
10. Cutten, *Silversmiths of Virginia*, 124.
11. *Ibid.*, 77; Federal census for 1800, Allegheny County, Maryland; Boultinghouse, *Silversmiths*, 272; Swannee Bennett, "A Biographical Sketch of Silas Toncray," ms, courtesy of Swannee Bennett.
12. Bennett, "Biographical Sketch," ms.
13. James D. Davis, *History of the City of Memphis* (Memphis, Tenn., 1873), 34, 312.
14. J. M. Keating, *History of the Town of Memphis and Shelby County*, vol. 1 (Syracuse, N. Y., 1888), 174–5.
15. Davis, *History of Memphis*, 312.
16. *Somerville Reporter*, 16 May 1840.
17. *Nash. Repub.*, 21 Dec. 1834; 26 Jan. 1836; 8 Mar. 1837; 17 Mar. 1837.
18. *MCD*, 1859, 166.
19. *MCD*, 1855, 178; 1856, 107.
20. *Maury, Williamson, Rutherford, Wilson and Marshall Counties*, 863.
21. Federal census of manufactures for 1820, Bedford County, Tennessee.
22. *Shelbyville Times Gaz.*, Sesquicentennial Issue, 7 Oct. 1969, 58.
23. Shelbyville *West. Intelligencer*, Shelbyville, 29 Aug. 1828.
24. *Shelbyville Times Gaz.*, Sesquicentennial Issue, & Oct. 1969, 29.
25. *Ibid.*, 29, 58.
26. Stephen G. C. Ensko, *American Silversmiths and Their Marks* (Southampton, N.Y., 1937), 31.
27. *Clarksville Patriot*, 23 June 1869; Jerome Redfearn, letter to the author, 30 Jan. 1982.

(W-Y)

1. *NBD*, 1860, 272; 1875, 247.
2. *Ibid.*, 1853, 57; 1855, 122.
3. Redfearn, *Indiana Silversmiths*, 180.
4. Mitchell, *State Gazetteer*, 441.
5. Nash. *Dem. Clarion & Tenn. Gaz.*, 8 Oct. 1811.
6. *The New-York Directory, and Register, for the Year 1790* (New York, 1790); William Duncan, comp., *The New-York Directory, and Register, for the Year 1791* (New York, 1791); Norfolk, Virginia *Herald*, 18 Oct. 1794, 17 June 1800, 22 Jan. 1801; Richmond *Virginia Gazette and General Advertiser*, 3 Sept. 1803.
7. *MCD*, 1860, 335.
8. Federal census for 1850, Shelby Ct., Tenn.; *MCD*, 1850, 40.
9. *MCD*, 1860, 336.
10. Federal census for 1850, Davidson Ct., Tenn; *Nash. Union*, 25 Apr. 1846; Nash. *Daily Cen. St. Am.*, 28 Feb. 1850.
11. Kovel and Kovel, *American Silver*, 283.
12. Federal census for 1850, Robertson County, Tennessee; Jerome Redfearn, *Indiana Silversmiths*, 101–2; *Nash. Union*, 27 May 1835.
13. Federal census for 1850, Robertson Ct., Tenn.; Mitchell, *State Gazetteer*, 441.
14. *Nash. Union*, 27 May 1835.
15. Mitchell, *State Gazetteer*, 71, 441.
16. Nash. *Daily Cen. St. Am.*, 7 June 1848.
17. Federal census for 1850, Sumner Ct., Tenn.; Edythe Whitley Rucker, *Marriages in Davidson County, Tennessee, 1789–1847* (Baltimore, 1981), 80; *Nash. Whig*, 29 June 1823; 26 Jan. 1824; Nashville *National Banner*, 27 Jan. 1826; 7 Apr. 1826, 26 Apr. 1828.
18. Appendix I.
19. Sharpe, List of Taxable Property; Whitley, *Marriages*, 188 (the marriage took place on 17 Mar. 1841); *MCD*, 1853, 173.
20. Federal census for 1850, Hardeman Ct., Tenn.; Jackson *South. Statesman*, 23 Jan. 1833; *Bolivar Free Press and Farmers Herald*, 29 Mar. 1834; 14 Jan. 1835.
21. Federal census of manufactures for 1850, Hardeman Ct., Tenn; Federal censuses for 1860, Hamilton Ct. and Hardeman Ct., Tenn.
22. Derita Coleman Williams, *A View of Tennessee Silversmiths*, a loan exhibition catalog, Dixon Gallery and Gardens, 18 Mar. 1983, Memphis, Tenn., 25; Hardeman County Court Records, microfilm, Roll 35, Book 5, 381, Tenn. St. Lib. & Arch.
23. Federal census for 1850, Blount Ct., Tenn.
24. Jackson *South. Statesman*, 23 Jan. 1833; *Bolivar Free Press*, 29 Mar. 1834, 14 Jan. 1835.
25. Nash. *Dem. Clarion & Tenn. Gaz.*, 2 Apr. 1811.
26. Caswell County, North Carolina, Apprentice Indentures, 20 March 1780, North Carolina Department of Cultural Resources, Division of Archives and History.
27. *NBD*, 1866, 261; 1875, 254.
28. Federal census for 1850, Shelby Ct., Tenn., under John H. Krafft; *MCD*, 1855, 184.
29. *MCD*, 1855, 184; 1856–57, 207; 1859, 175; 1872, 362.
30. *Maury, Williamson, Rutherford, Wilson, Bedford, and Marshall Counties*, 874; Mitchell, *State Gazetteer*, 288, 441.
31. Federal census for 1860, Maury Ct., Tenn.; *Nash. Clarion*, 27 Sept. 1808.
32. *Maury, Williamson, Rutherford, Wilson, Bedford, and Marshall Counties*, 768; *Columbia Observer*, 2 Oct. 1834.
33. Garrett, *Obituaries*, 216; Maury Ct. Court Rec., microfilm, Roll 184, Book F, 516–17.
34. Federal census for 1850, Shelby Ct., Tenn.
35. *MCD*, 1856, 212.
36. *Ibid.*, 1860, 343; 1866, 195; 1867–68, 251; 1868–69, 225; 1872, 364.
37. Federal census for 1850, Davidson Ct., Tenn.
38. *NBD*, 1853, 66; 1855, 126; 1857, 166, 222, 355; 1859, 157.
39. Mitchell, *State Gazetteer*, 316, 483.
40. *NBD*, 1855, 126; 1857, 166, 222.
41. *MCD*, 1855, 185: 1856–57, 209; 1859, 208; 1860, 166.
42. Federal census for 1860, Davidson Ct., Tenn.; *NBD*, 1860–61, 276.
43. Mitchell, *State Gazetteer*, 194, 483.
44. *NBD*, 1870, 330.
45. Federal census for 1850, Davidson Ct., Tenn.; Kovel and Kovel, *American Silver*, 186.
46. *Nash. Daily Union*, 28 July 1850; Federal census for 1850, Davidson Ct., Tenn.
47. Federal census for 1850, Shelby Ct., Tenn, under James S. Wilkins; *MCD*, 1855, 44; 1860, 343.
48. *NBD*, 1860, 343.
49. Mitchell, *State Gazetteer*, 1860, 441.
50. *Nash. Rep. & St. Gaz.*, 16 Nov. 1833, 4 Jan. 1834; 15, 25, 27 Feb. 1834.
51. Nash. *Impart. Rev. & Cumberland Repos.*, 29 Sept. 1808.
52. *Robinson's Original Directory for 1817* (Philadelphia, 1817), 483; John A. Paxton, comp., *The Philadelphia Directory and Register for 1818* (Philadelphia, 1818); *1819* (Philadelphia, 1819) Edward Whitely, comp., *The Philadelphia Directory and Register for 1820* (Philadelphia, 1820).

Bibliography

Books

Abernethy, Thomas Perkins. *From Frontier to Plantation in Tennessee*. Reprint. 1932. Chapel Hill, N. C.: Univ. of North Carolina Press, 1955.

Acklen, Jeannette Tillotson, comp. *Tennessee Tombstone Inscriptions and Manuscripts*. Baltimore: Genealogical Publishing Co., 1976.

Adair, James. *The History of the American Indians*. London: Printed for Edward & Charles Dilly in the Poultry, 1775.

Armstrong, Zella. *Notable Southern Families*. Vol. 1. Chattanooga, Tenn.: Lookout Publishing Co., 1918.

Beach, Ursula Smith. *Along the Warioto. A History of Montgomery County, Tennessee*. Nashville, Tenn.: McQuiddy Press, 1964.

Beckman, Elizabeth D. *Cincinnati Silversmiths, Jewelers, Watch and Clockmakers Through 1850, Also Listing the More Prominent Men in These Trades from 1851 until 1900*. Cincinnati, Ohio: B. B. & Co., 1975.

Belden, Louise Conway. *Marks of American Silversmiths in the Ineson Bissell Collection*. Charlottesville, Va.: University Press of Virginia for the Henry Frances du Pont Winterthur Museum, 1980.

Bohan, Peter, and Philip Hammerslough. *Early Connecticut Silver, 1700–1840*. Middletown, Ct.: Wesleyan University Press, 1970.

Bond, Octavia Zollicoffer. *Old Tales Retold or Perils and Adventures of Tennessee Pioneers*. Nashville, Tenn.: Methodist Episcopal Church, South, 1906.

Boultinghouse, Marquis. *Silversmiths of Kentucky, 1785–1900: Jewelers, Watch and Clock Makers*. Lexington, Ky.: Marquis Boultinghouse, 1980.

Brandau, Roberta Seawell, ed. *History of Homes and Gardens of Tennessee*. Nashville, Tenn.: Parthenon Press, 1936.

Burton, E. Milby. *South Carolina Silversmiths*. Charleston, S. C.: The Charleston Museum, 1942.

Campbell, Rev. Jno. P. *The Nashville, State of Tennessee and General Commercial Directory*. 4 vols. Nashville, Tenn., 1853–59, various publishers.

Clayton, W. W. *History of Davidson County, Tennessee*. Philadelphia: Tennessee Historical Society, 1880.

Coppock, Paul R. *Memphis Sketches*. Memphis, Tenn.: Friends of Memphis and Shelby County Libraries, 1976.

Craig, James H. *The Arts and Crafts in North Carolina, 1699–1849*. Winston-Salem, N. C.: Museum of Early southern Decorative Arts, 1965.

Crew, H. W. *History of Nashville, Tennessee*. Nashville, Tenn: Methodist Episcopal Church, South, 1890.

Curtis, George Munson. *Early Silver of Connecticut and Its Makers*. Meriden, Ct.: International Silver Co., 1913.

Currier, Ernest M. *Marks of Early American Silversmiths with Notes on Silver, Spoon Types and List of New York City Silversmiths, 1815–1841*. Harrison, N.Y.: Robert Alan Green, 1970.

Cutten, George Barton. *The Silversmiths of Georgia, Together with Watchmakers and Jewelers—1733 to 1850*. Savannah, Ga.: Pigeonhole Press, 1958.

———*Silversmiths of North Carolina, 1696–1850*. Raleigh, N. C.: North Carolina Department of Cultural Resources, Division of Archives and History, 1973.

———*Silversmiths of Virginia (Together with Watchmakers and Jewelers) from 1694 to 1850*. Richmond, Va.: Dietz Press, 1952. Second printing, 1975.

Dykeman, Wilma. *The French Broad*. New York: Rinehart and Co., 1955.

Ensko, Stephen G. C. *American Silversmiths and Their Marks*. Southampton, N. Y.: Cracker Barrel Press, 1937.

Fales, Martha Gandy. *Early American Silver for the Cautious Collector*. New York: Funk and Wagnalls, 1970.

Fink, Paul M. *Jonesborough: The First Century of Tennessee's First Town*. Washington Co., Tenn.: Tennessee State Planning Commission, 1972.

Flynt, Henry N. and Martha Gandy Fales. *The Heritage Foundation Collection of Silver with Biographical Sketches of New England Silversmiths, 1625–1825*. Old Deerfield, Mass.: The Heritage Foundation, 1968.

Frank, Fedora Small. *Beginnings on Market Street*. Nashville, Tenn: A Bicentennial Book from the Jewish Community of Nashville and Middle Tennessee, 1976.

———*Five Families and Eight Young Men*. Nashville, Tenn.: Tennessee Book Co., 1962.

Fredyma, Paul J. and Marie-Louise Fredyma. *A Directory of Massachusetts Silversmiths and Their Marks*. White River Junction, Va.: Paul J. and Marie-Louise Fredyma, 1972.

Free, George D. *History of Tennessee from Its Earliest Discoveries and Settlements*. 1895. Nashville, Tenn.: University Press Printers, rev. ed., 1896.

Garrett, Jill L. *Obituaries from Tennessee Newspapers*. Easley, S. C.: Southern Historical Press, 1980.

Gibbs, James W. *Dixie Clockmakers*. Gretna, La.: Pelican Publishing Co., 1979.

Gilmore, James R. *The Advance-Guard of Western Civilization*. Spartanburg, S. C.: Reprint Co., 1974.

Goodspeed Histories of Tennessee:

(These reprints are given varying titles by their different publishers. Those reprinted by Woodward and Stinson and the Ben Lomond Press are The Goodspeed Histories, *and those reprinted by Charles and Randy Elder and the Reprint Company are* Goodspeed's History.*)*

Cannon, Coffee, DeKalb, Warren, and White Counties. . . . 1887. Reprint. McMinnville, Tenn.: Ben Lomond Press, 1972.

Containing Historical and Biographical Sketches of Thirty East Tennessee Counties. . . . 1887. Reprint. Nashville, Tenn.: Charles and Randy Elder, 1972.

Fayette and Hardeman Counties. 1887. Reprint. Columbia, Tenn.: Woodward and Stinson Printing Co., 1973.

General History of Tennessee. 1887. Reprint. Nashville, Tenn.: Charles and Randy Elder, 1973.

Giles, Lincoln, Franklin and Moore Counties. 1886. Reprint. Columbia, Tenn.: Woodward and Stinson, 1972.

Hamilton, Knox and Shelby Counties. 1887. Reprint. Nashville, Tenn.: Charles and Randy Elder, 1974.

Lauderdale, Tipson, Haywood, and Crockett Counties. 1887. Reprint with new material by Rev. Silas Emmett Lucas, Jr. Easley, S.C.: Southern Historical Press, 1978.

Madison County. 1887. Reprint. Columbia, Tenn.: Woodward and Stinson, 1972.

Maury, Williamson, Rutherford, Wilson, Bedford and Marshall Counties. 1886. Reprint. Columbia, Tn.: Woodward and Stinson, 1976.

Shelby County. 1887. Reprint. Nashville: Charles and Randy Elder, 1974.

Sumner, Smith, Macon, and Trousdale Counties. 1886. Reprint. Columbia, Tenn.: Woodward and Stinson, 1971.

Gower, Herschel, ed. *Pen and Sword. The Life and Journals of Randal W. McGavock.* Nashville, Tenn.: Tennessee Historical Commission, 1959.

Grady, Jamie Ault. *William Bean, Pioneer of Tennessee and His Descendants.* Knoxville, Tenn.: Jamie Ault Grady, 1973.

Guild, Jo C. *Old Times in Tennessee with Historical, Personal and Political Scraps and Sketches.* Nashville: Tavel, Eastman and Howell, 1878.

Hailey, Naomi. *A Guide to Genealogical Research in Tennessee.* Owensboro, Ky.: Cook and McDowell, 1979.

Hamer, Philip M., ed. *Tennessee, A History, 1673–1932.* Vol. 1. New York: American Historical Society, 1933.

Hammerslough, Philip H. *American Silver.* Vol. 3. Privately printed, 1970.

Harris, George Washington. *Sut Lovingood's Yarns.* Edited by M. Thomas Inge. New Haven, Conn.: College & University Press, 1966.

Haywood, John. *The Natural & Aboriginal History of Tennessee.* Jackson, Tenn.: McCowt-Mercer Press, 1959.

———*The Civil and Political History of the State of Tennessee from its Earliest Settlement up to the Year 1796 including the Boundaries of the State.* 1823. Reprint. Knoxville, Tenn.: Tenase Co., 1969.

Henderson, Archibald. *The Conquest of the Old Southwest.* Spartanburg, S.C.: Reprint Co., 1974.

Hiatt, Noble W. and Lucy F. *The Silversmiths of Kentucky together with Some Watchmakers and Jewelers, 1785–1850.* Louisville: Standard Printing Co., 1954.

Hood, Graham. *American Silver, A History of Style, 1650–1900.* New York: Praeger Publishers, 1971.

Imlay, Gilbert. *A Topographical Description of Western Territory of North America; Containing a Succinct Account of Its Soil, Climate, National History, Population, Agriculture, Manners and Customs. With an Ample Description of the Several Divisions in which the Country is Partitioned.* London: J. Debrett, 1793.

Kimball, John F. *Kimball and James' Business Directory for the Mississippi Valley, 1844.* Cincinnati, Ohio: Kendall and Barnard, 1844.

Knittle, Rhea Mansfield. *Early Ohio Silversmiths and Pewterers, 1787–1847.* Cleveland, Ohio: Calvert-Hatch Co., 1943.

Kovel, Ralph M. and Terry H. Kovel. *American Silver, Pewter and Silver Plate.* New York: Crown Publishers, 1961.

Lewis, Marcus W. *Development of Early Emigrant Trails in the United States East of the Mississippi River.* Washington, D. C.: National Genealogical Society, 1972.

Looney, Louisa Preston. *Tennessee Sketches.* Chicago: A. C. McClurg and Co., 1901.

Lucas, Rev. Silas Emmett, Jr. *Obituaries from Early Tennessee Newspapers, 1794–1851.* Easley, S. C.: Southern Historical Press, 1978.

Lynch, Louise G. *Early Obituaries of Williamson County.* Privately published, 1977.

———*Miscellaneous Records of Williamson County.* Vol. 2. Privately published, 1978.

Michaux, F. A. *Travels to the Westward of the Allegany Mountains in the States of Ohio, Kentucky, Tennessee in the Year of 1802.* London: Bernard and Sultzer, 1805.

Mitchell, John L. *John L. Mitchell's Tennessee State Gazetteer and Business Directory for 1860–1861.* Nashville: John L. Mitchell, 1860.

Moore, John Trotwood, ed. *Tennessee, The Volunteer State, 1769–1923.* Vol. 2. Nashville, Tenn.: S. J. Clarke Publishing Co., 1923.

Morris, Eastin. *The Tennessee Gazetteer, or Topographical Dictionary.* Edited by Robert M. McBride and Owen Meredith. 1834. Reprint. Nashville, Tenn.: Gazetteer Press, 1971.

Morse, Jedidiah and Richard C. Morse. *A New Universal Gazetteer or Geographical Dictionary, Containing a Description of the Various Counties, Provinces, Cities, Towns, Seas, Lakes, Rivers, Mountains, Capes, Etc. in the Known World.* New Haven, Ct.: S. Converse, 1823.

Myer, William E. *Indian Trails of the Southeast from the Forty Second Annual Report of the Bureau of American Ethnology to the Secretary of the Smithsonian Institution.* Washington, D.C.: U. S. Government Printing Office, 1924–1925.

Nashville City and Business Directory. Vol. 5. Nashville, Tenn.: L. P. Williams and Co., 1860.

Nashville City Directory. The Eleventh Annual Issue. Nashville, Tenn.: Wheeler, Marshall and Bruce, 1974.

Owsley, Harriet Chappell, comp. *Index to Interments Nashville City Cemetery.* Nashville: Tennessee State Library and Archives, 1964.

Paschall and Riggs. *First Annual Memphis City Directory & General Business Advertiser for 1856–1857.* Memphis: Eagle and Enquirer Printing House, 1856.

Phelan, James. *History of Tennessee: The Making of a State.* Boston & New York: Houghton Mifflin, Riverside Press, 1889.

Pleasants, J. Hall and Howard Sill. *Maryland Silversmiths, 1715–1830, with Illustrations of Their Silver and Their Mark and with a Facsimile of the Design Book of William Faris.* Harrison, N.Y.: Robert Alan Green, 1972.

Putnam, A. W. *History of Middle Tennessee or Life and Times of Gen. James Robertson.* Knoxville, Tenn.: University of Tennessee Press, 1971.

Rainwater, Dorothy T. *American Silver Manufacturers.* Hanover, Pa.: Everybody's Press, 1966.

Rainey, W. H. *W. H. Rainey's and Co.'s Memphis City Directory and General Business Advertiser for 1855–1856.* Memphis: D. O. Dooley and Co., 1855.

Redfearn, Jerome. *Indiana Silversmiths, Clockmakers and Watchmakers, 1779–1900.* Georgetown, Ky.: Americana Publications, 1984.

Roach, Ruth Hunter. *St. Louis Silversmiths.* n. p., 1967.

Robert, Charles E. *Nashville and Her Trade for 1870*. Nashville: Roberts and Purvis, 1870.

Rogers, George H., comp. *The Nashville and Edgefield Directory*. 14th ed. Nashville: Marshall and Bruce, 1878.

Rothrock, Mary U., ed. *The French Broad—Holston Co.: A History of Knox County*. Knoxville, Tenn.: Knox County Historical Committee of the East Tennessee Historical Society, 1946.

Royall, Anne Newport. *Letters from Alabama, 1817–1822*. Reprint. University, Ala.: University of Alabama Press, 1969.

San Antonio Museum Association. *Early Texas Furniture and Decorative Arts*. San Antonio, Tex.: Trinity University Press, 1973.

Sistler, Barbara and Byron Sistler, comps. *Index to Early Tennessee Tax Lists*. Evanston, Ill.: n. p., 1977.

Smith, Daniel. *A Short Description of the Tennessee Government. 1793*. Reprinted in *Tennessee Beginnings*. Spartanburg, S. C.: Reprint Co., 1974.

Smith, Felix Randolph Robertson. *Alphabetical List of the Dead in the City Cemetery, As Shown by Existing Monuments and Headstones*. Nashville, Tenn.: n. p., 1909.

Smith, J. Gray. *A Brief Historical, Statistical and Descriptive Review of East Tennessee, United States of America: Developing Its Immense Agricultural, Mining, and Manufacturing Advantages, with Remarks to Emigrants*. 1842. Reprint. Spartanburg, S. C.: Reprint Co., 1974.

Smith, Jonathan K. T. *An Historical Survey of the Road System of Benton Counry, Tennessee*. Memphis, Tenn.: Jonathan K. T. Smith, 1976.

Statistical View of the U.S. Embracing Its Territory, Population, Moral and Social Condition, Industry, Property, and Revenue; The Detailed Statistics of Cities, Towns and Counties. Washington: Beverly Tucker, Senate Printer, 1854.

Stow, Millicent. *American Silver*. New York: Gramercy Publishing Co., 1950.

Tanner, Halpin and Co., comps. *Memphis City Directory for 1859*. Memphis: Hutton & Clark, 1859.

Thomas, Jane. *Old Days in Nashville*.1897. Reprint. Nashville, Tenn.: Charles Elder, 1969.

Trollope, Frances (Milton). *Domestic Manners of the Americans*. 1832. With a history of Mrs. Trollope's adventures in America by Donald Smalley. 1st Borzoi ed. New York: Alfred A. Knopf, 1949.

Twyman, R. B. T. *Twyman's Memphis Directory and General Business Advertiser for 1850*. Memphis, Tenn.: R. B. Twyman, Printer, 1849.

Vaught, Nathan. *Old City*. In *Historic Maury*. Vol. 1. Columbia, Tenn.: Maury County Historical Society, 1964.

Victor, Stephen K., "'From the Shop to the Manufactory,' Silver and Industry, 1970." In *Silver in American Life: Selections from the Mabel Brady Garvan and Other Collections at Yale University*. Edited by Barbara McLean Ward and Gerald W. R. Ward. Boston: David R. Godine, 1979.

Whitley, Edythe Rucker, comp. *Marriages of Davidson County, Tennessee, 1789–1847*. Marriage Book II. Baltimore: Genealogical Pub. Co., 1981.

Williams' Clarksville City Guide and Business Mirror, 1859–1860. Vol. 1. Clarksville, Tenn.: C. O. Faxon, 1859.

Williams' Knoxville Directory, City Guide, and Business Mirror, 1859–1860. Vol. 1. Knoxville, Tenn.: C. S. Williams, 1859.

Williams' Memphis Directory, City Guide and Business Mirror. Memphis, Tenn.: Cleaves and Vaden, 1860.

Williams, Samuel Cole. *Dawn of the Tennessee Valley and Tennessee History*. Johnson City, Tenn.: Watauga Press, 1937.

———*Early Travels in the Tennessee Country, 1540–1800*. Johnson City, Tenn.: Watauga Press, 1928.

———*Tennessee During the Revolutionary War*. 1944. Reprint. Knoxville, Tenn.: University of Tennessee Press, 1974.

Woodring, T. V. *The City Cemetery of Nashville, Tennessee, Facsimile of Original Records of Deaths and Burials*. Presented to the Tennesee Historical Society by the City of Nashville, 1955, now in the holdings of the Society at the Tennessee State Library and Archives.

Wyllie, Bertie. *Sheffield Plate*. Reprint. London: B. T. Batsford, 1913.

Wyler, Seymour B. *The Book of Sheffield Plate*. New York: Bonanza Books, 1949.

Young, W. A. *The Silver and Sheffield Plate Collector*. London: Herbert Jenkins, n. d.

Catalogs

American Art Association. *Personal Relics. Silver, China, and Glass from The White House, Books from the Hermitage and Other Association Items Once Owned by President Andrew Jackson (1829–1837) Inherited by His Great Grandson, Andrew Jackson IV of Los Angeles, California*. New York: American Art Association, 1927.

Anglo-American Art Museum, Louisiana State University. *Crescent City Silver, an Exhibition of Nineteenth-Century New Orleans Silver*. Baton Rouge, La.: Anglo-American Art Museum, 1980.

Association of the Corcoran Gallery of Art. *A Century of Silver, 1750–1850*. Washington, D. C.: Corcoran Gallery of Art, 1966.

Dulin Gallery of Art, East Tennessee Historical Society. *The Arts of East Tennessee in the Nineteenth Century*. Knoxville, Tenn.: East Tennessee Historical Society, 1971.

Metropolitan Museum of Art. *Catalogue of an Exhibition of Silver Used in New York, New Jersey and the South with a Note on Early New York Silversmiths by R.T. Harnes Halsey*. Reprint. New York: Arno Press, 1974.

Steiner, Mary Ann, ed. *St. Louis Silversmiths*. St. Louis, Mo.: The St. Louis Art Museum, 1980.

Tennessee Fine Arts Center at Cheekwood. *Made in Tennessee. An Exhibition of Early Arts and Crafts*. Nashville, Tenn.: Tennessee Fine Arts Center, 1971.

Warren, David B. *Southern Silver, An Exhibition of Silver Made in the South Prior to 1860*. Houston, Tex.: Museum of Fine Arts, 1968.

Williams, Derita Coleman. *A View of Tennessee Silversmiths, A Loan Exhibition*. Memphis: Dixon Gallery and Gardens, 1983.

Journal and Magazine Articles

Bacot, H. Parrott and B. B. Lambden, "Nineteenth-Century Silver in Natchez." *Antiques* 99 (March 1971): 412–17.

Caldwell, Benjamin H., Jr. "Tennessee Silversmiths." *Antiques* 100 (September 1971): 382–5.

Farnham, Katherine Gross. "Early Silversmiths and the Silver Trade in Georgia." *Antiques* 99 (March 1971): 280–5.

Fink, Paul M. "The Great Seal of the State of Tennessee. An Inquiry into Its Makers." *Tennessee Historical Quarterly* 20 (1961): 381–3.

Floyd, William Barrow. "Kentucky Coin-Silver Pitchers." *Antiques* 105 (March 1974): 576–80.

Harned, Henry H. "Ante-bellum Kentucky Silver." *Antiques* 105 (April 1974): 818–24.

Lee, Nathaniel Newcomer. "The New England Teachers in Nashville, 1818." *Tennessee Historical Quarterly* 19 (1960): 76–9.

Rogers, Tommy W. "Origin and Destination of Tennessee Migrants, 1850–1860." *Tennessee Historical Quarterly* 27 (1968): 118–22.

Scott, Thomas A. "The Impact of Tennessee's Migrating Sons." *Tennessee Historical Quarterly* 27 (1968): 123–25.

Smith, Sidney Adair. "Mobile Silversmiths and Jewelers, 1820–1867." *Antiques* 99 (March 1971): 407–11.

Newspapers

Athens Courier
Athens *Hiwassee Patriot*

Bolivar Free Press
Bolivar Free Press and Farmers Herald
Brownsville District Herald

Carthage Casket
Carthage Gazette
Carthage *Western Express*
Chattanooga Gazette
Clarksville Chronicle
Clarksville Gazette
Clarksville *Tennessee Weekly Chronicle*
Cleveland Dispatch
Columbia Beacon
Columbia Observer
Columbia *Western Mercury*

Daily Nashville American
Dresden *Jacksonian*

Elizabethton Republic and Manufacturer's Advocate

Fayetteville Observer
Fayetteville Republican
Fayetteville *Village Messenger*
Franklin *Independent Gazette*
Franklin *Western Balance*
Franklin *Williamson County News*

Gallatin *Examiner*
Gallatin Journal
Gallatin *Republican Sentinel and Sumner, Smith, and Jackson Intelligencer*
Greeneville Democrat

Hiwassean and Athens Gazette
Huntingdon Advertiser

Jackson *District Telegraph*
Jackson *District Telegraph and State Sentinel*
Jackson Gazette
Jackson Madisonian
Jackson Republican
Jackson *Southern Statesman*
Jackson *West Tennessee Whig*
Jonesboro(ough) *East Tennessee Patriot*
Jonesboro(ugh) *Farmers Journal*
Jonesboro(ugh) *Whig*
Jonesborough Whig and Independent Journal

Knoxville Enquirer
Knoxville Gazette
Knoxville Journal
Knoxville Register
Knoxville Standard
Knoxville Times

Lewisburg *Democratic Mirror*
Lincoln Journal

Maryville Intelligencer
Memphis *Commercial Appeal*
Memphis Enquirer
Memphis Weekly Appeal
Murfreesborough Courier
Murfreesborough *Jeffersonian*

Nashville Banner
Nashville Clarion
Nashville *Clarion*
Nashville *Clarion and Tennessee Gazette*
Nashville *Clarion & Tennessee State Gazette*
Nashville *Daily Center-State American*
Nashville *Daily Gazette*
Nashville Daily Gazette
Nashville Daily True Whig
Nashville Daily Union
Nashville *Daily Union*
Nashville Gazette
Nashville *Impartial Review and Cumberland Repository*
Nashville Patriot
Nashville Republican
Nashville Republican and State Gazette
Nashville *Tennessean*
Nashville *Tennessee Gazette*
Nashville *Tennessee Gazette and Mero District Advertiser*
Nashville True Whig
Nashville Union
Nashville Whig
Nashville Whig Banner
Nashville Whig and Tennessee Advertiser
National Banner and Nashville Whig

Paris *Patriot*
Paris *Republic*
Paris Sentinel
Pulaski *Whig Courier*

Randolph Recorder
Rogersville *East Tennessean*
Rogersville *Western Pilot*

Shelbyville *Peoples Advocate*
Shelbyville Times
Shelbyville *Western Freeman*
Somerville Reporter
Sparta Recorder and Law Journal
Sparta Review

Trenton Southern Standard

Washington Advertiser

Public Documents

Federal Census Records

Federal Census for 1820. National Archives Microfilm M-33, Rolls 122–5.

Federal Census for 1830. National Archives Microfilm M-19, Rolls 174–82.

Federal Census for 1840. National Archives Microfilm T-5, Rolls 164–71.

Federal Census for 1850. National Archives Microfilm M-432, Rolls 869–901 (Free Schedules).

Federal Census for 1860. National Archives Microfilm T-7, Rolls 271–8 (Free Schedules.)

Federal Census of Manufacturers for 1820. National Archives Microfilm M-279, East Tennessee Counties, Roll 26. Tennessee Western District, Roll 27.

Federal Agriculture and Manufacturing Census Records for 1850. National Archives Microfilm. Roll 72.

Federal Agricultural and Manufacturing Census Records for 1860. National Archives Microfilm. Roll 79.

Tennessee County Records

(All of the following may be found at the Tennessee State Library and Archives.)

Davidson County court records on microfilm. Wills. Rolls 56–9. Knox County court records on microfilm. Wills and Settlements. Roll 155.

McMinn County court records on microfilm. Wills. Roll 104.

Madison County court records on microfilm. Wills. Rolls 53–63.

Maury County court records on microfilm. Wills. Rolls 179–81.

Montgomery County court records on microfilm. Wills. Rolls 91–3.

Smith County court records on microfilm. Inventories. Rolls 79–81. Wills. Roll 104.

Washington County court records on microfilm. Inventories of Estates. Roll 113.

Index

The locations of Tennessee silversmiths and related tradesmen are listed under county headings; "tradesmen" refers only to those in the silver trades, such as silversmiths, jewelers, retailers, etc. The names of Tennessee silversmiths and related tradesmen identified as having begun work *after* 1860 are accompanied by their trades and locations. Bold-faced page numbers following an entry for an individual indicate the page containing his biographical data. Italicized page numbers indicate illustrations.

Designed by Kachergis Book Design, Pittsboro, N.C.
Typeset by Marathon Typography Service, Durham, N.C.
Printed and bound by Dai Nippon, Tokyo